Third World
Mass Media
and Their Search
for Modernity

BERMUDA

UNITED STATES

BAHAMA ISLANDS

TURKS & CAICOS ISLANDS

PUERTO RICO

BRITISH VIRGIN ISLANDS

ANGUILLA

BARBUDA

ST KITTS
NEVIS

ANTIGUA

MONTSERRAT

DOMINICA

ST LUCIA

ST
VINCENT

BARBADOS

GRENADA

TOBAGO

TRINIDAD

CUBA

JAMAICA

CAYMAN ISLANDS

BRITISH HONDURAS

GUATEMALA

HONDURAS

NICARAGUA

COSTA

COSTA

Third World
Mass Media
and Their Search
for Modernity

The Case
of Commonwealth Caribbean,
1717-1976

John A. Lent

Lewisburg
Bucknell University Press
London: Associated University Presses

OTHER BOOKS BY John A. Lent:

The Asian Newspapers' Reluctant Revolution
Philippine Mass Communications: Before 1811, After 1966
Broadcasting in Asia and the Pacific
Asian Mass Communications: A Comprehensive Bibliography
Asian Newspapers: Contemporary Trends and Problems
Philippine Mass Communications Bibliography
Newhouse, Newspapers, Nuisances

Associated University Presses, Inc.
Cranbury, New Jersey 08512

Associated University Presses
Magdalen House
136-148 Tooley Street
London SE1 2TT, England

Library of Congress Cataloging in Publication Data

Lent, John A
    Third World mass media and their search for modernity.

    Bibliography: p.
    Includes index.
    1. Mass media—West Indies, British—History.
2. Mass media—Bermuda—History. I. Title.
P92.W4L4   301.16′1′09729   75-39110
ISBN 0-8387-1896-5

PRINTED IN THE UNITED STATES OF AMERICA

Contents

List of Tables

9

Preface

This study had its beginnings in 1968 with what started out as a pleasure trip to the Dutch West Indian islands Aruba and Curaçao. After a couple of restless days on the Aruban beaches, I decided to take up some of the slack by looking into media operations on the island. Before the end of the two-and-a-half week work-vacation, I had visited each of the mass media plants and had talked with most communications managers on both islands. It was all very fascinating, learning firsthand about communications on small, developing islands. I found that some of these islands' mass media problems and their solutions were unique. For example, on Curaçao, in an effort to protect the privacy of individuals, newspapers identify arrested citizens only by their initials. Yet, in other cases, I found that problems of mass media on Aruba and Curaçao differ very little from those of other developing, and many developed nations. For instance, both islands have experienced difficulties with freedom of the press that are similar to those of other regions of the world.

Upon returning to the United States, I tried to find written materials on the mass media of these, as well as the nearby British and French islands. Except for a few scattered items, not much meaningful literature existed on the region's press. It was at that stage that I decided to explore the mass media situation in one group of islands —the Commonwealth Caribbean. In the fall of 1970 and again in the spring of 1971, I visited the major British islands in the Caribbean to gather primary data on mass communications, through interviews, library research, and observation. This study is the result of those efforts. It is an attempt to examine historical, cultural, economic, and political aspects of all Commonwealth Caribbean mass media, from the time of the first newspaper in 1717 until 1972. As a result of interviews conducted in January 1976 on Jamaica, Barbados, and St. Lucia, the manuscript was updated. Instances of known changes in the structure and function of the region's mass media since 1972 have been recorded in footnotes.

A number of West Indians were particularly helpful in making my research trips fruitful. First of all, I am heavily indebted to the approximately seventy-five media personnel who talked with me and showed me around. Especially helpful were Jack Dodge, Sir Etienne Dupuch, and Benson McDermott in the Bahamas; Fred Seal Coon on Jamaica; Ian Gale, Neville Grosvenor, Frank Collymore, and John Wickham on Barbados; Leo de Leon and Lenn Chongsing on Trinidad; Atlin Harrigan, Nathaniel Hodge, Stanley Procope, and Everard Richards in the Leeward Islands; Phyllis and Robert Allfrey, Edward Scobie, Winston Hinkson, Ken Archer, Stanley Reid, John Whitmarsh, Cameron King, Leslie Seon, A. Michael Cruickshank, and Reggie Clyne in the Windward Islands. A number of other individuals and organizations provided valuable information through correspondence. Among them were Canon C. R. G. Carleton, John Barsotti, Robert Devaux, Dorcas White, W. W. Bodden, Paul Fisher, Don Rowlands, Monty Parrott, Jack Rickel and Associates, UNESCO, United States Information Service, Caribbean Broadcasting Association, and Freedom of Information Center. I am also thankful for the assistance given by personnel at fifteen libraries in the islands and in the United States.

In addition, I would like to thank Professors Lester Benz, Hugh Cordier, Harry Duncan, William Zima, Herbert Schiller, and James Canel of Inter American Press Association, and David Renwick of *Trinidad Express*, for being kind enough to read and comment on the manuscript.

And to my family—wife, Martha; children, Laura, Andrea, John, Lisa, and Shahnon; parents, John and Rose Lent; and parents-in-law, Howard and Jane Meadows—I extend my appreciation for their tolerance and sacrifice.

Finally, I have incurred special debts to Leslie G. Moeller and James W. Markham. Professor Moeller, whose stimulation and criticism were particularly useful, spent many hours straightening out errors of grammar and logic, as well as encouraging the author. The imprint of his vast knowledge of mass communications is stamped on these pages. Professor Markham, my mentor at the University of Iowa until his death on February 7, 1972, also provided many insights and words of encouragement when they were needed most. To these fine scholars, for their guidance and friendship, I dedicate this book.

John A. Lent

Third World
Mass Media
and Their Search
for Modernity

1

Introduction

A very pertinent question concerning the Commonwealth Caribbean (formerly known as the British West Indies or British Caribbean) is: Why have not these isolated, but closely knit, populations on individual islands come in for their share of attention from mass communication scholars? Why have not diffusion-of-information studies been attempted in these societies that still depend heavily on informal communication channels to obtain and spread news? Why have not more studies been performed on the unique communication situations that are inherent in island cultures that have learned to devise their own information channels? Or, why have scholars not ventured into the study of the communicative capabilities of calypso, steeldrum bands, and political meetings that are endemic to the area?

Upon close scrutiny, one finds that not even the beginning stages of communication research—that is, gathering the historical and descriptive data on the mass media—have been accomplished in regard to the Commonwealth Caribbean.

Possible explanations for this lack of communication research in the Commonwealth Caribbean are: (1) European and American scholars have felt the islands too small and insignificant for serious exploration; (2) the islanders under colonial tutelage may never have thought they possessed institutions worthy of investigation; (3) the day-to-day humdrum of making a living has not allowed the educated elites in the islands to indulge in the luxury of research; (4) developing cultures often do not have an atmosphere in which the scholarly research approach is encouraged; (5) the diffuseness of this group of tiny islands dotting the sea has been responsible for deterring scholars.

The last point is very important. Not including the Bahamas and Bermuda, the rest of the Commonwealth Caribbean is strung out in a 1,250 mile arc, containing the British or former British colonies of Antigua, Barbados, the British Virgin Islands, Dominica, Grenada, Jamaica, Montserrat, St. Christopher (also known as St. Kitts) and its dependencies Nevis and Anguilla, St. Lucia, St. Vincent, and Trinidad and Tobago.[1] Although the Bahamas and Bermuda are out of the geographical sphere of the West Indian archipelago, for the sake of convenience they are usually accepted as West Indian. With their inclusion, the Commonwealth Caribbean extends from Bermuda off the coast of South Carolina to Trinidad and Tobago off the coast of Venezuela (see fig. 1).

The former British West Indies have about 13,500 square miles, or about one-seventh of the total land area of the Caribbean, and approximately 3.9 million population, about one-sixth of the total of the region. As an indication of the small size of most of the islands, the five Leewards, four Windwards, and Barbados together cover 1,317 square miles, not much more than the size of Rhode Island.

The largest land area of the islands belongs to the Bahamas. Few people have bothered to count the islands, but it is said that the Bahamas are made up of 29 islands, 661 cays, and 2,387 rocks for a total land mass of 5,400 square miles, more than Jamaica's 4,411 square miles, or slightly more than the area of Connecticut. On the other extreme are islands the size of Montserrat, Anguilla, and Nevis, with 32½, 35 and 36 square miles respectively.

PURPOSES

In the present multi-media and interdisciplinary study, emphasis is on the contemporary[2] mass media of the region and on the societies in which they function. An attempt has been made to explain present-day characteristics and practices of Commonwealth Caribbean mass media in terms of the history of the region and the media themselves and to relate these traits to the theories of communication and national development wherever applicable.

A sociological approach to history[3] has been utilized, making it possible to investigate the political, cultural, social, geographical, technological, and economic subsystems of mass media in the islands. Traditionally, media have been studied as isolated institutions not related to society or "the societal environment of which they are an indisseverable part."[4] In this study, however, the mass media of the Commonwealth Caribbean have been studied not only according to their internal structural and functional designs, but in their social, economic, cultural, and political settings as well. In other words, an effort has been made here to avoid what Markham depicted as:

> the pedestrian description of the mass media out of context, as if we picked the stuff out of UNESCO data. It should be woven into the narrative and related graphically to the various social and political dimensions. Mass media exist as integral parts of society and must be so treated.[5]

At times, comparisons are made between mass media of the various islands, and also with mass media of other developing areas. This results from a conscious effort to produce generalizations of a more comprehensive nature, generalizations which will lend themselves to a fuller understanding of the present and future meaning of mass media in the Commonwealth islands. On the other hand, however, generalizations will not be made at the cost of a careful consideration of the diversity that exists among the islands' media.

C. E. Black has said that the purposes of comparison are to organize and classify complex materials and then offer explanations of them.[6] Thus far very little has been done to classify and explain mass media of the islands, even though the history of the press of the region dates to the earliest United States printers, some of whom served apprenticeships in places such as Antigua, Barbados, and Jamaica.

Any studies attempted in the past dealt strictly with one island, never leaping barriers of nationalistic thinking. According to Nichols, to be able to avoid nationalistic prejudices leads to a new phase of generalization where a conceptualization within the framework of universal history can be reached.[7]

THEMES

Themes have dealt with the extent of the impact of these various factors: (1) Influences of British and American ways of life upon West Indian mass media; (2) Avenues of communication existent between individual West Indian states and London or New York rather than between West Indian states themselves; (3) Geographic and cultural distances in the islands; (4) Informal communications systems; (5) Government, political parties, and foreign enterprises as owners of mass media; (6) Government relationship with free expression of media; (7) Economic conditions of the media.

SOURCES

Written materials on many aspects of Commonwealth Caribbean life are lacking, either because they were carted off to England, left unprotected for the elements and insects to devour, or were never recorded by the settlers who were too busy selling and buying slaves, privateering, or raising sugar. Today, the research materials that do remain in the islands oftentimes appear to carry the stamp of governmental doctoring, or, if not that, then at least the nationalistic biases of the authors. I am very much aware, and desirous to inform the reader, that certain writers on the Commonwealth Caribbean hold very pronounced points of view. DaBreo, for example, is very anti-imperialist, anti-British colonialism and pro-West Indian nationalism, whereas Williams and Lewis, although they lean in those directions, attempt to give other viewpoints as well.

Of course, the paucity of literature on mass media of the region is even more serious (see Bibliography). For example, the only book-length treatment of a medium in the islands is *Tribune Story*, an autobiographical account of Sir Etienne Dupuch's struggles during fifty years as editor of the *Nassau Tribune*.

To gather firsthand information, I visited the islands in August and September 1970, April and May 1971, and January 1976. During these field trips, interviews[8] were conducted with seventy-six editors, publishers, and general managers of newspapers and magazines; general managers and sales and program directors of broadcasting systems; government information officers; legislators and even the president of Anguilla. The accomplished objective was to interview in depth at least one top executive on each medium on each island visited. These islands included the Bahamas, Antigua, St. Kitts-Nevis, Anguilla, Dominica, St. Lucia, St. Vincent, Grenada, Barbados, Trinidad, and Jamaica. I did not get to Bermuda, Montserrat, and the Caymans, although correspondence with media personnel on the latter two islands provided the necessary information (see Bibliography for a list of individuals who provided data through letters).

Questions asked of communication personnel were oriented around these aspects of mass media: their problems, roles in national development, audiences and needs, relationships with government and the society at large, cooperation with other media, penetration into different societal strata, cultural influences impinging upon them, content and distribution, personnel training, professionalization, and technological quality of media.

A problem encountered with some interviewees was their fear

of speaking out. In these cases, anonymity was assured and, as Singham had observed on Grenada, usually the information given under the protection of anonymity was verified later by another source not afraid of direct quotation.[9]

Gottschalk has written that "other things being equal, the historian who has experienced the most is the best historian."[10] With that rationale in mind, I felt it mandatory to experience, be it ever so briefly, as many as possible of the cultures about which I was to write. Without firsthand experience of this type, whole areas of behavior may be overlooked. The most isolated bits of behavior, according to Benedict, "have some systematic relation to each other."[11] Therefore, the talking did not end when I left the offices of media personnel. People in the parks, taverns, guest houses and hotels, at work and at play, provided tips about the culture, information which sometimes cannot be dug out of the formal structure of an interview. How else, except to meet them in their own environment, would it have been possible to find out that many lower-class Kittitians with poor eyesight cannot afford eyeglasses, and therefore are unable to read the newspapers that use small type, wrong fonts, and irregular spacing. Without being on the scene, how else would it have been possible to witness the informal communication network function on Grenada or Anguilla?

Besides interviews, external sources such as handbooks, travelogues, histories, and textbooks were used for data collection, as were the copies of newspapers and magazines, broadcasting program schedules, and market profiles. An informal content analysis to determine the relative emphasis on and frequency of communication phenomena was carried out to form the generalizations discussed in chapter 5.[12] Saturday, April 24, and Monday, April 26, 1971, were the newspaper sample dates; in the case of weeklies, the two issues closest to April 24 or 26 were reviewed. The most current program schedules of radio and television stations were surveyed to determine the category and origins of broadcasting content. In some cases, a tape recorder was used to monitor routine newscasts and local programming.

The chapters that result from this data gathering are organized according to historical, cultural, economic/technological, and political themes. Chapter 2 traces the history of Commonwealth Caribbean mass media from the first newspaper in Jamaica (first in the region, too) through emancipation and the personal journalism period, while chapter 3 brings the story of island journalism from the birth of the labor movements through the advent of broadcasting, federation, and to the present. Chapter 4 discusses ownership of regional media, and chapter 5 explores flow of news, media content, and its origins. In chapter 6, linguistic, psychological, and cultural factors related to communications problems in the region are discussed. Among the most perplexing problems facing Commonwealth Caribbean mass media, as well as most institutions of the area, are those in the realm of economics; there are not enough money, technology, and trained personnel to operate the media. Chapter 7 deals with these problems. Governmental and political relations of and with mass media make up the contents of chapter 8, and the final chapter synthesizes the various aspects of Commonwealth Caribbean mass media, drawing conclusions that might prove useful in the future for the region's communications industry.

NOTES TO CHAPTER 1

1. Generally, Honduras and Guyana are classified as Commonwealth Caribbean. This study will concentrate on the islands alone, not the former British colonies of Central or South America.

2. By *contemporary* is meant the 1960s and early 1970s.

3. See Sydney Kobre, "The Sociological Approach in Research in Newspaper History," *Journalism Quarterly* 22(1945):12–22; idem, "Productive Sociological Methods for Research of Press History," mimeographed (Paper presented at Association for Education in Journalism convention, Berkeley, California, August 1969).

4. **Ibid.**

5. Memorandum to "Internationales," August 7, 1969.

6. C. E. Black, *Dynamics of Modernization* (New York: Harper & Row, 1967), pp. 35–36.

7. Roy Nichols, "The Genealogy of Historical Generalizations," in Louis Gottschalk, ed., *Generalization in the Writing of History* (Chicago: University of Chicago Press, 1963), p. 139.

8. Personal interviews were used because, as Kerlinger says, they are the most powerful and useful tool of social scientific survey research. Fred N. Kerlinger, *Foundations of Behavioral Research* (New York: Holt, Rinehart & Winston, 1964), p. 395.

9. A. W. Singham, *The Hero and the Crowd in a Colonial Polity* (New Haven: Yale University Press, 1968), p. 338.

10.   Louis Gottschalk, *Understanding History* (New York: Alfred Knopf, 1969), pp. 96–97.

11.   Ruth Benedict, *The Chrysanthemum and the Sword* (Cleveland, Ohio: World, 1969), p. 10.

12.   Such as used by Wilbur Schramm, *One Day in the World's Press* (Stanford, Calif.: Stanford University Press, 1959); by Jacques Kayser, *One Week's News* (Paris: UNESCO, 1953), and by James W. Markham, *Voices of the Red Giants* (Ames, Iowa: Iowa State University Press, 1967).

2

The Beginnings

Apparently the printing press was not so vital to the colonization process of the Caribbean as it was in other parts of the world where printed materials were used for proselytism, as well as for the dissemination of European news to the colonists.

In parts of Latin America and the Philippines, for example, the Spanish set up presses as early as the sixteenth and seventeenth centuries; this was not accomplished in the West Indian islands of Trinidad and Jamaica, the former held by the Spanish for three centuries, the latter for a century and a half. If anything, the Spaniards discouraged a press in Trinidad. On at least two occasions they attempted to introduce the Inquisition there, once nearly a century and a half before Trinidad's first press. One historian has explained Spain's dilatory action concerning a press for Trinidad as follows:

> Spain had never been in very close contact with her colony. At times only once in every twenty years did a ship pass between Trinidad and the Mother Country. It was not until after the capitulation (to Great Britain) that anything like a regular service of packet ships connected the islands with her new owners.[1]

The Dutch did not bring printing to their Caribbean islands until 1790;[2] the French islands of Martinique and Guadeloupe did not have presses until 1727 and 1765 respectively.[3] Elsewhere in the Caribbean, printing was also late, arriving in Santo Domingo between 1750 and 1762,[4] in Cuba between 1696 and 1723,[5] and in Puerto Rico, not until 1806.[6]

Nor were the British colonizers in a hurry to establish West Indian presses. The first British settlement in the Caribbean, St. Christopher (also known as St. Kitts), was occupied in 1623 and had its first press in 1747.[7] In 1624[8] John Powell landed at Barbados and the second British colony in the region was established; over a hundred years later the island had its first press. Nevis was claimed by the British in 1628, but available records do not list a newspaper there before 1871; Antigua and Montserrat, settled in 1632, did not issue their first newspapers until about 1748[9] and 1876, respectively. Bermuda and the Bahamas had their first presses in the mid-1780s, hundreds of years after those islands were discovered.

Printing had a late start in the British Windward Islands as well. Dominica came under British sovereignty by cession from France in 1763; the first newspaper appeared two years later. In St. Vincent, the first newspaper was published in 1817, in St. Lucia in 1788, and in Grenada about 1765.

Jamaica's record was a little better than those of the other islands in that after the Spanish-held island was captured by Great Britain in 1655, only 62 years lapsed before the first known press.[10] An extreme case of procrastination in setting up a press involved the Leeward island of Anguilla, visited by British seamen in 1609, settled since 1688, but without a newspaper or press until 1967.

NOT AN ECCLESIASTICAL PRESS

Possibly the islands were so small and intrapersonal in nature that a press was not necessary to disseminate information, or the colonizers felt that the islanders, mostly slaves, were not important or intelligent enough to deserve the luxury of the written word. Or possibly the unstable nature of the islands (St. Lucia, for example, had thirteen changes of government before the final British takeover) did not allow for the establishment of permanent institutions. Still another reason for the late media development might be attributed to administrative fears of the press.

Jamaican newspaper historian Frank Cundall believed it was simply a case of the settlers being too preoccupied with other business to worry about developing printing facilities. He said:

This long period may partly be explained by the fact that a large number of those who came over in the army of occupation merely looked for plunder and not towards settlement, and that later the chains of buccaneering appealed to many, including those in high places, and that it was probably only when it became apparent that the printing of reports of legislative enactments and commercial intelligence and the like was a crying necessity, that a press was established.[11]

Cundall's explanation seems plausible. Whereas Spanish colonial presses were developed to print ecclesiastical works, the first British printing in the Caribbean was used to issue and make known the latest laws and proclamations. This was so in at least St. Christopher, Dominica, Trinidad, Tobago, Barbados, and Jamaica. The necessity for a printing press to produce such public documents was recognized in Barbados as early as 1678 when Governor Jonathan Atkins attributed the delays in transmitting copies of laws passed by the Legislature to the lack of a printing press on that island.[12] Not until 1730 did David Harry bring the first press to Barbados.

Some of the earliest evidence of Trinidadian printing testified that the craft was practiced to circulate ordinances that regulated the treatment of slaves and the maintenance of order.[13] In fact, the earliest extant product of printing in Trinidad was a 12-page booklet, bearing the imprint "Chacón, José María. *Ordenanza Publicada* en el Puertó España, el 11 de Agosto de 1786. Colophon: Del Puertó de España De La Imprinta de Don Juan Cassan" (italics mine).

The governor on isolated Tobago, as early as 1798, was urged to print that island's laws, to which he replied, "the acts of this island have not been printed for many years and there is at present no printing office."[14] Later in that year, the Assembly resolved to have the laws printed in London, but before the transaction could take place, the Tobago governor informed London authorities "that a printing office is now established at Scarborough." Earliest printing from that press was "An Act to Establish and Regulate a Small Coinage for This Island"; the first and one of the only newspapers on Tobago was a weekly inaugurated shortly after, in 1807, The Tobago *Gazette*.

The first press on Dominica, initiated by William Smith at Charlotte-town (now Roseau) in 1765, printed not only that island's first newspaper, The Dominica *Gazette*, but also "various proclamations and documents relative to registration of land titles."[15] Again, Thomas Howe, St. Christopher's first printer, was producing laws and government publications before he started that island's first newspaper, The St. Christopher *Gazette*, in 1747.

Before the advent of the newspaper, governmental notices on some islands, such as Jamaica, were made public "at the next Grand Court,

Quarter Sessions, and in the churches throughout the island, or in such manner as his Excellency should think fit."[16] On Trinidad, the means of publicizing orders was for the town crier, after the sounding of the drum, to read them aloud in specified public places, after which they were affixed to the church doors.[17]

Administrative authorities in Jamaica, in a 1716 memorandum to the Lords Commissioners for Trade and Plantations, gave as their reason for wanting a press the squelching of rumors and lies:

> In order to effect these extraordinary Benefits to the Island, numberless lies and stories have been industriously spread about the country, which are not easily answer'd where there is no press.[18]

A year before, however, the Council of Jamaica requested the Jamaican Assembly's support in "establishing a printing press for publishing the Minutes of both bodies."[19] The first printing on Jamaica was also useful in spreading mercantile notices. Previous to the newspapers, written lists of arrivals of marketable goods were attached to the doorposts of respective stores or proclaimed in the streets by Negro hawkers.

The government also campaigned for the development of a press on Bermuda. By 1771 the Bermuda House of Assembly resolved to encourage a press in that colony, transmitting such a resolution to London. The same recommendation was made in 1781 and 1783 before Joseph Stockdale, in 1784, accepted the challenge and issued the Bermuda *Gazette and Weekly Advertiser*.[20] In a number of instances, such as in Bermuda, considerable prodding on the part of government was necessary before a printer would come forth.

PUBLISHED WITH AUTHORITY, OR ELSE

Because of this governmental role in early British Caribbean printing, many of the first editors on the islands—as in most colonized areas of the world—were official employees who published with authority. For example, in Jamaica a number of the first editor-pressmen were "printers to the House of Assembly," "to the Corporation of Kingston," or "to the Honorable Council in Harbour Street."[21] The profusion of governmental printing these men produced was analyzed by Cundall: of 184 books and pamphlets published on Jamaica prior to 1820, 55 were the votes of the House of Assembly;

NUM. XLVII.

THE WEEKLY
Jamaica Courant.
With News Foreign and Domestick.

Publish'd by Authority.

Wednesday, April 15. 1719.

GREAT BRITAIN.

London, January 14.

HIS Day his Grace the Archbishop of York preach'd a Charity Sermon at the Parish Church of St. Paul Covent-Garden, for the Benefit of the British Charity School, lately erected by Subscription, for the pious Education of poor Children descended of Welch Parents, in and about the Cities of London and Westminster, and for providing them all necessary Apparel, and placing them (when qualify'd) to useful Trades.

Yesterday His Majesty was pleased to confer the Honour of Knighthood upon John Askew of Liddiard Millicent Esq; High Sheriff of the County of Wilts for this present Year, being introduc'd to His Majesty by his Grace the Duke of Kingston, Custos Rotulorum of the said County, and the Right Honourable the Lord Viscount St. John.

Madrid, January 3. N. S. The King grows better and better, having been purged several times with Success, and recover'd his Sleep and Stomach; so that there is grounds to hope his Majesty's Health will soon be entirely re-establish'd.

Paris, January 18. N. S. The Marshal de Villeroy is very ill of the Gout. The Duke of Chartres, the Regent's Eldest Son, is made President of the Council of Regency. Mr. Law hath bought the fine Palace of Nevers, which hath a long Gallery painted by Rubens; and is going to employ Two hundred Workmen to repair the House and Gardens. [*The following is more fully express'd than in our last.*]

Paris, January 21. N. S. On the 16th Instant, the Parliament made an Arret, which orders the Suppression of a Printed Paper, Entitled, A Declaration made by the Catholick King, December 25. 1718. The King's Advocates represented, that that Paper, which bears so awful a Name, being fill'd not only with the most injurious Terms and Expressions, but also with Maxims directly contrary to the Principles of the Government, they were far from thinking it was the Work of a Prince instructed in the Rights of Sovereigns, and educated in the Kingdom: That the Authors seem'd to design to excite Division and Revolt, having advanced their Temerity against the most Sacred Laws of the Land, and disown'd the Lawful Authority by which we are govern'd. The Court of Parliament hath order'd that Paper to be suppress'd as Seditious, tending to Revolt, and impugning the Royal Authority; enjoining all such as have Copies thereof, to bring them to the Registry, and forbidding all Persons to print, sell, utter or otherwise distribute it, upon pain of being prosecuted as Disturbers of the
Pub-

The first newspaper in the Commonwealth Caribbean, The Weekly Jamaica Courant, 1719.

From Saturday April the 14th, to Wednesday April the 18th, 1733.

BARBADOS.

AT a Meeting of His EXCELLENCY in Council at *Pilgrim* on *Tuesday* the 17th Day of *April*, 1733 being the Day inCourse.

PRESENT,
His EXCELLENCY the Right Honourable the Lord Viſcount *HOWE.*

The HONOURABLE

James Dottin,
William Terrill,
Ralph Weekes,
John Frere,
Joseph Pilgrim,   Eſqrs;
William Leſlie,
Thomas Maxwell,
John Aſhley,
Othniel Haggat, and
Thomas Applewhaite

Then His EXCELLENCY was pleaſed to order the Aſſembly to be called in, and made the following Speech to the Council and ſaid Aſſembly, *viz.*

Gentlemen,

WHEN His Majeſty did me the Honour to appoint me Governour of this Iſland, I was in Hopes I ſhould have been able to have attended the Service of it immediately, but the ſetling my Affairs took up a much greater Time than I expected which was the Reaſon I had not the Satisfaction of ſeeing you ſooner; but even during that Delay, I endeavour'd to make my ſelf as uſeful to you as I cou'd, by repreſenting the many Hardſhips and Diſadvantages the Trade of this Iſland now labours under, and by ſolliciting for a ſpeedy Redreſs: How fortunate I may have been in my earneſt Endeavours for obtaining it, I can't ſay. Cou'd the Succeſs be equal to the Deſire I have of ſerving you, you wou'd ſoon have all your Expectations anſwer'd, and all your Wiſhes granted: But this with Pleaſure I can aſſure you, ſeveral Reſolutions have already been agreed to in your Favour, and I do not in the leaſt doubt, from the known Goodneſs of our moſt gracious King, and from the Aſſiſtance you may expect from the Juſtice of the Britiſh Parliament, you will have a conſiderable Relief in a very ſhort Time.

Gentlemen of the Aſſembly,

ALtho' it may have been a Cuſtom for ſome Governours upon their firſt coming to call a New Aſſembly, the Confidence I have in your Wiſdom and Care for the Publick Good, and the Deſire I have that the neceſſary Buſineſs of this Iſland ſhou'd have all imaginable Diſpatch, determin'd me not to follow their Example, but call you together the firſt Opportunity, (I am ſure this Iſland will find the Good Effects of it) I fix'd upon the Day to which you ſtood adjourn'd, it being the moſt agreeable to me becauſe I thought it would be the moſt convenient to you.

I have Orders from His MAJESTY to lay before you ſeveral Inſtructions tending to the Honour, Security and Advantage of this Iſland: All theſe at proper Times ſhall be communicated to you.

I have alſo receiv'd an Additional Inſtruction relating to me, and the Support of the Dignity of this Government, but being unwilling to enlarge upon an Affair which in ſo great a Meaſure, relates to my ſelf, and relying wholly upon you, you ſhall now have a Copy of it.

I believe you will all agree that the preſent State of the Fortifications of this Iſland requires your utmoſt Attention, your own Security depending ſo much upon their being put and kept in good Repair, I need not make Uſe of any Arguments to enforce the Neceſſity of it.

Gentlemen of the Council, and Gentlemen of the Aſſembly,

I Have nothing more at Heart than the Proſperity of this Iſland; my Incli- nations,

The Barbados Gazette, *1733, a newspaper with many ties with United States.*

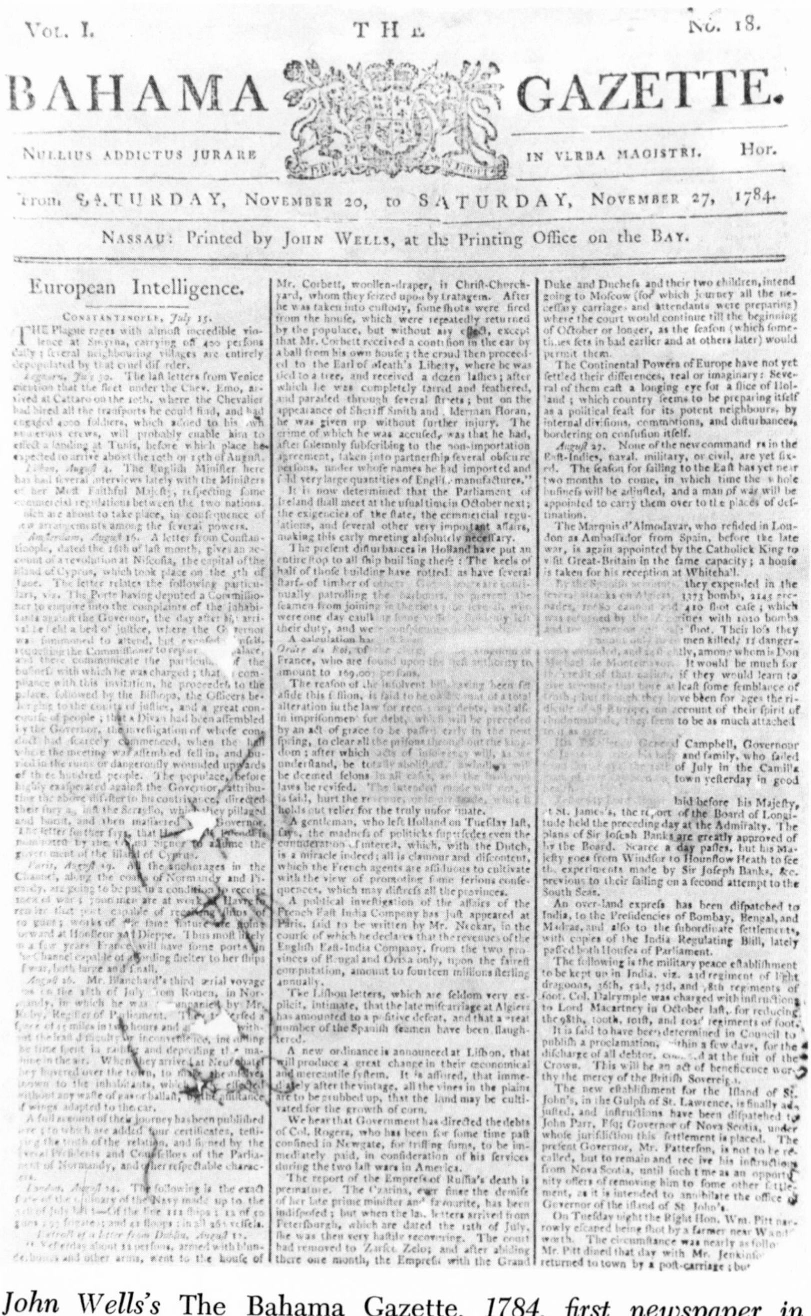

VOL. I. THE No. 18.

BAHAMA GAZETTE.

NULLIUS ADDICTUS JURARE IN VERBA MAGISTRI. Hor.

From SATURDAY, NOVEMBER 20, to SATURDAY, NOVEMBER 27, 1784.

NASSAU: Printed by JOHN WELLS, at the Printing Office on the BAY.

European Intelligence.

CONSTANTINOPLE, *July* 15.

THE Plague rages with almoſt incredible violence at Smyrna, carrying off 400 perſons daily; ſeveral neighbouring villages are entirely depopulated by that cruel diſorder.

Leghorn, July 30. The laſt letters from Venice mention that the fleet under the Chev. Emo, arrived at Cattaro on the 10th, where the Chevalier had hired all the tranſports he could find, and had engaged 4000 ſoldiers, which added to his own numerous crews, will probably enable him to effect a landing at Tunis, before which place he expected to arrive about the 10th or 15th of Auguſt.

Liſbon, Auguſt 4. The Engliſh Miniſter here has had ſeveral interviews lately with the Miniſters of her Moſt Faithful Majeſty, reſpecting ſome commercial regulations between the two nations, which are about to take place, in conſequence of new arrangements among the ſeveral powers.

Amſterdam, Auguſt 16. A letter from Conſtantinople, dated the 16th of laſt month, gives an account of a revolution at Niſcoſia, the capital of the iſland of Cyprus, which took place on the 5th of June. The letter relates the following particulars, viz. The Porte having deputed a Commiſſioner to enquire into the complaints of the inhabitants againſt the Governor, the day after his arrival he held a bed of juſtice, where the Governor was ſummoned to attend, but excuſed himſelf, requeſting the Commiſſioner to repair [illegible] palace, and there communicate the particulars of the buſineſs with which he was charged; that [illegible] compliance with this invitation, he proceeded to the palace, followed by the Biſhops, the Officers belonging to the courts of juſtice, and a great concourſe of people; that a Divan had been aſſembled by the Governor, the inveſtigation of whoſe conduct had ſcarcely commenced, when the hall where the meeting was aſſembled fell in, and buried in the ruins or dangerouſly wounded upwards of three hundred people. The populace, before highly exaſperated againſt the Governor, attributing the above diſaſter to his contrivance, directed their fury againſt the Seraglio, which they pillaged and burnt, and then maſſacred [illegible] Governor. The letter further ſays, that [illegible] nominated by the Grand Signor to aſſume the government of the iſland of Cyprus.

Paris, Auguſt 19. All the anchorages in the Channel, along the coaſts of Normandy and Picardy, are going to be put in a condition to receive men of war; 7000 men are at work at Havre to render that port capable of receiving ſhips of 70 guns; works of the ſame nature are going forward at Honfleur and Dieppe. Thus moſt likely in a few years France will have ſome ports in the Channel capable of affording ſhelter to her ſhips of war, both large and ſmall.

Auguſt 26. Mr. Blanchard's third aerial voyage was on the 18th of July from Rouen, in Normandy, in which he was accompanied by Mr. Boby, Regiſter of Parliament. They traverſed a ſpace of 15 miles in two hours and [illegible] without the leaſt difficulty or inconvenience, including the time ſpent in raiſing and depreſſing the machine in the air. When they arrived at Neufchatel they hovered over the town, to make themſelves known to the inhabitants, which [illegible] effected without any waſte of gas or ballaſt, by the aſſiſtance of wings adapted to the car.

A full account of their journey has been publiſhed here; to which are added four certificates, teſtifying the truth of the relation, and ſigned by the ſeveral Preſidents and Counſellors of the Parliament of Normandy, and other reſpectable characters.

London, Auguſt 24. The following is the exact ſtate of the [illegible] of the Navy made up to the [illegible] of July laſt:—Of the line 112 ſhips; 12 of 50 guns; [illegible] frigates; and [illegible] ſloops; in all 265 veſſels.

Extract of a letter from Dublin, Auguſt 17.

"Yeſterday about 12 perſons, armed with blunderbuſſes and other arms, went to the houſe of Mr. Corbett, woollen-draper, in Chriſt-Church-yard, whom they ſeized upon by ſtratagem. After he was taken into cuſtody, ſome ſhots were fired from the houſe, which were repeatedly returned by the populace, but without any effect, except that Mr. Corbett received a contuſion in the ear by a ball from his own houſe; the croud then proceeded to the Earl of Meath's Liberty, where he was tied to a tree, and received a dozen laſhes; after which he was completely tarred and feathered, and paraded through ſeveral ſtreets; but on the appearance of Sheriff Smith and Alderman Horan, he was given up without further injury. The crime of which he was accuſed, was that he had, after ſolemnly ſubſcribing to the non-importation agreement, taken into partnerſhip ſeveral obſcure perſons, under whoſe names he had imported and ſold very large quantities of Engliſh manufactures."

It is now determined that the Parliament of Ireland ſhall meet at the uſual time in October next; the exigencies of the ſtate, the commercial regulations, and ſeveral other very important affairs, making this early meeting abſolutely neceſſary.

The preſent diſturbances in Holland have put an entire ſtop to all ſhip building there: The keels of half of thoſe building have rotted, as have ſeveral ſtacks of timber of [illegible] are continually patrolling the harbours, to prevent the ſeamen from joining [illegible], who were one day caulking [illegible] left their duty, and were [illegible]

A calculation has [illegible] *Ordre du Roi*, of [illegible] France, who are found upon the [illegible] authority to amount to 169,000 perſons.

The reaſon of the inſolvent bill having been ſet aſide this ſeſſion, is ſaid to be on account of a total alteration in the law for recovering debts, and alſo in impriſonment for debt, which will be preceded by an act of grace to be paſſed early in the next ſpring, to clear all the priſons throughout the kingdom; after which acts of inſolvency will, as we underſtand, be totally aboliſhed. Swindlers will be deemed felons in all caſes, and the bankrupt laws be reviſed. The intended mode will not, it is ſaid, hurt the revenue, or injure trade, while it holds out relief for the truly unfortunate.

A gentleman, who left Holland on Tueſday laſt, ſays, the madneſs of politicks ſuperſedes even the conſideration of intereſt, which, with the Dutch, is a miracle indeed; all is clamour and diſcontent, which the French agents are aſſiduous to cultivate with the view of promoting ſome ſerious conſequences, which may diſtreſs all the provinces.

A political inveſtigation of the affairs of the French Eaſt India Company has juſt appeared at Paris, ſaid to be written by Mr. Neckar, in the courſe of which he declares that the revenues of the Engliſh Eaſt-India Company, from the two provinces of Bengal and Oriſsa only, upon the faireſt computation, amount to fourteen millions ſterling annually.

The Liſbon letters, which are ſeldom very explicit, intimate, that the late miſcarriage at Algiers has amounted to a poſitive defeat, and that a great number of the Spaniſh ſeamen have been ſlaughtered.

A new ordinance is announced at Liſbon, that will produce a great change in their economical and mercantile ſyſtem. It is aſſured, that immediately after the vintage, all the vines in the plains are to be grubbed up, that the land may be cultivated for the growth of corn.

We hear that Government has directed the debts of Col. Rogers, who has been for ſome time paſt confined in Newgate, for trifling ſums, to be immediately paid, in conſideration of his ſervices during the two laſt wars in America.

The report of the Empreſs of Ruſſia's death is premature. The Czarina, ever ſince the demiſe of her late prime miniſter and favourite, has been indiſpoſed; but when the laſt letters arrived from Peterſburgh, which are dated the 12th of July, ſhe was then very haſtily recovering. The court had removed to Zarſco Zelo; and after abiding there one month, the Empreſs with the Grand Duke and Ducheſs and their two children, intend going to Moſcow (for which journey all the neceſſary carriages and attendants were preparing) where the court would continue till the beginning of October or longer, as the ſeaſon (which ſometimes ſets in bad earlier and at others later) would permit them.

The Continental Powers of Europe have not yet ſettled their differences, real or imaginary: Several of them caſt a longing eye for a ſlice of Holland; which country ſeems to be preparing itſelf as a political feaſt for its potent neighbours, by internal diviſions, commotions, and diſturbances, bordering on confuſion itſelf.

Auguſt 27. None of the new commanders in the Eaſt-Indies, naval, military, or civil, are yet fixed. The ſeaſon for ſailing to the Eaſt has yet near two months to come, in which time the whole buſineſs will be adjuſted, and a man of war will be appointed to carry them over to the places of deſtination.

The Marquis d'Almodavar, who reſided in London as Ambaſſador from Spain, before the late war, is again appointed by the Catholick King to viſit Great-Britain in the ſame capacity; a houſe is taken for his reception at Whitehall.

By the Spaniſh accounts, they expended in the ſeveral attacks on Algiers, 3273 bombs, 2145 grenades, [illegible] cannon and 410 ſhot caſe; which was returned by the Algerines with 1010 bombs and [illegible] ſhot. Their loſs they [illegible] men killed, 11 dangerouſly wounded, and [illegible] ſlightly, among whom is Don Michael de Monteinavon. It would be much for the credit of that nation, if they would learn to give accounts that bore at leaſt ſome ſemblance of truth; but though they have been for ages the ridicule of all Europe, on account of their ſpirit of [illegible], they ſeem to be as much attached to it as ever.

His Excellency General Campbell, Governour of [illegible] and family, who ſailed [illegible] of July in the Camilla [illegible] town yeſterday in good health.

[illegible] laid before his Majeſty, at St. James's, the report of the Board of Longitude held the preceding day at the Admiralty. The plans of Sir Joſeph Banks are greatly approved of by the Board. Scarce a day paſſes, but his Majeſty goes from Windſor to Hounſlow Heath to ſee the experiments made by Sir Joſeph Banks, &c. previous to their ſailing on a ſecond attempt to the South Seas.

An over-land expreſs has been diſpatched to India, to the Preſidencies of Bombay, Bengal, and Madras, and alſo to the ſubordinate ſettlements, with copies of the India Regulating Bill, lately paſſed both Houſes of Parliament.

The following is the military peace eſtabliſhment to be kept up in India, viz. 23d regiment of light dragoons, 36th, 52d, 73d, and 78th regiments of foot. Col. Dalrymple was charged with inſtructions to Lord Macartney in October laſt, for reducing the 98th, 100th, 101ſt, and 102d regiments of foot.

It is ſaid to have been determined in Council to publiſh a proclamation, within a few days, for the diſcharge of all debtors, confined at the ſuit of the Crown. This will be an act of beneficence worthy the mercy of the Britiſh Sovereign.

The new eſtabliſhment for the Iſland of St. John's, in the Gulph of St. Lawrence, is finally adjuſted, and inſtructions have been diſpatched to John Parr, Eſq; Governor of Nova Scotia, under whoſe juriſdiction this ſettlement is placed. The preſent Governor, Mr. Patterſon, is not to be recalled, but to remain and receive his inſtructions from Nova Scotia, until ſuch time as an opportunity offers of removing him to ſome other ſettlement, as it is intended to annihilate the office of Governor of the iſland of St John's.

On Tueſday night the Right Hon. Wm. Pitt narrowly eſcaped being ſhot by a farmer near Wandſworth. The circumſtance was nearly as follo[ws]: Mr. Pitt dined that day with Mr. Jenkinſo[n] returned to town by a poſt-carriage; bu[t]

John Wells's The Bahama Gazette, *1784, first newspaper in Nassau.*

49 were bills, acts, and laws of the island; and 27 were the minutes, proceedings, and journals of the Assembly or courts.[22]

In the other islands too, government printing consumed a good portion of the printers' time. Printing the minutes of the House of Assembly was one of the chores Barbados's first printer was commissioned to undertake. When John Wells started the first newspaper in the Bahamas, The Bahama *Gazette*, he automatically assumed the position of government printer as well. On Dominica and Grenada, the linkage of the press with the Crown was evident in the first newspapers, which used logotypes bearing the word "Royal" or a line drawing of the king's arms.

Most of the early printing on Trinidad was accomplished by government printers, two of the first being Matthew Gallagher of The Trinidad *Courant and Commercial Gazette*, and William Lewer of The Trinidad *Gazette*. After April 25, 1825, the imprint in these papers was changed from "government printer" to "government press," hinting that the printing operations were henceforth the property of the colonial administrators. Not until the following year did Trinidad have an independent printing plant.

One can glean who was responsible for printing on St. Lucia by looking down a list of the first newspapers there. On the first through sixth newspapers, logotypes carried some variation of the line, "printed under contract at the Government Printery." Some of these periodicals were so government prone that they printed only administrative news and advertisements. Finally, with the seventh paper, *The News* of 1836, St. Lucia had an independent paper. Historian Breen, in his 1884 volume *History of St. Lucia*, described *The News* as "a laudable attempt to get rid of the shackles which continued in the British Colony to crush down the energies of the press to the level of its servitude in the reign of Louis XVI."[23] Its editor, Charles Wells, was rewarded for his stand on freedom of the press with jail sentences on at least two occasions, as well as dismissal from his post as deputy postmaster. In fact, Wells, along with some friends on the outside, edited his second newspaper, *The Palladium and St. Lucia Free Press*, from a jail cell, where he spent a year for libeling the chief justice. Even Wells started these first independent newspapers on St. Lucia while "contractor for the government printing work, availing himself of the materials at his disposal."[24]

Wells's difficulties with the officials were neither unusual nor unexpected. Printers in the Commonwealth Caribbean had hints from the beginning that their governments were not about to tolerate criticism. The governor of Jamaica made that clear even before the first press was developed on the island, setting down limits on printing. In a 1717 letter to the Council of Trade and Plantations, he wrote:

> But to prevent abuses, that might attend such a Liberty, there should be but one [printing press], and that to be licenced to the government for the time being.[25]

We learn indirectly of the first newspaper on Trinidad when reading that the island's governor had informed the king on January 27, 1790, that he (the governor) had deported Jean Viloux, editor of the weekly *Gazeta*. Viloux was accused of printing without the governor's permission "various articles from the foreign newspapers about the present revolution in France, in which were published items calculated to spread discussion, corrupt the true faith, and disturb the good order of our rule."[26] Trinidad's second printer had a more permanent tenure, though he spent some of it in prison for his articles against the chief justice.[27]

In discussing the state of freedom of the press in colonial Trinidad, Carmichael has said:

> The British Governors or officials exercised a strict control over the Press. Governor Woodford, when annoyed by any articles published, would send a polite note to the editor asking for the loan of the handle of the printing press, thus virtually suspending publication until its return.[28]

Methods of harassing editors were not always executed as subtly as borrowing a press handle. Judicial procedures sometimes were very harshly carried out. For example, St. Lucian editor Charles Wells was tried without a jury and found guilty by the judge he supposedly libeled. Samuel Keimer was charged with defamatory libel by a member of the King's Council of Barbados, and, even though the attorney general ruled that there was nothing libelous in Keimer's paper, Barbados *Gazette*, he was still "bound to keep the peace during six months."[29] In 1811 a St. Kitts paper was fined twenty-five pounds and its editor imprisoned one month for libel after publishing a resolution against a man who had committed an act of barbarity. Even though the House of Assembly and Council endorsed the resolution, the libel suit was still successfully prosecuted.[30]

Breach of privilege was the charge frequently brought against the colonial printer in Jamaica. Authorities felt it vital to protect administrative organizations from derogatory exposures in the press. In 1787, for example, libel charges were filed against the Kingston *Morning Post* and the Jamaica *Gazette* for "grossly reflecting upon the proceedings of the select committee of this house [Assembly] . . . ."[31] Apparently realizing what was in store for them, the editors went into hiding and escaped conviction.

An 1806 breach of privilege proceeding against The Kingston *Chronicle and City Advertiser, The Daily Advertiser,* and *The Courant* has been featured as one of the most significant cases in Jamaican press history,[32] although a reason for such a description has not been afforded. The editors, as in the above case, were accused of printing resolutions of the House that showed this prestigious body in a negative light. The long drawn-out case ended with the editors being reprimanded and the dignity of the House vindicated. The significance of the case might have been due to the fact that three of the printers involved were important government employees, Alexander Aikman, Sr., Alexander Aikman, Jr., and George Strupar. Strupar's defense of his right to publish the House proceedings[33] has been quoted in some Jamaican sources with the same reverence Americans have given to remarks by Andrew Hamilton in his defense of John Peter Zenger.

The perturbation that officials felt as a result of the press can be gauged from this 1732 letter to the Barbados *Gazette,* written by a member of that island's House of Assembly:

> Thus are we brought, by that accursed machine of yours, unknown to our forefathers, under the miserable dilemma of either dropping our ancient and undoubted privilege, or becoming the ridicule of phlegmatick [sic] Londoners. . . . if you do not speedily change your pernicious trade of printing . . . I will move the House . . . for leave to bring in a bill for the utter demolition of all printers and printing-shops.[34]

Paradoxically enough, many colonial printers thought that they were supporting the government at the time charges were brought against them. Keimer repeatedly indicated that his newspaper was pro-government, even choosing his correspondents by the criterion that they, too, were for the government. He wrote on December 30, 1732, " 'Tis a peculiar pleasure to me to observe that all my new correspondents, worthy of notice, are favourers of government." In turn, prospective correspondents wanted to be certain of the newspaper's politics, as this excerpt from the Barbados *Gazette* indicates:

> As we have observed nothing in your Papers which relates to this island but what tends to promote the real welfare of it . . . we do not think it beneath us to become your joint correspondents.

THE CONTENT: LAWS, LETTERS, LITERARY

With steady pressure from the authorities, it would seem likely that the contents[35] of colonial newspapers would include a generous amount of governmental information, and indeed they did. Laws, minutes of meetings, speeches, and essays pertaining to governmental matters usually filled at least page one.

But not all the newspapers acted as stooges for the governments; there were those which took stands on public issues, and there were those, too, which went in for sensationalism.[36] In his "Letters on Slavery," William Dickson pointed out that Jamaican newspapers were discussing the touchy subject of emancipation back in 1789:

> The spirit, good sense and humanity of the printers of the Jamaica newspapers ought not to be forgotten: for they have shown themselves superior alike to the taints of the "profligate" and the malevolence of the "unmerciful"; discouragements which all good men must expect to meet with in the discharge of their duty. Were I to give a similar account of the Barbadoes printers and their worthy correspondents, it would be said I courted their applause. Let the humane enquirer into this Subject compare the Barbadoes *Gazette and Mercury* with the other West Indian prints, and judge for himself.[37]

Much of the controversy in colonial newspapers resulted from the numerous letters to the editors, usually signed with pseudonyms, as they still frequently are. Thus, one reads letters in the first issues of the Barbados *Gazette* signed by "Dorothy Doubt," "Publicola," "Philalethes," "Charles Meanwell," or "Henry Hinter." Editor Keimer played a guessing game in print, with notes over the letters such as "The following letter comes from a hand that I remember to have seen twice before," or "What I shall give, for the entertainment of this day, came, if I mistake not, from a gentleman who. . . ."[38]

Some of the most intense controversy in the colonial West Indies appeared in the essayistic books and pamphlets that dominated the literary scene. Subjects of these works included masonry, the militia, religion, slavery, and, most popular of all, medicine. Professional rivalry among doctors was so keen that duels were fought because of what doctors said of one another. For example, one of the first pamphlets in Jamaica, *Essays on the Bilious Fever, Containing the Different Opinions of Those Eminent Physicians John Williams and Parker Bennet of Jamaica,* caused a duel between Williams and Bennet that terminated both of their lives.[39]

Passin[40] has said that the roles of the writer and journalist in traditional and transitional societies are usually close together, sometimes indistinguishable. This was so (and still is) in the Commonwealth Caribbean. Keimer in colonial Barbados thought of himself as a poet, as did a number of the contributors to his newspaper.[41] John Rippingham, editor of the Jamaica *Journal* in the early nineteenth century, was a book author, as were a number of his press colleagues.

In most of the West Indies, the early printers wore the hats of editor, pressman, writer, literary agent, and sometimes politician and postmaster as well. Before magazines, books, and almanacs were printed in quantity, newspapers served as the only outlets for literary fare. Some newspapers, such as *L'Impartial Journal Politique, Commercial et Litteraire de Ste. Lucie,* displayed in their nameplates the close liaison between journalism, literature, and politics that Passin discussed.[42] Other papers used literary works to convey news and express opinions, as these poems in the Barbados *Gazette* emphasize: "To Miss ——— on Her Dancing at Mr. Frith's Ball in Bridge-Town, December 18, 1732," or "To the Reverend Mr. Gordon, on His Success in the Complaints Against the Late Governor of Barbados. Written in the Year 1720," or "To Mr. ——— on His Having Resolved To Write No More. By Clio."[43]

EARLY AMERICAN MEDIA INVASION

The global media invasion by the United States that Herbert Schiller[44] feared in the late 1960s had its rudimentary counterpart in the colonial West Indies. For example, the first printers in Antigua, Bahamas, Barbados, and Jamaica were either exports or exiles from the United States. Also, the most famous United States printer, Benjamin Franklin, along with three printing partners in the Commonwealth Caribbean, was responsible for the first newspaper absentee ownership in that part of the world.

A number of the United States printer-emigrants wandered south at the time of the American Revolution, dissatisfied with political affairs in the thirteen colonies. The manager of the American Theatre, David Douglas, left for political reasons and ended up in Jamaica as printer when the American war for independence commenced. The Revolution also forced Alexander Aikman, Sr., a South Carolina printer, to Jamaica, where he became a partner with Douglas and William Aikman on the Jamaica *Mercury*.[45] Another South Carolina printer, John Wells, fled Charleston when the British Army left that city,[46] and by 1784 had drifted to Nassau where he developed The Bahama *Gazette*.

Isaiah Thomas, ranked with the Franklins and Bradfords as a distinguished colonial printer, almost became Bermuda's first printer. In 1772, when American politics became quite perplexing to the editor of the Massachusetts *Spy*, Thomas thought about moving his press to his wife's home on Bermuda. In a letter to his father-in-law, Joseph Dill, Thomas wrote on March 18, 1772, that he could be encouraged to come to Bermuda:

> If Sir, you and the gentlemen of your Island are still willing to encourage me, I beg you would favor me once more with a Line, as soon as it shall seem agreeable to you, that I may settle my affairs here so as to come over in the fall.[47]

For business rather than political reasons, Benjamin Franklin had many contacts with the British Caribbean. Two of his many partnerships were in the West Indies—one supposedly with William Daniell,[48] printer to the Assembly in Kingston, Jamaica, the other with Thomas Smith, and later Benjamin Mecom, in Antigua. Some question has been raised about the Daniell-Franklin partnership. If they were not partners, then it is certain that Franklin was Daniell's newsprint and equipment supplier. In a letter dated July 21, 1755, Daniell sent Franklin copies of Jamaican newspapers, and in turn pleaded that the American printer "let me know as soon as possible ab't your supplying me constantly [with reams of paper] as I am obligated to wait your answer persuant [sic] to your Desire."[49] In addition to supplying printing materials in exchange for coffee, sugar, rum, and money, Franklin on other occasions also printed almanacs for Jamaicans and Barbadians. *The Barbados Almanack for 1752*, for example, was prepared by Franklin & Hall at Philadelphia; ten years previously, Franklin was charging a "Joseph Grover of Jamaica" for "printing and paper 1200 Almanacks."[50]

The Franklin partnership in Antigua has been verified by a number of historians, including Isaiah Thomas[51] and Franklin[52] himself. In 1748 Thomas Smith was sent to Antigua by Franklin with the purpose of developing a press. Franklin thought highly of his partner at that point, calling him "a very sober, honest and diligent young man," but apparently had reason to revise his assessment later when he wrote, "Smith grew careless and got to sitting up late in taverns."[53] When Smith died in 1752, Franklin sent his own nephew, Benjamin Mecom, to continue the operation of the press and The Antigua *Gazette*. Within a few years, Mecom grew dissatisfied with the partnership, not liking the arrangement whereby he paid fixed annual sums to his mother as well as to his uncle.[54] He left Antigua for Boston, taking his equipment with him.

Franklin's name appears in the story of the meanderings of the first printers of Barbados, too. Both Franklin and David Harry, Barbados's first printer, had been apprentices of Samuel Keimer in Philadelphia.[55] Later, when Harry bought out Keimer's operation and Franklin had his own shop, the latter proposed a partnership with Harry. Harry refused the partnership and continued running in the red until, by 1730, he followed Keimer to Barbados, taking his press with him. Eventually, Harry employed Keimer to work the press, thus inspiring Franklin to write "the master became the journeyman of his former apprentice."[56] Harry did no better in Barbados than he had in Philadelphia and resold the press to Keimer. A year later, in 1731, Keimer started the first newspaper in all of the Americas to publish twice a week, the Barbados *Gazette*.

FOR SALE:
NEWSPAPERS, SNUFF, CRIBBAGE BOARDS

Subscriptions and advertisements certainly did not keep newspaper ledger books in the black. Newspapers were expensive in the colonial West Indies. For example, *The Royal Gazette and Bahama Advertiser*, published twice weekly, cost its subscribers $7½ (Bahamian) annually, at a time when a slave in that colony, depending on his age and strength, could be purchased for $200 to $300. The weekly *Gleaner*, when it first appeared in 1834, cost 2 pounds yearly, whereas special magistrates hired to oversee apprentice help were paid only 300 pounds yearly. A more frequently published Jamaican newspaper at the time cost 5 pounds yearly. To cite one other example, *The Liberal*, published twice a week in Barbados, in 1858 charged $8 a year for a subscription. "First class laborers" were being paid 30 cents a day in Barbados, "second class laborers," 15-20 cents. Of course, before Emancipation in 1833, most of the residents of the islands were slaves with no earning power to purchase newspapers. For example, in 1787 Jamaica's population included 210,894 slaves and 25,000 whites. Because of these factors, circulations were small. In Jamaica during the volatile 1830s, the largest circulation was that of the Jamaica *Despatch*, with 500 subscribers; the average newspaper had 100 customers.

First issue of The Gleaner, *Kingston, Jamaica, one of oldest surviving newspapers in the islands.*

Lack of a well-developed mercantile community did not allow for large advertising linage, either. On innumerable occasions, West Indian editors had to seek help elsewhere—from their governments, from the local citizenry through ingenious business deals, or from outsiders such as Franklin, who helped in obtaining newsprint and equipment, in addition to books, stationery, and other salable goods. Even today, the largest newspapers on Barbados, St. Lucia, and St. Vincent are supported in part by their bookstores.

Printers made space available in their shops for all sorts of merchandise, and they advertised these goods in their papers. Here is an advertisement that appeared in The Bahama *Gazette* of September 4–11, 1784:

> For sale at the printing office, drawing, writing and musick paper, scaling [*sic*] wax and wasers, German and common flutes, pocket books, merchants account books, memorandum books, pounce and pounce boxes, red and black ink powder, maps and charts, pewter and ebony ink stands, black bonds, bills of sale, bills of lading, powers of attorney, seamen's articles, apprentice indentures, etc., etc., etc. Printing work, done with accuracy and dispatch.[57]

Within the year, the *Gazette* editor increased his items for sale to about 200, adding foodstuffs, cases, ox tongues, clothing, medicines, ivory, and cribbage boards.

The editor of the Barbados *Gazette* in 1787 was bottling spirituous drinks for sale at his shop, for he advertised in the November 17–21 issue:

> Four bitts a doz. will be given, for 50 or 60 dozen of empty Quart Bottles. Apply to the Printer. Who wants to hire, an honest, sober negro man who can attend in a family; if he has been used to a liquor store, he will be more acceptable.

A few weeks later in the December 8–12 issue, the same editor was selling

> London particular and London market wines by the gallon. Port wine by the dozen, ale by the dozen . . . a few bottles of genuine muccadau snuff, etc., etc.[58]

A set of curious advertisements was inserted in The Bahama *Gazette*, causing one to wonder what Printer Wells was marketing. In the October 30, 1784, issue, he wrote:

> Wanted to purchase, a NEGRO WOMAN who is a good washer and ironer. Enquire of the printer.

In less than three months, he was selling:

> A Negro wench, who is a good seamstress, washer and ironer, with her two female children.

Besides merchandising these diversified products, the colonial printers also sought as much job printing as they could get, printing government documents, almanacs, and literary works. An example of the amount of printing some island governments supported is the fact that in 1829, the Jamaican Assembly contracted with eight different printers.[59]

The profitable almanacs were among the first publications of the Commonwealth Caribbean; in fact, an almanac for Jamaica was printed in London as early as 1672. Two of the first Jamaican printers, John Letts and M. Baldwin, entered the almanac publishing business almost immediately, issuing the first *Jamaica Almanac,* in broadsheet format, in 1734. The oldest Jamaican almanac in book form (and the earliest Jamaican book) was published in 1751, the *Merchant's Pocket Companion; or, An Almanac for the Year of Our Lord 1751.* Bermuda had an almanac from the first year of a press on that island,[60] and Dominica had an *Almanac and Register* at least as early as 1825.

Another source of revenue was through the printing of books and pamphlets, many of which were written for vainglorious purposes, others to settle controversial arguments mentioned earlier. The earliest book published in the islands appeared in Barbados in 1741, printed by William Beeby and entitled *Some Memoirs of the First Settlement of the Island of Barbados.* Shortly after, in 1749, the first book printed on Antigua was commissioned by the Reverend William Shervington when he wished to circulate more widely his *Occasional Poems;* the island's second book dealt with the popular subject of medicine.[61]

Even with these sideline projects, the colonial printer of the West Indies faced the prospect of a bleak existence. Devaux said of the situation on St. Lucia:

> Even if they [printers] had the ability or desire to undertake the duties of a purveyor of news and opinion, the prospect of a decent livelihood in that venture was such as to discourage anyone from taking the step.[62]

Jamaica Daily Telegraph, *1907, announcing earthquake that hit Kingston. Note warning to vendors in bottom center.*

The editors pleaded, in prose and verse, subtly and rudely, that subscriptions be paid on time, but usually to no avail. Thus, we read in the *Royal Gazette* of Jamaica in 1780:

> The Publishers of this Paper find themselves at last under the disagreeable necessity of giving Notice to their Subscribers who reside in the Country, that they shall, after one Month from this date, discontinue the News-Paper of those Gentlemen whose Subscriptions are not paid up to the First of May last.[63]

Keimer, in his Barbados *Gazette* of May 4, 1734, resorted to poetry in an attempt to embarrass delinquent subscribers. A few lines from "The Sorrowful Lamentation of Samuel Keimer, Printer of the Barbadoes Gazette" follow:

> What a pity it is that *some* modern Bravadoes,
> Who dub themselves Gentlemen here in Barbadoes,
> Should, Time after Time, run in Debt to their Printer,
> And care not to pay him in Summer and Winter![64]

Despite these handicaps, the printers continually established and nurtured new periodicals, as witnessed in the number of competing newspapers some islands had as early as the late eighteenth and early nineteenth centuries. Jamaica had at least four newspapers publishing in 1756; Antigua and St. Christopher, two in 1768 and 1769 respectively; Trinidad, four in 1831; Barbados, six in 1848; Dominica, four in 1790, St. Lucia, two in 1839; St. Vincent, two in the 1820s. One can get an idea of the strain under which competing newspapers operated by observing that in 1838, when the Bahamas had more than one newspaper, "there was no more patronage than would support one paper respectably and the rivals came out on blotting paper, wrapping paper, seidlitz powder and turmeric paper."[65]

By the beginning of the nineteenth century, the West Indies had seen the birth of forty-four newspapers,[66] including at least two dailies, *The Daily Advertiser* and The Kingston *Morning Post*, both published in Jamaica. In addition, at least four magazines commenced publication—all in Jamaica—during the eighteenth century. Probably the first magazine of the Commonwealth Caribbean was *Jamaica Magazine or Monthly Chronicle*, which appeared first in 1781 with articles on "History of Jamaica" and "Methods of Preparing Wood to Resist Fire," poetry, monthly occurrences, and death notices. By 1793 the second Jamaican magazine, *The Bon E'Sprit Magazine, or Abstract of the Times*, was initiated by William Smart. By the fourth edition, the magazine was in financial trouble and Smart wrote, "He finds himself also under the necessity to say that his finances are so very limited as to preclude every idea of running upon tick."[67] Smart also published the third magazine on the island in 1796, *The Colombian Magazine; or Monthly Miscellany.*

CRISES-ORIENTED PRESS

Sherlock[68] listed three watershed dates, or periods, in the history of the Commonwealth Caribbean: 1650, when it became clear that sugar would become the main crop of the region "with the estate owner dispossessing the smallholder and the African slave the white bondservant"; 1834, when the British Parliament enforced the Act of Emancipation, ending slavery in the islands; and 1938 to 1944, "marking the end of the post-emancipation period of colonial rule and the establishment of popular governments through universal adult suffrage, with independence and nationhood as accepted goals."

Up to the time of the second watershed period, the press of the Commonwealth Caribbean islands fitted into a traditional model of communications, being limited in information and channels it could provide, lacking professionally trained media personnel, suffering under an authoritarian rule, and utilizing content colored by the "status relationships between communicator and recipient."[69]

At about the time of Emancipation, British West Indian presses entered a transitional period that they are still partly in today, incorporating a great deal of face-to-face, communal, communications but also taking on some modernistic traits. Among some of the latter were an independent, crusading spirit, an awareness of the problems of society and an interest in curing them, and the use of modern technology in providing better mail services, the telegraph, and, later, after the 1930s, electronic media.

Curtin[70] discusses the role of mass media in Jamaica during this transitional period, pointing out the continued use of traditional communications:

> The news was spread through the overheard conversations of the whites, by rumor from slaves who had been in Britain with their masters, by occasional literate slaves or people of color who were willing to read newspapers aloud.

At the same time, Curtin believes that enough accoutrements of a modernistic nature—schools, periodicals, improvement societies, libraries, book publishers, and newspapers—were available to create a Jamaican public opinion. One of the opinion formulators, the newspaper, certainly was available, to the extent that Curtin complained that the island was "decidedly over-papered."[71] For example, during the immediate Emancipation era, 1830–34, more than twenty different periodicals were published in Jamaica, all with small circulations, most of an amateurish nature.

All of the dozen or so newspapers, with one exception, followed the tone of the Jamaica *Despatch*, a tone of "violence and scurrility against the emancipators, the government, the Negroes, and the missionaries."[72] The exception to this planter-class press was the *Watchman*, an organ of the "coloureds," edited by Robert Osborn and Edward Jordan. By 1832, as the crisis over Emancipation deepened, Jordan was indicted for "constructive treason" because of an anti-slavery article in the *Watchman*. Curtin felt that had Jordan been convicted, a white-colored racial war would have ensued.[73]

Most contemporary references to the *Watchman* are characterized by glowing, idealistic terms. However, in 1835 a Jamaican writer thought this of the paper:

> An inferior publication edited by persons of colour; but, from the virulence and indecency with which it attacked the respectable part of the community, it received but little patronage.[74]

Bitterness prevailed over the emancipation issue in Jamaica and, to a lesser degree, in the other islands. Pro-slavery writers predominated, using any one of three arguments to defend the continued use of slavery: (1) slavery was beneficial to Great Britain and therefore could not be given up easily; (2) the evils of slavery did not really bother the Jamaican slaves; (3) the results of Emancipation would be disastrous.[75]

The severity of this regional dispute was borne out by a Jamaica *Courant* article of 1831, expressing what was passed off as the opinion of Jamaicans on anti-slavery advocates:

> Shooting is . . . too honourable a death for men whose conduct has occasioned so much bloodshed, and the loss of so much property. There are fine hanging woods in St. James and Trelawney, and we do sincerely hope that the bodies of all Methodist preachers who may be convicted of sedition, may diversify the scene.[76]

Civil rights campaigns have always moved a little more slowly in Barbados.[77] Not until 1836 did the blacks of that island have their first newspaper, *New Times*. Samuel Prescod, known as the father of franchise reform in Barbados, served as editor without pay for eight months before being relieved of his duties because he was considered too outspoken for conservative Bridgetown.[78] Prescod, although at different times a judge, politician, and statesman, really came into prominence with *The Liberal*, a newspaper started in 1837 that was the spokesman for the laboring and middle classes of all colors.

In the Bahamas political dissension over the emancipation issue came to the fore after 1829,[79] when a section of the community set up George Biggs as editor and publisher of the Bahamas *Argus*, a violently anti-Emancipation, anti-government semi-weekly.

As Emancipation, and later colonial status, sparked heated debate, newspapers exploded onto the scene in Commonwealth Caribbean territories, to the extent that the number of papers in the first half of the nineteenth century (104) more than doubled the total of the eighteenth century (44) (see table 1). Some islands had more newspapers in those crises-laden times than they do today. For example, one writer attributed the demise of the *Royal Gazette* of Bahamas in 1857 to the fact that "the community did not require and could not support three newspapers."[80] In 1848 Barbados supported six newspapers, spread over six days of the week: *The Mercury and Gazette* on Tuesday and Thursday, the Barbados *Globe and Colonial Advocate* on Monday and Thursday, *The Barbadian* on Wednesday and Saturday, in addition to *The West Indian* and *Agricultural Reporter*.[81] The trend continued into the latter half of the Victorian Century until by 1886 Kingston, Jamaica, had four dailies, two more than exist today in any Commonwealth Caribbean nation.

Frustrations caused by the Crown Colony system also stimulated the growth of newspapers, especially in Trinidad and St. Lucia. As early as 1845 the Trinidad *Spectator* attempted to obtain representative government for that island, and in 1862, when the income tax was introduced into Trinidad, the Trinidad *Colonist* argued vigorously against taxation without representation.[82] In the main, Trinidadian newspapers were effective with their crusades: for example, a governor was recalled in 1880, an attorney general relieved of his office in 1870, and a chief justice censured in 1892, all because of newspaper campaigns. One editor, Georges Numa Dessources of the *Trinidadian*, was so disenchanted with Crown Colony rule in 1852 that he tried to found a republican state on the banks of the Orinoco, much to the displeasure of Venezuelan officials.[83]

In addition to these anti-colonial organs, a St. Lucian newspaper, *The Daylight*, started publication in 1898 "in the interest of our fel-

TABLE 2.1
NUMBER OF COMMONWEALTH CARIBBEAN NEWSPAPERS

Country	1700–49	1750–99	1800–49	1850–99	1900–71	Total
Bahamas	0	1	6	6	18	31
Barbados	1	1	12	13	22	49
Bermuda	0	1	4	5	4	14
Virgin Islands (British)	0	0	0	0	2	2
Caymans, Turks	0	0	0	1	1	2
Jamaica	2	13	43	34	64	156
Leewards						
Anguilla	0	0	0	0	2	2
Antigua	0	4	5	4	9	22
Montserrat	0	0	0	2	4	6
Nevis	0	0	0	2	3	5
St. Kitts	1	4	1	12	8	26
Trinidad-Tobago	0	2	10	19	18	49
Windwards						
Dominica	0	10	5	9	16	40
Grenada	0	3	5	9	9	26
St. Lucia	0	1	8	8	11	28
St. Vincent	0	0	5	8	6	19
Grand Total	4	40	104	132	197	477

SOURCE: Compilation by author (see Appendix A).

lowmen who live in the Crown Colonies and for the instruction of those who are not acquainted with the evils of the Crown Colony system of government," despite its motto, "for the queen, the law and the people."[84]

St. Kitts also had its crusading editor, Richard Cable, who in the 1880s published the dailies *The Daily Express of the St. Christopher Advertiser* and the St. Kitts *Daily Express*, plus the monthly organ of the St. Kitts Mutual Improvement Society, *Reporter*. All were published with political motives in mind. Cable was described as a man with a "stinging pen who was qualified to cope with his many contemporaries, or even surpassed them in his editorial role."[85]

The newspapers and editors during this independent-press period did suffer recriminations because of what they wrote. Jordan, the Jamaican editor, spent six months in jail because of a libel charge, and Prescod suffered a similar fate in Barbados. In 1832 the Port of Spain *Gazette* was refused any further court advertisements because it had run afoul of the chief justice[86] and because at about the same time editorials in the *Gazette* were dated from No. 1 Clarence Street, site of the jail. Subscriptions to the Trinidad *Sentinel* dwindled in number when in 1858 that paper wrote about the prejudice among Trinidadians.

ADVENT OF THE TELEGRAPH

Although newspapers seemed to be prospering during the nineteenth century, they did not do much to alleviate the inter- and intra-island communication problems of the British West Indies. Most newspapers were published in, and meant for, the island capital, oftentimes never reaching outlying areas, let alone neighboring islands. For example, on an island as small as St. Vincent (its greatest length, 18 miles; greatest breadth, 11 miles), communication with rural people in the mid-nineteenth century entailed the following:

> Over these roads, rough at all times and muddy when rains fell, letters and other messages were conveyed by messengers on foot or on horseback, a foot messenger taking six to eight hours to go between Kingstown and Georgetown. In the case of England's Crimean War, news of the fall of the Sebastopol fortress in September 1856 was received in St. Vincent by the Government some weeks after. On the day when the news came a messenger, sent from Kingstown on horseback, went proclaiming the tidings up the Windward highway. The sun went down and he was still going. Weary and worn he reached Georgetown in the shades of the night shouting "Sebastopol is taken!"[87]

The communication situation improved slightly with the growth of trade between Great Britain and the West Indies during the nineteenth century.[88] For example, by 1837 a regular fortnightly mail service existed between Falmouth and the West Indian ports. By 1873 mail from Great Britain was landed in St. Christopher fortnightly; letters for neighboring Montserrat were brought there by small schooners, which were then met by rowboats put off to bring the mail ashore to impatient colonists.[89]

But it was really up to the telegraph, and later, broadcasting, to link the islands internally as well as with the rest of the world. However, the deplorable communication systems within and between islands notwithstanding, telecommunication machinery was accepted on some islands with the greatest reluctance. When Grenada was being connected telegraphically with the world in 1871, a score of years after its success in Europe, the House of Assembly was so unimpressed that it debated naming the telegraph act "Act to tax the whole community and to benefit only a few interested parties."[90] Telegraph service in Jamaica was opposed by the propertied class, who observed that foreign news was uninteresting. A telegraph act was not passed in the Bahamas until 1891.

Once it was accepted, the telegraph had profound influences upon Commonwealth Caribbean printed media, giving the traditionally insularist press a chance to glimpse the outside world, if it cared to do so. To make sure that more than just a "few interested parties" benefited from the telegraph, the West Indian and Panama Telegraph Company and, in one case, an island government, supplied a free daily bulletin of world news, posted outside their offices. This type of medium was described by a Barbadian pressman as highly important for reporting on British cricket matches:

> Until then [1935] news travelled slowly, and the sole sources in the various islands were the bulletin boards outside the cable offices in the principal towns. Brief news reports were telegraphed thrice daily, at start of [cricket] play, luncheon intervals and when stumps were drawn. These bulletins seldom appeared less than an hour after the event and long queues of fans would line up for the momentous tidings.[91]

The Trinidad Public Works Department in 1881 erected a building to house a "Commercial News Room" and the offices of the West Indian and Panama Telegraph Company. The newsroom served as a meeting place for merchants, shippers, and other businessmen, who could study the latest foreign newspapers and periodicals and see telegraph news from Europe that was posted upon arrival.[92]

On Dominica a newspaper resulted from the daily posting of news items by the telegraph company. When in 1902 the elites of Roseau tired of walking to the wireless office to read overseas news, they persuaded the Roman Catholic bishop, who had a print shop, to issue a newspaper. This predecessor of today's Dominica *Chronicle*, called the *Cable News*, virtually reproduced the wireless items.[93]

PERSONAL JOURNALISM

By the end of the nineteenth century, personal journalism had grown so rampant in the region that newspapers on an island such as Barbados seemed more bent on destroying each other than destroying the evils of the society. Until the Barbados *Advocate* changed the tide in 1895, it was not uncommon to read of one Barbadian paper labeling another as a "dirty son of Ananias" or "a filthy excrescence on responsible journalism."[94]

In many cases the newspapers lived only as long as their editors or their editors' causes, a trait not unusual in Commonwealth Caribbean journalism even today. Because of such fly-by-night appearances by newspapers, one can count on one hand the number of contemporary papers that pre-date the twentieth century. They are the Nassau *Guardian* (1844), Barbados *Advocate-News* (1895), *Daily Gleaner* (1834), *Royal Gazette* of Bermuda (1828), and *Voice of St. Lucia* (1885).[95]

Some editors, whose personal causes were defended and promoted in their journals, joined their journalistic careers with political and public aspirations;[96] thus one finds Edward Jordan and Robert Osborn both serving in the Jamaica Assembly, with Jordan holding the additional titles of mayor of Kingston, member of Council, Island Secretary, and Receiver-General. Samuel Prescod was a public official, as were members of the Moseley family, owners and editors of the Nassau *Guardian*. Jamaican hero George William Gordon owned a paper; the Speaker of the Dominican House in 1850 edited the *Dominican Colonist*, while the clerk of the same House started the *New Dominican* in 1870.

At the dawn of the new century, the Commonwealth Caribbean editors attached themselves to issues that included questioning the status of crown government, developing trade and labor unions and political parties, and driving the people to nationalism and, ultimately, independence. Among these crusading editors were: Etienne Dupuch of the Nassau *Tribune*, Clennel Wickham and Clement Inniss of the Barbados *Herald*, Valence Gale and Charles Lynch Chenery of the Barbados *Advocate*, and T. A. Marryshow of *The West Indian* of Grenada.

Even in Jamaica, where the *Gleaner* helped perpetuate a tradition of conservatism, changes toward a more activist press were developing.[97] At the forefront of the activist press movement on Jamaica was Marcus Garvey, internationally known leader of black nationalism, who used journalism to promote his personal image as well as his radical ideas. Garvey began his career as a printer but lost this job in 1907 because of his participation in a printers' strike. His firing helped guide him to "a lifelong career as an organizer for members of his race to improve their social, political, and economic condition," according to Wolseley.[98] The first of a series of periodicals Garvey was to sponsor was *Garvey's Watchman*, started while he was employed at the Jamaica government printing office in 1910. Although he supported a series of short-lived periodicals, his only other Jamaican-based publication was a political fortnightly, *Our Own*. His Jamaican, as well as Costa Rican and United States, periodicals were all designed to promote Garvey's desires for a Black House (instead of the White House), black legislators, black generals, and even a black God. No doubt Garvey's motives were questioned often, especially when his publications advertised him as the world's greatest Negro.

On the other hand, very few questions were asked about the motives of two Barbadian idealists, Clennel Wickham and Clement Inniss, who published the Barbados *Herald* from 1919–30. Both men were unselfish in their devotion to the causes of the masses, expecting neither material nor prestigious rewards for their services. This type of concern for the common man and his suffering was indeed unique in Barbados, where the people really did not care much about changing societal ills. Lewis has said, "Even the liberals took for granted the colonial social structure, seeking solely to soften its harsh edges."[99] Traditionally, the press there had been unresponsive to social problems. For example, when the Duke of Devonshire released his 1923 report on the unsatisfactory sanitary conditions in the colony, the story was ignored by all of the press except for the *Herald*.

On several occasions, when advertisers sought to starve out the *Herald*, Inniss and Wickham tightened their budget and kept right on, usually saved by generous donations from the more liberal businessmen of Barbados. However, the paper folded in 1930, not able to withstand the vindictive judgment of the Barbados Grand Jury, which awarded staggering damages in a libel suit that the *Herald* lost. The *Herald*, next to Prescod's *Liberal*, has been called the "greatest radical journal" in the island's history. If not that, then the paper probably deserved this accolade:

> It may be said without exaggeration that one of the most important events in Barbados after the first world war was the foundation of the weekly *Herald*.[100]

The Bahamians, as well as a number of other islanders, could not expect their newspapers to expose the ills of government in the same fashion that Wickham and Inniss did, especially when the government was still a chief advertiser, job printing customer, or legal threat. The newspaper in the Bahamas that did (and still does) oppose government was the *Tribune*, edited by Etienne Dupuch.* Because of its

* In 1973, at the age of 73, Sir Etienne retired.

incessant fight to break the color lines of that colony (which it succeeded in doing by the 1950s), the paper was harassed by a number of deprivations, some of which were captured by Dupuch in his *Tribune Story:*

> All kinds of things happened. Most of the time I locked horns with the all-powerful financial and political interests in the town, or I was facing a ruinous libel suit brought on me by an excess of enthusiasm for a cause the *Tribune* had espoused, or all my property was being wrecked by a hurricane.[101]

Still other editors dedicated to something other than the pound note were Valence Gale and his brother-in-law, Charles Lynch Chenery, on Barbados and T. A. Marryshow on Grenada. At a time (1895) when the Barbados economy was at its lowest point, Gale, dissatisfied with the politically oriented, personal scandal sheets of the time, started his *Advocate*. One of his first goals was to hinder the government's plan to federate, not wanting his island to lose its long tradition of representative government.

Meanwhile, over on Grenada, statesman and politician T. A. Marryshow was fired up over the idea of West Indian nationalism during a period when that subject was quite unpopular. He used *The West Indian*, which he founded in 1915, and his public offices to push his paper's motto, "West Indies must be West Indian." He also used it to pioneer the labor movement of the region with Arthur Andrew Cipriani of Trinidad. Marryshow had a gift for oratory that made the "colonial office people weep," as well as a penchant for poetry—which he published in his paper, according to a contemporary editor of *The West Indian*.[102]

SUMMARY

The story of the first two centuries of newspapers in the Commonwealth Caribbean has many parallels with press development in other colonized societies. At the outset there was the yoke of government control upon newspapers. In the British West Indies it was possibly stricter than, say, in the United States colonies because so many Commonwealth Caribbean presses were initiated and stimulated by government.

There was the close relationship between government, press, and literature of which Passin speaks, oftentimes causing conflicts of interest as well as the investiture of too much power and influence in one man. But because intellectuals were in such short supply in these colonies, it was understandable how one man might be mayor, editor, and man of the arts all rolled into one. Of course, there was the ever-present financial problem of finding subscriptions, advertisements, job printing, and sideline work to keep newspapers functioning.

Slow in initiating social and economic reform, island editors did not get around to questioning taxation without representation and their peoples' generally subservient role to Crown and slavery until the mid-nineteenth century. On Jamaica revolts had occurred earlier over the emancipation of slaves, during which time the newspapers prospered as lively, sometimes controversial, media.

Large numbers of Commonwealth Caribbean newspapers have appeared (sometimes ever so shortly) during crises such as emancipation, the nationalist and labor movements, and independence drives. It was during such times that some of the giants of West Indian journalism emerged—Wickham, Inniss, Gale, Prescod, Jordan, and Marryshow. These same periods produced a type of personal journalism, possibly resulting from the strong-man editorships, that for a brief time, at least in Barbados, was self-defeating. Newspapers solely dependent upon one man's energies and causes usually died when the editor succumbed or his cause célèbre disappeared.

NOTES TO CHAPTER 2

1. Gertrude Carmichael, *The History of the West Indian Islands of Trinidad and Tobago, 1498–1900* (London: Alvin Redman, 1961), p. 199.

2. John A. Lent, "Mass Media in the Netherlands Antilles," *Gazette* 17, nos. 1–2 (1971): 51.

3. Arthur E. Gropp, *Guide to Libraries and Archives in Central America and the West Indies, Panama, Bermuda, and British Guiana* (New Orleans, La.: Tulane University, 1941), p. 99.

4. Frank Wesley Pitman, *The Development of the British West Indies 1700–1763* (London: Frank Cass & Co., 1967); Peytraud, *L'Esclavage aux Antilles Francaises avant 1789* (Paris: 1897), p. 455; Adolphe Cabon, "Un Siecle et Demi de Journalisme en Haiti," *Proceedings of American Antiquarian Society* (April 1939), p. 123.

5. John Clyde Oswald, *Printing in the Americas* (New York: Gregg Publishing Co., 1937).

6. Gropp, *Guide to Libraries*. . . , p. 644.

7. Stanley Procope, "History of the Press (of St. Kitts)" (Unpublished manuscript in Procope's files, Basseterre, St. Kitts). Thomas listed the date of the first press on St. Christopher as 1746 and added that the press "may have been introduced two or three years sooner." Isaiah Thomas, *The History of Printing in America with a Biography of Printers and an Account of Newspapers* (Albany, N.Y.: Joel Munsell, 1874), p. 190.

8. Dates of island discoveries are from: Philip Sherlock, *West Indies* (London: Thames and Hudson, Ltd., 1966), p. 23.

9. Thomas, *History of Printing*, p. 182. At that time, Benjamin Franklin in a letter to his sister on September 14, 1752, pointed out that the Leeward Islands had only one press, the one at Antigua operated by his nephew. He wrote: "Antigua is the Seat of Government for all the Leeward Islands, to wit, St. Christopher, Nevis, and Montserrat. Benny [his nephew] will have the Business of all those Islands, there being no other Printer." Wilberforce Eames, "The Antigua Press and Benjamin Mecom, 1748–1765," *Proceedings of the American Antiquarian Society* 38 (1928): 308.

10. Frank Cundall, "Jamaica Almanacs" (Manuscript in Institute of Jamaica files, Kingston, Jamaica).

11. Frank Cundall, "The Press and Printers of Jamaica Prior to 1820," *Proceedings of the American Antiquarian Society* 26 (1916): 290.

12. E. M. Shilstone, "Some Notes on Early Printing Presses and Newspapers in Barbados," *The Journal of the Barbados Museum and Historical Society* (November 1958), p. 19.

13. Douglas McMurtrie, *Notes on the Beginning of Printing on the Island of Trinidad* (Fort Worth, Tex.: National Association for Printing Education, 1943), p. 1.

14. "The First Printing on the Island of Tobago" (Manuscript in Institute of Jamaica files, Kingston, Jamaica).

15. Douglas McMurtrie, *The First Printing in Dominica* (London: Privately printed, 1932).

16. Cundall, "The Press and Printers. . . ," p. 292.

17. Edward W. Daniel, *The Introduction of Printing into Trinidad de Barlovento* (Port of Spain: Historical Society of Trinidad and Tobago, 1949), p. 1.

18. Cundall, "The Press and Printers. . . ," p. 291.

19. Frank Cundall, "Early printing in Jamaica," *The West India Committee Circular* (April 22, 1926), pp. 150–51.

20. Peter Lund Simmonds, "Statistics of Newspapers in Various Countries," *Statistical Society of London Journal* (July 1841), p. 123.

21. Thomas, *History of Printing*, p. 185.

22. Cundall, "The Press and Printers. . . ," pp. 377–407.

23. Quoted in Robert Devaux, "History of Newspapers in St. Lucia, 1788–1970" (In preparation as publication of St. Lucia Archeological and Historical Society), p. 7.

24. H. H. Breen, *History of St. Lucia* (1844), p. 267, quoted in Devaux, p. 7.

25. Frank Cundall, *A History of Printing in Jamaica from 1717 to 1834* (Kingston: Institute of Jamaica, 1935), p. 3.

26. McMurtrie, "Notes on the Beginning. . . ," p. 2.

27. Carmichael, *Trinidad and Tobago*, p. 88.

28. Ibid., p. 369.

29. Thomas, *History of Printing*, p. 189.

30. Sir Alan Burns, *History of the British West Indies* (London: George Allen & Unwin, 1954), p. 602.

31. Cundall, "The Press and Printers. . . ," p. 323.

32. Ibid., p. 337.

33. Ibid. What he actually said was that "if he had not published the resolution, he might as well have shut up his office altogether."

34. *Barbados Gazette*, August 12, 1732, quoted in *Caribbeana. Containing Letters & Dissertations, Together with Poetical Essays, on Various Subjects and Occasions; Chiefly Wrote by Several Hands in the West Indies, and Some of Them to Gentlemen Residing There* (London: Printed for T. Osborne and W. Smith, 1741), p. 34.

35. A look at the contents of one of the earliest extant issues of The Antigua *Gazette* gives some idea of the colonial newspaper's contents. The April 12, 1755, issue of the *Gazette* included: essays entitled "Of the Use, Abuse, and Liberty of the Press, with a Little Salutary Advice," by "Reflector," and "Of the Waste of Life"; extracts from the Barbados *Gazette, Tattler* and *Spectator;* news items from Boston, New York, Philadelphia, Annapolis, Williamsburg; three columns of advertisements and a humorous column, "A Catalogue of Sundry Grievances, Which Require Immediate Redress in New York." Eames, "The Antigua Press. . . ," p. 325.

36. For example, accounts of crimes were usually given in vivid, gory details.

A murder story in the June 17, 1732, Barbados *Gazette,* contained this paragraph: "That the Child in the Womb was stabbed in several Places, that its Guts came out, and that the Deceas'd's Caul and Entrails being out of her Belly, being cut and torn in a most Lamentable manner. . . ." Quoted in *Caribbeana,* p. 26.

37. Quoted in Cundall, "The Press and Printers. . . ," pp. 326–27.

38. Quoted in *Caribbeana,* pp. 207, 321.

39. H. V. Ormsby Marshall, "The Press and Us," *Sunday Gleaner,* October 16, 1955.

40. Herbert Passin, "Writer and Journalist in the Transitional Society," in Lucian Pye, ed., *Communications and Political Development* (Princeton, N.J.: Princeton University Press, 1963), pp. 114–15.

41. Some contributors used poetry to attack Keimer, one enlightening the editor that the reason he was not making money was his lack of education:

> Magician Keimer, tho' thyself unlearn'd,
> Since by Instruction Money may be earn'd,

etc. Quoted in *Caribbeana,* p. 17.

42. Passin, "Writer and Journalist. . . ," p. 110.

43. All contained in *Caribbeana.*

44. Herbert Schiller, *Mass Communications and American Empire* (Boston: Beacon Press, 1971).

45. Douglas McMurtrie, *A History of Printing in the United States* (New York: R. R. Bowker Co., 1936), pp. 328–29.

46. Thomas, *History of Printing,* p. 194.

47. Douglas McMurtrie, *A Project for Printing in Bermuda, 1772* (Chicago: Privately printed, 1928).

48. Oswald, *Printing in the Americas,* p. 127.

49. Frank Cundall, "Benjamin Franklin's Connection with Jamaica," Jamaica *Mail,* September 26, 1929.

50. George S. Eddy, "B. Franklin and Jamaica," Jamaica *Mail,* July 27, 1929.

51. Thomas, *History of Printing,* p. 182.

52. Franklin's letters to his sister, quoted in McMurtrie, *A History of Printing,* pp. 414–15.

53. Ibid.

54. Letter of Franklin to his sister, June 28, 1756, quoted in Eames, "The Antigua Press. . . ," pp. 310–11.

55. Shilstone, "Some Notes. . . ," p. 20.

56. Quoted in Thomas, *History of Printing,* pp. 188–89.

57. Bahama *Gazette,* September 4–11, 1784, in Nassau Public Library, Nassau, Bahamas.

58. Both quotes from Shilstone, "Some Notes. . . ," p. 24.

59. Cundall, *A History of Printing in.* . . , p. 29.

60. George Watson Cole, *Bermuda in Periodical Literature* (Boston: The Boston Book Co., 1907).

61. Eames, "The Antigua Press. . . ," pp. 305, 307.

62. Devaux, "History of Newspapers. . . ," p. 5.

63. Cundall, "The Press and Printers. . . ," pp. 310–11.

64. Thomas, *History of Printing,* p. 189.

65. Mary Moseley, "Newspapers of the Bahamas, 1784–1944," Nassau *Guardian,* November 23, 1944.

66. For a complete list of newspapers of Commonwealth Caribbean, see Appendix A.

67. Cundall, "The Press and Printers. . . ," p. 329.

68. Sherlock, *West Indies,* p. 53.

69. Lucian Pye, "Models of Traditional, Transitional, and Modern Communications Systems," in Pye, ed., *Communications and Political Development,* p. 24.

70. Philip D. Curtin, *Two Jamaicas: The Role of Ideas in a Tropical Colony, 1830–1865* (Cambridge: Harvard University Press, 1955), p. 39.

71. Ibid., p. 57.

72. Ibid., p. 58.

73. Ibid.

74. Quoted in Cundall, *A History of Printing in.* . . , pp. 30–31.

75. Curtin, *Two Jamaicas*, p. 66.

76. Jamaica *Courant*, January 6, 1831.

77. Gordon K. Lewis, *The Growth of the Modern West Indies* (London: Macgibbon & Kee, 1968), pp. 86, 233.

78. H. A. Vaughan, "Samuel Prescod: The Birth of a Hero," *New World* (1966–67), p. 60.

79. Moseley, *"Newspapers. . . ,"*

80. Ibid.

81. Jimmy Cozier, "Barbadian Representatives of the Fourth Estate," Barbados *Advocate-News*, October 1, 1970, p. 3.

82. George Barrat, "Our Fighting Editors," Trinidad *Express*, June 9, 1968, pp. 45–46.

83. Donald Wood, *Trinidad in Transition* (London: Oxford University Press, 1968), p. 305.

84. Devaux, "History of Newspapers. . . ," p. 10.

85. Procope, "History of the Press. . . ."

86. Carmichael, *Trinidad and Tobago*, p. 163.

87. Ebenezer Duncan, *A Brief History of Saint Vincent* (Kingstown, St. Vincent: Graphic Printery, 1970), p. 66.

88. Carmichael, *Trinidad and Tobago*, p. 244.

89. E. C. Baker, *A Guide to Records in the Leeward Islands* (Oxford: Basil Blackwell, 1965), p. 39.

90. Kay Frances, *This — Is Grenada* (Trinidad: Caribbean Printers, 1966), p. 21. Another isolated state had problems in accepting the telegraph. When the telegraph was introduced to Japan in the 1870s, superstition and fears abounded to the extent that the people felt that the wires were coated with the blood of unmarried women.

91. Thomas A. Archer, "Radio in Barbados," *The Bajan* (March 1964), p. 29.

92. Carmichael, *Trinidad and Tobago*, p. 300.

93. Personal interview, S. A. W. Boyd, Editor, Dominica *Chronicle*, Roseau, Dominica, May 5, 1971.

94. Cozier, "Barbadian Representatives. . . ."

95. Two Catholic organs, *Catholic Opinion* (1896) of Jamaica, and *Catholic News* (1892) of Trinidad might be included except for the fact they never had to depend solely upon circulation and advertising to survive.

96. Passin said this was necessary in colonial nations because very few nations could "afford the luxury of an extreme differentiation of elite function"; thus poets, writers and artists must take part in politics, administration, and education. Pye, ed., *Models*, p. 113. See following for contemporary situation: "The Pace-Setters Who Have Passed Through Our Doors," Trinidad *Guardian*, September 24, 1967.

A contemporary journalist-turned-politician explained why many journalists end up in politics in these islands. "By the very nature of journalistic work, you find yourself becoming involved in the political life of the country. Journalists are freer to do that. Businessmen, for example, cannot take sides; it might affect their businesses." Personal interview, W. St. C. Daniel, Speaker of the House, former ed. *Voice of St. Lucia*, Castries, St. Lucia, May 8, 1971.

97. At that time, there were figures such as Dr. Robert Love who, as editor of the Jamaica *Advocate*, "had employed the Negritude that he had learned in prolonged Haitian residence in the service of the idea of black representation in the Legislative Council of the period." There were newspapers in Jamaica at the turn of the century such as the Jamaica *Times*, which reflected the views of the new peasantry "rising out of the throes of slavery and the Emancipation: a Jamaican middleclass paper, with an unmistakably local flavour and bias." Basil McFarlane, "The Rise and Fall of 'The Times,'" *The Welfare Reporter* (February 1963), p. 26.

98. Roland Wolseley, *The Black Press, U.S.A.* (Ames, Iowa: Iowa State University Press, 1971), pp. 47-8.

99. Lewis, *Modern West Indies*, p. 233.

100. F. A. Hoyos, *Our Common Heritage* (Bridgetown, Barbados: Advocate Press, 1953), pp. 142-43.

101. Sir Etienne Dupuch, *Tribune Story* (London: Ernest Benn Ltd., 1967), p. 32.

102. Personal interview, Reggie Clyne, Editor, *The West Indian*, St. George's, Grenada, May 12, 1971.

3

The Awakening (1938–44) and After

A number of writers would agree with Sherlock that "in 1938 the West Indies moved out of the nineteenth into the twentieth century."[1] It was in that watershed year that, at the cost of forty-seven dead and hundreds injured, West Indian masses decided that the road to equality of opportunity was through active protest. Workers, feeling that they had been neglected too long, demanded higher wages, better general living conditions, and constitutional changes that would take the power out of the hands of the propertied class and place it with the masses. When these demands were not met immediately, strikes and riots resulted on Trinidad, Barbados, Jamaica, and St. Kitts.

Out of the riots emerged an organized labor movement, able to get more labor legislation passed between 1938 and 1941 than in the preceding century. It was led by a number of labor organizers involved in the strikes and riots—men who eventually became national leaders, some remaining in control of individual islands until the 1970s. Men such as Alexander Bustamante and Norman Washington Manley of Jamaica, Grantley Adams of Barbados, Uriah Buzz Butler of Trinidad, Vere Bird of Antigua, and Robert Bradshaw of St. Kitts-Nevis awakened the masses and then moved them toward one goal after another.

During the following decade a number of reforms resulted. For example, beginning with Jamaica in 1944, universal adult suffrage was guaranteed by constitutional change in most of the islands. Another goal of the 1940s, self-government for each island as a step toward independence, was not accomplished until the abortive West Indies Federation (1958–62) collapsed.

These popular movements for trade unionism and nationalism, like the emancipation cause of the 1830s, were stimulators of media growth in the Commonwealth Caribbean. In Jamaica at least thirty-two publications appeared between the 1920s, when unionism and nationalism sparks were struck, and the 1940s, when the movements were conflagratory in nature.

The type of journalist practicing in Jamaica during this period was characterized by Lewis as follows:

> The beloved Tom Redcam created a popular journalism at once Jamaican in theme and professionally ethical in tone, first in the old Jamaica *Post* and later in the Jamaica *Times*. Likewise, the English expatriate editor William J. Makin made himself, during the 1930s, into what one local admirer termed the economic abolitionist of the downtrodden people of Jamaica. Not least of all, O. T. Fairclough's formation of the weekly journal *Public Opinion* in 1937 provided a forum for the publication of every progressive idea. All of these, indeed, gave a new life to radical journalism.[2]

During the same period the first labor, or union, newspapers were established in the islands. Later they were to make up what one writer described as "one of the major developments of the 1940s and 1950s."[3] The labor press was significant because its spirit was contrary to the spirit of the press of earlier times, which had represented the "conservative sugar-owning interests" or the primarily personal desires of the editor.

To trace the origins of the labor press in the Commonwealth Caribbean, one must return to the post-World War I era when unions, and their newspapers, were organized somewhat clandestinely because of the laws that had been passed prohibiting the formation of unions. For example, on St. Kitts-Nevis a union had been organized as a friendship society. To carry out its propagandistic work for the masses, this society, the St. Kitts-Nevis Benevolent Association, started a monthly periodical in 1921, *Union Messenger*. The paper became so popular that it eventually became a daily.[4] By 1942, when unions were much more acceptable, another St. Kitts labor paper, the *Workers Weekly*, organ of the St. Kitts Workers League, was issued.

In Antigua the labor press emerged in 1943, when Edward Mathurin, a printer and former officer of the Antigua Trades and Labour Union, printed a newspaper in pamphlet form to disseminate working class information as well as to advance the union.[5] The following year the same organization established *The Workers Voice.*

The union press became an important mouthpiece of the mass movements led by men such as Arthur Andrew Cipriani, father of Trinidadian labor causes. Cipriani organized his Trinidad Labour Party shortly after World War I. By 1935 he was regularly using three forums to promote his organization, one of which was the party journal, *Socialist,* initiated in that year. What he said in his other forums—the Legislative Council and the Port of Spain City Council[6]—was usually given verbatim in the *Socialist.* Cipriani was successful also in garnering the favor of the popular Trinidad periodicals.

A WEST INDIAN IDENTITY

The strikes and riots of 1938 that occurred on Trinidad, Barbados, St. Kitts, and Jamaica[7] and their aftermath have been credited with steering the West Indian through his first real identity crisis. As he recognized who he was, the West Indian intellectual wanted to extol his cultural virtues to the rest of the world. Thus for the first time, newspapers, books, magazines, and art works took on the task of describing and portraying the West Indian—in newspapers such as *The West Indian,* in anti-colonial novels such as Adolphe Roberts's *The Single Star,* in books like Nembhard's *Jamaica Awakening,* and in social protest poetry such as that of Campbell and McKay. Before this time the West Indian intellectual was mute. In fact, West Indian literature did not exist before the 1930s.[8] For example, not until upper-class norms came under attack in the 1940s did Trinidad develop its native writing through struggling and obscure cultural clubs and little magazines.

The establishment in 1943 of *Bim* literary magazine and, at about the same time, the BBC radio program, "Caribbean Voices," provided regular outlets for the sudden outpouring of West Indian literary work. Interpretative newsmagazines also appeared for the first time with Jamaica's *Spotlight* in 1939, to be followed later by *Newday* (1957) and *West Indian Review: Magazine of the Caribbean,* both of Jamaica, and *Bajan* (1953) of Barbados. *Spotlight* came about when a *Gleaner* writer, Evon Blake, realized that he could not say what he wanted in someone else's paper. Fired by the *Gleaner*, Blake borrowed one pound and lived on it for a month until he sold his first advertisement for *Spotlight*. He ran the magazine single-handedly for 18½ years.[9]

If the results of this labor and nationalist unrest provided the West Indian with an identity, they also gave Great Britain some anxious moments. Therefore, immediately after the 1938 demonstrations, a commission was formed by the secretary of state for the colonies to examine the situation in the normally placid Commonwealth Caribbean. In the commission's report of 1944 the authorities apparently recognized and disapproved of the prominent role the press had played.

> It is an unfortunate feature of public life in the West Indies that attacks are all too often directed not so much against the policy of the Government as against individual officers who are thus treated as the designers and not the instruments of that policy. At times these criticisms, particularly in the Press, are ill-informed and amount to personal abuse, while other public attacks on officials may be actuated by motives of spite or personal gain.[10]

The report emphasized that in many cases government officials were debarred from replying to the media; at other times they could not do so because of inexperience and lack of suitable staff. To overcome these handicaps it was proposed that:

> Every available means of influencing public opinion and, where the means now available are inadequate, should introduce new methods of explaining their (public officials') policy. . . . Much more active steps can, and should, be taken to make known to the masses of the people the point of view of government on all the major problems of the day.[11]

Actually, the establishment of the important role of government information services in the islands can be traced to this report.

FEDERATION: A FOURTH WATERSHED

The 1958 birth of the West Indies Federation must be added as a fourth watershed period (at least for the mass media) to Sherlock's dates of 1650, 1834, and 1938–44 (see "Crises-Oriented Press" in chap. 2).

Whereas in other watershed periods the mass media blossomed intra-island, during the federation years (1958–62) communications took on a regional look. The role of the press was described by Hallett, who in 1957 said:

The press is being stimulated not only by federation plans but by the awakening of the whole area. There is a stir and excitement in the entire British Caribbean of a people striving for a larger identity which must find its expression journalistically.[12]

As federal planning progressed during the 1950s, newspapers such as the *Gleaner* and Barbados *Advocate*, realizing how unaware West Indians were of each other, initiated West Indian news columns. The *Gleaner* even sent correspondents to other islands to write series of articles on the region. Smaller papers such as the *West Indian, Voice of St. Lucia,* and *Vincentian*, also carried regional news columns for a time.

Once the Federation was operating, radio hookups permitted federal elections, inaugurations, and subsequent openings of the Federal Parliament to be broadcast throughout the region. The Federal Government Information Service also produced ten radio programs, each featuring a different island, for regional broadcast.[13]

But these attempts at news regionalization were not enough, as indicated by this newsman's lament at the time:

When at this late date, a picture of the Roseau Sugar Factory, St. Lucia, is used to illustrate an article on Dominica; when a radio announcer can refer to "Chuh-Chuh, Barbados," in acknowledging a letter from Thornberry Hill, Ch. Ch.;—or perhaps it should be explained that this abbreviation stands for Christ Church; when such mistakes are daily journalistic fodder; it is obvious that the time has come for newspapers to include Caribbean desks.[14]

Suggested as media necessities were not just Caribbean desks on individual media, but also a cooperative news bureau at the federal capital, a Caribbean news agency, regular newspaper service to all islands, regional journalistic associations to uplift ethical standards, and a national newspaper for the federation. Unfortunately, most of these innovations never left the dream stage. Caribbean news desks for most newspapers of the region were too expensive; the cooperative news agency at the federal capital could not be realized because of the lack of cooperation among the media. A regional news agency was not successfully launched until January 1976. The lack of a daily air schedule between islands in 1958 prohibited daily circulation of newspapers to other islands, as well as hindering the idea of a national newspaper for the Federation. Trying to determine which newspaper should be the national organ became a problem, too. The *Gleaner* was ruled out because Jamaica is too remote from the other islands, and for a time the Trinidad *Guardian* was considered the Federation paper.

Newspapers were often chastised for their stands on the merits and demerits of federalization. A *Gleaner* reporter wrote in 1957:

> There appears . . . at this time to be in existence a kind of political hysteria among our politicians which finds expression in statements deploring the activities, outlook and critical appraisal of the West Indian press.[15]

For example, Grantley Adams, later named Federation head, criticized the "nasty aspects" of Jamaican journalism in a speech before the Barbados House of Assembly; Prime Minister Eric Williams of Trinidad attacked first the Jamaican and later the whole West Indian press for handicapping the proper development of the Federation.

The editor of the *Gleaner* felt that his paper's stand on federation gave politicians little reason to complain:

> For weeks we ran stories when the referendum for federation was the subject of discussion. We discussed the pros and cons, slightly favoring the pros. The *Gleaner* was slightly pro because we felt federation would provide better security. Once federation came about, we were critical of Jamaica's under-representation however. Jamaica had one half of the land and one half the people of the federation but a minority of the government. When the referendum came in 1962 to decide whether to quit the Federation, we ran a forum for weeks with equal space for both sides. For example, we would give each side one half a page and down the middle we would run a historical account of Federation's development. When Jamaica quit the Federation, we took this as a valid decision and lived by it.[16]

The Barbados *Advocate-News* has always been for federation, according to the paper's general manager. Even in 1964–65, two years after the Feederation was scrapped and when Barbados was up for independence, the *Advocate-News* promoted federation, pointing out that none of the islands could afford independence. For that stand the paper was temporarily boycotted by government advertisers.[17]

BROADCASTING: FROM HAMS TO
JAMAICA BROADCASTING CORPORATION

Radio and television, media that psychically brought West Indians out of their small villages, came late to the region. A number of theories might be postulated for this lateness: the financially insecure position of the people, which made them unable to afford the media; the insularity of the islands; the lack of awareness of the benefits of advertising on the part of merchants, and the lack of extensive electrification on most islands. An amateur radio operator who wanted to develop a radio station on Barbados to announce the 1935 cricket matches gave still another reason:

> The legislators and advisors failed to recognize the power of the modern media at their disposal and adamantly refused to grant any applications for licenses which were submitted. . . . Numerous applications for stations were turned down by government because broadcasting "supported by sponsored programs is not in the interests of the people."[18]

Broadcasting in the British West Indies owed its inception to the local people's interest in cricket. The visit of a foreign cricket team to the Caribbean in 1934 prompted a group of amateurs in Georgetown, British Guiana to broadcast commentaries on the matches for the benefit of radio listeners in other parts of the Eastern Caribbean.[19] Until then the only English-language broadcast stations audible in the region were BBC's Empire Service and the United States shortwave stations, which were operating experimentally.

On the individual islands local radio service did not arrive in Barbados until 1934–35, Trinidad in 1935, Bahamas in 1936,* Jamaica 1939, Bermuda 1943, Montserrat 1952, Antigua 1955, and the Windward Islands 1954–55.[20] Again, Anguilla, which did not have a newspaper until 1967, entered the broadcasting field latest among the islands. In March 1969 that island had its first radio service when a limited broadcast took place from HMS Rhys, a British ship anchored offshore during Anguilla's revolt against St. Kitts. The shipboard station was so successful that immediately the British Foreign Office established a more permanent station on Anguillan soil, thus giving the people something they could call their own.[21]

---

* Started in a hat shop, broadcasting two hours daily (see: *Combroad* (April–June 1975), pp. 71–72).

Amateur operators developed the first broadcasting on some islands, such as St. Vincent and Jamaica. A recent editor of the *Vincentian* owned a small transmitter in 1937, which he turned into an amateur station. When federation talks were proceeding twenty years later, the St. Vincent government borrowed his transmitter to propagandize for federation and to give hurricane warnings.[22] Later the station was turned into a substation of Windward Islands Broadcasting Service.

Jamaica's broadcasting story* also resulted from the efforts of one man, in this case a wealthy planter, John F. Grinan. An amateur radio operator, Grinan went on the air in late 1939 with his ZQI, broadcasting initially for only one hour a week.[23]

The first broadcasting station in the region was a rediffusion service,[24] and until mid-century most of the Commonwealth Caribbean broadcasting was through wired systems. Comdr. Mansfield Robinson, RN (ret.) formed this first station in 1934 on Barbados; the first subscriber was not connected until the following year.

Other islands that had broadcasting services in the 1930s included Trinidad, with a wired broadcasting system dating to 1935, and Bermuda, where a small medium wave station was initiated in the 1930s by private enterprise but died within a few months. In the Bahamas a government-supported broadcasting service of 500 watts was opened in 1936 under the call sign of ZNS. Before that time special broadcasts were made over a. telecom transmitter in the Bahamas.

It was World War II that spurred the development of Commonwealth Caribbean broadcasting. Small government stations were established "for the duration." In a number of cases these stations remained on the air after the hostilities. The Bermuda government in 1940 commenced broadcasting with a 20-watt transmitter on the high frequency band, its purpose being to relay to the public news of the war in Great Britain, information on the responsibility of Bermudians concerning the war, data on the setup of the local government and governmental policy, and entertainment and educational material.[25] The same year Grinan presented his ZQI to the Jamaican government to be used as "a source of war news, a means of supporting morale, and a prop for cultural and community activities severely hampered by war conditions."[26] In 1943 and again in 1945, ZNS in

---

* For a recent account of Jamaica's broadcasting history see: Dwight Whylie, "The Future of the Jamaica Broadcasting Corporation," *Combroad*, (April–June 1975), pp. 13–14.

the Bahamas increased its wattage and, in the latter year, its hours of operation as well, presumably to reach more Bahamians with increased war coverage.[27] Barbadian Rediffusion expanded its service during the war, too, giving regular war bulletins to its 1,500 subscribers.

Despite this war-stimulated expansion, when the West India Royal Commission Report was released toward the end of the war, a need was shown for more local broadcasting in the islands. The people wanted their BBC programs supplemented with local stations, which would allow island governments to get their policies across to the people, spread education and, the Report continued, provide more recreation for the elderly.[28] Anxious to get these local stations organized during this turbulent period in West Indian history, the writers of the Report even recommended that the British pay all expenses for the creation of local broadcasting.

The Report was heeded, obviously, for by the 1960s there were a number of local stations in the Commonwealth Caribbean, many of which had been backed by outside money, but most of them being controlled by government. The governments of the islands were using the stations to get official views over to the people, demanding in license requirements that certain periods of the broadcast day be put aside for government news and views.

The mother country's influence on British Caribbean broadcasting was apparent; one had only to examine program formats and ownership patterns. Overseas Rediffusion Ltd. of London, through local subsidiaries, took control of the Jamaican and Barbadian sole outlets in 1950 and 1951 respectively. On Trinidad and Bermuda, Broadcast Relay Services (Overseas) Ltd. of London was granted franchises to operate both of those broadcasting systems in 1947. Two years after its creation in 1961,[29] Radio Caribbean International on St. Lucia was also associated with London Rediffusion. And for a stretch of time in the 1960s, press lord Roy Thomson of Fleet Street owned numerous broadcasting interests in the region before selling them to island governments (See chap. 4 on ownership for fuller discussion of Thomson interests).

During the 1950s, as local governments and national leaders came on the scene, so did government radio. By 1958 the Jamaican government established a public corporation to cater to public service broadcasting and took the name Jamaica Broadcasting Corporation, while the original JBC turned into Radio Jamaica Ltd., still a rediffusion station. From the outset, ZNS in Bahamas was government operated, as was Windward Islands Broadcasting Service in Grenada, started in 1955 to service St. Lucia, St. Vincent, Dominica, and Grenada, and discontinued in late 1971. Still other local, government-owned stations existed on Antigua after 1956, on St. Kitts after 1961, on Barbados after 1963, on Trinidad after 1969, and on Dominica, Grenada, St. Vincent, and St. Lucia after 1971. Radio Montserrat, developed in 1952 and owned and maintained by a voluntary Broadcasting Committee, has become a semi-official station as well.

THE MEDIA TODAY: A SURVEY

Approximately fifty-nine newspapers, a scattering of magazines, nineteen radio systems, seven television corporations, and the beginnings of an educational and documentary film business served the Commonwealth Caribbean in 1972.

Thirty-nine of the contemporary newspapers for which 1970 and 1971 statistics were available are distributed to 528,302 people.[30] Circulation figures for the other twenty newspapers, all very small operations and some very erratic in frequency of appearance, would not bring the total circulation of British West Indian newspapers to much over 550,000, this in an area of approximately 3.9 million population (see tables 3.1, 3.2).

In nearly every instance, these media are concentrated in the capital cities of the islands, so that the secondary cities and rural areas seldom have their own media. This is probably because in no other part of the world does one consistently find the most populated city to be so many times larger than the secondary cities.[31] Thus, unlike other developing regions, there have not been many recent attempts to build a provincial press. Jamaica has a weekly at Montego Bay, and Bahamas has two newspapers at Freeport, but otherwise the print media are centered in the chief cities. The broadcasting systems are also capital-centered, except for relay stations on the more mountainous islands.

The smallness of some islands makes it impractical to have more than one media center. Media personnel on most islands felt that they were penetrating all strata of their populations with the messages. The *Evening News* of Trinidad sets its final deadline at noon so that the paper can be distributed to the oil workers in rural areas before they leave work at 5 P.M.; the *Herald* of Dominica keeps ten agents in rural areas whose job it is to come to town once a week to pick up the paper and then deliver it in the villages. Political parties on St. Kitts distribute their organs through party officials who reside in the rural areas, and the Dominica *Star* hopes to get at least one copy in each village that will be read to the peasants by a village reader.

Despite these efforts, the majority of subscribers to the printed media on most islands are urbanites, a characteristic Rogers attributes to most developing peoples. He said that mass media messages in less-developed countries are of low interest and relevance to rural receivers because of the strong urban orientation of the mass media in these nations, even though rural people constitute the majority of the population.[32]

Television's advent in some of the islands was thought to be a panacea for all communication problems, especially those of insularity and parochialism among the rural people.[33] Government radio and television stations on Jamaica and Trinidad, in particular, have concentrated on improving the farmer's image of himself by having more programs aired for him.[34]

Daily Newspapers

Thirteen of the fifty-nine contemporary newspapers in the islands are dailies. They are: Antigua *Workers Voice,* Nassau *Guardian, The Tribune* and Grand Bahama *Tribune* of the Bahamas, Barbados *Advocate-News,* Bermuda *Royal Gazette, The West Indian* of Grenada, Jamaica *Daily Gleaner* and *The Star,** *The Labour Spokesman* of St. Kitts-Nevis, and *Guardian, The Evening News,* and *Express* of Trinidad. Only in Trinidad, Jamaica, and the Bahamas do dailies exist that are owned by different corporations competing with each other. A UNESCO team working in the islands in 1968 said that in a developing area such as the Commonwealth Caribbean, too much should not be made of competition between media. Instead,

> While each medium should be kept alert by the awareness of its own limitations and the need to develop its own particular area of strength, the greatest possible co-operation between the media should be sought and ensured, with a view to avoiding unnecessary duplication and wastage of limited human, technical and financial resources.[35]

---

* Jamaica has a new daily, *The Jamaica Daily News,* launched in May 1973.

TABLE 3.1

COMMONWEALTH CARIBBEAN DAILY NEWSPAPERS, 1972

Name	Morning-Evening	Circu-lation[1]	Ownership	Political Affiliation
Antigua:				
Workers Voice		4,200#	local, party	Labour
Bahamas:				
Tribune	evening	10,930	local, private	independent
Grand Bahamas *Tribune*	morning	3,000#	local, private	independent
Guardian	morning	6,169#	foreign, Perry	independent
Barbados:				
Advocate-News	morning	22,036	foreign, Thomson	independent
Bermuda:				
Royal Gazette	morning	11,131#	local, private	independent
Grenada:				
West Indian	daily, exc. M, F	1,000*	local, private†	independent
Jamaica:				
Daily Gleaner	morning	59,349	local, private	independent
The Star	evening	64,037	local, private	independent
St. Kitts:				
Labour Spokesman		1,500*	local, union	St. Kitts Trades & Labour Union
Trinidad & Tobago:				
Guardian	morning	52,717	foreign, Thomson	independent
Evening News	evening	53,793	foreign, Thomson	independent
Express	morning	35,872#	local, private	independent

[1] Circulation figures in most cases are from Benn's Guide to Newspapers, Periodicals of the World, *Newspaper Press Directory 1971* (London: Benn Brothers, 1971). Where no designation appears, the source is Benn's.

Circulation figures from *Editor and Publisher International Yearbook* (New York: Editor & Publisher, 1971).

* Circulation figures from interviews conducted by author.

† Indicates that individual owning newspaper has strong political ties.

The bulk of the daily circulation is derived from eight newspapers located in five countries—three in Trinidad, two in Jamaica, and one each in Barbados, Bahamas, and Bermuda. Together, these eight dailies represent nearly two-thirds (309,865) of the total newspaper circulation of the islands (528,302). Gleaner publications have the largest circulations in the region: *The Star* with 64,037 and *Daily Gleaner* with 59,349, followed by Trinidad *Guardian* with 52,717, its sister the *Evening News* with 53,793, and the *Express,* also of Trinidad, with 35,000. Relatively large circulations also are maintained by weekend editions published in the region: *Sunday Guardian* with 87,796; *Sunday Gleaner* with 83,674; *Weekend Star* (Friday) 75,853; *Sunday Express,* 54,000 and *Sunday Advocate-News,* 30,321. A Trinidadian editor explained that Sunday is a "big day for rural readership as many people buy one paper (the Sunday edition) for the week and read it then."[36]

Circulation figures mean very little when listed one after another in a press handbook or yearbook; they take on meaning when they are related to other statistics. For example, a cursory look at the largest circulation in the islands, that of the *Sunday Guardian,* would mean very little to a person who has just left the United States or another developed nation where circulations run into the millions. But as the editor of the *Evening News* of Trinidad pointed out, the *Sunday Guardian*'s circulation of 87,796 might rank proportionately among the top in the world in that almost one-tenth of the total population of Trinidad and Tobago purchase the paper.[37] Circulation figures of the newspapers on Bermuda are equally deceptive. The largest daily there does not have more than 12,000 circulation, yet in the early 1960s the island had more copies of newspapers available per 100 people (41.9) than do most nations of the world. For example, the highest at the time was claimed by Great Britain (50 copies per 100 people), followed by Sweden, Luxembourg, and East Germany, all with 40 or more.

Nondaily Newspapers

Passin has said that an adequate communications system needs an infrastructure of other media too, both mass and specialized journals, weeklies, and quarterlies. It is in this area that the "great weakness of journalism in the underdeveloped countries shows up most strongly,"[38] he pointed out. This journalistic weakness is a trait of the British West Indies, where weekly newspapers, not known for large circulations and unable to compete with larger dailies for the advertis-

Trinidad's two tabloid dailies, independent Express *and Thomson owned* The Evening News, *1971.*

ing dollar, must depend on sponsorship by political parties, unions, and other vested-interest groups.

On Jamaica, Trinidad, Barbados, and the Bahamas, a plethora of political nondailies surround the somewhat independent dailies. On Jamaica there is *Public Opinion*, left-of-center political weekly, as well as *Voice*, Labour Party, *New Nation*, PNP, *The Bell*, JLP, and the *Chinese Public News*. Barbados's weeklies include *Observer*, edited by an ex-member of Parliament, *The Beacon*, organ of Barbados Labour Party, and the *Democrat*, pro-government weekly.* At least five weeklies or fortnightlies are published on Trinidad, most of them representing some shade of island political life: *The Nation*, People's National Movement; *Vanguard*, Oil Field Workers Trade Union; *The Statesman*, Democratic Labour Party; *The Bomb*, United Democratic Liberation Party; and *Anglican Review*. *Bahamian Times* had been the main political sheet of the Bahamas for a number of years until the launching of *Torch* in 1971.

---

* In November 1973, *The Nation* was started on Barbados as an independent, locally owned weekly.

Thomson morning daily on Trinidad, Trinidad Guardian, *1971.*

The largest, and one of the oldest, dailies in region, The Daily Gleaner, *Kingston, Jamaica, 1971.*

Advocate-News

ESTABLISHED 1895   BARBADOS, WEST INDIES   MONDAY, APRIL 26, 1971   10 CENTS

● Problems, Progress To Be Outlined

CARIFTA Team
To Tour Islands

Week-end Deaths Put Toll at 21

What makes you think the Earthmen are building it?

Cosmonauts Back After Space Link-up

MOSCOW, SUNDAY—

W. Germany May Give Bank Aid

ST. JOHN'S, Antigua.

Manufacturers to Point Out Dangers of Bureau

KINGSTON, Jamaica, Sunday.

CDB Puts Off Study of Colombia's Entry

ST. JOHN'S, Antigua.

Conference Opens Today

Pornography By Mail May Be Stopped

COPENHAGEN.

BYC Leader Calls for Commissioner for Youth

THE Barbados Youth Council has called on the Government to appoint a Commissioner for Youth.

Barnard May Quit Hospital

CAPE TOWN, Sunday—HEART transplant pioneer Professor Chris Barnard.

Radical Groups Take Over Demonstrations

WASHINGTON, Sunday.

India Issues Strong Protest to Pakistan

NEW DELHI, Sunday.

Six Americans Killed

Call for Change

West Indians Guilty of Murder

ST. THOMAS, US Virgin Islands, Sunday.

'T' Official Due

April 30

Your Date With Your

Income Tax

File Now . . . Pay Now

Few Back on Job

GEORGETOWN, Guyana, Sunday.

13 Die in Fire

SEATTLE, Washington.

TODAY'S WEATHER

Advocate-News, *Bridgetown, Barbados, 1971, owned by Thomson.*

GREETINGS
TO DEAR FRIENDS

Our usual Xmas gift is once more open to you. Caskets of all classes A B and C can be obtained at reasonable prices from the Anglo American Funeral Agency, 73 Melville Street, St. George's and not to mention the influx of ornaments and Tombstones to be laid at the grave of your departed ones.

Also specialise in Embalming and all classes of Caskets, Canadian and American Designs also Monuments and statues.

We now take this opportunity to loan One free Coffin to any Relative of the departed ones buried by Anglo American Funeral Agency Co. Bills must be presented of the departed ones buried by the above name Company not later than 6 a.m. on the 25th, December 1961 . Also all Caskets purchased 20% discount will be given from 26th, December 1961 to 31st December 1961 We are now in a position to offer the new designs.

Anyone purchasing one of the new design Caskets will be given One Case

Whisky free. Don't be prejudiced you can purchase your Coffin before death, come in and select. We are at your service Day and Night.

We also offer you Oak Caskets with glass face also Steel Casket for burying at sea.

We can also supply Hymns for all Religions, who pay for them will have them; also Last Rite Sets, canned juices and best Burgess Bateries for Radios Flashlights and Satellite from U.S.A.

Also pocket Radio Batteries.

We now take this opportunity to wish everyone a Merry Christmas and a Brilliant 1962.

Oh God our help in Ages past

Our Hope for years to come.

Family Guest House can also be obtained within.

JAMES LAQUA

Funeral Director and Undertaker, Anglo American Funeral Agency.

73 Melville Street St. George's Grenada, W.I.

Phone 2302

Unusual advertisement carried in The West Indian, *Grenada, on Christmas Eve, 1961.*

TABLE 3.2

Commonwealth Caribbean Nondaily Newspapers, 1972

Name	Frequency[1]	Circu-lation[2]	Ownership	Political Affiliation[3]
Antigua:				
Antigua *Star*	Wed, Sat	3,500*	local, private†	Peoples Labour Movement Antigua Workers Union
Antigua *Times*	3 x week	5,000*	local, party	Antigua Peoples
Bahamas:				
Torch	Sat	3,000	local, party	Free PLP
Freeport *News*	M, W, F		foreign, Perry	independent
Barbados:				
Barbados *Observer*	Sat	1,000	local, private†	
The Beacon	Sat		local, party	Labour
Truth	2 x week	3,000	local, private†	Labour
Democrat	Fri	6,000	local, party	Democratic Labour
Bermuda:				
Mid-Ocean News	Sat	12,000#		
Bermuda *Recorder*	Fri			
Bermuda *Skyliner*	Fri		U.S. Navy	
Bermuda *Sun*	weekly			
British Virgin Islands:				
Island Sun	Sat			
Cayman Islands:				
Caymanian Weekly	Thurs	3,700*	local, private	
Dominica:				
Dominica *Chronicle*	Sat	2,500*	local, Catholic Church	
Dominica *Herald*	Sat	2,000*	local, private†	Freedom Party
Star	Sat	1,800*	local, private†	Freedom Party
Grenada:				
Torchlight	W, F, Sun	1,000*	local, private	independent
Vanguard	weekly	1,500*	local, party	Grenada National

TABLE 3.2 (Continued)

COMMONWEALTH CARIBBEAN NONDAILY NEWSPAPERS, 1972

Name	Frequency[1]	Circu-lation[2]	Ownership	Political Affiliation[3]
Jamaica:				
The Beacon	weekly		local	
Children's Own	weekly	76,406	local, private	
Jamaica Weekly Gleaner		27,462	local, private	
Catholic Standard	Fri		local, church	
Public Opinion	weekly	6,500*	local, party	People's National Movement
Voice	weekly		local, party	Labour
The New Nation	weekly		local, party	People's National
The Bell	weekly		local, party	Labour
Montserrat:				
Mirror		700*	local, private	independent
St. Kitts-Nevis-Anguilla:				
Democrat	Sat	3,600*	local, private†	People's Action Movement
Nevis Review	Fri		local, party	United National Movement
Anguilla Beacon	weekly	900*	local, private†	
St. Lucia:				
Voice of St. Lucia	W, Sat	4,000*	local, private	
Crusader	Sat	1,500*	local, party	Forum
Catholic Chronicle	weekly	2,000*	local, church	
Herald	weekly		local, private†	Labour
Standard	weekly	1,500*	local, private†	Labour
St. Vincent:				
Vincentian	Sat	3,500*	local, private	independent
Trinidad & Tobago:				
The Nation	weekly	12,500	local, party	People's National Movement
Catholic News	weekly	16,000	local, church	
Vanguard	fortnightly		local, party	Labour, Oil Field Workers Union

TABLE 3.2 (Continued)

COMMONWEALTH CARIBBEAN NONDAILY NEWSPAPERS, 1972

Name	Frequency[1]	Circulation[2]	Ownership	Political Affiliation[3]
Tapia	weekly		local, party	Tapia
Democrat	weekly			
The Statesman			local	Democratic Labour
The Bomb			local, private†	United Democratic Liberation
Moko			local, party	United National Independence
Anglican Review			local, church	

[1] If frequency is not noted, publication appears on nonregular schedule.

[2] Circulation figures in some cases are from Benn's Guide to Newspapers, Periodicals of the World, *Newspaper Press Directory 1971* (London: Benn Brothers, 1971). Where no designation appears, the source is Benn's.

[3] If no entry is listed, political affiliation was undeterminable.

° Circulation figures from interviews and correspondence with editors.

† Indicates individual owning newspaper has strong political ties. For example, he might be a parliamentarian, senator, member of council, organizer or leader of party or union that paper supports.

Circulation figures from *Editor and Publisher International Yearbook* (New York: Editor and Publisher, 1971).

The Leeward and Windward Islands, for the most part, are served by weeklies. In some ways it is a wonder that a press exists at all in these smaller islands. Economic and political pressures, along with the heavy influx of foreign media and the regionalization of Barbadian and Trinidadian papers, would seem to dictate against them. They do exist, however, and oftentimes in such quantities as to choke the newspaper industry. For example, Dominica, with approximately 60,000 population, has three weekly papers with the possibility of a fourth; St. Lucia,° with 100,000 people, publishes five newspapers

---

° In late 1975, another newspaper, *The St. Lucia Star,* was started on that island.

at least weekly; Grenada (90,000) three; Antigua (60,000) three, and St. Kitts (57,000) two. St. Vincent° (92,000), Montserrat (13,000), Cayman Islands (10,000), and Anguilla (6,000), each have one newspaper.

On at least St. Kitts and Antigua one finds that the number of newspapers matches the number of political parties. On Dominica two of the three papers are opposition-party supporters, the third a Roman Catholic organ. On Grenada all three papers are anti-government, one being the organ of the opposition party. On St. Lucia three of the papers are politically oriented, a fourth is a Catholic paper. One, *Crusader,*°° is a Black Power paper and organ of a radical group called the Forum.[39]

When one considers that these papers are concentrated in one city on each island, which because of literacy and commercialization is the main supporter of the newspaper industry, the competitiveness takes on even more serious ramifications.

Total circulation for twenty-four of the forty-four nondailies for which figures were available was 98,700. When circulations of two Jamaican weeklies, *Children's Own* and *Jamaica Weekly Gleaner,* were added, the total was more than doubled, 202,568 (see table 3).

Magazines

Magazines in the Commonwealth Caribbean suffer a more precarious existence than even nondaily newspapers. Although they have been printed in the region since 1781, magazines have never really found a niche for themselves. One of the reasons for this is that they have been priced out of the reach of the masses. Many magazines in the islands today cost one East Caribbean dollar. Second, West Indian magazines must compete with British and American periodicals, as well as with Sunday supplements of regional papers. Finally, the lack of a clearly defined advertising market has hindered the medium's growth. For example, *Bim* depends on twenty personal friends who purchase advertisements to keep it going.

An editor of *The Bajan,* a newsmagazine published on Barbados,

---

° Two other newspapers appeared on St. Vincent in 1975: *The Star* and *The Tree,* the latter a mimeographed, Democratic Freedom Movement monthly.
  °° The *Crusader,* since 1970, has been the organ of the opposition Labour Party.

listed even more reasons why magazine publishing has not been successful in the islands:

> Sheer tropical laziness is one reason there have not been more magazines attempted in the islands. In addition, the insularity of the region has kept the birth of regional magazines down. When a magazine does develop here, it is usually the brainchild of one man. If he leaves the publication, it dies. The smaller islands are either too small or unsophisticated to have magazines.[40]

Newsmagazines run the risk of not being newsy by the time they are published, there not being enough advertising or circulation money for such periodicals to come out more frequently than monthly. Still, at least three* newsmagazines are published in the area.[41] A fourth one is being planned by four West Indians who hope to be able to circulate 10,000 copies of their proposed fortnightly to all islands of the Caribbean.[42]

The type of magazine that has appeared most frequently in the islands has been the literary periodical. Since the birth of the most famous Commonwealth Caribbean literary journal, *Bim*, others such as *Weymouth* on Barbados, *Opus* and *Voices* on Trinidad, *Dawnlit* on Dominica, and *Thoroughbred* on Jamaica have made brief appearances. Besides *Bim* the only other literary magazine that publishes regularly in the islands is *Link*,** edited on St. Lucia by the editor of the weekly newspaper, *Crusader*.

Other magazines that maintain regularity of issue are: the newsmagazines, *Spotlight* on Jamaica and *The Bahamian Review; Caribbean Quarterly* and *Social and Economic Studies*, both scholarly journals edited at the University of the West Indies; and *Jamaica Journal*, quarterly of the Institute of Jamaica[43] (see table 3.3).

In addition, there is a whole array of magazines published by departments of government, especially units involved with tourism. The tourist market is so important that even the newsmagazines are designed with the foreign visitor in mind. In the Bahamas Etienne Dupuch, Jr., is in business to print tourist magazines, yearbooks, brochures, and maps.

Other magazines of some importance in the islands have been the

---

* *Caribbean Contact,* published monthly in Trinidad by the Caribbean Conference of Churches, also qualifies as a newmagazine. It was started in 1974.

** *Link* is now defunct. A new literary magazine is *Savacou*, a quarterly published in Jamaica by the Caribbean Artists Movement.

Trinidad Chamber of Commerce's *Enterprise,* Dominica Social Development's *Dominica Welfare Review,* Jamaica Government Public Relations' *Jamaica Now,* Trinidad Central Statistics Office's *Quarterly Economic Report, The Jamaican Historical Review,* and the *Journal of the Barbados Museum and Historical Society,* the latter in print now for over 30 years.*

TABLE 3.3

Commonwealth Caribbean Magazines, 1971

Name	Frequency	Category	Founded	Circu-lation	Owner
Bahamas:					
Bahamas	5 x year	general	1933	100,000	local, private
Bahamas Weekly and					
Nassau Tourist News	weekly	travel	1962	6,000	local, private
Bahamian Review	monthly	news	1952		local, private
Barbados:					
Bajan and South					
Caribbean	monthly	news	1953	3,000	local, private
Barbados Museum and					
Historical Society					
Journal	quarterly	history	1933		local, private
Bim	semi-annual	literary	1943	750	local, private
Bermuda:					
Bermudian	monthly	general	1930	6,500	local, private
Jamaica:#					
Caribbean					
Challenge	monthly	religious	1957		local, church
Caribbean Educational					
Bulletin	3 x year	education	1968		local, govt.
Caribbean					
Quarterly	quarterly	scholarly	1949	1,000	local, university

---

* As well as *People: The Magazine of the Caribbean,* a monthly started in 1975 by Imprint Caribbean Ltd. in Trinidad, and *Islander,* published by Virgin Islands Publishing Co. at Tortola, British Virgin Islands.

TABLE 3.3 (Continued)

COMMONWEALTH CARIBBEAN MAGAZINES, 1971

Name	Frequency	Category	Founded	Circulation	Owner
Jamaican and West Indian Review	quarterly		1963		local, private
Jamaica Chamber of Commerce Journal	quarterly	business		4,000	local, private
Jamaica Industrial Review		industry			local, private
Jamaica Journal	quarterly	quality	1966		local, private
Jamaican Nurse	3 x year	scholarly		2,000	local, private
Jamaica Public Health	quarterly	health			local, govt.
Social and Economic Studies	quarterly	scholarly	1953		local, university
Spotlight	monthly	news	1939		local, private
West Indian Medical Journal	quarterly	medical	1951		local, university
St. Lucia:					
Link	quarterly	literary	1969		local, private
Trinidad & Tobago:					
Caribbean Labour	quarterly	labor	1960		local, union
Enterprise	quarterly	business	1962		local, private
Central Statistics Office Economic Report	quarterly	economic		600	local, govt.
Outside Region:*					
West Indies Chronicle		industry	1886	3,300	foreign

SOURCES: Personal interviews by author; *Ulrich's International Periodicals Directory, 1971–72* (New York: R. R. Bowker Co., 1971).

Jamaica has a few other publications that publish on a more infrequent schedule. Some of these are: *Pepper Pot, Thoroughbred, Jamaican Woman, Caribbean Farming, West Indian Economist.* Source: Interview, Fred Seal Coon, Editorial Manager, *Daily Gleaner.*

* Although *West Indies Chronicle* is published in London by the West Indies Committee, it can be found in a number of Caribbean bookstores. *Caribbean Business News,* published in Canada, is included in this category also. However, it circulates only to business people, not to the general public.

Radio, Television, Film

Electronic media have been more secure than print, possibly because they have been supported for the most part by considerable outside capital (see chap. 7 for further discussion of economics of mass media).

Among the largest radio systems in the islands today are: Jamaica Broadcasting Corporation and Radio Jamaica, with eight and four transmitters, respectively, for full-island coverage; Radio Antilles, the "mystery station"[44] of 200–250 KW on Montserrat; Windward Islands Broadcasting Service, with substations on each Windward island;* Radio Caribbean, with English and French broadcasts directed to St. Lucia, Martinique, and Guadeloupe; both Radio Trinidad and Tobago National Broadcasting System (known also as 610 Radio and Radio Guardian); ZNS of Bahamas; and Caribbean Broadcasting Corporation.[45] Neither JBC nor CBC has been showing a profit, depending for financial support on its television stations.

Bermuda, Barbados, Antigua, Trinidad, Jamaica, and St. Lucia have television systems of their own.** Caribbean Broadcasting Corporation on Barbados has had television relay stations on St. Lucia (since 1966), and St. Vincent and Dominica, more recently, and Leeward Islands Television Services of Antigua maintains translator stations on Montserrat and the Dutch-French island of St. Maarten. Two different television companies operate on Bermuda, Capital Broadcasting Co., Ltd. and Bermuda Radio and Television Ltd. Other islands, especially Trinidad and Jamaica, would probably have a second television system if the governments allowed another franchise. Color television exists on Bermuda, Barbados, and Trinidad.

Local television service, except for Bermuda (see Appendix B

---

* When WIBS was dissolved December 31, 1971, each Windward island soon after started its own broadcasting system, each financed by a combination of government subsidy and commercial advertising. Radio St. Lucia covers the whole island with a new transmitter installed in 1971. Radio Dominica is a government-owned entity operating as a division of the premier's office. The station began operations independently of WIBS on November 1, 1974. Radio St. Vincent and the Grenadines operates 11 hours daily, Monday to Saturday. The 500-W transmitter provides about 80 percent island coverage. Radio Grenada came into existence January 1, 1972. (*Commonwealth Broadcasting Association* [London: Commonwealth Broadcasting Association, 1974].)

** St. Kitts-Nevis received its own television service on December 3, 1972, when the government-owned and operated ZIZ Television came into being. ZIZ-TV has one transmitter and four translators to cover St. Kitts-Nevis and the entire Leeward Islands four to five hours daily. (*Commonwealth Broadcasting Association* [London: Commonwealth Broadcasting Association, 1974].)

for the story of Bermuda television), was unknown in the Commonwealth Caribbean until the independence era of the 1960s. Jamaica,
Trinidad, Barbados, and Antigua, just before or upon donning independent or associated statehood status, felt that they needed the
gadgetry of modernity that television offered.

Film production has been introduced into the islands very
slowly. At least one island, Jamaica, would like to develop a local
film industry. A Motion Picture Industry (Encouragement) Law was
passed on Jamaica as early as 1948 and was designed to provide
generous tax concessions to recognized film producers. Still, like most
of the islands, the main film producers on Jamaica are government
agencies.

Barbados, Bermuda, and Trinidad, in addition to Jamaica, have
small documentary and institutional film industries, but all feature
films shown in the Commonwealth Caribbean are imported, mainly
from the United States. Trinidad, because of its racial mixture, brings
in films from India, Great Britain, Malaysia, Sweden, Hong Kong,
and France, but still obtains over 70 percent of its movie fare from
the United States.[46] Most governmental public relations or information offices maintain mobile units and educational film libraries that
they use to take the movies to the villages.

SUMMARY

Since the dawn of the twentieth century, nearly 200 newspapers
(see table 2.1), at least 19 radio stations, and 7 television systems
have been launched in the Commonwealth Caribbean. A considerable
amount of this media development, especially in the case of printed
media, revolved around the promotion of trade unionism, independence, black awareness, and nationalism.

This was especially so during the turbulent 1930s and 1940s when
mass media played activist roles in the search for a West Indian
identity. Newspapers and literary magazines such as *Bim* more and
more served as outlets for the numerous West Indian-oriented works
coming from the pens of the pioneer crop of Caribbean authors. The
pre-World War II birth of two new media—radio and newsmagazines
—provided additional opportunities for the West Indian to expand
his previously parochial outlook.

If the strikes and demonstrations of the 1930s were responsible
for leading to the creation of West Indian identities, the federation
attempts two decades later were designed to solidify the disparate

peoples into one West Indian culture. Again, mass media played significant roles, arousing interest or ire for the federated state concept. As in the past, the media matured as a result of the participation—in this instance, by the efforts to provide more regional cooperation in the exchange of news and programs.

The story of the recent development of mass media in the islands is characterized by traits such as these: capital-city centralization of channels, struggle for a West Indian cultural identity, and insularist, rather than regional, attitudes toward media goals.

NOTES TO CHAPTER 3

1. Philip Sherlock, *West Indies* (London: Thames and Hudson Ltd., 1966), p. 82.

2. Gordon K. Lewis, *The Growth of the Modern West Indies* (London: Macgibbon & Kee, 1968), p. 173.

3. Robert Hallett, "Newspaper Growing Pains in New Nation," *IPI Report* (February 1958), p. 3.

4. Stanley Procope, "History of the Press [of St. Kitts]" (Unpublished manuscript in Procope's files, Basseterre, St. Kitts).

5. Novelle H. Richards, *The Struggle and the Conquest* (St. John's, Antigua: Workers Voice Printery, n.d., but probably 1964), pp. 32–33.

6. Eric Williams, *History of the People of Trinidad and Tobago* (London: Andre Deutsch, 1964), p. 222.

7. St. Vincent, St. Lucia, and Antigua also had mass strikes in the 1930s.

8. Sherlock, *West Indies,* p. 155.

9. "Recollections of Evon Blake," *Spotlight* (December 1964), pp. 7–8.

10. *West India Royal Commission Report* (Presented by the Secretary of State for the Colonies to Parliament by Command of His Majesty [London: His Majesty's Stationery Office, June 1945]), pp. 58–59.

11. Ibid.

12. Robert Hallett, "Newspaper Growing Pains in New Nation," *IPI Report* (November 1957), p. 4.

13. Willy Richardson, "The Place of Radio in the West Indies," *Caribbean Quarterly* (December 1961), pp. 158–62.

14. Edward L. Cozier, "The Press in the New West Indies," *The Bajan* (April 1958), pp. 22–23.

15. "West Indian Politicians and the Press," *Sunday Gleaner*, April 28, 1957.

16. Personal interview, Theodore Sealy, Editor, *Gleaner*, Kingston, Jamaica, August 26, 1970.

17. Personal interview, Neville Grosvenor, General Manager, *Advocate-News*, Bridgetown, Barbados, September 7, 1970.

18. Thomas A. Archer, "Radio in Barbados," *The Bajan* (March 1964), p. 29.

19. G. V. de Freitas, "Press and Radio," *The Statist* (September 1956), p. 69.

20. All dates taken from Information Department of Colonial Office, *Handbook on Broadcasting Services in the Colonies Etc. 1956* (London: Information Department of Colonial Office, 1956), pp. 4–167.

21. Personal interview, Roy Dunlop, Director, Radio Anguilla, The Valley, Anguilla, April 29, 1971.

22. Personal interview, W. H. Lewis, Editor, *Vincentian*, Kingstown, St. Vincent, May 10, 1971.

23. "John Grinan—He Showed the World," *Spotlight* (December 1964), p. 79.

24. Rediffusion is a wired radio system. Lines are strung from the broadcasting studios to individual homes, which are equipped with loudspeakers. Subscribers to Rediffusion pay a rental rate for the service. Maintenance is one of the serious drawbacks of the system.

25. *Handbook on Broadcasting*, p. 11.

26. H. P. Jacobs, "The Press and Radio," *Gleaner* Independence Supplement, July 28, 1962.

27. "Radio Bahamas Announcing Course" (News release in ZNS files, Nassau, Bahamas).

28. *West India Royal Commission Report*, pp. 58–59.

29. Radio Caribbean was initiated by Michel Ferry, a colorful Frenchman who has been called a legend on St. Lucia. He apparently set up the station as an offshore broadcast unit for Martinique and Guadeloupe. Personal interview, John Whitmarsh, Station Manager, Radio Caribbean, Castries, St. Lucia, May 7, 1971.

30. All circulation statistics in this chapter were obtained from interviews with editors, Benn's Guide to Newspapers, Periodicals of the World, *Newspaper Press Directory 1971* (London: Benn Brothers Ltd., 1971), and *Editor & Publisher International Yearbook, 1971* (New York: Editor & Publisher, 1971).

31. This media centralization resulted from colonial days, according to one author. Pearcy said, "In colonial times the key institutions of government and church were located in one city, the capital. Commercial enterprises, desiring to be near the source of power, clustered nearby, while transportation [and communication] lines formed out from them." Pearcy said that the justification for the primatial city in these smaller islands is that they could not support two or three large cities. So one finds in Jamaica that Kingston has 376,520 people and the secondary city, Montego Bay, only 25,000. J. Etzel Pearcy, *The West Indian Scene* (New York: Van Nostrand, 1965), p. 55.

32. Everett Rogers, "Mass Media Exposure and Modernization Among Colombian Peasants," in David Berlo, ed., *Mass Communication and the Development of Nations* (East Lansing, Mich.: International Communication Institute, 1968), p. III-3.

33. "Television Will Publicize Life in Rural Jamaica," *Daily Gleaner*, July 31, 1963, p. 8.

34. Personal interview, L. H. Stewart, Assistant General Manager, Jamaica Broadcasting Corporation, Kingston, Jamaica, August 28, 1970; Personal Interview, Leo de Leon, Program Director, 610 Radio, Port of Spain, Trinidad, September 1, 1970.

35. Guy Roppa and Neville E. Clarke, *The Commonwealth Caribbean: Regional Co-Operation in News and Broadcasting Exchanges* (Paris: UNESCO, 1969), p. 18.

36. Personal interview, Lenn Chongsing, Editor, *Guardian*, Port of Spain, Trinidad, September 1, 1970. In the Bahamas, the people purchase the newspapers daily and save them to read on the weekend. Personal interview, Benson McDermott, Vice President, *Guardian*, Nassau, Bahamas, August 24, 1970.

37. Personal interview, Compton Delph, Editor, *Evening News*, Port of Spain, Trinidad, September 1, 1970. On Barbados, the *Advocate-News* is sold to one in ten of the 250,000 population. But there are about five members in each household, hence the paper is read by every other Barbadian. Interview, Grosvenor, Bridgetown, September 7, 1970.

38. Herbert Passin, "Writer and Journalist in the Transitional Society," in Lucian Pye, ed., *Communications and Political Development* (Princeton, N. J.: Princeton University Press, 1963), p. 105.

39. Forum is an organization that stresses psychological and spiritual qualities that the third-world man will need as the twenty-first century begins. It is not so radical as some groups in the United States, and the *Crusader* is not a "kill the pigs" type of newspaper. Personal Interview, Stanley Reid, ed., *Crusader*, Castries, St. Lucia, May 8, 1971.

40. Personal interview, John Wickham, Editor, *The Bajan*, Bridgetown, Barbados, May 14, 1971.

41. *The Bajan, Spotlight, Bahamian Review.*

42. Personal interview, Randolph Rawlins, Radio Jamaica commentator and co-founder of newsmagazine, Basseterre, St. Kitts, May 1, 1971.

43. See Irene Zimmerman, *A Guide to Current Latin American Periodicals: Humanities and Social Sciences* (Gainesville, Fla.: Kallman Publishing, 1961).

44. So called by many West Indians because of the rumors that circulate about its aims, e.g., "Communist agitator," "station made up of German collaborators from World War II," etc. However, one source said the station was set up in 1963 to "provide advertising to the Caribbean." Sir Harold Mitchell, *Contemporary Politics and Economics in the Caribbean* (Athens, Ohio: Ohio University Press, 1968), p. 171.

45. The other radio operations in the islands are Antigua Broadcasting Service and ZDK on Antigua, Radio Anguilla, Barbados Rediffusion (also Radio Barbados), ZBM 1 and 2 and ZFBI on Bermuda, Radio Montserrat, ZIZ on St. Kitts, and ZBVI on Tortola in the British Virgin Islands.

46. UNESCO, *World Communications: Press, Radio, Television, Film* (Paris: UNESCO, 1964), p. 153.

4

Mass Media Ownership

Ownership of Commonwealth Caribbean mass media, especially radio and television, is very much like that of Africa. Two types predominate:* ownership by foreign enterprises and, for most of the remaining media, ownership by local governments and local political parties.[1]

For example, among Commonwealth Caribbean broadcasting systems, it is indeed rare for a station to be both locally and privately owned. Radio station ZDK on Antigua is owned by the family of the immediate past premier of the island, while St. Lucia Television, a subsidiary of Caribbean Broadcasting Corporation of Barbados, is owned by the proprietors of a St. Lucia television rental firm. Bermuda Radio and Television is a private company owned by publishers of the island's newspapers and the Bermuda Broadcasting Co. However, controlling interest in the latter company is owned by a British firm. Otherwise, radio and television stations in the region are owned either by foreign entrepreneurs, local governments, or a combination of both. On six of the seven islands with competing radio stations,[2] the pattern is such that one station is owned by government, the second by Rediffusion or another foreign enterprise.

The picture is somewhat different among newspapers. Although two-thirds of the island newspapers[3] are owned, or significantly controlled, by outside entrepreneurs and local political or church interests,[4]

---

* At a meeting in 1974 of Caribbean developmental communicators, acceptable alternatives to present media ownership structures were suggested as follows: exclusive state ownership; diversified forms of public ownership, representative of various interest groups; and local private ownership, which should not be motivated solely by profit incentives (Supplement to *Intermedia* 2, no. 4 [1974]:iv.)

the majority of the region's circulation is in the hands of local, privately owned papers. The six dailies under local, private owners have a combined circulation of 184,319, or over 56 percent of the total daily circulation. Four dailies owned by foreign groups have a total circulation of 134,715, 41 percent of total, and three political party dailies circulate to 6,700, 2 percent.

Of the 46 nondailies, less than 20 percent (9) could definitely be classified as local, privately owned newspapers. However, they control approximately 63 percent (128,768) of the known nondaily circulation (202,568).[5] The largest proportion, 26 of 46 papers, was made up of political organs. The 15 politically owned nondailies for which figures were available circulated to 53,000 people, and three of the five church-owned nondailies had a combined circulation of 20,500. Circulation figures of the two foreign-owned nondailies were not available but would not be more than a few thousand each.

In the following discussion, ownership will be broken down into these categories: foreign, local and private, local and political, local and government, and consortium.

FOREIGN

It has not been difficult to get foreign conglomerates to invest in the islands' media, especially radio and television. For example, all the Commonwealth Caribbean nations had to do was flirt with the idea of television and foreign investors came courting. As a result, all of the television stations in the region were developed with generous amounts of American dollars and British pounds.

Even today, as the smaller islands contemplate television of their own, they find their first big decision is to decide which foreign offer of assistance they should accept. That is the case with Dominica, now in the process of choosing, from among a number of foreign bids,* the best offer for the franchise there.[6] St. Kitts-Nevis has made its decision, accepting a $1¼ million (EC) loan from the British-owned Cable and Wireless to develop a governmental television system.[7] If St. Lucia Television Service ever decides to expand its operations, at

---

* However, in 1974 Premier Edward Le Blanc chaired a meeting to discuss a proposed television service for Dominica with a number of private interests such as hotels, tourism, mercantile, and commercial sectors. The proposal called for few locally originated programs at the outset, but regular transmissions from Barbados. (*Combroad* [July–September 1974], p. 50.)

least Cable and Wireless, Rediffusion, and Bermuda television will be around to render a bid.[8] And in the Bahamas efforts to initiate local television service in the late 1960s were supported by $250,000 (US) of KOCO-TV (Oklamoma City) capital.* The United States station had signed a controversial agreement with the Bahamian government to provide a variety of training, management, and equipment services, but in 1968 the Bahamian government stopped its television plans without explanation.[9]

Besides United States and British media concerns, the Canadian government has been more than mildly interested in developing electronic media in the region. In the mid-1960s, at the request of the Canadian government, the Canadian Broadcasting Corporation conducted a feasibility study on the possibility of establishing a radio network to service the Commonwealth islands.[10] After studying the report, the Canadian government made an offer of $8 million (EC) to create a Canada-Caribbean Broadcasting Center and a string of stations in the British West Indies. The offer was not accepted because a decision could not be reached concerning the location of the Center (island jealousies standing in the way), and because the project was not coming from within the islands themselves. The head of the Caribbean Broadcasting Union said of the project:

> First of all, I have learned that the Center could not be centered anywhere; it would have to move about. Secondly, the offer from CBC was handled from political levels, instead of broadcasting levels and thus it fizzled out. Island governments also feared the project would cost them too much.[11]

The outside financial help may be readily available, but the need for this foreign ownership is ambivalently accepted by small islands, many of which are newly independent nations feeling compelled to collect television as part of the paraphernalia of nationhood. Incapable of raising necessary investment and equipment capital, of producing their own program content, or of providing required training and skills, these governments must resort to foreign ownerships or partnerships in consortia. Meanwhile, the nationalists on the islands continually cry out against this form of modern-day colonialism. In a rare case or two, after the new medium became a success, the local government has asked that the outside entrepreneurs remove them-

---

* In 1974 there were still no immediate plans for developing television in the Bahamas.

selves. Thus, in 1969 when the prevailing mood of Trinidad was to "get things out of foreign hands," Prime Minister Eric Williams was able to persuade Roy Thomson to "take the initiative in giving up"[12] his radio and television holdings there to the government. Yet, at an earlier time, Williams had asked Britisher Cecil King to do the opposite —come to the island with his money and develop a third daily for Trinidad, the *Mirror*.[13]

Rediffusion

Among the very first instances of near dominance of Commonwealth Caribbean mass media by a foreign enterprise was that of Overseas Rediffusion (also known as Rediffusion International). By the early 1950s Rediffusion already controlled radio stations on the three most populated islands, Jamaica, Barbados, and Trinidad. With the advent of the 1970s, broadcasting companies on Jamaica, Barbados, Trinidad, St. Lucia,* Bermuda, and Tortola (in the British Virgin Islands) were owned by Rediffusion.

The London-based corporation also had a small hand in the development of television in the region. For a time, before its takeover by the government in 1969, Trinidad and Tobago Television was partly owned (40 percent) by Radio Trinidad, a Rediffusion outlet. On Antigua, as mentioned before, Leeward Islands Television Services is owned by a consortium that includes Rediffusion as a chief shareholder.** In the 1960s Rediffusion made an unsuccessful bid for the TV franchise on Jamaica, which subsequently was awarded to the government broadcasting unit.

From the outset, Overseas Rediffusion, in its agreements with local governments, included clauses that allowed for local autonomy in editorial matters.[14] On each island a local company, whose ordinary shares[15] are owned by Rediffusion, is formed with its own board of directors. All planning and broadcasting decisions are made locally; however, responsibilities for coordinating the business and financial matters rest with a Rediffusion regional manager for the Caribbean area.[16]

---

* Radio Caribbean on St. Lucia was sold to French enterpreneur Guy Noel. Rediffusion sold the station because it was not making the profit expected.

** In June 1975, the Antigua government became sole owner of Leeward Islands Television Services when Rediffusion liquidated its holdings. The Walter government paid EC $760,000 for ZAL-TV.

Thomson and King

Dwarfing Overseas Rediffusion in overall media penetration in the British West Indies have been the interests of Roy Thomson. Lord Thomson, who owns at least 400 worldwide businesses, most of them related to communications, has been active in radio, television, and newspaper ownership in the islands. He still maintains control over two of the few region-oriented newspapers, the Barbados *Advocate-News* and Trinidad *Guardian*, as well as the *Guardian*'s mass-circulation sister, *Evening News.** Together, Thomson's three papers represent 39 percent (128,546) of the total daily circulation in the Commonwealth Caribbean. But his interests in the region have dwindled significantly in recent years. At various times he has been involved financially with the *Voice of St. Lucia*, Antigua *Star*, Trinidad *Mirror*, and Barbados *Daily News*, in addition to broadcasting units on Trinidad, Jamaica, Barbados, and Bermuda. His name has come up occasionally in discussions of Bahamian media; at different times he has tried to purchase the Nassau *Tribune*,[17] Nassau *Guardian*, and ZNS. And in 1960 he made an unsuccessful bid for the Jamaica *Daily Gleaner*, a decade after his rival, Cecil King, had surveyed Kingston as to the possibility of developing a third daily there.[18]

Rivaling Thomson in the Commonwealth Caribbean, as he has done in Great Britain and parts of Africa, has been Cecil King, whose International Publishing Corporation in the late 1960s controlled 250 newspapers and periodicals. In the mid-1960s, when Thomson seemed invulnerable on Trinidad, owning both dailies (*Guardian* and *Evening News*), the only Sunday paper (*Sunday Guardian*), half of the radio interests (Guardian Radio), and shares in the only television system (TTT), King established another newspaper there, the *Mirror* and its Sunday edition. Within a few months King's International Publishing Corporation, in conjunction with the Liverpool Post and Echo, Ltd., had also succeeded in acquiring the Barbados *Advocate*[19] and its subsidiaries, *Voice of St. Lucia* and Antigua *Star*.[20]

However, by 1966 King, realizing that his profit margin was being sliced,[21] sold all his Caribbean interests to Thomson who, as a result, owned all three dailies on Trinidad, the only daily on Barbados, and

---

* In March 1975, the Trinidad *Guardian* and *Evening News* effected an operating merger with the McEnearney-Alstons Group, a predominantly Caribbean conglomerate. McEnearney-Alstons reportedly paid TT $4 million for nearly two-thirds ownership. The general manager of the Barbados *Advocate-News* told me in 1976 that the Barbadian government would probably purchase that Thomson newspaper.

the chief newspapers of St. Lucia and Antigua.[22] Thomson's subsequent sale of the *Mirror* plant and equipment to a Canadian firm led to the paper's death,[23] followed by a labor controversy that saw *Mirror* employees demonstrating in Port of Spain, publishing their own "phantom paper," and taking their case to industrial court.[24] However, from the ashes of the *Mirror*, a new Trinidadian daily, *Express*, emerged, staffed by a number of former *Mirror* employees. The *Express* is both privately and locally owned. Thomson did not hang onto the *Voice of St. Lucia* or Antigua *Star* very long, either. In 1969 he sold the *Star* to an Antiguan (who is now leader of the Antigua People's Party) after industrial unrest and work stoppages on that island affected the paper; the following year he resold the *Voice* to its former St. Lucian owner, Sir Garnet Gordon.*

Thomson, much like S. I. Newhouse in the United States, sees his job as a technical one—to provide the capital resources to allow media to perform their social role effectively. This is the reason he gave in the mid-1960s for wanting to expand his operations in the developing world:

> If the newspapers and magazines and television stations which I own are making money, then I know that they are rendering a social service; and the bigger the operation grows, the greater the service being rendered. . . . if the Thomson organization goes into the newly emergent countries of Africa, Asia and the Caribbean, this is because we feel that we have a *technical* job to do. We do not regard it as our function to interfere in *their* social or political affairs. . . . all we insist on are the two basic principles . . . 1. operate your newspapers in the best interests of the people of your community, 2. tell the truth and report all news and happenings factually and without bias.[25]

Dizard, commenting on Thomson Television International's (TTI) technical job, confirmed the organization's success in "attracting profitable business by offering developing countries a full range of technical and program services tailored to local needs."[26] Others, however, wonder how much of a social service is provided by media empire-builders such as Thomson, Newhouse, and King. They question the realness of the local editorial autonomy policy these men espouse;

---

* Sir Garnet Gordon died in 1975, but the Gordon family still owns the paper. Director Michael Gordon told me in 1976 that the family plans to keep the paper "for the time being," but hopes the Trinidad *Express*, which provides a consultancy service to the *Voice*, will purchase shares in the paper.

that is, as long as a medium is making money, the editorial policy is not bothered.

In Thomson's house biography, his policy toward editorial content was explained in this fashion:

> Editorially the properties could print what they liked, attack whom they chose (short, as he had stipulated, of God and the Monarchy) and support whichever party politically the community most favored; but if they spent a dollar a month more on lead or typewriter ribbon . . . than the budget prescribed, they must answer to him.[27]

And one of Thomson's Caribbean editors agreed that his boss adheres to that stated policy:

> Anything affecting revenue, Thomson is interested in; anything hurting advertising and circulation, he is interested in, but his local editors and the people of the country should be the ones who know what's good for the country.[28]

On the other hand, critics such as Ainslie feel that the real significance of foreign ownership of news media does not lie in this fear that daily policies will be dictated from abroad. It is something more subtle,

> something less concrete, and more pervasive, in the general orientation of the media (dictated in part by where they buy their material, and how they train their journalists) and in the "cast of mind" of the editorial staff, which in turn influences that of the reader.[29]

The cast of mind of a radio station in Trinidad formerly owned by Thomson was described by that station's program director, who said:

> Up to now there have been no editorial programs on this station because the previous owner, Thomson, did not want to hurt anyone. We will change that policy now that we are government owned. Under Thomson, we were not permitted nor encouraged to do local programs either.[30]

Yet, the general manager of Thomson's Barbados *Advocate-News* saw the reverse effect, that under local ownership the *Advocate-News* had "parochial influences exerted upon its functions."* He went into more detail:

> I have worked on both sides of the fence and feel there is much more progress when the paper is under foreign owned groups than when it was under a local concern. I remember that before 1961, any friend of the Gale family (owners of the paper then) could get stories withheld. Now the editor and I decide what is fit to publish without any fear of a backlash. Under Gale the paper published day to day and hoped it did not hurt anyone. Besides, in the last nine years, circulation has increased over 50 per cent.[31]

Brushing aside some of the above praise or criticism as being motivated by vested interests, one must still grapple with some realistic foreign-ownership problems facing developing nations. For example, there is the fact that foreign-owned media are commercially oriented, depending on mass sales and advertising volume, which developing nations are not prepared to provide.[32] Additionally, the urge for profits brings a tendency on the part of media to stress the entertainment rather than educational, developmental, or investigative aspects of journalism, the latter traits desperately needed in developing cultures.

Because London- or New York-owned media in the British West Indies are there only at the beck and call of local governments, it seems that they feel that caution must be exhibited during controversial situations, especially those of a political nature. This was the criticism leveled at the Thomson newspapers of Trinidad by the general manager of the independent *Express* on that island. He said that during the Black Power campaigns of early 1970, the *Guardian* was mute, not saying anything editorially for ten days about the riots and state of emergency. On the other hand, the *Express* editorialized daily, he added.[33]

Reliance upon the ledger book as the sole indication of a medium's success is not conducive to the needs of a developing nation, where sacrifice must be encouraged for longer-term goals. For example, a UNESCO team surveying West Indian mass media in 1968 felt that Thomson could do more sacrificing financially to insure that the

---

* When I interviewed him in 1976, the general manager maintained his earlier position, saying that under Thomson ownership, there was no editorial interference and that employees "know where they stand."

smaller newspapers in the region survived. The UNESCO survey team was critical of Thomson's relinquishing of the *Voice of St. Lucia* because of what they considered his inadequate reasons: its poor financial showing and the fact that he himself had already established a preponderance in the region with his Trinidad and Barbados dailies and no longer needed the smaller *Voice*. Such behavior by outsiders, UNESCO feared, would destroy small island media.[34]

Hinged to this fear has been the danger that a foreign entrepreneur such as Thomson, with some strategically placed purchases, could have a virtual stranglehold on mass media in the archipelago. That was nearly the case in the Eastern Caribbean when Thomson owned the main newspapers of Trinidad, Barbados, St. Lucia, and Antigua, issued special editions of the *Advocate-News* designed for each island of the region, and participated in numerous broadcasting consortia. But because of the tightening of foreign ownership by some island governments, this fear is no longer realistic. Complaints are still voiced, however, that Thomson media monopolize certain areas. For example, Grenada editors cannot compete with Thomson's regional dailies, which exchange photographs and news between their Barbados, Trinidad, and Guyana offices;[35] the *Express* on Trinidad cannot obtain certain syndicated feature and comic materials because Thomson's London outlets control their distribution.[36]

Despite these criticisms, there are those who feel that the foreign publishers and broadcasters have provided, at least technologically, a standard of journalism that the Commonwealth Caribbean could not have had otherwise. But even this positive note has been blemished by the UNESCO team's report, which illustrated that the "top quality of Jamaica's 'Gleaner' and the liveliness of Trinidad's 'Express'" were accomplished without much, if any, outside help.[37]

LOCAL, PRIVATE

The Jamaica Gleaner Company is the largest local, privately owned mass media enterprise in the Commonwealth Caribbean. Besides publishing the two largest dailies in the region, *Daily Gleaner* (circulation 59,349) and *Star* (64,037), Gleaner Company also produces newspapers for children (*Children's Own*,[38] 76,406), overseas Jamaicans (Jamaica *Weekly Gleaner*, 27,462),[39] and the weekend audience (*Weekend Star*, 75,853, *Sunday Gleaner*, 83,674, and its supplement, *Sunday Magazine*). With the largest and most modern newspaper plant in the region, Gleaner Company also operates its own book-publishing division, publishes a Wednesday supplement for the western portion of Jamaica, and issues special farmer's, food, and plaza (shoppers') supplements to the *Gleaner* three times a week. Since 1963 the firm has also published a legal journal of the more important judgments of the Jamaica Court of Appeals. The company does not own broadcasting stations, however, because their applications for franchises have been rejected repeatedly,* according to the paper's general manager.[40]

During its formative years the firm was in the hands of its founders, Jacob and Joshua de Cordova, or their descendants. Now a public limited company, the Gleaner has dissolved the family element of control completely.

Because of its near monopoly over the printed media of the island, the Gleaner Company does come in for considerable criticism. The editorial manager of the *Daily Gleaner* replies that actually no monopoly exists because no exclusive license was awarded the paper.** He added:

> Anyone with five million pounds can start his own paper here. Our attitude at the *Gleaner* is to welcome competition but when it appears, set out to kill it.[41]

Both Gleaner dailies claim to be apolitical, although individual directors of the corporation tend to support the Jamaica Labour Party. Fred Seal Coon, editorial manager of the *Gleaner*, explained why:

> The directors as individuals support Labour because People's National Party is tinged with communism and socialism, and businessmen generally fear the socialistic influence. However, every government in power considers the *Gleaner* an arch enemy.[42]

The apolitical nature of the papers is emphasized in the company's statement of policy, which disclaims for the dailies any ambition to be history-makers or kingmakers. According to that statement:

> Its objectives are public. It grinds no axes. It seeks to record, to inform, and to entertain; and to promote and encourage the best advancement and progress for Jamaica and all its public.[43]

---

* The general manager of the *Gleaner* told me in 1976 that his company, Rediffusion Jamaica Radio, and a foreign firm had submitted another request to the government for a color television franchise. He did not think the application would receive a favorable reaction because the government, as it leans closer to socialism, wants to maintain its TV monopoly.

** Of course, since the appearance of *The Jamaica Daily News* in 1973, the *Gleaner* does not have a monopoly in Jamaica.

Second largest of the privately owned, indigenous newspapers of the region is the Trinidad *Express,* with a circulation of 35,872. The *Express* was created in 1967 when former *Mirror* employees, bitter about that paper's death, obtained public support for a new daily. The tabloid is completely controlled by local shareholders, the largest of whom is a Trinidadian businessman, Vernon Charles. Proud of its indigenousness,* the *Express* thinks of itself as the only Trinidad daily not afraid to speak out. Its general manager said that because the foreign-owned. *Guardian* and *Evening News* do not get involved in local controversy, the *Express* must act as the island's forum of dissent.[44] He gave this example to support his statement:

When the black power movement was coming in 1970, we were accused of fanning the flames. When it broke in February, the *Guardian* did not say anything editorially for ten days. And the government did not say anything either. We editorialized daily. We said we could sympathize with people who seemed dispossessed, who felt hopeless. But we also said we condemned violence that was happening around the demonstrations.[45]

During the ensuing riots the Port of Spain business community, bent on finding a scapegoat according to this *Express* official, boycotted the *Express* for two months, placing advertisements in the Thomson papers only.[46]

Despite such harassment, the *Express* refused to bow to the business or governmental elements of Trinidad. The editorial policy of the paper since the riots was described by its general manager as follows:

The big problem of the *Express* is that we are outspoken in a community where the establishment of this outspokenness is not apparent. Here they have always been assured that the papers would say what the community wanted them to say. Our problem is to communicate with the business community and tell them to deal in a realistic way with the social problems of the nation. What we are doing is to stimulate thought to throw up truth. In a society where the establishment is a minority, if you don't show society they may have hope, then you are playing with an explosive situation.[47]

---

* The *Express* has promoted an indigenous press for other islands as well. In order to keep out foreign ownership, the *Express* has provided consultancy services (and in some cases, material aid) to *The Nation* on Barbados, *The Jamaica Daily News, The Voice of St. Lucia,* and *The Torchlight* on Grenada.

The Nassau *Tribune*, its sister in Freeport (Grand Bahama *Tribune*), and the *Royal Gazette* and *Mid-Ocean News* on Bermuda are the other major newspapers devoid of both foreign and political ownership or control.*

Owner of the *Tribune* for over fifty years has been Sir Etienne Dupuch, whose father founded the paper in 1903. Apparently the paper will continue as a family business; Sir Etienne's daughter and her husband are the heirs-apparent for the proprietor-publisher-editor post. A son, Etienne, Jr., in a separate enterprise, publishes Bahamian tourist magazines and the *Bahamas Handbook and Businessman's Annual*.

Bermudian newspapers are owned by Bermuda Press Ltd., a local corporation that also publishes a weekly magazine supplement, *Happening*, and owns part of the island's television interests. In fact, Bermuda Press Ltd. is the only Commonwealth Caribbean newspaper firm with broadcasting stock.

Magazines in the region, except for informational and propagandistic periodicals issued by governmental agencies, are owned privately by West Indians. General-interest magazines, although owned by West Indians, are designed oftentimes for non-West Indians, the tourists. In fact, claiming the largest circulation among periodicals is the tourist-designed *Bahamas*, operated by Bahamas Magazine Ltd. *Bahamas*, published five times a year, lists a circulation of 100,000.[48] In a number of cases, Commonwealth Caribbean grammar and high schools, universities, and cultural groups (e.g., Barbados Museum and Historical Society and Institute of Jamaica) are responsible for publishing the bulk of an island's magazines.

The absence of foreign ownership of magazines in the islands stands out rather conspicuously. This fact is partially attributable to the unprofitable nature of the magazine industry in these small islands. Also, in a few cases, conscious efforts are made to keep periodical ownership at home. In the late 1960s, for example, when the Barbadian newsmagazine *The Bajan* was up for sale, a small group of Barbadian businessmen purchased it, not because of their interest in news and literature, but to keep ownership on Barbados.[49]

---

* Of course, since this was written, *The Jamaica Daily News* has appeared as another major, locally owned, independent newspaper. The *Daily News*, a morning tabloid, is owned by the Communications Corporation of Jamaica Ltd. The cost of starting the daily was Jam.$1.27 million, $900,000 of which was raised through share capital, $370,000 through loan capital. Two local firms, Desnoes and Geddes Ltd. and National Continental Corporation, took up $140,000 and $260,000 of the equity, respectively. The balance of $500,000 was offered to the public.

Among the few indigenous, privately owned broadcasting units in the region is ZDK Radio (corporate name is Grenville Radio Ltd.) on Antigua. The station is wholly owned by the former premier, V. C. Bird, and his two sons. Originally, it was partly financed by Canadian entrepreneurs. Manager Ivor G. T. Bird told how he obtained a license for ZDK:

> A few years ago, I wrote two letters to my father (premier of Antigua then) asking to set up a second station. He turned me down because it was the government's policy not to have a second station competing with its own outlet. I was able to convince my father another station was needed. One reason I got a license was I promised him I would sell shares to the public.[50]

ZDK went on the air for the first time in December 1970, approximately two months before the Antiguan national elections that swept his father out of office. Station personnel, as well as other Antiguan media managers, claim that the station was not used for political purposes by the Birds, and that the terms of the license forbid the station's use politically.

The other broadcasting medium in this category is St. Lucia Television Service, Ltd. Its owner is Ken Archer, a St. Lucian who originally came from Great Britain. Archer operates the television service as a subsidiary of his St. Lucia Rental, Ltd.

According to Archer, the premier of St. Lucia would like to form a corporation that would include both radio and television, but only if Windward Islands Broadcasting Service, of which St. Lucia is a member, is abandoned.*

> If any island pulls out of WIBS, the premier feels he could dissolve the St. Lucia WIBS substation and form a St. Lucia government broadcasting system. But for political reasons, he cannot take that step unless another island drops out of WIBS first. The new radio station that would then be formed, and St. Lucia Television (which would remain as a privately owned concern), would form a corporation for the purposes of using joint facilities and equipment and seeking outside funding.[51]

---

* In 1971 WIBS was dissolved, and St. Lucia did set up its own broadcasting service. In 1976 plans were being made to combine Radio St. Lucia and St. Lucia Television Service into one corporation. The government will finance the transmission equipment for the TV service and probably ask St. Lucia Television Service to operate it.

LOCAL, POLITICAL

Determining political ownership of Commonwealth Caribbean newspapers is an elusive exercise. Take the cases of the St. Kitts *Democrat* and Antigua *Star*, for example. One can pick up a copy of the St. Kitts *Democrat* and read literally nothing except information on People's Action Movement activities, manifestos, and policies. Yet, listening to the paper's editor, one learns that the paper does not belong to PAM, is neither subsidized nor owned by the party, but does actively support its tenets and candidates.[52] However, upon closer scrutiny, one finds that the chief stockholder of the paper is also the top leader of PAM.

The Antigua *Star* editor explained that his paper's chief owners are two ministers (home affairs and public utilities) in the governing People's Labour Movement cabinet, plus a former PLM official. He said that the *Star* is affiliated with PLM and Antigua Workers Union and that during the previous election it had published daily editorials and news stories supporting PLM candidates. But on the other hand, he insisted that the paper was not the organ of PLM or AWU.[53]

Similar situations exist in other islands, especially the Leeward and Windward chains. Self-styled "independent" weeklies are often owned by parliamentarians, mayors, senators, and party leaders. And although content of the papers is saturated with political viewpoints and invectiveness, the editors claim that their papers have always been oppositionist and definitely do not favor one particular party.

On Dominica the *Herald** is owned by Edward Scobie, mayor of Roseau and co-founder and vice-president of the four-year-old Freedom Party. Scobie said that the paper, acting as a platform for the aggrieved, is oppositionist in character, but *Herald* policy is not dictated by the party secretariat. He added:

> I am solely responsible for the *Herald*. I have never sought help from the party on any points. In fact, our editorial line has not coincided with Freedom Party at times.[54]

Of the two other Dominican newspapers, the *Star* is privately owned by Robert and Phyllis Allfrey, the latter an organizer of the Freedom Party and prominent West Indian political figure, while the *Chronicle* is the property of the Roman Catholic diocese of Dominica.

---

* The *Herald* folded a year after Scobie was arrested in 1972 on charges of committing violence and inciting to violence.

Antigua's third and most recent newspaper, *Times*,* was initiated by the Antigua People's Party as its mouthpiece. Although 100 shareholders control the paper, a chief owner is Reuben Harris, a local nightclub proprietor. Acting editor of the *Times* in 1971 was Harris's wife, top adviser to the minister of education at the time. On leave from her governmntal post, Mrs. Harris steered the *Times* along an anti-government, pro-APP line.[55]

Among other examples, the Anguilla *Beacon* is owned by a member of the Anguilla Council (main governing body of the island), while the *West Indian* of Grenada is in the hands of a local solicitor who was once a senator.**

Of course, newspapers making no pretense about their political ownership do exist in the islands. In this classification are Antigua *Workers Voice*, St. Kitts *Labour Spokesman*, Grenada *Vanguard*, and St. Lucia *Crusader*, along with the party press of Trinidad, Barbados, Jamaica, and Bahamas (see chaps. 3 and 5 for further discussion of the party press on the larger islands).

In at least two cases these newspapers serve dual roles, acting as the voice of a trade union as well as that of a political party. For example, the daily *Workers Voice* serves both the Antigua Labour Party and Antigua Trades and Labour Union, and St. Kitts *Labour Spokesman* is the newspaper of both the labor union and the labor party on that island. It is not unusual for political newspapers to be edited by high party officials. Editor of the *Voice* is general secretary of Antigua Trades and Labour Union; in the late 1950s the paper's editor was George Walter, now premier of Antigua.

Finally, Grenada *Vanguard* admits to being owned by the Grenada National Party, and St. Lucia *Crusader* is the property of the Black Power group, Forum.***

Although the combined circulation of newspapers owned by political parties (probably not much more than 70,000) is less than 14 percent of the total, this figure should not be slighted. On some of the smaller islands the political newspapers, since they are the only ones available, appear to be the national press.

Political party ownership of broadcasting in the Commonwealth Caribbean does not exist (at least not in an observable manner),

---

* Closed in 1971 because of the financial burdens placed on the paper by the press laws of that year.
** The *West Indian* is now owned by the Grenada government.
*** *Vanguard*, not able to cope with government interference, has ceased publication. *Crusader* is now owned by the St. Lucia Labour Party.

probably because the governments, as significant broadcasting owners themselves, deny parties broadcasting franchises.

In the case of Trinidad, the government, in its Third Five-Year Plan, emphasized that political party influences had to be kept out of government ownership of radio and television. To insure that this would happen, the government planned to set up a broadly based authority to supervise and regulate all sound and visual broadcasting and to continue operation of government-owned Trinidad and Tobago National Broadcasting System and Trinidad and Tobago Television on a commercial basis with a representative board of directors.[56]

LOCAL, GOVERNMENT

Whereas Commonwealth Caribbean nondailies are owned/controlled to a great degree by political parties, electronic media* in the region operate under an umbrella of government ownership and control.[57] This link of state-owned media includes four of the area's seven television systems and 11 of the 19 radio stations.

On the three largest islands, Jamaica, Trinidad, and Barbados, local governments own both a radio and a television station; in at least five other instances (Bahamas, Dominica, Grenada, St. Kitts, and St. Vincent), the government radio stations are the only broadcasting outlets on the islands.

On the most populated island, Jamaica Broadcasting Corporation** owns the only television station, one of the two radio stations, and educational television. JBC radio and television, although publicly owned and operated by a statutory corporation, receive neither taxpayer money nor license fees. All financing is derived from advertising and loans.

Caribbean Broadcasting Corporation, Trinidad and Tobago National Broadcasting System, St. Kitts ZIZ, and Bahamas ZNS also are public broadcasting systems that support themselves by advertising.[58]

Government purchase of broadcasting interests on Trinidad in

---

* For another review of ownership (as well as administration, audience size, source of revenue, and technical operating standards) of television services of Jamaica, Trinidad and Tobago, Barbados, and Antigua, see Everold Hosein, "Regional Television Programming for the Commonwealth Caribbean," *Combroad* (October–December 1973), pp. 13–17.

** For an overview treatment of Jamaica Broadcasting Corporation, see Lorna Gordon, "The Jamaica Broadcasting Corporation Geared to Serve a Developing Nation," *EBU Review* 23, no. 3: 25–27.

November 1969 alarmed some West Indians who, like DaBreo, felt that Prime Minister Eric Williams is transforming the Trinidad economy from a capitalist to a socialist form. According to DaBreo, the Trinidad government has "more shares in, or complete ownership of, more major concerns than any other Caribbean island with the exception of Cuba."[59] Among these financial concerns were Trinidad and Tobago National Broadcasting System (formerly 610 Radio,* and earlier still, Radio Guardian) and Trinidad and Tobago Television. The purchases not only brought a large portion of broadcasting under government control, but also took it from the foreign control of Thomson and others.[60]

TTNBS remains a commercial enterprise, profits being used to increase local programming and staff and to repay the government its capital investments.[61] The station, although state-owned, is a civilian, independent agency with no government control over day-to-day operations, according to one official.[62]

An official at TTT, describing the relationship between government and TTT as "very cordial indeed," said that that station has been allowed to carry on as it did before government take-over.[63]

The writers of the Third Five-Year Plan for Trinidad, anticipating the criticism that would result from government ownership, pointed out that very few democracies of the West did not have public broadcasting and fewer still allowed media to be owned by foreigners.

A third large government-owned broadcasting medium is Caribbean Broadcasting Corporation, the commercial[64] radio and television stations on Barbados. CBC is administered by a nine-member statutory board appointed by the cabinet for three-year terms. Government personnel and politicians are not members, except for one representative of the prime minister. The CBC board is charged with leading the corporation "in accordance with the Act, the License and the Broadcasting Rules and is responsible to the Minister in charge of broadcasting." The transient nature of board members has stimulated criticism. One writer said:

> As long as the control of radio and television in Barbados depends on boards appointed for short periods by a minister of government in power, it is unlikely that stimulation will occur in any fields other than entertainment and sports.[65]

---

* 610 Radio was incorporaated as a private company from January 1973, with the government holding all shares either directly or through nominated subscribers. The new name became National Broadcasting Service of Trinidad & Tobago Ltd.

Windward Islands Broadcasting Service,* with main headquarters on Grenada and substations on Dominica, St. Lucia, and St. Vincent, is the fourth large public broadcaster in the region. In the past WIBS has been a noncommercial network subsidized by the four governments concerned. The regional organization is administered by the West Indies Broadcasting Council, which is made up of the four island premiers. Between meetings[66] of the Council, the premier of Grenada acts on behalf of the Council, after consultation with individual members.[67] All members of the WIBS staff are part of the Grenada civil establishment.

WIBS chief program officer, Claude Theobalds, admitted that the administrative structure of the network left the substations open to considerable criticism:

> The criticism of WIBS is that it is controlled by the premiers, and thus by politicians. The individual premiers have a lot of influence on local substations and policy depends on the disposition of these premiers. On each island, the substation is responsible to that island's premier through his cabinet secretary. WIBS rules, however, are set down by WIBS Grenada. The theory is that the overall policy is set by the four premiers, but the manager of WIBS Grenada is responsible for day-to-day decisions.[68]

Because so much of the control is left to Grenada personnel, managers on the other three islands go about their jobs without even knowing the terms of the licenses under which they work. The substation manager on St. Lucia said that he had never seen his station's license, and that if a problem should come up, he would refer it to Grenada or to the St. Lucian cabinet secretary[69] (see chap. 8 for further discussion of government relationships with WIBS, as well as with other Commonwealth Caribbean mass media).

Since there has been talk recently of dissolving the network[70] and setting up individual island stations, WIBS since 1969 has been in the process of reorganizing. The proposed restructuring provides for four independent local stations and a network organization owned by, and providing engineering, sales, and program services to, the stations. Both the network and stations would be operated as commercial entities, and all revenues derived from the network operation would be divided equally among the four stations.

---

* The following information on WIBS is history now that that service has been discontinued.

In addition, the proposal stipulates that employees of the network staff be made members of a statutory corporation that would be a wholly owned subsidiary of the local stations. Individual stations would be administered separately by statutory boards on the respective islands, and the network would be controlled by a broadcasting board comprised of a representative from each station.[71]

The above plan may never see fruition. For example, at least one substation (Dominica) is in the process of making a complete break with WIBS. Radio Dominica is a 10,000-watt, commercial enterprise, housed in new facilities paid for by the Dominican government. Manager-designate of the new station, Jeff Charles, explained government's thinking:

> The Dominican government felt its purposes would best be served by having greater autonomy in radio programs and more physical control of the system. It also would like to promote local identities and provide island-wide coverage.[72]

Even before Radio Dominica went on the air, the opposition political party predicted that it would be too government prone and made up only of government employees.[73]

The state-owned Bahamian stations, ZNS-1 and ZNS-2, are under the supervision of an independent five-man commission, appointed in consultation with the prime minister. Actually, however, the prime minister does the appointing of personnel to the Bahamas Broadcasting and Television Commission.* The commission itself is responsible to the minister for internal affairs. ZNS personnel think of the station as neither a public service department nor a public corporation, but something in between these structures. The station pays its own debts, collects no money from the public treasury, and has its own bank account.[74]

A common characteristic of the island governments is a determination to protect their exclusive broadcasting rights. Amid requests[75] and pleas for a second television service, the Jamaican government refuses to grant another license, arguing that the island is too small to support two television systems.

On Trinidad and in the Bahamas, it is unlikely that the govern-

---

* Recently, the commission became the Broadcasting Corporation of the Bahamas (BCB), operating three radio stations: ZNS-1, in Nassau, designed to cover the nation; ZNS-2, in Nassau, primarily for residents of New Providence Island; and ZNS-3, in Freeport, designed to cover Radio Bahamas' Northern Service.

ments will grant additional broadcasting licenses. A Trinidadian official said that he saw no possibility of competition in the field of television because "no one will be allowed a TV license unless the government wants him to have one."[76] The Bahamian government also feels that it must protect its station from competition, and has denied numerous radio applications over the years.[77]

The other mass medium owned by various island governments is the magazine. However, most periodicals issued by the governments have limited interest and circulation among the general population. A few titles will explain why this might be so: for example, there is the *Quarterly Economic Report,* a 600 circulation Trinidad government periodical; Jamaica *Public Health,* quarterly of the Ministry of Health; *Winban News,* publication of the Windward Islands Banana Association; and the Jamaica Department of Statistics *Rural Retail Price Index.* The St. Vincent Government Information Service, among others, has attempted to reach a wider audience through its fortnightly called *St. Vincent Today,* but the magazine suspended publication after one issue because of a lack of staff.

CONSORTIUM

Because of the need for financing from a number of sources, a favorite Commonwealth Caribbean ownership format, especially for broadcasting, has been the consortium, made up of local and foreign financial interests. Usually the foreign part of such consortia provides needed outside capital, training, and programming, while the local participants keep some of the ownership at home.

Involved prominently in British West Indian media consortia has been London press magnate Roy Thomson, whose Thomson Television International (TTI) usually provides programs, sells advertising time and supplies, and operates and maintains equipment in exchange for a fee and commission.[78]

On Trinidad, consortium partners of TTI were Rediffusion, Columbia Broadcasting Company, and the Trinidad government; on Barbados, TTI served as managing agent for Caribbean Broadcasting Corporation, and on Jamaica, in another consortium, Thomson arranged a half-million pound loan, on the guarantee of the Jamaican government, to develop Jamaica Broadcasting Corporation radio and television. The latter agreement, which guaranteed Thomson seven percent of television revenues as an agency fee, was dissolved in 1970 when a commercial bank loan was secured.[79] Thomson also owns part of Capital Broadcasting on Bermuda.

Besides Thomson, the three United States commercial broadcasting networks have been involved in at least five Commonwealth Caribbean broadcasting consortia. Columbia Broadcasting System (CBS) continues to own 10 percent of the Trinidad and Tobago Television (TTT) —the other 90 percent is owned by the Trinidad government*—and part of Leeward Islands Television Services on Antigua.** National Broadcasting Company (NBC) holds membership in consortia that operate a television station in Jamaica and a radio station in Barbados, and American Broadcasting Company (ABC) has a financial involvement in Capital Broadcasting Company, owners of ZFB-TV on Bermuda.[80]

In addition, other broadcasting systems of the region funded by consortia include Leeward Islands Television Services and Radio Antilles. The consortium governing Leeward Islands Television Services until 1975 was made up of Rediffusion, Bermuda radio and television, a local business, the Antigua government, and CBS. On Montserrat, the 200,000-watt Radio Antilles, which broadcasts in French, Spanish, and English to most of the Caribbean, was reportedly supported by a group of Swiss religious organizations aiming to offset Roman Catholicism in the area.[81]

SUMMARY

The ownership pattern among Commonwealth Caribbean mass media appears to follow these lines: electronic media, developed as parts of consortia, are increasingly becoming government agencies, while daily newspapers remain as either foreign or local, privately owned media, and nondailies as political party newspapers.

Although foreign enterprises are still enthusiastic about investing in Commonwealth Caribbean mass media, indications are that the maturing, newly emergent West Indian states are contemplating the development of communications channels with minimum, if any, outside help. Such nationalistic thinking, especially on an island like Trinidad, does not do much good for foreign entrepreneurs such as Roy Thomson and Cecil King. Thomson's Caribbean holdings have

---

* In 1974 negotiations were underway for the government to acquire the ten percent shares held by Columbia Broadcasting System.
** The Antigua government is the sole owner now.

dwindled considerably during the past half-decade, while King has sold all his holdings in the region. The two largest foreign concerns remaining in the islands—Thomson, who controlled 39 percent of the total daily circulation until recently, and Rediffusion, owner of six radio stations—may attribute their survival to the local autonomy principles they espouse.

Without foreign capital, however, mass media development must depend on either governmental or political party support, there being very few business concerns willing and able to undertake financing of such expensive, long-term projects as radio and television stations and newspapers. Already, approximately 60 percent of the broadcasting systems, including most of the largest, are government owned, and the majority of the nondailies evidence strong political backing. Dailies on Jamaica, Trinidad, Bahamas, and Bermuda represent the most significant privately owned, local media in the islands.

NOTES TO CHAPTER 4

1. Wilson Dizard, *Television: A World View* (Syracuse, N.Y.: Syracuse University Press, 1965), pp. 62–68; Rosalynde Ainslie, *The Press in Africa: Communications Past and Present* (New York: Walker & Co., 1968), p. 235. The comparison can be taken a step further in that the same communications empires that invaded Africa—Rediffusion, Thomson, and *Mirror* Group—have also, at varying times, descended upon the West Indies. The difference lies in the fact that Commonwealth Caribbean media are also under United States ownership nets.

2. St. Lucia, Barbados, Jamaica, Antigua, Montserrat, Bermuda, and Trinidad.

3. Seven of the 13 dailies; 33 of the 46 nondailies.

4. Included are newspapers which claim they are not owned by political parties, but where main stockholders are either politicians or political party leaders. In all of these cases, the newspapers support the party of this individual.

5. This figure has been inflated by the 103,868 total circulation of Jamaica's *Weekly Gleaner* and *Children's Own*.

6. Personal interview, Jeff Charles, Manager Designate, Radio Dominica, Roseau, Dominica, May 6, 1971.

7. Personal interview, Ken Archer, Director, St. Lucia Television Services, Castries, St. Lucia, May 8, 1971. Archer guessed that the reason Cable and Wireless invested the money was to get an opportunity for further involvement in the island's financial future. Cable and Wireless already owns a 200-watt station on the Turks Islands, plus all telegraph facilities in the Commonwealth Caribbean.

Cable and Wireless also owns virtually all telecommunications facilities in the area. Besides owning all country-to-country cable and radio links, C & W operates internal telephone and telegraph services of a number of territories. Most island governments realize it would not be reasonable to think of taking over this foreign-owned organization's functions; they do not have the skilled personnel. Some governments, however, especially that of Trinidad and Tobago, are thinking of asking for partnerships with C & W.

8. Ibid.

9. Personal interview, Jack Dodge, General Manager, ZNS, Nassau, Bahamas, April 26, 1971. See also P. Anthony White, "The Shameful Blackout," Nassau Guardian, April 23, 1971, p. 2.

10. The contents of that study are confidential. Letter to Author, W. Y. Martin, Executive Assistant, Canadian Broadcasting Corporation, Ottawa, October 1, 1970. See Advertising Age (October 31, 1966), p. 94.

11. Personal interview, Ray Smith, Head, Caribbean Broadcasting Union, St. George's, Grenada, May 12, 1971.

12. Personal interview, Lenn Chongsing, Editor, Trinidad Guardian, Port of Spain, Trinidad, September 1, 1970.

13. L. Hunt, "Mass Media in the West Indies," The Democratic Journalist (4/1967), p. 53.

14. Central Rediffusion Services Ltd., Commercial Broadcasting in the British West Indies (London: Butterworth's Scientific Publications, 1956), pp. 14–15.

15. Equivalent to common stock in United States.

16. Guy Roppa and Neville E. Clarke, The Commonwealth Caribbean: Regional Co-Operation in News and Broadcasting Exchanges (Paris: UNESCO 1969), p. 54. The managers of Rediffusion stations on Barbados and Trinidad said that their local outlets made all editorial decisions for the stations on those islands. Personal interview, Gary Duesbury, General Manager, Radio Rediffusion Service Ltd., Bridgetown, Barbados, September 7, 1970; Personal interview, Lloyd de Pass, General Manager, Radio Jamaica, Kingston, Jamaica, August 27, 1970.

17. Sir Etienne Dupuch, Tribune Story (London: Ernest Benn Ltd., 1967), p. 116.

18. Personal interview, Theodore Sealy, Editor, Daily Gleaner, Kingston, Jamaica, August 26, 1970.

19. The paper became the Advocate-News in 1968 when Thomson bought out the rival Barbados Daily News and merged the names.

20. The Advocate had conducted a feasibility study in 1961 and learned it

was not profitable to have a newspaper on each Commonwealth Caribbean island; therefore, a year later the newspaper bought the *Star* to serve the Leewards and the *Voice* for the Windwards. "Meeting a Need in the Islands of EC," Barbados *Advocate-News*, October 1, 1970.

21. Hunt, "Mass Media in the West Indies."

22. Thomson also picked up the Guyana *Graphic*, *Sunday Graphic*, and Berbice *Times* in that deal.

23. "The 'Mirror' Closes. . . ," Trinidad *Guardian*, September 3, 1966; "A Sad Day," Trinidad *Guardian*, September 4, 1966.

24. "Former 'Mirror' Workers Backed," Trinidad *Guardian*, September 7, 1966; "Former 'Mirror' Workers March," Trinidad *Guardian*, September 6, 1966; " 'Down the Drain' Goes a Career in Journalism," Trinidad *Guardian*, January 31, 1967; "Ex-Worker Surprised at 'Mirror's' Loss," Trinidad *Guardian*, February 1, 1967; " 'Mirror' Workers March in City," Trinidad *Guardian*, September 11, 1966; "Survival or Suicide?," Trinidad *Guardian*, December 31, 1966.

25. Russell Braddon, *Roy Thomson of Fleet Street* (London: Collins, 1965), p. 282.

26. Dizard, *Television*, p. 63.

27. Braddon, *Roy Thomson*, p. 130. Thomson verified his local autonomy principle in an interview published in the Trinidad *Guardian* when he visited that island. "Press Baron on Trinidad," Trinidad *Guardian*, December 11, 1965.

When Cecil King purchased the Barbados *Advocate* in 1961, he said basically the same thing, that his main concern was to make money and that the "long tradition of the island's leading newspaper will be maintained." "Who Owns the Advocate?," Barbados *Advocate*, November 21, 1961.

28. Personal interview, Neville Grosvenor, General Manager, *Advocate-News*, Bridgetown, Barbados, September 7, 1970.

29. Ainslie, *Press in Africa*, p. 241.

30. Personal interview, Leo de Leon, Program Director, 610 Radio, Port of Spain, Trinidad, September 1, 1970.

31. Interview, Grosvenor. And, of course, in an interview with Ian Gale, general manager of Caribbean Broadcasting Corporation and former editor of the newspaper his grandfather founded, one learned that the *Advocate-News* has had many criticisms since it fell into foreign hands.

32. See Ainslie, *Press in Africa*, p. 242.

33. Personal interview, Ken Gordon, General Manager, *Express*, Port of Spain, Trinidad, September 2, 1970. Foreign-owned media in Trinidad have felt the

pressure of criticisms that they do not represent the interests of the people. The *Guardian* and *Evening News* periodically run editorials or stories boasting of the public services they provide, how their "roots are deeply sunk in the community," and explaining that the expatriate owner of the *Evening News* is "not here to peddle the propaganda of the country of which he is a citizen." Trinidad *Guardian*, September 24, 1967; *Evening News*, August 23, 1963; *Daily Mirror*, September 29, 1964.

34. Roppa and Clarke, *Commonwealth Caribbean*, p. 12.

35. Personal interviews, Reggie Clyne, Editor, *West Indian*, and Elcon Mason, Editor, *Torchlight*, St. George's, Grenada, May 12, 1971.

36. Interview, Gordon.

37. Roppa and Clarke, *Commonwealth Caribbean*, p. 11.

38. Published 36 times during school term. Copies purchased by the schools for distribution to students.

39. Mats for the overseas edition are sent to London and a larger issue of the *Weekly Gleaner* is published there. The *Weekly Gleaner* published in Kingston is distributed to North and South America. The paper takes on importance because of the large Jamaican population living abroad. Over one-quarter million Jamaicans immigrated in the 1960s.

40. Personal interview, G. A. Sherman, General Manager, Gleaner Company, Kingston, Jamaica, August 26, 1970.

41. Personal interview, Fred Seal Coon, Editorial Manager, *Daily Gleaner*, Kingston, Jamaica, August 26, 1970.

42. Ibid.

43. Quoted in souvenir edition of *Daily Gleaner*, December 31, 1966, pp. 8–9.

44. Interview, Gordon.

45. Ibid.

46. Ibid.

47. Ibid.

48. Because of the erratic nature of Commonwealth Caribbean magazines, it is not possible to determine total number and circulation of British West Indian periodicals. However, combined circulation of nine periodicals for which figures were available was 27,250. These magazines are listed in table 3.3.

49. Personal interview, John Wickham, an editor of *The Bajan*, Bridgetown, Barbados, May 14, 1971.

50. Personal interview, Ivor G. T. Bird, Manager, ZDK Radio, St. John's, Antigua, May 4, 1971.

51. Interview, Archer.

52. Personal interview, Nathaniel Hodge, Editor, St. Kitts *Democrat*, Basseterre, St. Kitts, May 1, 1971.

53. Personal interview, Bentley Cornelius, Editor, Antigua *Star*, May 4, 1971.

54. Personal interview, Edward Scobie, Editor, Dominica *Herald*, Roseau, Dominica, May 5, 1971.

55. Personal interview, Mrs. Reuben Harris, Acting Editor, Antigua *Times*, May 4, 1971.

56. It was also stated that no political party criteria would be used in the appointment of staff members.

57. Davison said that among emerging nations there is usually a tendency for media to come more and more under governmental control because of the economic factor and the inability of new nations to tolerate media criticism. W. Phillips Davison, *International Political Communication* (New York: Frederick A. Praeger, 1965), p. 139.

58. Broadcasting personnel in the islands felt that this type of arrangement was unique to their islands.

59. D. Sinclair DaBreo, *The West Indies Today* (St. George's, Grenada: Published by Author, 1971), p. 45.

60. That this latter point is important can be gleaned from looking at the Third Five-Year Plan (1969–73) of Trinidad. The plan suggested: (1) no new media be allowed onto the island, (2) no foreign enterprise be allowed to buy out existing media, (3) sale of any existing foreign-owned media to another enterprise must have government permission, (4) government will take complete ownership of Radio Guardian and controlling interest in television, (5) advertising content of all media will be controlled with the view to ensuring that a national image is projected and local goods and services are more forcefully projected.

61. Interview, de Leon.

62. Ibid.

63. Letter to Author, John Barsotti, Assistant Program Director, Trinidad and Tobago Television, Port of Spain, Trinidad, August 10, 1971.

64. Originally CBC was financed by bank loans guaranteed by the government. Today the company's revenues come from a TV license fee of two pounds yearly, import duty of TV sets, and advertising.

65. "Broadcasting and Television," *Bajan* (July 1965), p. 10.

66. Meetings are held every 12 to 18 months.

67. Roppa and Clarke, *Commonwealth Caribbean.*

68. Personal interview, Claude Theobalds, Chief Program Officer, WIBS, Kingstown, St. Vincent, May 11, 1971.

69. Personal interview, Winston Hinkson, St. Lucia WIBS Director, Castries, St. Lucia, May 8, 1971.

70. Reasons given were: the substations have insufficient local programming, are not powerful enough to penetrate the entire length and breadth of their islands, and costs their governments too much money in the absence of any advertising revenue. Source asked for anonymity.

71. Source asked for anonymity.

72. Interview, Charles.

73. Ibid.

74. "A Brief History of ZNS" (Unpublished manuscript in ZNS files).

75. Interview, Sherman. See also "Sherman Decries TV Ban on Jamaica," *IAPA News* (July 1971), p. 2; "Wants Government To State Radio, TV Policy," *Daily Gleaner,* February 20, 1958.

76. Personal interview, Sam Ghany, Sales Manager, Trinidad Broadcasting, Port of Spain, Trinidad, September 2, 1970.

77. Interview, Dodge. A former newspaper executive in the Bahamas said the government keeps the radio monopoly because it is a money-maker. He said the Nassau *Tribune* and Nassau *Guardian,* among others, have sought a TV license, but they don't even receive the courtesy of a reply from the government. Personal interview, Chris Evans, Former General Manager, Nassau *Guardian,* Nassau, Bahamas, August 24, 1970.

78. Roppa and Clarke, *Commonwealth Caribbean,* p. 54; Dizard, *Television,* p. 68.

79. Personal interview, L. H. Stewart, Assistant General Manager, Jamaica Broadcasting Corporation, Kingston, Jamaica, August 28, 1970.

80. Herbert Schiller, *Mass Communications and American Empire* (Boston: Beacon Press, 1971), p. 82; Dizard, *Television,* p. 63.

81. Interview, Archer. In May 1971, the Montserrat *Mirror* reported that the station was sold to a German firm. "Antilles Changes Hands," *Mirror,* May 14, 1971.

5

News Flow and Media Content

It was Merrill who said that the popular press "calls the people of the world to play. It does not call them to think, to assess, to become concerned, involved or empathic."[1] He could have been assaying the majority of the Commonwealth Caribbean printed media when he made that categorical statement. Most island newspapers use liberal amounts of crime, sports, and tourist-directed information, along with foreign-oriented entertainment features. Most of them also emphasize another national pastime of West Indians, island politics.

As for electronic media content, a statement by Schiller might be appropriate for both radio and television in the islands, although he specifically referred to television. According to Schiller, American television is setting the tone for programming throughout the world.[2]

If not made in the United States, shows aired in the British West Indies have at least been patterned after American prototypes. Thus, sitting in a guest house in Barbados, one can view a local television quiz show that not only copies an American format but even uses questions about the United States, rather than about Barbados. And the reward for winning the quiz is a trip to the United States.

In this chapter news flow into the region will be reviewed first, followed by discussions of the content of printed and electronic media.

NEWS FLOW

Commonwealth Caribbean mass media readers/viewers/listeners must, for the most part, depend upon foreign agencies for information from both abroad and neighboring islands.[3]

At the beginning of the 1970s the chief sources used by Commonwealth Caribbean media for their foreign news were: Reuters, Associated Press (AP), United Press International (UPI), and foreign broadcast services. Radio Caribbean on St. Lucia, which broadcasts in French as well as English, also takes Agence France Press, and the *Gleaner* occasionally uses New York Times Service and United Features. Television news is provided by Reuters, AP, and UPI, in addition to Columbia Broadcasting System, VISNEWS, and Central Office of Information in London.[4] No medium in the area subscribes to more than two news agencies; those which receive Reuters dispatches usually pick up AP or UPI, also.

Of the four major news agencies operative in the Commonwealth Caribbean, only one, Reuters, has attempted regionalization of news. Originally serving the region from London, the Reuters Caribbean Desk was switched to Barbados in January 1968 to serve as a news-gathering center and distribution network for the region. The operation includes reediting the London-to-South American Editing Service for Caribbean consumption and the reception, editing, and retransmission of messages from stringers in thirteen island territories.[5] The messages of these stringers reach Barbados by reverse radio circuit from Jamaica, Guyana, and Trinidad and by commercial cable or telex from Antigua, Belize, Dominica, Grand Cayman, Grenada, Montserrat, St. Kitts, St. Lucia, St. Vincent, and Tortola. Totaling twelve hours a day in five newscasts, the service consists of about 25,000 to 30,000 words of world news to which is added 5,000 words of regional news. Reuters also transmits regional news to London for worldwide use.

Reuters Caribbean Service is fed to the six largest newspapers—*Daily Gleaner,* Jamaica *Star,* Barbados *Advocate-News,* Trinidad *Express,* or approximately 52 percent of the total British West Indian circulation—and to the eight biggest broadcasting companies—Jamaica Broadcasting Corporation Radio-TV, Radio Jamaica, Caribbean Broadcasting Corporation Radio-TV, Barbados Rediffusion, Radio Antilles, Radio Trinidad, Trinidad and Tobago National Broadcasting System, and Trinidad and Tobago Television.[6]

According to the UNESCO report, Reuters is able to pick up these top media because of its reputation for objectivity, as well as its being suited to the character and feelings of the region.[7]

For the smaller media unable to afford the full service, Reuters, together with Cable and Wireless, makes available in a half-hour newscast, "Reuterpress," a daily summary of world and regional news consisting of approximately 1,000 words in twenty news items.

Larger media subscribe to Reuters Caribbean Desk through a block contract arranged by the Caribbean Publishers and Broadcasters Association.[8] The CPBA "package deal" stipulates that overall costs of the service be divided among the country-members according to their populations. According to the 1968 UNESCO report, the administration of its members' subscriptions to Reuters, along with sponsorship of two journalism training programs, accounts for CPBA's main accomplishment (see discussion of CPBA activities regarding training in chap. 7).

The Caribbean Service does have limitations, chiefly that it does not reach far enough geographically, owing to the high costs of telecommunications facilities. According to the 1968 UNESCO report:

A recent attempt to extend the Caribbean Service to Antigua, St. Kitts, Tortola and Montserrat radios failed despite the comparative proximity of those islands and the fact that on Montserrat, Radio Antilles was already receiving the Reuters Service. Their distance from Barbados was so great that the quotations given for the lease of the necessary circuits proved well beyond the radio's financial capabilities.[9]

Other weaknesses are its lack of in-depth, feature and photograph coverage and its foreign origins. The latter handicap has been partially offset by the employment of local personnel to work the service.[10]

Besides Reuters, other organizations have attempted regional news services. For example, the fourth conference of heads of Commonwealth Caribbean governments in October 1967 talked about a news agency that would be independent of governments, large publishing outfits, and world news agencies. Although the proposals that developed from the conference were accepted unanimously by media personnel of the region, the project is still in the talking stage* of development.[11]

---

* At its fifth meeting in November 1974, the Caribbean Broadcasting Union devised a system for increasing the volume of regional news and information carried by radio and television systems in the islands. The system provides for automatic coverage throughout the area of important regional developments and a series of special productions to mark Caribbean Day 1975, held on July 7. The same assembly reviewed efforts being made to establish the Caribbean News Agency. (*Combroad* [January–March 1975], pp. 41–44.) On January 7, 1976, the Caribbean News Agency (CANA) was launched in Barbados. Sixteen media systems of the region affiliated with CANA; they are the shareholders in the agency. Of the 10,000 shares, 5,566 are held by privately owned media, and 4,434 are owned by government mass media. Some press operations of the Caribbean, notably the *Gleaner*, have declined to participate in CANA for fear it is just another government endeavor. Besides a general news service, CANA also offers specialized services such as "tourist news," "trade news," and "sugar production news." CANA handles 5,000 to 6,000 words of Caribbean news daily, and 15,000 words of foreign news (Personal interview, Harry Mayers, head, CANA, Christchurch, Barbados, January 12, 1976).

Associated Press subscribers in the islands are Trinidad *Guardian*, Bahamas *Tribune*, Trinidad and Tobago National Broadcasting System (formerly known as 610 Radio or Radio Guardian), Trinidad and Tobago Television, Jamaica *Gleaner*, Jamaica *Star*, Radio Jamaica, Jamaica Broadcasting Corporation Radio-TV, and Radio Caribbean. The six dailies affiliated with AP have a total circulation of 243,826, or 44 percent of the total circulation of area papers.

UPI goes into the offices of the Trinidad *Express*, Barbados *Advocate-News*, Bahamas *Guardian*, and Caribbean Broadcasting Corporation. Combined circulation of UPI newspaper affiliates is 64,077, or approximately 11 percent of all daily and nondaily circulations.

Workers Voice, *Labour Spokesman*, and *West Indian*, representing a total circulation of 6,700, 1 percent of total, do not subscribe to any news service.

AP and UPI both transmit their news for the Caribbean by radio teletype from New York, neither service providing regional bureaus. Recognizing the present telecommunications setup in the area, where Reuters uses the existing Cable and Wireless circuits, and the financial inability of most media to support an additional news service, AP and UPI do not plan region-wide operations in the foreseeable future.[12]

However, Associated Press has expanded its service to Central and South America by adding five hours of English-language transmissions to its bilingual (mostly Spanish) service. Known as the Latin America Wire, this service runs nineteen hours a day, consisting of 80 percent in Spanish and 20 percent in English. All transmissions are from New York by radio teletype and are picked up by all AP subscribers in the Commonwealth Caribbean. Some editors, particularly those on islands that have deep interests in the Spanish-, French-, and Dutch-speaking areas of the Caribbean and Central and South America, prefer AP because it offers a better news coverage of the wider region. UPI transmits by radio teletype from New York to the Caribbean its "World News Report," a fourteen-hour-a-day service. Both AP and UPI have a network of local stringers in the islands, some of whom are full-time employees of local papers or radio stations.

Only a half-dozen Commonwealth Caribbean newspapers use the AP or UPI photo services,[13] possibly because most photographs reach subscribers by air mail, sometimes too late to meet press deadlines. During special events, however, mobile radiophoto equipment is hired from Cable and Wireless. Only Jamaica Broadcasting Corporation and the Gleaner Company have their own radiophoto facilities.

Feature syndicates do not exist in the islands, most media obtaining comics, columns, movie and television personality sketches, and crossword puzzles from United States or British outlets.

Besides subscribing to the foreign news agencies, broadcasting systems use large amounts of news relayed from foreign studios, notably British Broadcasting Corporation (BBC), Voice of America (VOA), and Canadian Broadcasting Corporation. In a 1968 survey of island radio stations, it was found that 40 percent of all news presentations originated from studios abroad.[14] The difficulty with these foreign newscasts was explained by a WIBS program director who said that even if a BBC news show is beamed directly to the Caribbean (as is the case oftentimes), it will contain numerous items of little or no significance to West Indians. He said, "The West Indies make up a small area of the total audience of the Caribbean and South America which a BBC news program will be directed to."[15]

Dependence on foreign sources of information also permeates the smallest newspapers on the mini-islands, nondailies that by and large cannot afford subscription to wire services or maintenance of correspondents and stringers but that do rely heavily on cables and mailers from foreign organizations, as well as on local handouts. The resultant "handoutitis" that afflicts newsgathering in these islands is exemplified below. The *Vincentian* editor forms his nondomestic news budget from items collected from the United States Information Services (USIS), *News of India*, London *Express*, and Public Relations Associates of Barbados. The *Labour Spokesman* uses Reuters cables plus mail releases from British Information Services, USIS, United Nations, *Unesco Features*, and a Swiss press review. Regional news in the St. Lucia *Crusader* emanates from exchange of newspapers, "word-of-mouth knowledge of other islands' happenings,"[16] and radio monitoring.[17] Grenada's *West Indian* utilizes radio monitoring, cable services, and "Reuterpress," and the Anguilla *Beacon* listens to Radio Anguilla, a subscriber of Reuters, for its world news coverage.

PRINTED MEDIA CONTENT

Larger-Island Dailies

British West Indian dailies are located on the larger islands of Jamaica, Trinidad, Barbados and Bahamas, and on Bermuda. Dailies are published on three Leeward and Windward Islands, but usually as four-to-eight page newssheets full of the sponsoring political party's propaganda.

Newspaper managements in the islands said that they pattern their dailies after British and, in one case, American prototypes. The *Daily Gleaner* and *Star* on Jamaica are more British-prone because they place major emphasis on design, a *Gleaner* official pointed out.[18] The same reason was given by a Bahamas *Guardian* official for his paper's imitation of British dailies.[19] Trinidad *Guardian* personnel, however, said that their paper uses a combination of British and American approaches but follows the "more restrictive" British rules on reporting.[20]

Standard-size dailies of the region do look like transplants from London. For example, except for the Trinidad *Guardian*, they all carry front-page advertisements. The *Gleaner* runs at least two large display advertisements on page one, besides using the nameplate ears for smaller promotionals. The Bahamas *Tribune* and Barbados *Advocate-News* carry advertisements in the ears only, while the Bahamas *Guardian* has ear-size ads in all four corners of page one.

Front-page design on these dailies leans much more to traditional styles rather than modernistic ones. All six standard-size papers on Trinidad, Jamaica, Barbados, and Bahamas use top-of-the-page full nameplates, never varying that format; all print traditional photographic poses ("firing squad," check passing, and groundbreaking types), and all emphasize above-the-fold makeup, leaving the bottom half for weather, one-column stories, and news briefs. Yet, such papers as the *Guardian* and *Tribune* in the Bahamas show signs of changing to more modernistic makeup, using boxed stories, wider column widths, functional white space, and action-type photographs. Except for the *Daily Gleaner* and Trinidad *Guardian*,[21] standard-size papers in the islands use eight-column formats.

Daily tabloids published on the larger islands, Trinidad *Evening News,* Jamaica *Star,* and Trinidad *Express,* get the attention of the masses with abundant uses of crime, sensation, and politics. Large headlines (72 points and above), local photographs and stories, and small display advertisements make up front pages of these six-column dailies. The back page of the *Express* serves as a second front page with its own nameplate, photographs, and banner headlines; the *Evening News* and *Star* use 72-point headlines on their back pages, but there the resemblance to page one ends.

Jamaica

The Gleaner Company has designed its two dailies to penetrate both morning/evening and white-collar/mass audiences. The *Daily Gleaner* is considered the white-collar paper, a "hybrid between the London *Times* and Manchester *Guardian*," according to its editor; the *Star* is designed to appeal to the masses. *Gleaner* editor Theodore Sealy delineated the potential audiences in this fashion:

The shop girls, barmaids and boys on the sidewalks read the *Star*. When they get old and get a family, they graduate to the *Gleaner*.[22]

Aware of its dominance of the market, the *Gleaner* attempts to offer outlets for the various strata of society. Besides its Sunday edition[23] with color comics and *Sunday* magazine, the *Gleaner* provides its public with a second color comic supplement on Fridays. On Thursdays *Gleaner* readers receive a food supplement, on Fridays a plaza section for the numerous shoppers who come out on Saturdays. In fact, the paper's largest weekday circulation is on Saturday, the opposite of the situation in the United States, where Saturday editions are poor sellers. A *Gleaner* supplement designed for the western end of the island appears once a week,[24] as does a four-page farmer's section. The *Star* publishes its weekend edition[25] on Friday evenings, again meant to attract the Saturday marketers.

The *Daily Gleaner* publishes twenty-four to thirty-six pages a day, the larger editions appearing on supplement days and Saturdays.[26] The twenty-four page issue of April 26, 1971, gave top billing to a Reuters dispatch about the heaviest Vietnam fighting of the year. The second boldest headline, appearing beneath the Saigon story, discussed the USSR's Soyuz 10 flight. In the top right-hand corner of page one was a story from the *Gleaner* farm desk, while other prominent page-one stories reported the opening of a cricket match in Jamaica and the inauguration of Haitian leader Jean-Claude Duvalier. Two stories were printed denying rumors disseminated that concerned Jamaican business and investment. Besides the front page, page two and the opposite editorial page were used for international news.

Most inside pages contained large display advertisements topped by a few brief news stories. Two pages were devoted to sports and one to photographs under the heading "Highlights of News on Local Scene." The photo page lacked imagination in design, with pictures of similar sizes and shapes stacked atop one another. The photographs themselves either showed someone accepting an award (two of the pictures were nearly identical poses, only the award recipient being different), or sitting at his desk or around a banquet table. Only three comic strips ("Beetle Bailey," "Carol Day," and "Blondie") appeared, along with one-panel funnies of "Dennis the Menace" and "Dolly." The final seven pages of the issue were largely classified advertisements interspersed with society items and photographs.

The *Gleaner* runs one page of editorials daily, the contents coming from a number of outside sources. In the April 26, 1971, issue, United States Information Service provided an in-depth story on Congress pondering sugar quotas; New York Times Service discussed British business prospects and the war between East and West Pakistan; while United Features backgrounded United States-China ping-pong diplomacy. Local materials on the editorial page included a regular personal column called "You Can Quote Me," an editorial on inflation in Jamaica, a statement from the vice chairman of a University of West Indies group, and three letters to the editor. According to the *Gleaner* editor, the paper does "assessment editorials" that are more interpretative than crusading.

A thirty-four-page Saturday *Gleaner*[27] provided its market-day audience with two pages of entertainment features and advertisements, six pages of business and industry news, and full-page treatments of weekend comics, tourism, church services, and obituaries.

The *Gleaner* sister daily, *The Star*, led off its twelve-page issue of April 26, 1971, with stories headlined "Killed by Stone, Gun in City"; "Jockeying for Haitian Leadership," with photograph of Jean-Claude Duvalier; "Three More Held for Firearms"; "Held for Robbing His Aunt"; "Boys Held Up With Toy Gun"; and one-inch items about the Soyuz flight and a cricket flash.

Inside pages of the *Star* entertained readers further with stories from court like "Last Child Not His, Husband Tells Court" and "Son Accused: Mom Punched." Besides giving readers real-life crime stories, the *Star* also runs a regular mystery serial. Court stories are written in a lively style, as this lead from a divorce-court report indicates:

> The marriage of Dorothy Smith was very bad from the start, as her husband would go out at nights with other women and not return until early in the mornings. This was the evidence given in the Divorce Court.

The *Star* is made up as if the entertainment-seeking subscriber were a front-to-back-cover newspaper reader. For example, page two is sports; three, comics (all United States or British), radio-TV guide, and crossword puzzle; four, movie advertisements and movie personality profiles; five, court news, especially items from divorce court; the middle two pages, mystery serial; eight, world news, classifieds, and two comic strips; nine, local and foreign news photographs; ten and eleven, women's and home features and local government news;

and the last page, Vietnam story about heavy losses and two Jamaica accident accounts.*

Trinidad

The Trinidad *Guardian* is the daily for Trinidadian white-collar workers, although the paper wants to change its status slightly, hoping, with added comic strips and features, to bring in more young readers. The Guardian Company also issues a twenty-page *Sunday Guardian*, along with the sixteen-page tabloid *Sunday Guardian Magazine*[28] and four standard-size pages of color comics. The *Guardian*'s sister, the tabloid *Evening News*, makes regular use of photographs of beautiful girls (oftentimes in bikinis), and crime and sports news. The editor said that he publishes a great deal of fashion news and runs a weekly disc-jockey column with the aim of attracting young people to the paper.[29]

The twenty-page issue of the Trinidad *Guardian* for April 26, 1971, seemed to strive for a balance of local, regional, and international news on page one. Six columns, topped by a 72-point head, reported on a speech in which Prime Minister Eric Williams told some businessmen to use the talent of youth. Prominent front-page space was given to another Williams speech delivered to a taxi organization. The three page-one photographs included Williams watching as his car is refueled at a service station, Williams's daughter viewing a local art exhibit, and a political leader who pledged to legalize cockfighting if elected. Other page-one items included a story on the Soyuz 10 flight, another on the Indian-Pakistani conflict, and six news briefs.

The second page of the *Guardian* reported news from Guyana and southern Trinidad; page three, wire service news from around the world; and page five, society news featuring a "Talk of Trinidad" column by "Humming Bird." The editorial page concentrated on local matters with four letters to the editor, two editorials (one on Carifta, the other on divulging information in England), a memorandum text of the Agricultural Society of Trinidad discussing Britain's entry in the European economic community, and a policy statement of one

---

* An impressionistic analysis of the *Gleaner* and the *Star* in January 1976 revealed that not much had changed pertaining to the newspapers' formats and the types of contents they carried. A sample issue of the *Daily News* for January 16, 1976, contained 24 pages organized in this manner: national news on page one, the next three pages devoted to local and regional information, followed by an editorial page on local topics (including locally drawn cartoon), letters and columns page, four pages of international news, two pages of a photo essay, four pages on entertainment, a feature page, classifieds, and three pages of sports.

of the local political parties. The *Guardian* does not use editorial columns. In fact, the only columns in the paper, besides "Talk of Trinidad," were "London Diary" and "Washington Letter," both written by Trinidadians living in those cities and reporting on Caribbean expatriates. The paper lacks in-depth reporting, as do most Commonwealth Caribbean newspapers; the most likely place for such stories, the opposite editorial page, is devoted to general news items in the *Guardian*. Because it was election season in Trinidad, the April 26 edition contained three pages of lists of electors and two pages of political advertisements. The rest of the issue included a page of comics (all from the United States) and crossword puzzles, three pages of classifieds, and two of sports. Most display advertisements in the *Guardian* are locally produced.*

The *Evening News*, one of Trinidad's two mass tabloids, carried sixteen pages on April 26, 1971; most of the paper's contents emphasized local spot news, features, and entertainment. The main headline on page one described a United States accident that injured seven members of a Trinidadian steel band. But most of page-one emphasis was directed to Prime Minister Eric Williams. His speech to the businessmen under the heading "PM 'Digs' Some of Our Young Talent," was played up; a picture of him observing the same art exhibit at which the *Guardian* photographed his daughter was displayed on page one. The only world news on page one, and one of only two international stories in the entire issue, dealt with the change of power in Haiti. The other front-page news was a photograph and caption about a Trinidadian bishop observing ANZAC Day. Page two, entitled "This Page Is Just for You," was made up of society news and pictures plus a half-page "Business Services Directory," the latter full of advertisements.

Elsewhere in the paper, a full page was devoted to the commercial directory, similar to the yellow pages of United States telephone directories. Page three consisted of six small stories along with a photograph of three female defendants in the Manson murder case. The half-page designated as editorial page included a chit-chat column entitled "What We Think," two letters, two large advertisements, and a locally drawn cartoon. Two other pages in the front half of the *Evening News* dealt with remembrances of old Trinidad, society,

---

* An analysis of the *Guardian* in December 1975 and January 1976 showed that although there were changes made since 1971—e.g., some of the columns have been replaced with new ones—they were not substantive. The format and types of content remain basically unchanged.

fashion, recipes, and a help-to-the-lovelorn column. The middle spread gave play to Bennett Cerf's "Try and Stop Me," a local showtime feature, and local news stories. An astrological column, "Lady Luck," and radio-TV schedules made up "Your Cinema News Page"; United States comics and crossword puzzles filled still another page. Two pages each of classified advertisements (one called "Southern Services," promoting businesses in San Fernando, a southern city), and sports and the back page made up the rest of the paper.

The back page of the *Evening News* routinely is a local news page; in this issue a five-column photograph of an automobile accident, a story about the archbishop calling the nation to prayer, and news briefs were included. Evaluative statements are made throughout the stories in the *Evening News*: a woman in one dispatch is described as "trendily dressed"; an athlete in another contributed "handsomely" to his team's success.

The only locally owned daily in Trinidad is the tabloid *Express*, begun in 1967 when the Trinidad *Mirror* folded. Because it is locally owned, the *Express* thinks of itself as the national newspaper.

Contents of the *Express* reveal that it is dealing with local affairs in a more critical manner than the Thomson papers. Editorials and local political columnists regularly take stands that are unpopular with the government. For example, an editorial column discussing the prime minister in the April 26, 1971, issue was headlined, "If This Man is Christ, If This Is the Second Coming, Leave Me Out." Nevertheless, Williams's speeches and visitations, no matter of how little significance, are given prominent play in the *Express*, as they are in the Thomson papers. A picture of Williams's daughter visiting the art exhibit made the top spot of the *Express* front page for April 26, as did Williams's plea to the businessmen that young talent should not be allowed to die for lack of reward. (The photograph of Williams's watching as his car was fueled took up six columns of page three, as did his speech to the taxi drivers.) Only two other items, both about the impending national elections, were played on page one that day.

The *Express* differs from the Jamaica *Star* and Trinidad *Evening News* in that although it has a large budget of entertainment features, the paper also deals with serious political, economic, and governmental issues of the nation and region. Besides the editorial column on Williams, already mentioned, the April 26 *Express* also displayed on its middle two-page spread a Reuters analysis of the Haitian government changeover.

Other *Express* contents included a page of Reuters international dispatches, movie and society pages, and a lengthy installment of D. H. Lawrence's "Women in Love." A weekly photo page displayed six pictures taken at an art show, four of which showed the prime minister. A "Days of Judgment" page was devoted to "interesting judgments handed down by the Industrial Court of Trinidad and Tobago," while radio-TV schedules, comics, letters to the editor, a crossword puzzle, and astrology column made up two other pages. "Taxi Talk," a daily interview with a local cab driver, on anything from his hobby to his preference for political office, was featured on still another page. The remainder of the issue contained two pages each of sports[30] and classifieds and the back page with its own nameplate, bold banners, local and regional news, and photographs.*

Barbados

The only daily[31] on Barbados, the Thomson-owned *Advocate-News*, comes closest to being a regional newspaper in the Caribbean. The *Advocate-News* uses more regional items than any other daily in the region; as a result, it has become popular on other islands as well. Whereas the Jamaica *Gleaner* depends on Kingston proper, its place of publication, for the majority of its sales, only 20 percent of the *Advocate-News* circulation is in its city of publication, Bridgetown.** The paper can be purchased throughout the region; as far north as St. Kitts (350–400 air miles away), home delivery of the Sunday *Advocate-News* is possible the same day.

Advocate-News editorial policy stipulates that the paper should be a watchdog on government and a stimulator of national development. Stated more specifically by the general manager, the policy follows these tenets:

> We follow Parliament very closely and feel this is a contribution to national development. In newly-developed nations such as Barbados, the government has a tendency to introduce fairly strong legislature and become an almost semi-despotic regime. These new governments are very sensitive to criticism. If a measure is brought up in Parliament that might give too much power to certain people, we take a strong stand.[32]

---

* Looking at the *Express* in January 1976, I noted that the paper seemed to tone down its contents since 1971. Also, the *Express* seems to carry more regional news than it did five years ago.

** In 1976 this characteristic of the paper was missing. The general manager told me that the *Advocate-News* does not think it feasible to circulate to the small islands as the *Express* does. Also, the *Advocate-News* had numerous problems with distribution through local airline services.

The fourteen-page *Advocate-News* for April 26, 1971, included pages specified for certain types of news—one page each given to regional, international, local government, and tourism, and local business, commerce, and trade. In addition, the paper emphasizes society and women's news, devoting a page to each. The society page portrayed in words and pictures a ball held by the upper stratum of society; the women's page reported news in which females, including those convicted in the Manson murders, figured. The *Advocate-News* gives more space to society news than any other Commonwealth Caribbean daily.

The editorial content of another page of the *Advocate-News* was made up solely of stories and pictures about people receiving gifts and awards. One page each was taken up with comics (all from the United States) and local sports, and two with classified advertisements.

The editorial page of the April 26 edition included a long interpretative story on East Caribbean tourism, two letters to the editor, an editorial on the United States and China, and a remembrances-of-olden-days column. Reuters provided a good portion of the background writing for the page. The only editorial-type columns in the paper are "Topic for Today" and "Perspective," both critical discussions of Barbadian life.

Page-one emphasis was on regional and world news with datelines from Washington, New Delhi, Saigon, Port of Spain, Seattle, St. Thomas (U.S. Virgin Islands), Antigua, Jamaica, Capetown, Moscow, Copenhagen, and Guyana. Eighteen stories, one local photograph, and a cigarette[33] advertisement were played on the front page.*

Bahamas

Both Bahamian dailies, the Nassau *Guardian* and Nassau *Tribune*, seem to have promoting tourism and local development as their raison d'être, although at varying times each has taken the role of antagonist of the government.[34] Because of the Bahamas' prominence as an international resort, the papers regularly use interviews and photographs of visiting entertainment personalities appearing at the hotels and casinos, real estate stories about new beach areas opening up for development, and photographs of bathing beauties. Special industrial or real estate development supplements are regular attractions of the papers. Large portions of both papers resemble entertainment guides for tourists.

---

* As with previously mentioned dailies, there were not discernible differences between issues of the *Advocate-News* in 1971 and 1976.

Both dailies use most of their front pages for local political,* crime, and accident stories, usually allocating space for only one international story on the page.[35] Crime stories are detailed as graphically as they are in tabloids on Trinidad and Jamaica. For example, a rape story in the August 13, 1970, Nassau *Guardian* used this quote: "He pulled down my panties . . . while he was doing this, I was bleeding because he was fighting to do this."

Both the *Guardian* and *Tribune* maintain sister papers in Freeport (approximately 125 miles from Nassau) to keep residents of the second largest city informed. The six-page Grand Bahama *Tribune,* a daily, uses mostly stories and photographs that its Nassau namesake prints, except for a Freeport-oriented front page and a "News from Nassau-The Capital" page. Conversely, to keep Nassau residents knowledgeable about Freeport, the Nassau *Tribune* reports daily on Freeport with a one-page section "News from Grand Bahama." The *Guardian's* sister in Freeport is the *News,* published three times a week on its own offset presses.

Larger-Island Nondailies

A number of nondailies are published in Jamaica, Trinidad, Barbados, and the Bahamas, most of them pushing political aims. Their contents are either sensational or promotional or both. For example, some of the political organs were designed to attract the voting masses with a combination of political rhetoric and sex-crime-violence news. The *New Nation,* tabloid organ of the People's National Party on Jamaica, is in this category, as is the Barbados *Democrat,* weekly organ of the ruling party.

However, most of the political papers on the larger islands are serious, polemical organs, rather restrained in their efforts to tell the masses about their parties and leaders. In many cases they are not so interested in blasting the opposition or in entertaining the people as they are in propagandizing for their own candidates and policies. *Tapia,* organ of a group by the same name in Trinidad, is in this class. An organization campaigning for new nationalism, Tapia** uses its newspaper to reflect the aspirations of the group's leader, Lloyd Best,

---

* For a case study of newspaper coverage of elections in the region, see Vernon M. Darville, "The Bahamas Press: A Study of the Editorial Coverage of the 1967–1968 General Elections by the Two Nassau Dailies—*The Nassau Guardian* and *The Tribune*" (master's thesis, University of Florida, 1972).

** A similar group in Barbados, Manjak, has been publishing a weekly, also called *Manjak,* since November 1973. The 8-page *Manjak* is, in fact, printed by Tapia House in Trinidad.

a "father figure" who not only writes for the paper, but sells it on the streets as well. Other serious political newspapers are *Moko,* organ of the United National Independence Party, *The Nation,* journal of the ruling People's National Movement, and *Vanguard,* Trinidad Labour Party, all on Trinidad, and *The Torch,*[36] newspaper of the Free Progressive Liberal Party of Bahamas. Personality sketches of party leaders, their speeches and comments, and favorable remarks made about the party are the main contents of such papers.

Another type of nondaily prevalent in the larger cities is reminiscent of the New York *National Enquirer* of the 1960s. For example, in *Truth,* a Barbadian semi-weekly published by a member of Parliament, headlines proclaim "Jealous Lover Scalps Girlfriend So She Can't Visit Hairdresser," or "Jackie Is Haunted by J. F. K.'s Ghost." The Barbados *Observer,* weekly sponsored by an ex-member of Parliament, carries similar fare: "Boss Bugs John To Snoop on the Help," "Teenagers' Secret Sex Code," or this vividly descriptive headline: "Dog Bites Off Boy's Ear—Swallows It. Pop Shoots Pooch To Recover It. Then Doc Sews It Back On."

Smaller-Island Newspapers

As could be expected, newspaper content is chiefly political on the smaller islands, where political parties or politicians control a large proportion of the papers. For example, *Workers Voice* on Antigua makes it a point to print "news about government actions which are not in the people's interests." An editor of the *Voice* said, "We remind the people that this government is doing what it accused the previous administration of doing."[37] The St. Kitts *Democrat* editor said that during elections his newspaper publishes nothing but political items; the rest of the year the paper prints "accusations against the Labour Party and some overseas news."[38] Most of the Antigua *Star* contents are political, its editor said, although an attempt is made to give the other parties' views as well.[39] A rationale for the heavy usage of political materials in Grenada's *Vanguard* was offered by its editor: "The doings and undoings of this government are so enormous that we haven't the time to deal in anything but political activities."[40]

Examination of the newspapers[41] themselves showed that they lacked regional and foreign news, in-depth analyses, feature articles, photographs and, in some cases, editorials. However, possibly some papers felt that they did not need editorials as long as their headlines and news stories served evaluative functions. The St. Kitts *Democrat,* for example, bannered its April 24 and May 1 issues with "sweep

Major newspapers of St. Kitts, both political organs, 1971.

them out" headlines, based on the People's Action Movement election theme, and filled half of the twelve-page May 1 issue with the manifesto of that party. The other St. Kitts newspaper, *Labour Spokesman*, spent its entire news hole, except for two briefs, on politics and the forthcoming elections. The front-page banner of the April 24 issue warned, "Look Out for PAM To 'Cog'—They Have No Ideas." In the following edition, April 26, the *Spokesman* described a rally staged by its sponsor, the Labour Party, with this evaluative headline, "Labour Captures Pall Mall Square, Largest Public Meet Ever."

The April 24 issue of *Workers Voice* on Antigua, a supporter of the former premier, V. C. Bird, was political in tone with a page-one story entitled, "Bird Could Pay His National Debts, This Was Small Matters [*sic*]; Only Unemployment Is the Major Problem." The main headline in the April 27 issue also editorialized, "Unemployment Now Rapidly Rising While Bird Is Out, Antiguans Begin to Express Concern As Hundreds of Workers Are Being Laid Off." Carrying out its campaign against the economic policies of the new government, the *Voice* inserted this query into its daily "Question Box" of April 25: "Is it a fact that the so-called Walter government has taken less than three months to return Antigua back to the days of plantocracy or worse?" Periodically, the *Voice* reminds its readers that the premier had been convicted of smuggling at one time by referring to him in news stories as "Antigua's number one smuggler." The Antigua *Star*, handmaiden of the ruling People's Labour Movement, played up a speech and photograph of the new premier in its April 24 edition and complimented the government budget in its main story of April 28. Most of the *Star* contents were local and political, with only one brief international story in the two issues. The third newspaper on Antigua, *Times*, featured on its April 24 front page, stories on a development bank for the region and curtailment of a local airline service. Although it has very definite leanings to the Antigua People's Party, the *Times* strives for objectivity more than its competitors, emphasizing regional and Reuters world news, features, sports, and photographic essays. A regular page in the paper is called "The Reuters Press Bulletin."*

On Grenada all three papers act in opposition to the all-powerful Gairy administration. The *West Indian*, still living on laurels gained under Marryshow's editorship, is devoid of much meaningful content.

---

* In 1976, because of strict press laws, Antigua had two newspapers— *Leader*, a biweekly tabloid published by the Walter government since late 1975, and *Workers Voice*, the Labour Party paper.

THE WEST INDIAN

WEST INDIES MUST BE WEST INDIAN

Front Page EDITORIAL

A joint exercise by The Torchlight and The West Indian

DID THIS MAN SEE---
A PRISONER DRIVING BY NIGHT?

Discription fitted to driver and car

'Something can be done it there's proof' Says Official

Community centre opened at St David's

Bradshaw stays in St. Kitts saddle

SALES GROW N'GOODS GO VIA OUR ADS

The West Indian, *Grenada, 1971. Note misspellings and mixed type fonts used in headlines.*

For example, in the April 24 issue, only six small stories made up the editorial content of the five inside pages. Most of the pages are devoted to display advertisements and heavy headlines. For example, four columns of heads, four inches deep, were required for an average letter to the editor.[42] Writing in the *West Indian,* as in a number of British West Indian papers, leans on the use of clichés. An example was the arrest of local girls who, the paper reported, were "allegedly caught redhanded 'smoking' pot." The *Torchlight* devotes most of its space to local politics as well as to announcements of "comings and goings" of Grenadians. The *Vanguard,* voice of the Grenada National Party, is much more emotional than the other papers when discussing what it terms "Gairyism" and the "Gairy regime." The eight-page April 23 issue, for example, carried only stories and columns related to the "regime" and its weaknesses; the April 30 edition printed a full-page article likening Gairy's rule in Grenada to that of Hitler.*

Among Dominican newspapers, the *Herald,* organ of the Freedom Party, is the most vociferous politically. Like *Vanguard* on Grenada, it spares no epithet when discussing the premier, editorializing about "Our Magnanimous Leader" in the April 24 issue, while on other occasions comparing him to Hitler and Duvalier. The eight-page April 24 issue featured page-one stories about risks to dock workers, a letter to the editor, a small obituary, and four government notices. Inside pages contained plentiful legal and court notices but not much more.** The *Herald,* like a number of papers in the Leewards and Windwards, lacked news content, containing not more than a dozen small stories in the entire issue. An editorial feature of the *Herald,* and the *Labour Spokesman* and *Workers Voice,* is a question box in which the editor prints derogatory rumors.[43] The oldest Dominican paper, *Chronicle,* concentrates on local announcements and news of the sponsoring Roman Catholic Church. The main story of the May 1 edition dealt with this topic, "Church Contribution Put on Record." Providing the Dominican with his most varied fare is the *Star,* described more fully in Appendix D. Among the contents of the twelve-page April 23 *Star* were a guest editorial, "London Letter" column, short stories, local art work, a page of regional and world news, and an analysis of the local black power group.

St. Lucia is served by the *Voice of St. Lucia, Crusader, Standard, Herald,* and a Roman Catholic newspaper. Contents of the politically

---

* The *Vanguard* has ceased publication.
** The *Herald* has ceased publishing.

Two of the three main newspapers of Dominica, 1971.

oriented *Standard* and *Herald* are predominantly news briefs. *Crusader*, in existence since 1934, was taken over by Forum, a black power group, and subsequently the Labour Party, at the beginning of the 1970s. Believing that a very close relationship exists between ideological, economic, and cultural backgrounds and what the Forum wishes to accomplish, the editors of *Crusader* provide readers with agriculture pages, entertainment sections, satire written in patois, children's poetry, reviews of books and plays, and other cultural fare. Themes of many *Crusader* articles emphasize what the Forum considers to be St. Lucia's main problems: tourism and the unequal roles of blacks. The *Voice*, under local ownership again after going through King and Thomson transitions, is one of the few newspapers in the Commonwealth Caribbean that goes in for interpretative reporting. Editor Rick Wayne's* aim, since assuming his office in early 1971, is to "pull the St. Lucian's head out of the sand." In his first issue as editor, Wayne incurred the wrath of many St. Lucians by exposing the drug-abuse problem on the island. In other issues he investigated the sanitary

---

* Wayne, after a short stay at the *Voice*, became personal secretary to the premier and editor of the government's *Vanguard*. However, he ran afoul of the government and in 1975 started his own monthly, the St. Lucia *Star*. An analysis of the *Star* in 1975 indicated that Wayne was doing many things with this paper that he contemplated for the *Voice*.

state of the marketplace and conditions at a local prison.[44] He has been accused of being "too shocking and too American" in his news approach. "Because I make my stories as shocking as possible they say I took American sensationalism into little St. Lucia," he explained.[45] Wayne said that he does not editorialize; instead, he holds a mirror up to public officials and lets the people see them in their real roles. Wishing to attract the man in the street as a reader, Wayne plans to use more dialect writing, more "shocking to reality" reporting, and more information that people do not already have.*

A common complaint among West Indians is that, because of the face-to-face communication networks and importation of outside media, most of the news they see in the smaller papers they have already read elsewhere. For example, the *Torchlight* editor lamented the fact that Grenadians react to his paper with, "Oh, we saw that in the Trinidad *Express* or heard it on radio."[46]

Along the same lines, the Montserrat *Mirror* editor, discussing her paper's contents at the time she took over, said:

> The *Mirror* did not reach the average Montserratian because it did not reflect what was happening in the community. It did not contribute and as one radio announcer put it, "The *Mirror* was 40 percent advertising, 40 percent government notices and 20 percent trash." Unfortunately when this was said, the *Mirror* contained a speech by the Administrator. The announcer was accused of calling the Administrator's speech "trash" and he was transferred.[47]

St. Vincent's only** newspaper, *Vincentian*, is made up almost entirely of local news, a large portion of which emanates from the government. A story about regional chambers of commerce fearing nationalization attempts was featured on the front page of the twelve-page April 24 issue, along with four briefs and a catalog-type photograph of a small airplane used to ship produce to Great Britain. In the May 1 edition readers were given a long essay on heaven written by a local minister.***

---

* The *Voice* in 1976 seemed to devote a rather high percentage of its content to politics. The paper's director told me in 1976 that he favored the government, chiefly because the opposition was not constructive.

** Two new newspapers on St. Vincent—*The Star* and *The Tree*—are also primarily political sheets with the type of contents such newspapers usually carry.

*** Although the format of the *Vincentian* has improved, the contents are still very parochial. For example, the page-one banner for January 2, 1976, read, "Accidents and Cows." The story, describing an accident in which a cow was hit by an automobile, went into vivid details: "The windshield of the car was shattered and one of the cow's horns broke from the impact. No one was hurt."

The Montserrat *Mirror*, Anguilla *Beacon*, and *Caymanian Weekly* also concentrate solely on local happenings. The six-page April 30 *Mirror* included a story on the island's executive council, six other small items of local interest (among them a front page story about a woman who "lost a finger"), an editorial, one letter, and advertisements. Like many West Indian newspapers, the *Mirror* has a tendency to be highly specific in crime and accident stories. This excerpt is from a story in the April 23 issue:

> Crowds of curious school children and shoppers thumbed their noses as they gathered outside the house of deceased Sarah ——— who police discovered dead in her house.

Newspapers of Cayman Islands, Montserrat, and St. Lucia, 1971.

The Anguilla *Beacon* for February 6, 1971,[48] ran two front-page stories: one on a road project, the other about police dealing with drivers of vehicles with defective lights. Inside, the *Beacon* printed two letters, an editorial, Radio Anguilla schedule and story, a page of sports, and a government report. The twenty-page *Caymanian Weekly* for April 22 emphasized tourism by printing sailing features, tourist and society news, and photographs of visiting beauties attired in bikinis.*

---

* A more recent issue, that of May 24, 1973, indicates the use of basically the same format and content.

Metamorphosis of an island newspaper, The Beacon, *Anguilla; from ditto to mimeograph.*

Compared to United States and British standards, Leeward and Windward Island newspapers have quaint ways of phrasing, especially in headlines. The St. Lucia *Herald,* in one issue, headlined a bus accident, "Bus Turns Turtle; 4 in Hospital," while the Dominica *Chronicle* had these two headlines in the same issue: "Mental Man Interested in Dominica" and "Cave Man Marries Nurse." In the Grenada *Vanguard,* an obituary of a lawyer was announced as "Malcolm —— Crosses the Bar." A headline in the *Voice of St. Lucia* said "Marijuana Man Arrested," and the Dominica *Herald* bannered a top page-one story, a letter to the editor, with "No Water, Ward Toilets Cannot Flush." Letters to the editor are used as the main page-one stories in other papers as well, including *Torchlight, Workers Voice,* Montserrat *Mirror,* and *West Indian.* The characteristic does not result so much from editors' stressing the importance of letters as it does from the fact that newspapers do not have adequate reportorial staffs to do the newsgathering themselves.

In analyzing the unobjective nature of newspapers of developing regions, Pye said that evaluative news writing was endemic to these countries because the editors are unable to separate their roles of creative writer and journalist. Pye also felt that journalists in these territories, because they keep attuned to the modern world, become cynical about the performance gap they witness between local politicians and those of the modern world. As a result, Pye concluded,

> The press and radio in such situations are not likely to be inspired to communicate an objective, realistic, and compassionate view of the problems of political life.[49]

Specialized Publications

The few popular magazines that exist in the Commonwealth Caribbean usually whitewash negative societal features, promote financial or industrial development, and cater to the tourist. Newsmagazines even set their goals at promoting tourism, an example being *The Bajan* on Barbados. An editor of this newsmagazine explained:

> The magazine is tourist oriented now, catering to hotels. More copies are sent to the United States and Canada than to other Caribbean islands. If *Bajan* just runs pictures of beaches as it has in the past, this won't do anything for Barbados. The content must change, must become more Barbadian. We must publish materials which don't have tourist value but value for the region.[50]

A typical issue[51] of *The Bajan* includes a "Coming Events" column designed for the tourists, as well as tourist advertisements for hotels, resorts, and nightclubs. This particular issue featured a story about the banana industry, as well as the usual sections similar to *Time* magazine in format, except, rather than having departments designated "Nation," "Middle East," and so on, *The Bajan* uses "Landscape Gardening," "Seeing Stars," "Religion," "Scientific Farming," "The Arts in Trinidad," "Travel," "Books," "Sports," "Fashion," "Youth and Religion," and "People."*

The monthly newsmagazine of the Bahamas, *Bahamian Review*, is similar in format and purpose to *The Bajan*. Advertisements are geared to tourists as are numerous articles. An indication of the

---

* The format of the January 1976 issue of *The Bajan* is basically the same as five years previously. Still oriented toward the tourist, *The Bajan* has, however, regionalized some of its ten departments so that now they are termed "The Caribbean," "Tourism," "Conservation," "Bajan Happenings," "Religion," "People," "Sport," "Letters to the Editor," "Coming Events," and "Fun and Games." This issue contained 48 pages.

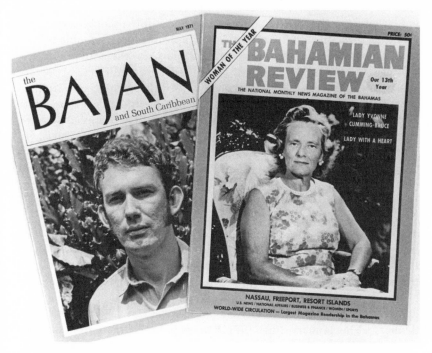

Newsmagazines published in Barbados and Bahamas, 1971.

audience for which the magazine is meant might be gauged from a cursory look at the photographs included. Most of the subjects of pictures in *Bahamian Review* are white tourists or investors, this in a predominantly black society. The February 1971 issue featured a woman-of-the-year cover story, honoring the wife of the governor. Besides stories on floating houses in the Bahamas and "Bahamas Big Drawing Card in New Concept for Vacations," the rest of the issue was devoted to regular departments, the largest being that of business and industry. Other departmental topics were: education, immigration, trade, tourism, science and art, women, entertainment, sports, and people.*

Still other publications published by private and governmental interests design themselves strictly around the tourist market. Maga-

---

* The previously mentioned *Caribbean Contact*, started in 1974, usually has in-depth, investigative articles on the region in its 24 pages. The magazine serves as a periodical of record on major Caribbean events.

zines such as *Bahamas* and *The Visitor* supplement the "what to see" guides while at the same time painting a beautiful, although sometimes superficial, picture of these islands. A typical issue of *Bahamas*[52] includes numerous photographs arranged around these departments: "Notes on Nassau," "Observant Eye," "Beautiful Brides," "Camera Closeup," "Freeport Flash-Point," "Notes on Freeport," and "Impact by Night" (fashion). Most of the people photographed are white tourists or investors. Featured stories in this issue emphasized the investment angle: "Why I Chose the Bahamas," by Sammy Davis, Jr., "Bright New Breed Boosts IAB To Success," "30 Million New Eleutheran Dream Will Boost Investment Flow," "New Image, Big Business for Lee Brothers," and so on. *The Visitor: Jamaica Resort Weekly* is a giveaway tourist guide placed in tourist hotels and guest houses.*

Literary periodicals relate more to local cultures than do the newsmagazines or tourist magazines. Chief among Commonwealth Caribbean literary journals is *Bim*, founded in 1943 by the Young Men's Progressive Club. Most of the literary figures of the region have contributed to *Bim*, some of them crediting their first publication to that magazine. The semi-annual takes neither political nor social stands, its editor said, just as most regional novels stay away from these themes.[53] The January–June 1971 *Bim* included extracts from a forthcoming novel by West Indian George Lamming, numerous poems and short stories, and advertisements.**

Link, the other main literary magazine of the islands, supplements its creative literary fare with essays containing political and social themes. Typical articles in this quarterly based on St. Lucia might include "Socio-Historical Background of the Caribbean," "Problems of the Artist in the West Indies," or "Photo-Play: Ti-Jean and His Brothers."

More esoteric journals are *Caribbean Quarterly*, published at the University of the West Indies, and *Jamaica Journal*, quarterly of the Institute of Jamaica. *Caribbean Quarterly* explores sociocultural, economic, and political problems of the West Indies in articles written by area scholars. *Jamaica Journal*, with full-color photographs, might

---

* A new magazine of this type is *Islander*, published in the British Virgin Islands. Among its regular sections are "Environment," "Yacht of the Month," "Travel," "Eating Out," and "Profile." Each island of the Caribbean is also given special treatment, but the emphasis is definitely pegged to the tourist business, as are the advertisements.

** The June 1975 issue of *Bim* was very similar to the 1971 version. A new literary magazine on Jamaica, *Savacou*, takes a different approach. One issue each year is devoted to creative work and artistic criticism; the other three issues are topic-oriented.

be compared to a magazine such as *American Heritage*. Although scholarly in subject matter, the magazine attempts to make history, science, art, literature, and music interesting to its readers.

ELECTRONIC MEDIA CONTENT

Television

Most Commonwealth Caribbean television viewing, except on weekends, commences after 4:30 P.M. The reasons given for concentrating television programs in the late afternoon and evening hours are: the working habits of West Indians do not allow for a large daytime audience, and the stations generally cannot afford staff and program production costs required for longer viewing periods. It is suspected that the second reason is more important, because radio has certainly found daytime audiences.

For example, Trinidad and Tobago Television (TTT) airs one hour of "Sesame Street" in the mornings, Monday through Saturday, but does not begin its regular broadcasts until 4 or 5 P.M.; on Sunday, its broadcasts begin at 2:55 P.M. Caribbean Broadcasting Corporation (CBC) has educational programs at 9 A.M. and 1:15 P.M., Monday through Thursday, but starts its evening schedule at 4:30 P.M. On Saturday and Sunday, the station maintains 9 A.M. to noon and 4 P.M. to 11 P.M. or midnight schedules. Jamaica Broadcasting Corporation (JBC) is on the air from 4 P.M. to 11:22 P.M. Monday through Thursday, 4 P.M. to 12:12 A.M. on Friday, 2 P.M. to 12:24 A.M. on Saturday, and 1:30 P.M. to 11:32 P.M. on Sunday. Leeward Islands Television Services commences broadcasting between 4 and 5 P.M. seven days a week, and signs off between 10:30 and 10:45 P.M. St. Lucia Television is on the air from 5 P.M. to 11 P.M. Bermuda Radio and Television (ZBM) broadcasts from 3 P.M. to midnight daily, and Capital Broadcasting (ZFB on Bermuda), from 2:30 P.M. to midnight Monday through Friday, 9 A.M. to noon and 3:30 P.M. to midnight on Saturday, and 3:30 P.M. to 11:30 P.M. on Sunday. Most television stations in the islands end their broadcasting relatively early, between 10:30 P.M. and, at the latest, 12:30 A.M. on weekend nights.*

Jamaica Broadcasting Corporation, Trinidad and Tobago Television, Caribbean Broadcasting Corporation (Barbados), Capital Broadcasting Company (ZFB on Bermuda), and Bermuda Radio

---

* By 1976 these schedules had not changed significantly.

and Television Company (ZBM) all broadcast between fifty-five and sixty hours per week, while Leeward Islands Television Services (Antigua) broadcasts forty-two hours and St. Lucia Television approximately thirty-one hours weekly.

On at least TTT, JBC, CBC, and Leeward Islands Television, the day's programming commences with educational shows, particularly "Sesame Street," which all four of these stations use, as does one of the Bermuda stations. Usually the next hour is devoted to children's shows, followed by a major news and sports program at 7 P.M. The fare after 8 P.M. consists of mystery and intrigue, light comedy, and variety and discussion programs, concluded with a newscast just before sign-off.

Program formats for the three largest television stations in the Commonwealth Caribbean look like this:

Jamaica Broadcasting Corporation usually spends the first one-and-a-half hours of its schedule on children's shows ("Sesame Street" and a local "Romper Room"), followed by adventure and light comedy ("Daniel Boone," "Joe 90," "Gentle Ben," "Daktari," "I Dream of Jeannie," "Bewitched," "Flying Nun," or "Real McCoys") until news and sports at 7 P.M. From 8 P.M. to 10 P.M., shows are designed for adult audiences* and include panels, mystery and intrigue shows, light comedy, and variety. Typical programs during this period include "Name of the Game," "Val Doonican Show," "Mod Squad," "Love American Style," "Lancer," "Hawaii Five O," "Ben Casey," and "Adam 12." After a ten-minute newscast the late-evening format begins at 10:10 P.M. with shows such as "Peyton Place," "Alfred Hitchcock," "FBI," "The Saint," "Dragnet," and movies.** "Late, Late News" ends the JBC broadcast day.[54]

Trinidad and Tobago Television,[55] during its late afternoon hours (before 6 P.M.), emphasizes children's fare with cartoons, travelogues, magic and crafts shows, "Flipper," "Skippy the Bush Kangaroo," "Flintstones," and two local children's shows, "Rikki Tikki" and "12 and Under." Panels, women's programs, documentaries, and magazine and news shows are used during the early evening hours, while the audience after 8 P.M. is provided "Ironside," "Peyton Place" (twice

---

* One writer felt that Jamaican television, even with a good program schedule, was very unsuccessful in "leading this idling, gossiping, joke-cracking crowd into spending a balmy evening indoors." (Al Stump, "Where the Goggle Box Strikes Out," *TV Guide* [June 17, 1972], pp. 45–46, 48.)

** The changes in the JBC schedule by 1976 were imperceptible. The format was the same; the shows changed to include titles such as "The Six Million Dollar Man" or "Dad's Army."

a week, 30 minutes each), "Andy Williams Show," "Issues and Ideas" (local panel), "Journey to the Unknown," "Mary Tyler Moore," "The Big Valley," "Sam Benedict," "Mr. Novak," "Alfred Hitchcock," "Showcase," "Please Don't Eat the Daisies," "Marcus Welby," "Mission Impossible," and an occasional locally produced variety or panel program.

Late-afternoon programs on Caribbean Broadcasting Corporation television[56] are also meant to attract the younger viewers. Shown before the 7:30 P.M. "Tonight" newscast are: "Sesame Street," "Mr. Ed," "Ivanhoe," "Leave It to Beaver," "Woody the Woodpecker," "The Monkees," "Flintstones," "Lone Ranger," "Magilla Gorilla," "McHale's Navy," "Colt 45," "Quick Draw McGraw," and "Zorro." A five-minute "Lions' Bingo" show, a play-at-home game sponsored by the Lions Club, follows the half-hour "Tonight" newscast. The rest of the evening log is filled with programs such as "Cheyenne," "Sports Magazine," "Run for Your Life," "Dragnet," "Honey West," "Government Programme," "Marcus Welby," "It Takes a Thief," "Gidget," "Iron Horse," "Alfred Hitchcock," "Love That Bob," "Time Tunnel," "Perry Mason," "The Virginian," "Jack Benny Show," "Mod Squad," and "English Wrestling."*

St. Lucia Television and Leeward Islands Television Services have similar formats.[57] Leeward Islands Television has a larger budget of soap operas, regularly placed in the hour period before "The World at Seven" newscast.

A perusal of television schedules in the Commonwealth Caribbean leaves very little doubt about the foreign origins of the programs.** At the time of analysis, all of the stations, with the possible exception of TTT, relied upon foreign sources for 60 to 80 percent of their content. For example, approximately thirty-nine of JBC's 58½ broadcast hours were foreign-originated programs, while thirty-four of Leeward Islands Television's forty-two and forty-five of CBC's fifty-six hours were in the same category. St. Lucia Television has one to

---

* The program schedule of CBC-TV for January 13, 1976, is used for comparison: "Sesame Street," "Electric Company," "Lions' Bingo," "Circus," "Family Affair," "Tips on Health," "CBC News," "Adam 12," "GIS Presents," "Mannix," "Follow the Rhine," "Checkmate," and "News Capsule,"

** For example, in a 1971 television audience survey on Jamaica, the following were the most popular shows during a sample week: "Julia," "Marcus Welby," "Family Quiz," "The Name of the Game," "Andy Williams Show," "Ironside," "Mannix," "It Takes a Thief," "Bonanza," and "Tom Jones." ("National Television Audience Survey Jamaica 1971," [prepared for the Jamaica Broadcasting Corporation by CRAM International].) In 1975, it was estimated that JBC-TV received two-thirds of its television programs from abroad. (*Combroad* [April–June 1975], p. 14.)

one-and-a-half hours (or approximately one-fifth) per day allocated for domestic programming, but can seldom fill more than 20 percent of that slot.[58] Although Bermuda television schedules were not available, it can be assumed that ZBM-TV, as a program affiliate of NBC, CBS, and Rediffusion, and ZBF-TV, associated with ABC and Thomson Television International, also use more foreign than domestic programs.

Probably at the forefront in its use of local productions is Trinidad and Tobago Television, which features one-third local shows now and, by mid-1972, hoped for equal proportions of domestic and foreign content.* Locally produced shows on TTT include formats besides the news, sports, panel, and government information types that Commonwealth Caribbean stations rely on as their only homemade programs. A partial listing will point out TTT's effort to penetrate various age, ethnic, and social groups: "Rikki Tikki," children's show; "Mainly for Women"; "Child Care"; "At Home," care for the home; "Best Village," variety show featuring performers from various Trinidad and Tobago villages; "Indian Variety Show"; "Steelband Concert"; and "12 and Under."[59]

Part of the reason TTT, and also Trinidad and Tobago National Broadcasting System radio, has been able to effect more domestic programming might have its roots in the Trinidad Third Five-Year Plan, 1969–1973. From the outset, the plan, which nationalized television and 610 Radio, emphasized local control, staff, advertising, and content. Realizing the costliness of local program production, the drafters of the plan recommended that, first, "immediate attempts" be made to substitute high-quality "canned" programs for the "present low quality canned" material, and that, gradually, a higher proportion of locally originated programs should be introduced. The government, through this plan, also stipulated that the station should instill a

---

* A content analysis of Trinidadian television programming in October 1975 revealed the quota was not met. Hosein reported that 70 percent of Trinidad TV shows were imported; of those in prime time, 53 percent came from abroad. If government information shows and news were excluded from prime-time totals, then only 19 percent of the programs were truly Trinidadian. On other islands, the 1975 figures were as alarming: on Jamaica, 72 percent were imported; on Barbados, 87 percent; and on St. Kitts-Nevis, 90 percent. During prime time, 62 percent of Jamaica's shows were imported, 84 percent of Barbados's and 90 percent of St. Kitts-Nevis's. Again, excluding news ond government information shows from prime-time schedules, on Jamaica, only 18 percent were locally produced; on Barbados, 3 percent; and on St. Kitts-Nevis, none (Everold Hosein, "Communication Issues in the Commonwealth Caribbean," [paper presented at Caribbean Studies Association, St. Lucia, January 8, 1976]).

national consciousness in the people by emphasizing Trinidadian values and styles, giving dignity to rural life, and providing broadcast opportunities for local talent.

Of course, this was not the first time an island government had said these things. For years, license agreements between governments and broadcasting stations had stated that efforts should be made to localize programming. But these agreements were extremely general, and the governments usually did not try to enforce them. The vagueness comes through in the Jamaican statute that states "that a proportion of the recorded and other matter included in the programs shall be of Jamaican origin and of Jamaican performance, the proportion to be prescribed by regulations from time to time." The Barbadian statement is as indefinite. It declared that "a reasonable portion of broadcast material is local or Caribbean in content and character and that such material includes programmes featuring the prose and poetry, drama, music and other arts of the said region."

The possible difference on Trinidad is that the island's premier, Eric Williams, is known for his emphasis on nationalistic aims, and once he and his government set broadcasting standards in regard to domestic programming, they see that they are carried out.

In addition to TTT, other television stations in the area are taking initial steps to localize at least their news and magazine shows.* UNESCO reported in 1968 that:

> The present state of news coverage by television stations in the Region is rather limited—consisting generally of one or two news bulletins a day. . . , with the exception of TTT which in addition to two-minute "nightcap" headlines, has an evening "Panorama" of 45 minutes.[60]

TTT's "Panorama" is still on the air, extended to one hour now, but since 1968 other stations also have expanded their news shows. CBC-TV has a half-hour daily news show in color, "The World Tonight,"

---

* The programs that result are highly criticized. A Trinidad columnist wrote of that island's hourly TV news shows, "[they] reveal a genius for irrelevance and inconsequence, for vagueness and obscurity" (Trinidad *Express,* January 12, 1976. p. 8). Analyzing the main news show of CBC-TV on Barbados for January 12, 1976, I would agree with the above comments. The half-hour CBC-TV show was divided into headlines, commercials, seventeen minutes of local and regional news, six minutes of international information, two minutes of weather reports, and five minutes of sports news.

while JBC-TV has two-minute headlines at 6 P.M. and 11:20 P.M., ten minutes of late news at 10:10 P.M., and a 30- to 40-minute news and sports program at 7:30 P.M. Leeward Islands Television features "The World at Seven," a half-hour of news produced locally six days a week, in addition to ten minutes of "News Spotlight," also local, just before sign-off. Large portions of these shows are made up of film produced elsewhere by foreign agencies.[61]

Very little local television drama has been produced in the islands,* mainly because of the cost and the lack of expertise on the part of personnel. To produce regional dramas, such as soap operas, meets with the obstacle of cross-cultural interpretations. Efforts to exchange radio drama, for example, failed when it was learned that Barbadians could not understand Jamaican dialect.

Of course, reasons exist for the abundant use of foreign television programs, the most important being that they are cheaper than local shows. A television official at JBC told how much cheaper:

> It costs us 20 times more to do a local show than if we import a program. Also, the local shows are not as good as the imported ones so the one place where we can excel in local productions is public affairs material.[62]

At a station as small as St. Lucia Television, money is not available to do local productions. For example, even if local steel-band entertainers were willing to perform free, St. Lucia Television could not afford to hire a truck to transport the musicians to the studios outside town.[63] CBC-TV on Barbados has a similar problem. Initially, local artists performed free to get the exposure on CBC-TV, but later, when they expected payment, the station could not accommodate them even modestly.[64]

In other instances, foreign programs are widely used because of

---

* The recently appointed general manager of CBC-TV has talked about using more local drama. During independence week in 1975, his station showed four locally produced shows, one of which was a drama. He hopes to show a half-hour local drama every Sunday, as well as a regular local dance program. An artist himself, the general manager said TV in a developing nation "does not have to be as slick as in North America. Instead of showing a finished play, we should present a rehearsal on TV" (Personal interview, Austin Clarke, general manager, CBC-TV, Bridgetown, Barbados, January 12, 1976).

inadequate equipment* or insufficient advertising support for domestic programming. Usually the only organization capable of television production in the Commonwealth Caribbean is the government, so that what a critic wrote about Jamaican television in 1964 applies today in most islands. He complained that "only on the government's regular half hour of TV time did local entertainers get a chance."[65]

On almost every island with its own television system, officials attribute their use of large segments of foreign materials to strong cultural ties existing between the United States and Great Britain and the islands. Some go as far as to insinuate that the people not only prefer but need American and British content.

The influences of American television upon Bahamians, for example, must be obvious. The over 25,000 TV-set owners in those islands, without the services of local channels, view a great deal of Floridian television. The broadcasting director of the Bahamas explained how intense the American influence has been, at least on part of the Bahamian population:

> The American influence is great here. We look to the United States not Great Britain. People travel to Miami frequently—even to see the World Series games on television there when reception is poor in the Bahamas. They go to Miami to see boxing matches on TV as well. So the Bahamian is familiar with United States media.[66]

The proximity of most Commonwealth Caribbean islands to the United States, which facilitates travel between the two territories, and the large number of West Indians now residing in the States were given as other reasons that broadcasting fare is patterned after Amer-

---

* For example, JBC-TV on Jamaica has reached the saturation point in local productions without better equipment, more money, and more personnel. The chief local TV programs on JBC-TV are news (45 minutes daily) and discussion types. Among the Jamaican-produced shows are "Focus," one hour Monday night panel; "Firing Line," one hour Tuesday night press conference; "Say It Loud," one hour Sunday youth panel; "Version," a religious panel; a weekly children's program; "Jazz," one hour Saturday night club show; "Where It's At," a teenager trends program; "Schools Challenge Quiz," one half-hour weekly; "Play Pen," half-hour weekly show of games and play for pre-school children; "Pulse," a weekly show about the "little man" in society, and "Sunday Report," one hour weekly documentary on Jamaica (Personal interview, Dwight Whylie, general manager, JBC, Kingston, Jamaica, January 14, 1976).

ican radio and television. The general manager of Radio Jamaica, while discussing radio's imitation of United States standards, made some observations that apply equally to television.* His statements were:

> Radio in Jamaica is patterned after United States or Canadian networks. The majority of the people here have traveled to the United States; Florida is just one hour and twenty minutes from here. People go there often and hear American radio styles and expect the same upon returning to Jamaica. . . . There's no getting around it. When the Jamaican government, for instance, said you had to have a license to import recordings into the island, the big United States recording companies sent master copies of records here and they were pressed and marketed locally nevertheless. And so, local singers and writers continue imitating North American singers in their style.[67]

On Antigua American television programs are better received than British ones because "Antiguan culture is tied to United States culture by way of the United States bases that have been here since 1940."[68] On Barbados the rationale for offering over 80 percent foreign (mostly United States) television content is as follows:

> People here have been brought up with United States films so they like them better. They understand them better than British films even though the latter are better produced.[69]

Despite the above rationale, it might be that British West Indian television, like that in other developing nations, has become enmeshed in the following cycle: a Caribbean island sets up its own television service and a number of people make an investment in a set. Now that they own the set, they want their money's worth and demand longer viewing times. But, because local productions are prohibitively expensive, the station must import a larger quantity of foreign shows that sometimes are irrelevant, if not injurious, to the island's development.

Radio

As in most emerging nations, radio has become the most popular medium in the Commonwealth Caribbean. Personal observation of

---

* In 1976 four out of every seven hours of JBC-TV programming originates from the United States.

the wide use of transistors and car radios would confirm that. So would the few statistics available.[70] On Jamaica a 1969 survey[71] found that, of the total adult[72] population (1,165,000), 63 percent (or 735,000) were regular daily listeners to the radio. The audience was split in this fashion: 67 percent listened to Radio Jamaica regularly and 37 percent to Jamaica Broadcasting Corporation. An earlier survey[73] conducted on Trinidad showed that, of the total adult population (586,000), 57 percent (or 333,000) were regular daily listeners to radio. Radio Trinidad, with an estimated listenership of 288,000, had the largest audience on that island; regular listeners of Radio Guardian (now known as Trinidad and Tobago National Broadcasting System) totaled 242,000. On the smaller islands Antigua Broadcasting Service, claiming to serve all of the Eastern Caribbean area, estimated listenership at 100,000, nearly double the population of Antigua, and ZNS in the Bahamas claimed 75,000 daily adult listeners out of an adult population of 95,000.[74] Radio Caribbean, which broadcasts in French and English, estimated a set count of 66,000 for its English Language Service, 100,000 for its French Language Service.

To satisfy this growing audience, stations in the region have increased their hours of broadcast, and most of them are now on the air approximately seventeen to eighteen hours a day. Jamaica Broadcasting Corporation is on the air for 19 hours and 45 minutes (4:45 A.M. to 12:30 A.M.), while Radio Jamaica has a broadcast day that commences at 4:45 A.M. and ends at 12:05 A.M. Both stations broadcast all night on Friday and Saturday. Radio Barbados (CBC) is on eighteen hours a day (5:28 A.M. to midnight, except Saturdays when sign-off is at 2 A.M.), as is Barbados Rediffusion. Radio Trinidad transmits 17 hours and 50 minutes daily (5:25 A.M. to 11:15 P.M.), while TTNBS is on the air 18½ hours (5:25 A.M. to midnight). The only twenty-four-hour daily service is provided by ZNS-1 in the Bahamas; its sister, ZNS-2, programmed as an FM station* would be in the States, broadcasts sixteen hours a day (7 A.M. to 11 P.M.). Windward Islands Broadcasting Service, and its three subsidiaries, does not come on the air until 11:45 A.M. and closes down at 10:15 P.M. Radio Antilles, the largest wattage station in the Commonwealth Caribbean, broadcasts sixteen hours a day.[75]

The peak listening period on most islands is between sign-on and

---

* Other FM stations have been started in the region by 610 Radio on Trinidad (October 1974), JBC and Radio Jamaica (both in September 1972). A check of radio schedules in January 1976 revealed that they are on the air approximately the same times as in 1971.

8 or 9 A.M. Audience surveys confirmed that fact in the Bahamas, and on Trinidad, Jamaica, and Barbados. The majority of the stations fill this time period with devotional shows, agricultural reports, world and regional news, obituaries, weather information, sea condition reports, soft music, a daily horoscope, turf tips, and other programming helpful in starting the day. Besides the early-morning period, other "A premium" times are[76] 11 A.M. to noon and 4:30 P.M. to 10:30 P.M. on Barbados; noon to 2 P.M. and 6–8 P.M. in the Bahamas; 11 A.M. to 1 P.M. and 4–7 P.M. on Trinidad; and noon to 1 P.M. and 9–10 P.M. on Jamaica.

To give the reader an example of a typical weekday of programming on a Commonwealth Caribbean station, a summary of Radio Trinidad's schedule follows:

5:30–9 A.M.   Transmissions begin with a religious feature followed first by an agricultural program and then by a morning disc jockey show interspersed with news headlines, weather information, sports feature, and participating spots.

9–noon.   Designed for housewives, this period contains women's features, news, and daytime serials. Particularly suitable for advertising of household and women's products. News of "hot" special events transmitted at this time.

Noon–2 P.M.   World news followed by commentary on local, Caribbean, and world affairs. Followed by daytime serial, news, sports, and quiz show.

2–4 P.M.   Traditionally the time when a selection of top BBC programs, chosen for their suitability for Trinidad, are broadcast.

4–6 P.M.   Heavily weighted with music. The commuter's period, it has been made flexible to accommodate live broadcasts of special events such as the opening of new establishments, prime minister's Best Village competitions and tours, farm shows, and live local talent programs.

6–7 P.M.   Indian music is listened to by a high proportion of this minority group. Followed by an educational program alternating on some evenings with light relaxing music.

7–8 P.M.   A magazine-type program incorporating local interviews and comments and BBC Caribbean tape services; recordings on West Indians in Britain are supplied by British Information Services and used on this program.

8–9:15 P.M.   Reserved for programs chosen by the Trinidad government.

9:15–11 P.M.   News, drama, outside broadcasts, and late-night music programs (including classical music).[77]

Breakdown of a regional station's content, that of Radio Antilles on Montserrat, indicates the cultural variety in the Caribbean. Radio Antilles divides its broadcast day into linguistic segments, broadcasting in English from 6–7 A.M., 9–10 A.M., 2–7 P.M., and 9–10 P.M., the intervening times devoted to French- and Spanish-language periods. The station is extremely popular in the Commonwealth Caribbean, especially in the Windwards, possibly because of its program versatility and relevance. For example, Radio Antilles presents a half-hour program for Dominicans that includes "Dominican music, mail and messages for our listeners in Dominica." In addition, the station's French-language fare is appealing to the many Windward Islanders who speak a French-derived patois.

Radio Caribbean, which, because of its transmitting to Guadeloupe and Martinique, has more French- than English-speaking listeners, programs similarly to Radio Antilles. French Service shows (all music) are aired between 6–8 A.M., 10:30 A.M. and 2:30 P.M., and 6 P.M. until 10:30 P.M. closedown.

Generally speaking, Commonwealth Caribbean radio programming consists of large blocks of disc-jockey or request shows, interspersed with news, weather, sports, and an occasional drama or government show. Even the stations on the larger islands, although progressing to more local and nonmusic programming, still rely heavily upon disc-jockey shows. For example, Jamaica Broadcasting Corporation* and Radio Jamaica devote their entire evening segments to two record shows, "Dynamic Records" and "Federal Records," with news headlines and weather bulletins inserted. Both stations also fill their afternoon schedules with this type of programming. Radio Jamaica devotes 3½ afternoon hours five days a week to music and request shows; Jamaica Broadcasting Corporation programming from 12:45 P.M. to 5 P.M. is made up of three disc-jockey shows, broken up with two five-minute newscasts and four two-minute news headlines. JBC and Radio Jamaica also have other music shows in the morning and early evening hours.

Radio Trinidad separates its extended blocks of music with ten-to-fifteen-minute governmental, news, or devotional programs, or a short soap opera. For example, "Matinee Top 100," a music show, is

---

* In 1974 JBC Radio cut back on its output of popular music and concentrated on the development of news, public affairs, and "intellectually stimulating features." Some of the new programs are "Here Comes Charley" (comedy-variety), "The Public Eye" (news-commentary-in-depth reporting), "Sparerib" (daily reports and interviews to "stimulate the mental, personal and social development of Jamaican women"), "Palaver" (panel on major topics of national interest). (*Combroad*, [April–June 1974], pp. 54–56.)

on from 1 P.M. to 4 P.M. daily, but during that three-hour period two short news bulletins, one five-minute Ministry of Agriculture show, a fourteen-minute daytime serial, and a fifteen-minute "Know Your Bible" program also are broadcast. TTNBS (610 Radio) programs two music shows taking up the period from 1 P.M. to 4:45 P.M. daily; the only interruptions are two minutes of news on the hour and one minute of weather on the half-hour. Basically the same formats predominate on the two Barbadian stations.

ZNS-1 (Bahamas) uses the same programs every day during its 5:30 A.M. to 7:30 P.M. schedule but varies the evening content from day to day. Early morning hours (6–9 A.M.) are centered around a music show, interspersed with weather, bank and labor exchange reports, news, sports, community announcements, and out-island weather. From 10 A.M. to noon the format is designed for women listeners and includes three soap operas (two from Australia, one from the United States). Afternoon programming is predominantly music, weather, and news, while the evening hours are taken up with soft music, news, and commentary. The midnight-to-dawn portion of the schedule is strictly music.

A characteristic common to the majority of the islands is the similarity of program content and hours of broadcast of competing stations. On Jamaica, for example, it seems that there is very little difference in JBC and Radio Jamaica content, except that the stations do give their music shows different names. Also, De Leon said that he saw very few differences in programming on the two Trinidadian stations. One island where the competing stations do differ in content and design is Antigua. ZDK, for example, has divided its entire schedule into six shows, each headed by a disc jockey.[78] From 6–10 A.M. the music show is "Morning Sound and Housewives Club"; from 10 A.M. to 2 P.M., "Merry Melodies"; 3–6 P.M., "Super-Bad Show"; 6–7 P.M., "Caribbean Sounds"; 7–11 P.M., "Jody and Friends"; and 11 P.M. to 1 A.M., "Soul Shack." On the other hand, Antigua Broadcasting Service features as many as forty-one short programs during a sixteen-hour day, a large number of them tapes of BBC drama, sports, daytime serial, news, and panel discussions.

Music also makes up the largest portion of the programming of Windward Islands Broadcasting Service.* Request shows are popular

---

* Since the dissolution of WIBS, each Windward Island has its own radio station. If Radio St. Lucia is typical, then the formats of the new stations have not differed much from that of WIBS. One bright spot has been the production of 66 fifteen-minute capsules on St. Lucia folk culture to be used on Radio St. Lucia (*Caribbean Contact,* [December 1975], p. 14).

among WIBS listeners, as they are throughout the region.[79] WIBS format is designed to allot approximately an hour of programming daily to the substations on St. Lucia, Dominica, and St. Vincent. Ten-minute news shows are broadcast daily from each of the four islands, so that a listener on Dominica must also take in the newscasts from St. Vincent, Grenada, and St. Lucia if he plans to listen to the noon news. The WIBS director said that the islanders enjoyed this format, that it gave them the feeling that they were eavesdropping on a neighboring island's news.[80] St. Lucia's share of the WIBS schedule, in addition to its newscast, includes the daily airing of a half-hour show, "From St. Lucia Today," and two-and-a-half hours weekly of Government Information Services programs, as well as half-hour segments devoted to interviews, sports, and "Week's News in Focus."[81]

WIBS allocates Dominica forty-five minutes daily, the other 11½ hours being direct relay from WIBS headquarters in Grenada. Thus, Dominicans hear thirty minutes of local features at midday and a fif-teen-minute package of news, Jaycee bingo, Caribbean news (relayed from Grenada), and local music at dinnertime.[82] St. Vincent is given seven to nine hours weekly as its portion of WIBS time. Half of the schedule is given to St. Vincent Government Information Services. In addition, over one-half of all local newscasts on St. Vincent are GIS releases.[83]

Two complaints continually leveled at Commonwealth Caribbean radio are: (1) that it is too frivolous, often neglecting its responsi-bilities to uplift the cultural level of the people and instill a national consciousness, and (2) that it is foreign-made and, thus, often irrele-vant.

The frivolity criticism probably results from the plethora of United States rock, pop, and soul* that is broadcast in the islands. One West Indian critic even associated United States and British pop music with the revolution of rising expectations, claiming that

> We have societies here which have no sense of identity; copying America has become as important as copying Britain was. We are transistorized people and pop panaceas are our salvation. This is why you see young boys walking and listening to transistors . . .

---

* The Caribbean Broadcasting Union, in its last two general assemblies, has stressed that broadcasting in the region must take a different form—one more similar to that of Trinidad. In his presidential address to the CBU in 1973, Leo de Leon stressed that broadcasting must operate less as a jukebox and more as an information exchange center and formulator of opinion. (*Combroad*, [March–April 1974], pp. 44–45.)

what are the radios playing . . . pop. Marx called religion the opium of the people. I think the transistor is in a sense intended to be this. . . . You have an ambivalence there, sort of double entendre people being fed with material in terms of pop, which will make them almost unaware of their poverty, and they are equally being fed with all the pictorial images of the white wealthy West which merely makes them discontent with their poverty.[84]

A Trinidadian program director lamented the lack of initiative taken by radio to form a Trinidadian or West Indian public opinion:

We lost so much in Trinidad by just playing music over the last couple decades. As early as 1950 we should have done analytical programs. If we had done this we would have changed the whole structure of society here. We have failed dismally. We lost a whole decade by not having varying program types. In the past, radio in these islands has treated news as the newspapers did. Media have not sought to pose or answer questions. There were no talk shows in the past, no public participation in the media.[85]

His station, TTNBS, in an effort to do something for the masses other than soothe them, has incorporated more news analysis and public affairs reporting in its schedule. So has Jamaica Broadcasting Corporation. Most stations have numerous newscasts but few that are in depth. For example, in 1968, among Commonwealth Caribbean stations, 12.5 percent of the programming was devoted to news, but the formats ran something like this: a two-minute news bulletin every hour plus two or three major ten-minute bulletins and possibly one or two longer BBC transcriptions daily.[86]

Concerning the second complaint, the Jamaica Broadcasting Authority, a governmental body that appraises broadcasting performance, yearly in its reports decried the use of American, British, and Australian shows. On one occasion the Authority characterized the majority of Jamaican listeners/viewers as "non-whites watching white faces and white mores and white attitudes";[87] at another time it chastised Jamaican announcers for mimicking the voices of American and Canadian colleagues.*

---

* The Board's 1972 report criticized the amount of foreign content. The report that year also lamented the lack of audience participation shows, mispronunciation in news shows, and the abundance of "reggae trash" (*Daily Gleaner*, August 2, 1973, p. 12). The 1973 report, as in previous years, complained about the frequency of advertisements at peak times, especially on TV, and said that news reading was still of a low standard, with some readers feeling a need to have a phony accent (*Daily Gleaner*, May 27, 1974, p. 12).

The island governments were responsible for some stations' policies on foreign content. For example, Rediffusion stations, under the terms of their licenses, were required to devote considerable amounts of time to British Broadcasting Corporation transmissions. As late as 1967 Trinidad Rediffusion was required to broadcast at least twenty-one hours per week (20 percent of air time) of British Broadcasting Corporation matter; Jamaica, ten hours. Both stations normally exceeded that standard. Although the Barbados Rediffusion outlet had no such obligation during the 1950s, the station still broadcast thirty hours weekly of BBC transcriptions.[88] In other cases island stations depended upon foreign content matter because it was inexpensive (relative to local productions) and easily available.

The majority of the radio programs broadcast in the islands today are foreign in content. Radio Trinidad, for example, still obtains over 70 percent of its materials from overseas,[89] while with smaller stations, such as Antigua Broadcasting Service and Radio Anguilla, the percentages are 75 and 95 percent, respectively. Oftentimes it is difficult to determine station managers' referent when they discuss local content. For example, when personnel at Antigua's ZDK boast 99.9 percent local programming,[90] what they are saying is that because Antiguan disc jockeys spin the records and read the news, then the station is predominantly domestic. They fail to take into account the origins of the music* and news. Actually, ZDK's only local shows are a weekly children's program and a Saturday night live presentation from a local night club.

The director of Bahamian station ZNS is more realistic, however, pointing out that on 67 percent of his station's shows, "the disc jockey is the only thing that is local."[91] The remainder of the ZNS log consists of 14 to 16 percent news (Voice of America, BBC, and Canadian Broadcasting Corporation relay), 10 to 12 percent religious, and 8 percent talk and interview. The station has made progress with at least three local shows: a weekly three-hour exploration of Bahamian music and musicians, a six-hour Sunday magazine show, and a Bahamian soap opera.[92]

Since the late 1960s efforts have been made to localize larger portions of Commonwealth Caribbean radio content, especially on

---

* Apparently broadcasters on Jamaica and Barbados have. JBC stipulates that one half of the music on radio be Jamaican (Personal interview, Dwight Whylie, general manager, JBC, Kingston, Jamaica, January 14, 1976). In its Barbadianization campaign, CBC radio requires that 75 percent of all music be Barbadian or Caribbean, and 25 percent North American (Personal interview, Austin Clarke, general manager, CBC, Bridgetown, Barbados, January 12, 1976).

Trinidad, Jamaica, Barbados, Bahamas, and St. Lucia. Since government takeover in 1969, TTNBS has increased its local fare to 40 percent, including more Caribbean music, two hours daily of Trinidadian-produced newscasts, three hours of news analysis every day (on Sundays, six hours), and more local drama productions, especially soap operas.

Radio Barbados (CBC) also has taken the step toward more local productions; for example, in an 18½-hour broadcast day in September 1970, only 3 hours and 45 minutes were devoted to foreign matter, most of which came from the BBC. The chief local programs produced by Radio Barbados included "West Indian Short Story" and the soap opera, "Braithwaites at Black Rock," the latter discontinued because of its high production costs.

Radio Caribbean on St. Lucia has formed a Community Development Service, designed "to promote the interests of the people of St. Lucia." In its early stages, the service sponsored two shows, "Talking Point" and "Listening Point," both of which depended primarily upon St. Lucian items.

Indications are that the Rediffusion stations will adhere more closely to their program policy, set down approximately two decades ago. That policy stipulated that the stations must have appeal for the audiences they served, give special importance to matters of local interest, use local talent to the maximum extent, and design programs that cater to all sectors of the community, including minorities.[93]

Especially hopeful are the efforts at domestic programming being made by Verbatim, Inc. and Caribbean Broadcasting Union. Verbatim, Inc. is a business organization of two Americans who hop from island to island interviewing interesting West Indians and then selling the tapes to Commonwealth Caribbean radio stations.[94] An advantage of Verbatim's service is that the organization uses taped material, a less costly process than direct linkups.*

More formidable as a regional programming outlet** is the Carib-

---

* By 1974 a regional television system was functioning. West Indies Television Network, calling itself "The Big One," simultaneously broadcasts to 16 islands, including the British Virgin Islands, St. Kitts-Nevis, Barbuda, Antigua, and Montserrat. The scheme was made possible by international licensing through the Dutch and British governments. Studios are on St. Maarten. The network is the joint venture of local island businessmen and the Screen Gems/WAPA, a division of Columbia Pictures. (*Combroad*, [July–September 1974], p. 50.)

** For a study of the feasibility of implementing a regional system of television programming in the Commonwealth Caribbean within the available resources, see Everold Hosein, "Regional Television Programming for the Commonwealth Caribbean," *Combroad* (October–December 1973), pp. 13–17. His findings coincide with those in this book.

bean Broadcasting Union, formed at the advent of the 1970s.* Membership in CBU is open to all broadcasting organizations in member countries of the Commonwealth Caribbean that "have been authorized to operate a national broadcasting service by the competent authority in each country." Thus, the main members are the public broadcasting services in the islands, although, according to the CBU head, "there is room for associate memberships for all broadcasting systems in the region." Among the objectives of the organization are: "to promote the building of a regional tradition in broadcasting," "to encourage and provide, through broadcasting, for fuller involvement of the peoples of the region in their common aspirations," "to encourage proper standards and ethics in regional and unit broadcasting," "to promote the building of a regional tradition in broadcasting, and to initiate, encourage and develop expertise, principles and facilities for the training of broadcasting staff," "to encourage the exchange of regional news and programming between member stations," "to act as a bargaining agent for members with regard to any commercial broadcasting rights of a regional nature," and to "encourage the technological development of modern broadcast communication within the region."[95] The CBU head said that the formation of the organization was possible at this time because the larger broadcasting units have become interested in the smaller ones and want to exchange programs, and because CBU is coming from within the region, that is, it is not foreign-sponsored.

Financing is expected to come from subscriptions of member stations, as well as from donations and payment for special services that CBU will provide for individual broadcasting units. Its first project, a series of documentaries (150 hours of taped shows) about member territories, completed in early 1971, was sponsored by two Commonwealth Caribbean airlines. The organization does not yet produce domestic drama shows but plans to do so later.[96]

All the foregoing talk about foreign content to the contrary, radio in the islands already has some unique characteristics that distinguish it

---

* Since CBU was established as a regional body in May 1970, it has held general assemblies in Guyana, Barbados, Bahamas, Antigua, St. Lucia, and Trinidad and Tobago. At its 1975 meeting, CBU agreed to produce a wide range of regional programs in 1976, including a thirty-minute "Humour in the Caribbean" show, separate programs on each of the 13 CARICOM nations, and a six-part series on the work of the Caribbean Community Secretariat. Through CBU, Antigua, St. Kitts-Nevis, and Montserrat radio stations continue weekly to exchange program material on simultaneous broadcasts in each territory. Also CBC, Radio St. Lucia, and Guyana Broadcasting Service sustain a weekly one-hour show (*Combroad* [October–December 1975], p. 47).

from that in other cultures. Among these are: "communication by radio," existing in the Bahamas particularly,[97] where the common man can send messages by radio much as people do by telephone in more developed nations; the index to the day's programming is broadcast periodically during the day (much as program schedules are printed in newspapers); and the obituaries.[98] Because of the emphasis on quick burial in these subtropical islands, the obituary or death announcement is an important service provided by radio. Some stations broadcast them as many as five times daily.

Also, not in very many parts of the world will the radio listener hear "Banana Cutting Notices," as he will in the Windward Islands. Information about the quality, acceptance, and loading time of bananas at various depot ships is sent by cable from the Banana Association branches to all WIBS substations. The service enables the farmer to cut the fruit at the right time and move it expeditiously to the closest depot for quick shipment.

SUMMARY

Both Commonwealth Caribbean news flow and media content are highly dependent upon foreign services and sources. Since there is no British West Indian news service, the larger-island media rely on United States, British, and Canadian wire services and broadcast agencies, and in some cases, their own stringers; the smaller-island media pick up their news from radio monitoring, private and governmental press releases, informal sources, and "Reuterpress."

Larger islands are served by dailies whose editors say that they use London journalistic techniques and United States and British news sources to fill most of their pages. Except for four tabloids, most of the dailies are traditional, rather than modernistic, in content and design. Nondailies on Jamaica, Trinidad, Barbados, and Bahamas contain mostly political or sensational material.

On the smaller islands, nondailies, in an effort to promote political parties and men, use evaluative news stories, highly descriptive headlines, and information that West Indians have already been exposed to in the larger papers and by the electronic media.

Magazines, even newsmagazines, are also very promotional, containing large quantities of material that is meant to show the tourist how beautiful West Indian beaches, casinos, and hotels are.

Television, still relatively young in the region, is limited to the late afternoon and evening hours, except for occasional educational shows in the mornings. Most stations are on the air between fifty-five and sixty hours a week, during which time they show 60 to 80 percent foreign shows, mostly variety and drama.

The average radio station in the islands is on the air seventeen to eighteen hours a day, broadcasting large segments of pop music, broken up with news, sports, and weather. On islands with competing stations, content does not differ much between the broadcasting units. Chief complaints leveled against radio have been that it is not meeting the needs of the island-nations and is too foreign-oriented.

However, since about 1968, local efforts have been made to create organizations that would encourage more indigenous and relevant media content for the islands. The Reuters Caribbean Desk, and more recently, the Caribbean News Agency, and Caribbean Broadcasting Union serve that function.

NOTES TO CHAPTER 5

1. John Merrill, *The Elite Press* (New York: Pitman, 1968), pp. 5–6.

2. Herbert Schiller, *Mass Communications and American Empire* (Boston: Beacon Press, 1971), p. 111.

3. There are, though, media in the islands that can manage their own regional coverage. The *Gleaner*, for example, maintains 400 stringers in its own territory, while the Trinidad *Guardian* operates bureaus in two secondary towns. Radio Jamaica and Jamaica Broadcasting Corporation keep stringers in rural areas and neighboring territories. One Radio Jamaica commentator, whom this author met in both St. Kitts and Antigua, said that his job is to island-hop to gather enough material to file three news commentaries a week.

Not only information entering the islands, but stories leaving the region are generally filtered through what Hachten terms "wire service nationalism," described by him as "reporting the news from the point of view of the correspondent's own reader's interests as well as the national interests and foreign policy considerations of his own government."

William Hachten, *Muffled Drums* (Ames, Iowa: Iowa State University Press, 1971), p. 86.

4. VISNEWS Ltd., a partnership formed of Reuters, BBC, and Australian, Canadian, and New Zealand broadcasting authorities, is a news film agency that provides a daily international news service.

British Information Service, mentioned earlier, functions primarily to give direct support to "current political and commercial activities" taking place in Great Britain.

Central Office of Information directs Great Britain's overseas film and television programs. Approximately 150 Commonwealth, colonial, and foreign lands receive COI films yearly.

Sir Harold Beeley, "The Changing Role of British International Propaganda," *Annals of the American Academy of Political and Social Science* (November 1971), p. 125.

5. The impact of the Reuters Caribbean Desk was emphasized by UNESCO. During a week in September 1967, heads of Commonwealth Caribbean governments surveyed newspapers in Barbados, Trinidad, Jamaica, and Guyana to determine how much hard news from other Commonwealth Caribbean territories was printed by these papers. They found that no features or photographs concerning the area were published during the week surveyed. At that time the daily average of regional items per paper was 2.6. Later, in November 1968, after the Reuters Caribbean Desk was created, the average per paper shot up to 11. Guy Roppa and Neville E. Clarke, *The Commonwealth Caribbean: Regional Co-Operation in News and Broadcasting Exchanges* (Paris: UNESCO, 1969), p. 7.

6. As well as a Guyana newspaper and two broadcasting concerns.

7. Roppa and Clarke, *Commonwealth Caribbean*, p. 38. Additional information provided author by letter from W. E. Parrott, Reuters Manager for the Caribbean, Bridgetown, Barbados, March 28, 1972. See also W. E. Parrott, "Reuters in the Caribbean," *The Bajan* (September 1971), pp. 20–21.

8. Roppa and Clarke, *Commonwealth Caribbean*, p. 41. The only association of mass media organizations in the region, CPBA, has members among the larger newspapers and radio and television stations of the British West Indies. Objectives of the organization include: promotion of the interests of media, holding of conferences of the association, facilitation of exchange of experience and opinions among media personnel.

9. Roppa and Clarke, *Commonwealth Caribbean*, p. 35.

10. Ibid., p. 34.

11. Ibid., p. 43.

12. Ibid., p. 37.

13. Ibid., pp. 18–19.

14. Ibid., p. 22.

15. Personal interview, Claude Theobalds, Chief Program Officer, WIBS, Kingstown, St. Vincent, May 11, 1971.

16. Personal interview, Stanley Reid, Editor, *Crusader* and *Link*, Castries, St. Lucia, May 8, 1971.

17. Radio monitoring is an important source of news even among the larger mass media. The Jamaican *Gleaner* monitors radio all day in case "they get

something we don't," according to Editor Theodore Sealy. And, according to Sealy, radio uses the newspaper as a news source, too. "Some of the first bulletins read over radio in the morning are read from the *Gleaner*," he said. Personal interview, Theodore Sealy, Editor, *Daily Gleaner*, Kingston, Jamaica, August 26, 1970.

18. Personal interview, Fred Seal Coon, Editorial Manager, *Daily Gleaner*, Kingston, Jamaica, August 26, 1970. A British journalist, Henry Fairlie, in 1966 criticized British newspapers for their going overboard for readability and presentation at the sacrifice of content. Tony Brenna, "Fairlie's Press Appraisal," *Editor and Publisher*, June 11, 1966, p. 77.

19. Personal interview, Chris Evans, General Manager, Nassau *Guardian*, Nassau, Bahamas, August 24, 1970.

20. Personal interview, Lenn Chongsing, Editor, Trinidad *Guardian*, Port of Spain, Trinidad, September 1, 1970.

21. Both use nine-column formats.

22. Interview, Sealy.

23. The Sunday *Gleaner* is usually 32 pages in addition to its Sunday magazine. A page of the Sunday edition reviews the week's world news; another page features a serialized portion of a novel popular in the United States or Great Britain. *Sunday Magazine* includes the United States color funnies, a TV schedule, crossword puzzle, and two or three features.

24. At one time the *Gleaner* also published Mid-Island and East Island supplements.

25. The *Week-End Star* is usually in the range of 24 pages, featuring stories headlined in a manner similar to this, "Killed in Fight Over Woman," as well as crime mysteries and one page of locally drawn cartoons with sexual overtones.

26. Content analyses among Commonwealth Caribbean mass media are indeed rare. Therefore, when one is done, it seems necessary to report the results, even though they may be dated. In 1962 Alleyne analyzed the content of the Jamaica *Daily Gleaner*. He found that the paper devoted 46.6 percent of its Saturday content to advertisements (50.5 percent on Mondays), 6.5 percent on sports (4.5 on Mondays), 12.5 percent foreign news (5.9 on Mondays), 5.4 percent local political news (4.3 on Mondays), and 29 percent other (34.8 on Mondays). Mervin Alleyne, "Communications and Politics in Jamaica," *Caribbean Studies* 3, no. 2: 34.

27. For April 24, 1971.

28. The May 9, 1971, edition of the *Sunday Guardian Magazine* featured five pages about a local shirt factory and two pages on Trinidad's tallest building. The rest of the magazine was made up of movie stories, an astrology column, a feature about a man who jumped 18,000 feet and survived, fashions, and a color comic section of United States funny-strip characters.

29. Personal interview, Compton Delph, Editor, Trinidad *Evening News,* Port of Spain, Trinidad, September 1, 1970.

30. On Saturdays the *Express* contains an eight-page special magazine section called "Boots: Saturday's Sports with Big Kick." Contents of this seection deal predominantly with racing for the benefit of the Saturday bettors.

31. Barbados does not have an evening newspaper. The *Advocate-News* does publish a Sunday edition with a magazine, *The Advocate Magazine.* Sunday's edition features a "Last Week in Review" page of local news items presented day by day. The 12-page magazine supplement for May 2, 1971, included local columns plus syndicated United States features.

32. Personal interview, Neville Grosvenor, General Manager, *Advocate-News,* Bridgetown, Barbados, September 7, 1970.

33. Cigarette, whiskey, and beer advertisements are common in Commonwealth Caribbean newspapers.

34. Personnel at the *Guardian* claim that the paper is "more or less anti-government editorially." But in 1970-71, the paper had neither editorial writers nor an editorial policy on anything, one official said. Personal interview, Benson Mc-Dermott, Vice-President, *Guardian,* Nassau, Bahamas, August 24, 1970.

35. The 12-page *Guardian* for April 26, 1971, for example, used these front-page stories: dry spell causes fires, anthropologist gets grant, support for resort pledged, murder suspect to court, year's exports and imports show increase, Haitian power challenge, public should have access to all beaches, treasury bills offer allotted.

36. In October 1970 two cabinet ministers and eight members of the House of Assembly disagreed with the Pindling government and resigned. They formed the Free PLP and took the organ of the PLP, *Bahamian Times,* with them. In the spring of 1971, the splinter group formed the new paper, *The Torch.* The fate of the *Times* is still undecided.

37. Personal interview, Leslie John, Chief Reporter, *Workers Voice,* St. John's, Antigua, May 4, 1971.

38. Personal interview, Nathaniel Hodge, Editor, *Democrat,* Basseterre, St. Kitts, May 1, 1971.

39. Personal interview, Bentley Cornelius, Editor, Antigua *Star,* St. John's, Antigua, May 4, 1971.

40. Personal interview, A. Michael Cruickshank, Editor, *Vanguard,* St. George's, Grenada, May 12, 1971.

41. Either the April 24 or May 1, 1971, issues were surveyed. Where newspapers had publishing dates other than Saturday, the issues nearest to these two dates were analyzed.

42. The largest page-one story in the May 11, 1971, issue of the *West Indian*, for example, told about a Grenadian bank employee who had finished a London course of study. Three lines of 72-point type were required to headline that story.

43. A tyipcal item from the "Is It True?" column of the *Herald*: "That . . . a remark was passed at police headquarters: if we ever get Scobie [*Herald* editor] in the cells, we would beat him unmercifully?" Grenada's *Vanguard* publishes "What the People Say," a rumor column of statements, rather than questions.

44. Personal interview, Rick Wayne, Editor, *Voice of St. Lucia*, Castries, St. Lucia, May 7, 1971.

45. Ibid.

46. Personal interview, Elcon Mason, Editor, *Torchlight*, St. George's, Grenada, May 12, 1971.

47. Letter to Author, Dorcas White, Editor, Montserrat *Mirror*, Plymouth, Montserrat, June 10, 1971.

48. This issue was used in the sample because it was the last *Beacon* published up to that time. The paper had been awaiting a new roller for its press.

49. Lucian Pye, ed., *Communications and Political Development* (Princeton, N.J.: Princeton University Press, 1963), pp. 80–81.

50. Personal interview, John Wickham, Literary Editor, *The Bajan*, Bridgetown, Barbados, May 14, 1971.

51. In this case, May 1971.

52. Volume 23, No. 1, 1971.

53. Personal interview, Frank Collymore, Editor, *Bim*, Bridgetown, Barbados, May 14, 1971.

54. Of course, not all of these shows are on the screen nightly. This is a sampling of most of a week's programs on each station. JBC's schedule was for September 1970. In each case these are weekday schedules. On weekends the stations use more religious, sports, panel, and movie content.

55. This schedule was for April 1971.

56. This schedule was for April and May 1971.

57. Schedules for the two Bermuda stations were not available.

58. Personal interview, Ken Archer, Director, St. Lucia Television Services, Castries, St. Lucia, May 8, 1971.

59. Letter to Author, John Barsotti, Assistant Program Director, Trinidad and Tobago Television, Port of Spain, Trinidad, August 10, 1971.

60.   Roppa and Clarke, *Commonwealth Caribbean*, p. 29.

61.   For example, in October 1968 TTT in its "Panorama," broadcast 2,712 feet of locally produced news film, as well as 2,165 feet of UPI-TN and 4,823 feet of CBS films. Footage received from the two foreign sources was 4,589 and 5,387, respectively, so that TTT used 68 percent of the foreign film received. Roppa and Clarke, *Commonwealth Caribbean*, p. 29.

62.   Personal interview, L. H. Stewart, Assistant General Manager, Jamaica Broadcasting Corporation, Kingston, Jamaica, August 28, 1970. Schiller gave some insights into the low costs of importing television films. The prices for American one-hour TV films are: on Bermuda, $25–40 (US); on Jamaica, $25–30 (US); and on Trinidad, $30–35 (US). Schiller, *Mass Communications*, p. 88.

63.   Interview, Archer.

64.   Personal interview, Ian Gale, General Manager, Caribbean Broadcasting Corporation, Bridgetown, Barbados, September 4, 1970.

65.   "Radio and TV," *Spotlight* (December 1964), p. 77.

66.   Personal interview, Jack Dodge, General Manager, ZNS Radio, Nassau, Bahamas, April 26, 1971.

67.   Personal interview, Lloyd de Pass, General Manager, Radio Jamaica, Kingston, Jamaica, August 27, 1970.

68.   Personal interview, Vernon G. Michaels, Manager, ZAL-TV, St. John's, Antigua, May 4, 1971.

69.   Interview, Gale.

70.   Audience surveys conducted in the region have been subjected to criticism by a number of broadcasting personnel. A JBC official said that the survey done on that island did not include lower age groups. The fact that a seven-day recall technique was used also distressed him. A Radio Trinidad sales manager complained that a market survey accomplished there recently did not bring out information about ethnic groups. He explained: "One type of people here (the Indians in central Trinidad) work on sugar plantations and don't want anyone in their homes while they are at work. These people were not surveyed, therefore, and they constitute 40 percent of the population here." Interview, Stewart; personal interview, Sam Ghany, Sales Manager, Trinidad Broadcasting, Port of Spain, Trinidad, September 2, 1970.

71.   *Jamaica Survey No. 6* (London: Rediffusion, 1969). Field work accomplished May and June 1969.

72.   Fifteen years and over.

73.   Survey field work done in August 1967.

74. The ABS figure was a station estimate; ZNS statistics come from: *Bahamas Radio Audience Survey No. 1* (London: Rediffusion, 1970). Field work done in September 1970.

75. Other examples: Radio Caribbean has a 16-hour-and-45-minute broadcast day, seven days a week; Antigua's ZDK, 19 hours, commencing at 6 A.M.; Antigua Broadcasting Service, 16 hours and 15 minutes (Sundays, 10 hours and 35 minutes). Radio Anguilla broadcasts 15½ hours a day, except on Sundays, when it closes down between 8 A.M. and noon.

76. Names for time ratings vary from island to island. "A premium" is considered the time period in which the most people are tuned in.

77. Adapted from *Market Profile Trinidad, Radio Trinidad* (London: Rediffusion, 1969).

78. News and community board announcements are broadcast hourly from 6:40 A.M. to 8:40 P.M.; weather six times a day and sports once in the morning and again in the evening. ZDK varies its weekend schedules to include religious and children's shows.

79. For example, tiny Radio Anguilla receives at least 150 request letters a day from a population of about 6,000.

80. Personal interview, Ray Smith, Head, Caribbean Broadcasting Union, St. George's, Grenada, May 12, 1971.

81. Personal interview, Winston Hinkson, Director, WIBS, Castries, St. Lucia, May 8, 1971.

82. Personal interview, Jeff Charles, Manager Designate, Radio Dominica, Roseau, Dominica, May 6, 1971.

83. Interview, Theobalds. In its reorganization plans of 1969, WIBS recognized that the amount of time allocated to the substations would have to be increased if they were to be enticed to stay in WIBS. Thus, it was proposed to break the 16-hour broadcast day into four 3-hour segments and a 3-hour-and-45-minute period. Each island would produce one 3-hour segment for distribution to all four islands. The longer period in the evening would be local broadcasting, each substation handling shows exclusively for its local listeners. This proposal came about as the other Windward Islands contemplated splitting from WIBS and establishing their individual national broadcasting systems.

84. R. Bobbie Moore, "Lecture on the Socio-Historical Background of the Caribbean," *Link* (April–September 1970), p. 13.

85. Personal interview, Leo de Leon, Program Director, 610 Radio, Port of Spain, Trinidad, September 1, 1970.

86. Roppa and Clarke, *Commonwealth Caribbean*, p. 22. Only 7.6 percent of

the weekly fare of the five television stations in the region in 1968 was devoted to news. This usually took the form of one or two news bulletins a day for a total of 20 minutes.

87. *Daily Gleaner,* September 23, 1964, p. 18. See also John Maxwell, "Towards Good Radio," *Public Opinion,* February 8, 1958; *Daily Gleaner,* November 6, 1962, p. 8; *Daily Gleaner,* January 25, 1966, p. 5.

88. Central Rediffusion Services Ltd., *Commercial Broadcasting in the British West Indies* (London: Butterworth's Scientific Publications, 1956), p. 37.

89. Interview, Ghany.

90. Personal interview, Jody Owen, Program Director, ZDK Radio, St. John's, Antigua, May 4, 1971.

91. Interview, Dodge.

92. The other Bahamian station, ZNS-2 also concentrates on a news-music format but includes a number of foreign comedy and drama series: "Clitheroe Kid," "Paul Temple and the Geneva Mystery," "Sing Along with the Country-men," "The Newcomers," and "Just a Minute," all BBC: "American Musical Theatre," "Scope—UN Magazine," "France Applauds," "Green Dolphin Country."

93. Central Rediffusion, *Commercial Broadcasting,* p. 12.

94. Personal interview, Chris Nuthall, Regional Programmer, Verbatim, Inc., St. John's, Antigua, May 5, 1971.

95. "Statutes of the Caribbean Broadcasting Union," mimeographed (Grenada, April 13, 1971).

96. Interview, Smith.

97. For example, the community announcements on ZNS Radio in the Bahamas include items such as: "To Reverend Smith: Make arrangements for my arrival at Abaco. Signed Reverend Jones"; "Mrs. Hinkle of Cat Island is asked to contact Mrs. Brown at General Hospital as soon as possible"; "To Sara Hopkins of Grand Bahama: Your father had a successful operation. Resting well." Besides these messages, the station also includes birth, death, wedding announcements, ship-loading and arrival times, lost and found and other classified-type notices.

98. Obituary announcements are preceded by funereal music. The announce-ments themselves list background on deceased, names of all relatives, and funeral plans.

Japanese on Hawaii advertise funerals by radio because of the distinctive characteristics of Japanese burial services there—the wake must be immediately after the death. See Donald W. Klopf and John P. Highlander, "The Radio Obituary: Cultural Phenomenon in Broadcasting," *Journalism Quarterly* (Summer 1964), pp. 440–42.

6

Mass Media and Major Cultural Aspects of West Indian Society

A former United States State Department official, Charles Frankel, classified cultural exchange in three categories. In the first stage (according to Frankel) "cultural exchange was simply an accidental by-product of the contact between different groups," while in the second period the process was planned, representing the

> triumph of one's own culture over the cultures of others. [It] was not accidental, but was deliberately sought and promoted. It was a motive as well as a consequence of war, of commerce, of imperial organization and imperial rivalry.[1]

The third stage was characterized by a heavier volume and intensity of cultural exchange, penetrating more deeply than earlier and including more organized institutions participating in the information flow.

In the Commonwealth Caribbean recorded cultural exchange commenced in stage two of Frankel's categories. As European explorers came to the islands, they superimposed their institutions and values on those of the Caribs and Arawaks, to the extent that the latter cultures were virtually demolished.

As the plantation system developed in the islands, millions of Africans were taken out of their societies and shipped to the British West Indies as slaves. In the process they, too, were stripped of their cultural identities.

This chapter will discuss the presence of a number of cultural

factors—many dating to the colonial period—that are directly or indirectly related to mass communications in the islands.

"VIEW FROM THE DUNGHILL"

Ayeast,[2] Sherlock,[3] and Lewis,[4] among others, have repeatedly
stated that, unlike Asian and African colonies, the West Indies, upon
receiving independence, had no previous culture with which they
could identify. The result, as Gordon K. Lewis, professor at the University of Puerto Rico, has made clear, is that the West Indian is a
"schizoid person, . . . *peau noir, masque blanc*,[5] the possessor of a
pseudo-European culture in an Afro-Asian environment."[6]

The confusion and contradiction of such an existence has afflicted
institutions and individuals alike, and it is not unusual to find examples
such as that of calypso king "Mighty Duke," who, on one hand sings
proudly,

> I am black and proud
> And I am glad that we are rid of this old slave
> mentality.
> And everybody young and old growing afro
> And telling the world that black is beautiful,

while at other times, he lets it be known that he scorns certain African
dress.

In the schools, children learned about Gladstone and the queen,
rarely about sugar and calypso; in the libraries, the litterateur read
novels set in London, not in Kingston or Port of Spain, there being no
West Indian literature until the second third of the twentieth century.

Williams,[7] Lewis,[8] and Singham[9] have shown the effects of an
imposed, metropolitan-type of education, with British curricula, textbooks, and examinations in island schools. Children struggled to sort
out the world of reality for themselves, as they read from books made
in England and usually irrelevant to the West Indian scene. They
learned arithmetic problems in terms of pounds and shillings when
the local currency was usually in dollars and cents; they sang about
"tripping through the snow to grandfather's house on Thanksgiving
Day," this, one author said, "in a Caribbean society where it is often
difficult to ascertain the father of the child."[10]

On the other hand, it is altogether possible that had the British
gone the other route and developed a locally based education, they
would have been accused of building an insular feeling to lock the

native into his current situation, thus depriving him of the world view that he needed.

When in 1962 television was proposed for Trinidad & Tobago, an editorial writer pointed out that the medium might help Trinidadians learn something about themselves. He felt that such knowledge was necessary, for

> It is probably true that there are no places in the world less known by many Trinidadians today than these same islands of Trinidad & Tobago, their people, and their potentialities.[11]

The results of exported education were sarcastically explained in a calypso, entitled "Dan the Man," written in 1963 by the "Mighty Sparrow." Here are a few stanzas:

> According to de education you get when you small
> You will grow up wid true ambition and respect from
>   one and all
> But in my days in school, they teach me like a fool
> The tings dey teach me a should be a block headed mule.
>
> Listen what dey teach me.
> Pussy has finished his work long ago and so he resting
>   and ting.
> Solomon O'Grundy was born on a Monday,
> The ass in the lion's skin.
> Winken, Blinken and Nod sailed out in a wooden sloop
> They say de goutie lose he tail and de aligator trying
>   to get monkey liver soup
> And Dan is de man in the van.
>
> De lessons and de poems dey write an' send from England
> Impress me they were trying to cultivate comedians.
> Comic books make more sense, you know it is fictitious
>   without pretense,
> C. O. Cutteridge wanted to keep me in ignorance.[12]

If we listen to the writers on West Indian education, then "Mighty Sparrow" was not far off the mark; the colonizers did aim to keep him and his fellow West Indians in ignorance. Elementary education, for example, was meant for the masses; secondary education only for the elites. Formal communications media designed their content for the elites, not for the poor, illiterate slaves, while literacy was limited to the whites, a few coloreds, and almost no blacks. According to Dizard, anywhere the European colonialists happened to be, the policy was the same. He felt that it was a method of control:

> The European colonialists controlled their empires by withholding literacy and more advanced education, a policy far more effective in stifling opposition than putting "the natives" in chains. Education was limited largely to the training of clerks to serve the colonial administrators.[13]

A result of the implanting of British culture on the West Indians has been the nurturing of false meanings of intellectualism on many islands. Even today many West Indians believe that the only good education is that which is gained abroad, and an intellectual is one "who writes letters to the local newspaper or possesses a 'certificate' from some third-rate commercial institute run by profit-hungry managers."[14]

Lewis felt that whole cultures in the West Indies were permeated with negative effects of the British cultural exchange, citing the examples of Barbados, the Leewards, and Caymans. According to him:

> The Puritan heritage perhaps also explains the cultural backwardness of Barbadian life, for there is no adequate civic centre, no modern museum, no evening newspaper, no good theatre. . . . So pervasive is "Bajan" provincialism, that a novelist like John Hearne can enlarge his creativity in Jamaica while George Lamming feels his genius would be stifled in Barbados.[15]

The Leewards, Lewis contended, were equally culturally neglected, perpetuating a philistine way of life where

> genteel respectability reigns supreme. There is the same song recital by the local soprano; the same church bazaar opened by the Administrator's wife; the same choral competition under official patronage; the same lecture on Keats or Shelley by the visiting American eminence; the same newspaper stories about the upbringing of the children of the Royal Family; the same ceremonial opening of the Legislature; the same state dinners and garden parties at Government House, religiously noted by the local newspaper gossip writers.[16]

Cultural traditionalism has been faulted as one of the main causes of the societal lag of the Caymans, Turks and Caicos, and Grenadines, to the extent that Carriacouan society copies cultural conditions that existed in Grenada sixty years ago.[17]

The problems created by the elites of colonial societies who assiduously imitate the language, dress, social customs, and political patterns of the colonizer have been discussed by numerous writers. For example, Singham noted this paradoxical situation, whereby

> despite rebuffs and his own ambivalence, the colonized individual continues to imitate, not only because it is necessary for the advancement of his career but because the authoritarian personality produced by colonialism encourages imitation rather than creativity.[18]

Singham[19] and Williams,[20] among others, have talked about the frustration inherent in imitation: no matter how high an individual may rise, he never knows if he did it on his own. And Lewis[21] has said that if there is a common West Indian culture, it was created not by the mimicking elites, but rather by the social classes at the bottom of the social ladder or, in his terminology, "the view from the dunghill."

In imitative societies, according to Eric Williams, the scholarly prime minister of Trinidad and Tobago, the "authentic and relevant indigenous formulations are either ignored or equated with subversion." Although examples of authentic works by West Indians abound—literature of a high standard by Lamming, Naipaul, and Walcott and the steel bands and calypso native to Trinidad—Williams nevertheless complained that

> artistic, community and individual values are not for the most part authentic, but possess a high import content, the vehicles of import being the education system, the mass media, the films, and the tourists.

The result, Williams added, is a psychological dependence on the outside world, thus crippling Caribbean self-confidence and reliance, and setting up a vicious cycle in which

> psychological dependence leads to an ever-growing economic and cultural dependence on the outside world. Fragmentation is intensified in the process. And the greater the degree of dependence and fragmentation further reduces local self-confidence.[22]

PATOIS, CREOLE, "ENGLISH ENGLISH"

Colonialist interference in the Commonwealth Caribbean stemmed not only from the British; the French and Spanish had left their marks before the English arrived. Trinidad until 1798 had been a Spanish colony inhabited by Spanish and French settlers; Jamaica had also been Spanish-controlled. During the incessant wars of the European powers during the eighteenth century, islands such as St. Lucia and Dominica had new occupiers regularly. Each change of government disrupted and modified the way of life, leaving impacts upon the government, economy, religion, and the individual himself.

For example, the Windward Islands, because of their French occupation as well as their rugged terrain, were never slave economies to the extent that other islands were. Whereas the Leewards and Barbados (which have had unbroken connections with England) have been Protestant, the Windwards are predominantly Roman Catholic. Even the personality of the Trinidadian, according to Lewis, has been affected by Trinidad's late entry into the British Empire. Lewis states that

> unlike his Barbadian or Kittitian brothers, [the Trinidadian] escaped the debilitating effects of centuries of bond slavery, which perhaps explains today his style of raucous ebulliency as compared to the social deference of those others.[23]

However, it was linguistically that the French and Spanish had their profoundest and longest-lasting effects upon the islands. Some would argue that the influence of these two languages on the region added to the complexities of fragmentation and separatism; others would claim that the result has been beneficial in that the masses were given their distinct languages. No matter which side one argued, he readily realized that in these English-speaking islands the masses were speaking something other than English. He also recognized, as have a number of scholars,[24] that the political boundaries were oftentimes at variance with the linguistic borders.

In the Windwards, the creole language is French patois; in Trinidad & Tobago, the creole takes on both Spanish and French accents. The result has been that many people of the Windwards who still speak French patois can communicate with their fellowmen on the French islands of Martinique and Guadeloupe but not with residents of Antigua or Barbados who speak a creole based on English. If linguistic groupings had been used as a basis for a cultural unit, it is more than likely that Dominica, St. Lucia, Martinique, and Guadeloupe would have formed one state.

Dependence upon the creole varies, but is probably most intense on Dominica and St. Lucia, where it has been estimated that more than 95 percent of the inhabitants use patois as their mother tongue; not more than a third of these can express themselves in English.[25] Lepage pointed out how the influences lingered longer in some islands than in others:

> For complex historical and sociological reasons, Creole French has been retained much longer in some islands than in others—it has virtually disappeared in St. Vincent, is rapidly disappearing in Trinidad & Tobago and Grenada, but is still widely spoken in St. Lucia and Dominica. . . . In Trinidad, Spanish is a small item in the inventory of complication; the Creole French patois of previous generations is now given way to Creole English, which in turn is full of Creole French loanwords and has also been influenced by the Tamil and Urdu of East Indian estate labourers.[26]

The degree of creole usage can be related to the social status attached to the language. On Jamaica, for example, creole is considered "just bad English"; on other islands, teachers and parents discourage its usage. Taylor said that because creole is identified with slavery, it is spoken of as a "monkey language" or as no language at all.[27]

Until 1941 it was illegal to use patois in St. Lucian and Dominican schools, and as late as 1953 schools still posted notices declaring "patois forbidden here." The low social status attributed to the language produces problems for children who, having heard the vernacular in their homes, mix it with the English they learn in school, the resultant mixture inhibiting them from any kind of creative expression.

Taylor believed that the future fortunes of the creoles are dependent upon their speakers' "ability to adapt them to new requirements of communication . . . in a changing world."[28] By this Taylor meant incorporating the creoles into mass media and official and business transactions. But so far, unlike Papiamentu, the creole of the Dutch West Indies, French patois and English creole have not been extensively adapted to modern mass media usage. For example, on Jamaica, where a person speaking basic creole has difficulty understanding messages in standard English, the media do not use the creole at all.

As a result, according to Alleyne (writing in the early 1960s), the masses do not understand the content of the mass media:*

> It is certain that the most severe difficulties are experienced in the comprehension of the communications of the formal media such as radio, the newspaper and of ceremonial occasions such as public broadcasting, legal proceedings, etc.[29]

Comprehension of the mass media is further hindered when editors and broadcasters not only refuse to use the creole, but also insist upon writing and speaking "English English." One broadcaster in the region complained that Windward Islands Broadcasting Service newscasts were couched in British ways of saying things. "You can't talk about 'fiscal' when talking to the masses about money matters," he explained.[30] He felt that radio communicates to the banana plantation owner, not to the banana worker. A television executive on Antigua refuses to use dialect in programming because he would "rather stick with proper English; that dialect is not the Antiguan's way of talking."[31]

The problem is not a new one. Traditionally, Commonwealth Caribbean elites had difficulty getting the attention or into the frames of reference of the masses,** to the extent that when democratization came to the area during the 1930s and 1940s, politicians resorted to employing journalists as their interpreters to the masses. Previously they had had no need to communicate with the common man.

A St. Lucian editor, Stanley Reid of *Crusader*, said that the situation has not improved much, that the number-one communication problem in the islands still results from language, that is, the majority of the people speaking patois or creole and the media speaking English.[32] His newspaper, along with two other media on St. Lucia, has attempted to alleviate or lessen the problem by using patois in its

---

* This point was apparent in research conducted in St. Lucia in 1974. A listenership survey revealed that 86 percent of those sampled preferred a St. Lucian/West Indian accent on radio (Everold Hosein, "Mass Media Preferences, Media Credibility and CARICOM Awareness in Urban St. Lucia," *Caribbean Monthly Bulletin* [July 1975], pp. 14–20). In another study, it was found that farmers on Dominica and St. Lucia did not listen to radio because they did not understand it. Eighty percent of the farmers favored patois as a broadcast language (T. H. Henderson et al., "Constraints to the Adoption of Improved Practices in the Windward Islands Banana Industry" [mimeographed report available at University of West Indies, Mona, Jamaica]).

** A group of Caribbean developmental communicators meeting in December 1974 agreed that a major problem of the region was the language dichotomy, "elite" versus "mass" traditional language. (Supplement to *Intermedia* 2, no. 4 [1974]: iii.)

pages. WIBS has also broadcast a few programs in the dialect, usually in an effort to reach the farmer.*

However, in most cases, media personnel said that the use of dialect is either too expensive, too limiting, or too unpopular. Radio Caribbean, located on St. Lucia but servicing the French islands· of Martinique and Guadeloupe as well, uses French as a second broadcast language, thus reaching the part of its audience that speaks the French-derived patois. But the station manager pointed out how expensive it was to maintain such a unique broadcasting situation, that is, using two languages to broadcast to two different types of culture on three different islands.[33]

A soap opera, "The Fergusons of Farm Road," is produced in Bahamian dialect and aired over ZNS once a week. It, too, is expensive to produce and, even with a sponsor for the show, the station only breaks even. The popularity of the show is uncontested, however. It is aired in the evening and repeated at noon on Thursday, courtesy of the tourist minister, who felt that people working in the tourist trade should be able to hear it too.[34] St. Lucia Television Service also has aired a few patois programs, but they were not popular.[35]

Nor has creole found its place in the literary output of the region. Frank Collymore, editor of the chief literary magazine in the islands and called by many the "father of West Indian literature," attributed the lack of creole works to the limiting characteristics of the language. "If the dialect is too narrow, it doesn't afford the work enough of an audience," he said.[36] The limiting aspects of dialect were pointed up a few years ago when Caribbean Broadcasting Corporation Television in Barbados was showing soap operas produced in Jamaican creole. Barbadians complained that they could not understand the dialogue.

All in all, the islands find themselves in the perplexing situation of many new nations; having no national language, they must carry out the business of modernization in the metropolitan tongue. A difference does exist between emerging nations elsewhere and those in the British West Indies. Alleyne, discussing it, wrote:

Nationalistic movements usually resurrect old national vernaculars. In most cases, though, the vernacular is not genealogically

---

* In 1976 Radio St. Lucia, Radio Caribbean, St. Lucia *Crusader*, and Radio Dominica were using patois. Radio Caribbean uses one-and-a-half hours daily of patois, including a weekly request show. The station hopes to broadcast as many as six hours daily in the dialect. Radio Dominica airs one-half hour of patois daily (Personal interview, Winston Foster, assistant manager, Radio Caribbean, Castries, St. Lucia, January 10, 1976).

related to the rejected language; not considered a sub-standard form of the literary and standard language, as in the West Indies. Rather the vernacular in those cases is an indigenous language, distinctively and genealogically different from the standard literary language.[37]

Thus, because the islands do not have an indigenous language to which to revert, the media may be doing the region a service by forcing audiences into a standard, recognized, and common area-wide language.

Although the motivations behind the perpetuation of English as a common region language may not be the finest, the fact that the people have an international base of communication could offset many of the disadvantages encountered.

MEDIA FOR THE WHITE-COLLAR WORKERS

Just as culture, education, and language were designed by the British for the British, so were the newspapers. Actually, they were probably founded for a market that, in this case, represented the upper-class buying power, or the British. Unless an editor was independently wealthy, he could not start a newspaper for the lower classes, which had neither the purchasing power nor the literacy level to support the medium. In addition, very little communication existed, or needed to exist, between the ruling elite and native population, the latter made up mostly of slaves. Alleyne said that in colonial days:

> The affairs of the colony were conducted largely in the interests of the Colonial Office and this elite. Communication within and between them was easily achieved through the medium of Standard English, and the masses of the population who spoke nonstandard English did not, or was [sic] not required to participate in discussion or decision making.[38]

Finally, foreign-imposed media were important to colonialism in that they sustained the occupant's culture and afforded the colonists channels through which they could speak to other colonists. Fanon, speaking more generally, said that the media were elite-oriented in colonized areas to keep occupants close to civilization, *their* civilization:

In the hinterland, in the so-called colonization centers, it is the only link with the cities, with the metropolis, with the world of the civilized. It is one of the means of escaping the inert, passive, and sterilizing pressure of the native environment. It is, according to the settlers' expression, the only way to still feel like a civilized man.[39]

Because newspapers have traditionally been perceived as an elitist symbol, especially in developing areas, a great amount of prestige has been attached to the reading or mere possession of them. Even today many Jamaicans pick up the *Gleaner* not so much for its information as for its prestige value. A Jamaican editor told the story of construction workers who regularly are seen with the *Gleaner*, "reading" it upside down. He said that the *Gleaner* is synonymous with the word *newspaper* in Jamaica, so that emigrants return from Europe saying continental "gleaners" are not as nice as they are in Jamaica.[40]

With some Commonwealth Caribbean media, the tourist has replaced the colonizer as the market for mass media. *The Bajan*, a newsmagazine published on Barbados, is designed for the white tourist, not for the black Barbadian. "It proclaims the white beaches of the island, pushes the products of hotels, airports and duty-free shops," according to one of the magazine's editors.[41] Bahamian magazines also are aimed at the tourists. And Caribbean Broadcasting Corporation, during peak tourist months, televises a preponderance of United States, Canadian, and European fare for the benefit of tourists who represent the buying power at which advertisers aim their messages.

Attempts are being made to reach a larger segment of the blue-collar workers through the formal media. Both the Trinidad *Guardian* and Jamaica *Gleaner* have mass-oriented evening papers, the *Evening News* and *The Star*, respectively. Radio stations such as ZDK on Antigua, Radio Antilles on Montserrat, Jamaica Broadcasting Corporation, ZNS in the Bahamas, and 610 Radio on Trinidad have taken the common man into consideration when designing programs. Radio Antilles has taken considerable Windward Island listenership away from the more elite-oriented WIBS, for example. A Dominican broadcaster said that the Montserrat station, with its popular fare, is hitting northern Dominica so hard that "you'd think the station were located on Dominica."[42]

"BLACK NEWSPAPER" AND RUMOR

One of the mistakes the modern world tends to make about the traditional and transitional worlds is that they do not have communications networks just because they do not conform to modernistic informational systems. But, in colonial times, while the elites had their mail boats, newspapers, and private clubs as communication centers, the West Indian slaves had talking drums, music, folktales, symbols, gossip, and rumor. Sherlock has said that "rooted in his holdings and villages, the peasant spoke through his folksongs and stories."[43] An offshoot of the folksong, the calypso native to Trinidad has been significant enough as a purveyor of information* that writer V. S. Naipaul has called calypso "the ballad, the broadsheet, the *Punch* and *New Yorker* of Trinidad."[44]

An interpersonal communications net is comfortable to the West Indian, who usually lives in small communities where "the myriad ties of kinship, friendship, neighborhood and associational membership bind everything into an elaborate complex of mutual obligation."[45] This is especially true on smaller islands with populations varying between 6,000 and 100,000. However, most of the populations on the larger islands also live in these small villages, there being only one major city on each island.

A Bahamian editor said that, because the islands are small, people feel an obligation to spread information so that everyone knows the news before his paper comes out. In fact, he lamented that his paper is often accused of being inaccurate because a reporter was not on the spot when something happened, whereas a number of the villagers were there.[46]

In the smaller islands the masses probably do not need formal media channels to carry on communications with each other and with their leaders, at least on local matters. Why would an Anguillan or Dominican have to inferentially feed back information to his leader through letters to the editor, talk shows, and so on, when all he has to do is confront the leader personally? For example, a St. Lucian youth told this author that when his parents could not get the mayor to move some garbage that was in front of their home, they went to the prime minister's office and presented their problem to him personally. When this author sought an interview with the head of the Anguilla government, a taxi driver drove him directly to Ronald

---

* As one professor of government at the University of West Indies said recently, "If you really want to know what is going on in Trinidad, go to the calypso tents." (Los Angeles Times Service dispatch in *Philadelphia Inquirer*, March 25, 1975, p. 8-A.)

Webster's office, and without any prior notification, the interview was granted.*

Lewis, writing about the features of West Indian society that make it more traditional[47] than modern, delineated a number of interpersonal communications traits:

> Passion for intrigue; malicious gossip, the famous Trinidad *mauvais langue;* the enormous public importance that accompanies every private event; even death becomes an important social event and funerals important social symbols so that, as one commentator has put it, "a death notice in the Trinidad *Guardian* can cause more uproar and indignation than a Rudranath Capildeo statement from London"; the public character of daily life that makes anonymity almost impossible, so that the habit of spiteful scandal-mongering, of the gazette neg, the backyard talk, leaves almost nobody untouched, at any social level; and the same quality explains why a well-kept secret is a West Indian rarity.[48]

Alleyne, studying Jamaican communicative processes, concluded that the significant communications on that island "would seem to be the stimulus of human speech rather than that of the subsystem of writing (newspaper) or of the secondary technique of radio."[49]

Yet, in an area populated by some 3.9 million people, about 550,000

---

* A December 1974 conference on developmental communications for the Caribbean also noted the importance of oral, person-to-person contact in the region, stating that there was too much emphasis given to mass media. "In numerical terms, Caribbean society is not a mass. Its people can be reached with relative ease and in comparatively short time. . . . Moreover, Caribbean society was seen basically as a participatory rather than a competitive society and its major form of communication as 'traditional' employing the methods of oral, person-to-person contact rather than those of the mass media." (Supplement to *Intermedia* 2, no. 4 [1974]: ii.) A recent research project in the Windwards showed that farmers in those islands do not utilize formal mass media to obtain new ideas on the growing of bananas. Part of the reason was that over one-half of the growers were illiterate, the remainder barely literate. The farmers said that they normally did not listen to agricultural programs on radio because they did not know about them, or the programs are aired at inconvenient times, or the farmers do not own radio receivers. The researchers concluded that the constraints in the persuasive communication process are: credibility of the communication source, source commitment, logic of the message, characteristics of the channel used to communicate, and characteristics of the farmers (T. H. Henderson et al., "Constraints to the Adoption of Improved Practices in the Windward Islands Banana Industry" [mimeographed report available at the University of West Indies, Mona, Jamaica]).

copies of newspapers circulate among them. And, as in many developing regions, a high proportion of these 550,000 copies are passed from hand to hand until they are almost tattered.

In most Commonwealth Caribbean societies, a combination of formal and interpersonal communication channels is utilized, so that on St. Vincent, for example, a few rural people pick up the weekly *Vincentian*, read it, and spread the news via the "black newspaper," the term used there for word-of-mouth communications.[50] On Dominica, as in most islands, nondaily newspapers are published on market day, Saturday, with the hope that rural people coming to town will pick up the newspapers and later share the contents with illiterates in the villages.[51] Radio also plays a significant role in this two-step flow of information. In the Windward Islands, banana-cutting notices are announced over radio, informing rural people of the best times to bring their bananas to market. Because the times are consistent, most people do not listen to the notices. When there is a change in the recommended banana-cutting time, those people who hear the radio announcement take it upon themselves to spread the vital information by word of mouth.[52] In the out islands of the Bahamas, people must listen to radio to find out when the mail boat will arrive with newspapers, mail, and supplies. Radio is used in place of nonexistent telephone service on some islands, especially in the Bahamas, where people use ZNS to send messages back and forth between Nassau and the out islands. Besides community service programs designed for this purpose, ZNS also airs "Hospital Calling," a Saturday evening program that allows hospital patients to talk over the air to their friends and relatives in out islands.

When radio and television made their debuts in the British West Indies, social commentators questioned the effects they would have on traditional communicative patterns. With television, for example, "will the good conversation in the homes come to an end?" or "will the folktales be dropped by the wayside?" they asked. One writer, fearing television, pointed out that thirty years previously "most families entertained themselves daily with good, witty and enlightened talk, and music performed by friends and members of each household," but radio changed all that.[53] On Trinidad another commentator[54] worried that television's advent would do away with bedtime stories and folktales, and instead, children would fall asleep to the sounds of "Huckleberry Hound" or "Lassie."

But as Fagen, among others,[55] has said, the modern media do not simply supersede or displace other channels; "rather they link existing networks while giving rise to a host of dependent nets which service, disseminate, and frequently transform their product." Probably conversation has not dwindled in the Commonwealth Caribbean since broadcasting began; it still goes on but now, in many cases, in response to speech sounds emitted by radio and television amplifiers rather than by human voice boxes. According to a 1968 UNESCO team that surveyed media in the region, even newspapers have stimulated a great deal of conversation. For example, on Dominica a large number of newspaper purchasers buy all three weekly newspapers on Saturday and "spend the Sunday happily arguing over them."[56] Rural people in Jamaica, sitting on the stoops of village shops watching television, will, during the course of a discussion program, argue about what they are seeing and hearing. "If the television said so, it usually is so among these rural people," a Jamaican broadcasting official said.[57] In Barbados this author observed patrons of a guest house vigorously discussing program content while the television show proceeded. The general manager of Caribbean Broadcasting Corporation said that this was a normal trait of Barbadians.[58]

Although, as we shall see later, West Indians are extremely hesitant about letting their views be known by way of formal media, they spend hours on end in rum shops, markets, pentecostal meeting halls, the "run-about," or barber shops discussing political and agricultural subjects. In St. Kitts rum shops, a Grenada guest house for the laborer, an Antiguan inn—nearly everywhere one might find the common man— the talk centers around political topics, people taking sides and voicing the slogans of their parties and leaders. Upon entering any public place on Anguilla, a native is immediately greeted with "What's new down there?" or "What's happening, mon?" and in each case one senses that the words are more than just greetings.[59] Certainly face-to-face communication is not absent in more technologically developed nations, but in basically nonreading communities such as most of these islands it is the principal means of disseminating political news.[60]

The accuracy of information that travels over these informal networks is seldom questioned in the islands. Pye, speaking about transitional societies generally, said that this results from the tendency in these cultures for people to appraise the reliability of the information "on the basis of their personal relationship with the source of information."[61]

The following example shows how false information was spread in Jamaica, without much questioning on the public's part. When two Russian ships docked in Kingston for refueling just four days before election day in 1962, the casual news of the ships' arrival was, within two days, transformed into a rumor and spread over the entire island. The rumor had it that there was a threat of Russian take-over in Jamaica should the ruling party be returned to power. The prime minister felt obligated to make hourly radio announcements denying the rumor; when his party lost at the polls, he attributed the defeat to the propaganda's effect.[62] DaBreo ascribed great importance to rumor in the West Indian social structure, saying that "certain official secrets have a tendency of becoming known unofficially to certain persons by means that only these persons know."[63]

There is unanimity about the swiftness with which information is dispatched over what I shall call *the palm-tree telegraph.* For example, tourists on Anguilla told me about their hotel reservations and car and boat rentals being made in advance without the use of formal media or the telephone or telegraph. In his studies Alleyne mentioned this characteristic also.[64] But, here a personal example experienced on a smaller island will be related. After trying unsuccessfully to contact a former information officer by telephone, I asked about him in the town square, leaving a message with three unsystematically chosen people that if they saw him, they were to tell him to look me up at my guest house. Two hours later, the former information chief was in my room, willing to talk with me. The message had reached him.[65]

ISOLATED, FRAGMENTED, AND SMALL

The lack of intercommunication among West Indian islands is not unique; such a phenomenon is a trait of most former colonies. However, the problem in the Commonwealth Caribbean is compounded by two additional factors: distances between islands, and water (see fig. 1).

Time and again, in Asia, Africa, and Latin America, it has been exemplified that transportation and communications in colonial units were meant to benefit the colonialists, not the colonized, and were designed to tie the colony to the mother country, not one island or colony to the other. Cable colonialism[66] was the rule. A colony could not talk easily with a neighboring state without the information first being filtered through Europe, so that as late as the 1920s it was quicker to send a letter from Jamaica to Barbados by way of England than to try to send it directly.

Schiller, speaking generally, felt that such outgoing communications reinforced the controls of a few Great Powers over subject territories and peoples. Like the fabled colonial railroads that continue to run from materials supply centers in the interior to coastal ports and are almost entirely useless for internal transport, non-Western communications also were primarily outgoing.[67]

In the Caribbean communications has been so outgoing—outgoing, that is, to Europe—that

> differences in metropolitan associations makes [sic] Martinique more remote from neighbouring Barbados than is distant London; and Curaçao, an hour's flight in the south from Barbados, is a foreign country as compared with Canada.[68]

Awareness of the problem goes back a number of years. For example, a British Royal Commission of 1882, studying public revenues of Jamaica, Grenada, St. Vincent, Tobago, St. Lucia, and the Leewards, concluded:

> It has been the custom to maintain an independence of others which may have been excusable in former days, when communication was infrequent and difficult, and when there were neither telegraphs nor steamers, when each island was actually separate from the others . . . a state of things entirely superseded by the present day.[69]

The only fault with this statement was the overly optimistic prediction of interaction after the advent of the telegraph and steamer.

West Indian isolation was strengthened by the colonial governments that found the island borders a convenient administrative and political unit. The result, according to Smith, has led to fragmentation in and among the islands, no cooperation for unitary states being available.[70] Sommerlad recognized the same pattern in Africa, where the colonial splitting of that continent created "a fragmentation which not only produces political tensions but hinders economic, political and social development."[71] Others, such as Hobson, saw sinister motives in colonial policies of isolation and fragmentation, saying that the expansion of the British Empire had been "compassed by setting the 'lower races' at one another's throats, fostering tribal animosities," and utilizing these factors for the benefit of imperialism.[72]

Federation attempts in the islands have failed largely because of this separatist mentality of the West Indian. As Sherlock said, "When a man says 'I am a Jamaican' or 'I am a Barbadian,' he is very likely expressing the broadest allegiance he knows."[73] As another author pointed out, it is difficult for the "ordinary Kittitian or Grenadian to feel that he and the Jamaican he has never met are both part of the same West Indian community."[74]

A poor communications system among the islands, resulting in the lack of trust and information territories have of each other, has led to the fragmentation dilemma, according to authors such as O'Loughlin[75] and Lewis. Lewis blamed the failure of federation in the late 1950s and early 1960s on the lack of contact among island peoples:

> For the degree of intimacy between societies depends upon the availability of cheap and frequent communications. The theory of the "two West Indies" will . . . disappear as communications facilitate regular and easy travel within the region.[76]

In turn, strong insular pride and rivalry have been nurtured by the isolation, some islanders feeling that their own nations are the center of the universe. Lewis said that on Barbados it is still "a hazardous enterprise to suggest that the other islands are better in some ways."[77] Size of island[78] and degree of urbanization have complicated the problem, developing a jealousy whereby the larger islands look down upon the smaller ones. The situation became so absurd that small islands such as St. Kitts and Antigua looked down upon smaller dependencies such as Nevis, Anguilla, and Barbuda. The smaller Leeward and Windward islands, feeling that they are the backwater of the West Indies, are always trying to catch up, collecting the paraphernalia of statehood and/or modernity in the process: Dominica, St. Kitts, Anguilla, and Antigua have set up expensive radio and television systems mainly for prestige.

Thus, attempts at regionalization must compete with national pride, and most island governments are still reluctant to expend their finances and energies for regional operations.* For example, in the area of broadcasting, the director of a region-wide radio network, WIBS, said:

> Any money individual islands spend must be earmarked as going to the island's people. Certain insularity on the part of government

---

* On March 2, 1975, the *New York Times* reported that regionalism was on the rise again in the English-speaking Caribbean, as evidenced by a proliferation of conferences among the heads of government and the formation of a new regional common market, Caribbean Community, or CARICOM.

leaders exists for political reasons, but the real insularity arises from the feeling that the smaller territories were "had" by the bigger ones who pulled out of the 1958 federation. So the small islands look after their own interests first.[79]

Traditionally, the larger islands, through their media, communicated with each other but not with the smaller territories. Although very little information about the Leewards and Windwards appeared in larger-island media, these small islands nevertheless had to use Trinidadian, Jamaican, and Barbadian media because they themselves did not possess such sophisticated and costly media.* The director of WIBS talked about this state of affairs, pointing out that he sees changes being made in the direction of more inter-island media use and reliance:

> During World War II, we listened to Trinidad radio, read Trinidad papers. No one in Trinidad reads our *West Indian* [on Grenada] but we read the *Express* of Trinidad today. Smaller units look to the larger but this trend is being reversed now with some regional operations. Also complicating the situation is the split between Eastern Caribbean and Western Caribbean spheres of interest. There has been an exchange of broadcast programs in East Caribbean for years but not with Jamaica. Jamaicans have a reluctance to give carte blanche to other East Caribbean stations. Jamaica would not have confidence and respect for East Caribbean stuff. The Bahamas also do not have a West Indian consciousness.[80]

Although smaller islands today have their own broadcasting operations, many still depend on larger-island newspapers to give them printed enlightenment. Thus, the Barbadian and Trinidadian newspapers are very popular in the East Caribbean and the *Daily Gleaner* of Jamaica in the Caymans. In one of the few surveys conducted, Singham found, a decade ago, that Grenada's most popular newspaper was the old *Mirror* of Trinidad, followed by the Trinidad *Guardian* and Barbados *Advocate*, and the most popular radio station was Radio Guardian of Trinidad, not WIBS of Grenada.[81] Media personnel on the

---

* The smaller islands are not in the immediate plans of the Caribbean News Agency. Subscribers are media from the larger islands. The CANA head said that although small-island media have inquired about linking up with the news agency, they really cannot contribute much to its success now (Personal interview, Harry Mayers, head, CANA, Christchurch, Barbados, January 12, 1976).

smaller islands still admit that among the most-read newspapers are those from the bigger islands, not their own weeklies.*

Insular megalomania, resulting from the pride, jealousy, and rivalry of the territories, oftentimes leads to a parochial attitude whereby island leaders, as well as the media, guard against outside criticism. Lewis touched upon this matter when he said:

> The small island complex, indeed, is a thorny prickle that can damage the hand of any careless outsider. There are political ministers who fear that their views may appear in public print and will say nothing to you.[82]

Partly for that reason, Eric Gairy, leader of Grenada, threatens outside media, including *Look* magazine, for what they have written about him and Grenada; Trinidad's Eric Williams refuses to see American reporters, still seething about the bad press he received at the hands of a *Wall Street Journal* reporter; Ronald Webster shows dissatisfaction that East Caribbean mass media did not take seriously enough Anguilla's stand against St. Kitts. Jamaica's former prime minister, Hugh Shearer,** had narrowed down the culprits causing his island's problems to the local bigots and the "sensational journalists who advertise them." One writer elaborated on Shearer's feelings about outside media covering Jamaican happenings:

> He has hotly scolded *Time* for its sensationalism and the Copley News Service for what he calls "irresponsible inaccuracies and dishonest statements." Shearer's particular bêtes noires are free-lance writers who "gravitate towards the mischievous, ill-equipped, and consequently disenchanted individuals in the society." Both free-lance writers and staff writers, according to Shearer, get their material in the air-conditioned bars of hotels where they ply their informants with liquor. Faced with a free press abroad and a run of problems at home, a government leader through the paranoiac mists,

---

* The results of a 1974 study on St. Lucia give a different picture. The sample of 100 St. Lucians answered that Radio Caribbean (40 percent), Radio Antilles on Montserrat (36 percent), and Radio St. Lucia (14 percent) were the most popular radio stations. For news programs, the St. Lucians chose Radio St. Lucia (37 percent), Radio Antilles (33 percent) and Radio Caribbean (20 percent). The most widely read newspapers, according to this survey, were *Voice of St. Lucia* (88 percent), Trinidad *Express* (25 percent), St. Lucia *Crusader* (16 percent), Barbados *Advocate-News* (6 percent), and Trinidad *Guardian* (6 percent) (Everold Hosein, "Mass Media Preferences, Media Credibility and CARICOM Awareness in Urban St. Lucia," *Caribbean Monthly Bulletin* [July 1975], pp. 14–20).

** He was succeeded by Michael Manley and his People's National Party, voted into power in 1972.

fancies witches brewing a conspiratorial plot. "We are tempted to wonder," Shearer has said, "if there is not a worldwide journalistic conspiracy to organize a campaign to discredit the achievements of countries such as ours, and to overemphasize our problems and deficiencies—a sort of lopsided defense of past imperialism."[83]

Bermuda, protecting her vital tourist trade, is hypersensitive to reports in United States and British newspapers about recent uprisings there. So are a number of other tourist islands worried about their social evils being exposed to the world. Any visitor to Bermuda or the Bahamas would be quick to recognize that his pleasure is paramount, "and anything likely to upset him is eschewed; hence, in fact, the colour bar and hence, too, the active censorship which helps insulate the Bahamian populace against knowing much about outside conditions."[84] Concerning the latter point, a Bahamian editor pointed out how unaware of the outside world many of his people are. He related the story of a Nassau man who visited Andros Island during World War II and realized that, when he mentioned the conflict, Andros Islanders thought he was talking about World War I, which they did not know had ended.[85]

The smallness of the islands has also had an impact upon reporting and advertising practices. A St. Lucian editor, among others, said that his paper's chief problem related to the personal relationships that develop on small islands. The problem he faces is that emotions intermingle with reporting and "reports become partial and prejudiced."[86] A Trinidadian editor felt that publication of a news story should not be based on whether it will affect a personal relationship between a reporter and the person he is writing about. He added:

> Papers tend to be in the firing line if they take an activist role. If the paper stumbles onto a good story that the people must know and if they feel the party of the story will be embarrassed by the story, the story must be published nonetheless. In a small country such as Trinidad, pressures are bigger and reporters must have more guts and publish the news, whether embarrassing or not.[87]

The personalness of small islands also enters into advertising practices.* On St. Lucia, for example, merchants advertise mainly to

---

* This book has not dwelt much on advertising. For an account of more formal advertising practices in Jamaica, see Cecil Lindo, "Jamaica," in *International Handbook of Advertising*, ed. S. Watson Dunn (New York: McGraw-Hill, 1964), pp. 280–82. The report stated that an Advertising Agency Association of Jamaica had been formed in 1955, but died soon for lack of support. The major problem of advertising on the island then was lack of trained staff.

save face, the feeling in the small communities being that "if you can advertise, then you must be someone important."[88] Other businessmen on the smaller islands feel that advertising is a type of charity that is chalked up alongside their names. They think of it as a way to help a friend in the media industry.

MICROPHONE AND PRINT SHYNESS

Among the personality characteristics of the British West Indian that have been attributed to British colonialism are anomie, rage, compulsion, and withdrawal. Singham talked about the hostility and rage:

> The basic pathological nature of the society is thus reflected and reinforced by the pathology in the individual personality structure. One of the most noticeable and widespread characteristics resulting from this situation is the considerable amount of hostility that is always latent and often expressed in the society and the polity; expression of which ranges from the constant character assassination that marks colonial life.[89]

Any sample of Commonwealth Caribbean newspapers, for example, will reveal the character assassination and rage felt by the people, in their attitudes toward the United States and Great Britain as well as in their internal political arguments.

The individual trait of the Commonwealth Caribbean that probably has the most pervasive effect upon mass media is that of withdrawal. Everywhere in the islands one notes what a UNESCO team surveying the region in 1968 discovered—the general reluctance of ordinary people to speak out in public. According to the report and as we have just seen, this attitude is also shared by government leaders and officials.[90]

Pseudonyms still trail articles and letters in British West Indian newspapers just as they did 200 years ago, although, because of the smallness of the islands, it is doubtful that much concealment takes place behind the pen names. Sources of information are very hesitant to share what they know, thus handicapping reporters and broadcasters.

Various reasons are offered for this mike-and-print shyness, but the most popular explanation is related to the authoritarian nature of the societies today and their repressive colonial experiences. Again, according to Singham, this factor exists with any colonized people. It is so well embedded in the social and personality structures that even "those who rebel against the repression of colonialism retain their authoritarianism when they achieve power and try to introduce change."[91]

Thus, a Dominican editor said that people will meet him in the sea or in church and give him information but refuse to write it for print;[92] Antiguan editors and broadcasters indicated that their biggest problem was getting local news because people were afraid to speak out, especially during the long Bird government. On Trinidad an opposition leader, A. N. Robinson, gave this assessment of public opinion there:

> Trinidad today, is moving towards a claustrophobic society in which the dominant characteristic is fear—fear to express a conviction and fear to stand up for things in which one believes.[93]

A Trinidadian broadcaster agreed with Robinson:

> One of the biggest problems in broadcasting is a populace which in general is not eager to speak its individual mind in public. Too many people are afraid to voice convictions openly and stand by them. Opinions are hard to come by that are honest and too often they are not for publication if they are honest.[94]

It is definitely fear of authoritarian reaction that keeps Grenadians from speaking anything other than positive attributes about their island and its leader, Eric Gairy.* One editor, who has suffered the wrath of the leader, said that Gairy gives himself God-like characteristics; the people reinforce his egocentric behavior by rushing to WIBS to outdo their neighbors in saying good things about Gairy.[95] Barbadian and St. Lucian editors[96] were more specific in describing the reason for this fear of government reprisals. They claimed that people are afraid to write about political matters because those most qualified to do so are also civil servants who stand to lose their positions.

Fear of being quoted was observed on most islands, but especially in Jamaica, the Leewards, and Grenada. A Jamaican broadcasting manager, for example, asked that he not be quoted on a national development question because the government would wonder what right he had to an opinion on the subject; a former governmental information officer on another island told this author to correspond with him

---

* Eric Gairy's party, United Labour, made an issue of full independence in the February 1972 election and was swept back into power.

in language couched with phrases such as "regarding the good things you had to say about your leader," when in actuality he had said the opposite of the administration. Another broadcaster gave me a document about his station, and asked that I not quote from it or tell anyone who cared to know that I found the paper in a wastebasket.

The editor of the *Labour Spokesman* on St. Kitts said that he was too busy to give me much time when I answered that I was going to write the interview down. Once he did consent to the interview, he answered many questions by claiming ignorance, having been on the job for only a year, or by laughing queries off, or by referring me to other offices that were closed, it being Saturday. A broadcaster said that he should not be quoted because he would lose his civil service job for being disloyal; still another media manager answered questions as though he were reading a release, being very deliberate in what he said. The manager of St. Kitts radio was busy and said that he would write down the "information you want" and deliver it. The following day one of his staff brought a one-paragraph description of the station to my guest house; the statement was made up of data that one could get from any world-radio handbook.

Editors on St. Kitts, Antigua, and Grenada were more secure if they had a colleague along for the interview. Media executives on Antigua and St. Kitts, in particular, answered questions with yes and no only, even to queries that required more than an affirmative or negative reply. WIBS personnel were hesitant to speak out about governmental control over the substations, and the man assigned to provide me information on WIBS broadcasting on St. Vincent was a Grenadian who was there helping to set up programs.

The severity of the problem in these tourist islands was discussed by Lewis:

> It is, all in all, a general picture of almost total economic and financial control used ruthlessly against anyone who dares oppose the oligarchies in business and politics. . . . Fear and intimidation, indeed, induce a climate of secrecy in the society as a whole.[97]

The British West Indian masses are definitely fearful of expressing viewpoints in public or, as they call it, being "read up" in the newspapers and on radio. Their concern is based on the repercussions they might face from the authorities, plus the ridicule they might receive within the closely knit communities. Listing his main programming difficulty as the inability to get people on the screen, a St. Lucian television director said:

They seem to fear TV. There are no professionals here and the amateurs are afraid their mistakes show up too easily on TV. They appear once, get a lot of criticism from friends and won't appear again.[98]

A St. Vincent broadcaster said that on the small islands people hesitate to express political views publicly because they are afraid that they will offend someone else who is on the other side of the issue. Thus, he said, politics is a very personal topic to them.[99] For the same reason, a former St. Lucian editor, now Speaker of the House, said that media must strike a "median between extremes and not be too rash one way or another."[100]

SUMMARY

Scholars enumerating the sociocultural influences upon the Commonwealth Caribbean nearly always start with the imprint that colonialism has left. They point out, and sometimes lament, that the implanting of foreign cultures, first Spanish and French and later British and African, obliterated the native Carib and Arawak institutions. In addition, they feel that British colonialism made mimics of the intellectual classes, imported too many "made in England" education-and-language patterns, and generally confused the West Indian, to the extent that even in the latter one-third of the twentieth century he has very little idea who he is.

Invariably these students of the cultures emphasize the key roles played by communication, or the lack of communication, during this process of cultural exchange. For centuries until not many years ago, the pattern in the region has been to create media for the elites and white-collar workers, not the laboring classes. However, in most cases, these same scholars fail to mention that because of the poverty and literacy levels of the masses, the development of the media could not have taken another course. Today the big mass-circulation dailies, as well as the electronic media, are reaching at least part of the blue-collar audience.

The fact that, for so many years, the masses could not afford or read newspapers did not preclude them from having their own communication networks. Even today interpersonal communication channels play a very important role in Commonwealth Caribbean life.

Although the diversity of language patterns of the region does not complicate communication as it does in India or the Philippines, there are still problems. Especially in the Windwards and Jamaica, media personnel complain that the language of the people is either a French-derived patois or English-based creole, while the language of the media is standard English. St. Lucia stands out as an island where mass media are occasionally printing and broadcasting in the language used by the majority of the people.

The isolated, fragmented, and small nature of the islands has also had effects upon the manner in which communication takes place in the Commonwealth Caribbean. For years, and to a certain degree now, the water and distance barriers as well as colonial philosophy made it more practical to communicate with or through London, rather than directly with neighboring islands. The fragmented characteristic of the region stymied efforts at more productive regional approaches, although this situation is gradually being remedied. Because of their smallness, these territories, along with their leaders and the mass media, have tended to guard against both external and internal criticism, fostering an inhibition in West Indians to say what is on their minds.

NOTES TO CHAPTER 6

1. Quoted in Herbert Schiller, *Mass Communications and American Empire* (Boston: Beacon Press, 1971), pp. 13–16.

2. Morley Ayeast, *The British West Indies: The Search for Self-Government* (London: George Allen & Unwin, 1960), p. 14.

3. Philip Sherlock, *West Indies* (London: Thames & Hudson Ltd., 1966), p. 13.

4. Gordon K. Lewis, *The Growth of the Modern West Indies* (London: Macgibbon & Kee, 1968), p. 393.

5. Loosely translated, "a little black, white mask." Probably closer to title of a book by Frantz Fanon, *Black Skin, White Masks*.

6. Lewis, *Modern West Indies*, p. 393.

7. Eric Williams, *From Columbus to Castro: The History of the Caribbean 1492–1969* (London: Andre Deutsch, 1970), p. 460.

8. Lewis, *Modern West Indies*, p. 87.

9. A. W. Singham, *The Hero and the Crowd in a Colonial Polity* (New Haven, Conn.: Yale University Press, 1968), p. 77.

10. Williams, *History of the Caribbean.*

11. "Television for Trinidad," Trinidad *Guardian,* November 1, 1962, p. 10. For a similar quote about Jamaica, see "Sir Alex Opens Television Service," *Daily Gleaner,* August 6, 1963, p. 1.

12. Quoted in Singham, *Hero and Crowd.* Cutteridge was an English writer of textbooks used in the West Indies.

13. Wilson Dizard, *Television: A World View* (Syracuse, N.Y.: Syracuse University Press, 1965), p. 229.

14. Lewis, *Modern West Indies,* p. 394.

15. Ibid., p. 254.

16. Ibid., p. 142.

17. Ibid., p. 337.

18. Singham, *Hero and Crowd,* p. 11.

19. Ibid.

20. Williams, *History of the Caribbean,* p. 501. See also John Hearne, "The Creative Society in the Caribbean," *Saturday Review,* September 14, 1968, p. 62.

21. Lewis, *Modern West Indies,* p. 28.

22. Williams, *History of the Caribbean,* pp. 501-2.

23. Lewis, *Modern West Indies,* p. 197.

24. For discussions on artificial political boundaries that have broken up linguistic groups, see Fred R. von der Mehden, *Politics of the Developing Nations* (Englewood Cliffs, N.J.: Prentice-Hall, 1964), p. 37; James W. Markham, "Investigating the Mass Communication Factor in International Behavior," in *Mass Media and International Understanding* (Ljubljana, 1968), pp. 125-26; Dankwart A. Rustow, "Language, Modernization, and Nationhood—An Attempt at Typology," in Joshua A. Fishman et al., *Language Problems of Developing Nations* (New York: John Wiley & Sons, 1968), p. 87; Sherlock, *West Indies,* p. 136.

25. Douglas Taylor, "New Languages for Old in the West Indies," in Joshua A. Fishman, ed., *Readings in the Sociology of Language* (The Hague, Netherlands: Mouton, 1970), p. 613.

26. Robert B. LePage, "Problems To Be Faced in the Use of English As the Medium of Education in Four West Indian Territories," in Fishman et al., *Language Problems of Developing Nations,* p. 434.

27. Taylor, "New Languages," p. 614.

28. Ibid., p. 616.

29. Mervin Alleyne, "Communications and Politics in Jamaica," *Caribbean Studies* 3, no. 2: 28.

30. Personal interview, Winston Hinkson, Director, WIBS, Castries, St. Lucia, May 8, 1971.

31. Personal interview, Vernon G. Michaels, Manager, ZAL-TV, St. John's, Antigua, May 4, 1971.

32. Personal interview, Stanley Reid, Editor, *Link* and *Crusader*, Castries, St. Lucia, May 8, 1971. This problem was discussed by a Government Information Service official on St. Vincent. He said that the people really enjoy West Indian films shown by government mobile film units because of the accent. "They don't understand the accent of the foreign movies so easily. They don't get upset about the films being portrayals of whites; it's the accent that bothers them." Personal interview, Leon Huggins, Head of Film Division, Government Information Service, Kingstown, St. Vincent, May 10, 1971.

33. Personal interview, John Whitmarsh, Station Manager, Radio Caribbean, Castries, St. Lucia, May 7, 1971.

34. Personal interview, Jack Dodge, General Manager, ZNS, Nassau, Bahamas, April 26, 1971.

35. Personal interview, Ken Archer, Director, St. Lucia Television Services, Castries, St. Lucia, May 8, 1971.

36. Personal interview, Frank Collymore, Editor, *Bim*, Bridgetown, Barbados, May 14, 1971.

37. Alleyne, "Communications . . . in Jamaica," p. 52.

38. Ibid., p. 28.

39. Frantz Fanon, *Studies in a Dying Colonialism* (New York: Monthly Review Press, 1965), p. 71.

40. Personal interview, Fred Seal Coon, Editorial Manager, *Daily Gleaner*, Kingston, Jamaica, August 26, 1970. Doob related similar African cases of media used for prestige purposes. One African "had to listen" to the 7 P.M. BBC news because he "had to be in the presence of BBC sounds" at that hour. Leonard W. Doob, *Communication in Africa: A Search for Boundaries* (New Haven, Conn.: Yale University Press, 1961), p. 286.

41. Personal interview, John Wickham, an Editor, *The Bajan*, Bridgetown, Barbados, May 14, 1971.

42. Personal interview, Jeff Charles, Manager Designate, Radio Dominica, Roseau, Dominica, May 6, 1971.

43. Sherlock, *West Indies,* p. 155.

44. James R. Ullman and Al Dinhofer, *Caribbean Here and Now* (London: Macmillan & Co., 1968), p. 95. Menzel would call the calypso a "quasi-mass communicator." He points out, for example, that speakers in election campaigns are quasi-mass communicators, possessing characteristics and payoffs that are "intermediate between those of mass and interpersonal communications." Herbert Menzel, "Quasi-Mass Communication: A Neglected Area," *Public Opinion Quarterly* (Fall 1971), pp. 406-9.

45. Lewis, *Modern West Indies,* p. 24. Doob theorizes that when life centers around the local community so solidly and contacts with the outside world are few, people are less interested in what they cannot perceive directly. "The amount of communication by people everywhere is roughly the same, only the depth and scope vary. Originally Africans communicated a great deal about a limited number of topics; now, as they widen contacts, they communicate much less about a larger number." Doob, *Communication in Africa,* p. 257. For other discussions of the important role of interpersonal communications in developing regions, see Daniel Lerner and Wilbur Schramm, *Communication and Change in the Developing Countries* (Honolulu, Hawaii: East-West Center Press, 1967), p. 11; Max Millikan and Donald Blackmer, eds. *The Emerging Nations* (Boston: Little, Brown & Co., 1961), p. 5.

46. Personal interview, Leon Turnquest, Editor, Nassau *Guardian,* Nassau, Bahamas, April 26, 1971.

47. One writer felt that it was difficult to label the West Indies a traditional society. Kroll said: "But even the term 'traditional' demands significant qualification in the West Indies, for no traditional society exists in the sense that such is found in Africa, Southeast Asia and elsewhere. Yet despite the heavy overlay of colonial rule, a sub-colonial, distinctively local, social system has developed, and this sub-system, with its origins in slavery, indenture, non-British commercial institutions, and the non-public reaction to colonial governance emerges in a prominent position in post independence." Morton Kroll, "Political Leadership and Administrative Communications in New Nation States. The Case Study of Trinidad and Tobago," *Social and Economic Studies* (March 1967), p. 18.

48. Lewis, *Modern West Indies,* p. 24. The loudspeaker is a communications tool used extensively on some islands. This author witnessed loudspeakers and public address systems in use at political meetings and parades in St. Kitts; Alleyne discussed their role in Jamaica. For example, during the revolt on Anguilla, the leaders said that their public address system was invaluable. "I had this PA system and traveled around the island, got people together and gave them the last reports. As long as I keep them informed, they know what to expect. They then in turn spread the information," Anguillan leader Ronald Webster said. Personal interview, Ronald Webster, The Valley, Anguilla, April 29, '1971.
Webster's public address system was one of the only means of reaching the

masses on an island that did not have a newspaper, radio station, telephones, or telegraph at that time. Since then, besides the development of a newspaper and radio station, the British have provided the people with another public address system.

The role played by the loudspeaker on St. Vincent is that of a barker, according to Government Information Service. When the GIS mobile film unit goes into the countryside to show educational and feature movies, the loudspeaker pulls the people together. "A good loudspeaker is a necessity," one official said. Interview, Huggins.

49.   Alleyne, "Communications . . . in Jamaica," p. 53.

50.   Personal interview, Weston H. Lewis, Editor, *Vincentian*, Kingstown, St. Vincent, May 10, 1971.

51.   Personal interview, S. A. W. Boyd, Editor, Dominica *Chronicle*, Roseau, Dominica, May 5, 1971.

52.   Ibid.

53.   Hugh Morrison, "Live Arts," *The Bajan* (February 1965), p. 26.

54.   "Bed Time Stories Days Are Over," *Sunday Guardian*, October 28, 1962.

55.   Richard Fagen, *Politics and Communication* (Boston: Little, Brown & Co., 1966), p. 45. Black said that the "means of mass communications are as efficient in sustaining the traditional as in disseminating the modern." C. E. Black, *The Dynamics of Modernization* (New York: Harper & Row, 1967), p. 160. Lerner and Schramm discussed the best mix of mass communications with interpersonal communications. Lerner and Schramm, *Communication and Change*, p. 28. Feliciano and Flores reported that in the Philippines mass media are used to reinforce oral channels. In Lerner and Schramm, *Communication and Change*, p. 296. Millikan and Blackmer believed, however, that face-to-face communications must give way to more impersonal systems if modernization is to take place. Millikan and Blackmer, eds., *Emerging Nations*, p. 21. Davison said that person-to-person communications is important in emerging nations as a way to give wide currency to ideas disseminated through the mass media. He said that it plays a role, too, because of the limited coverage of the media and because many people have not learned to rely on modern communications even when these are available. W. Phillips Davison, *International Political Communication* (New York: Frederick A. Praeger, 1965), p. 142.

56.   Guy Roppa and Neville E. Clarke, *The Commonwealth Caribbean: Regional Co-Operation in News and Broadcasting Exchanges* (Paris: UNESCO, 1968), p. 17.

57.   Personal interview, L. H. Stewart, Assistant General Manager, Jamaica Broadcasting Corporation, Kingston, Jamaica, August 28, 1970.

58.   Personal interview, Ian Gale, General Manager, Caribbean Broadcasting Corporation, Bridgetown, Barbados, September 4, 1970.

59. See African examples of same trait in Doob, *Communication in Africa,* pp. 125, 257.

60. Alleyne, "Communications . . . in Jamaica," p. 37. Almond and Coleman agreed that certain structures we usually consider part of "primitive societies" are found in modern systems and not always as marginal institutions, interpersonal communications being one example. Gabriel A. Almond and James S. Coleman, *The Politics of the Developing Areas* (Princeton, N. J.: Princeton University Press, 1970), p. 20. See also S. C. Dube, "A Note on Communication in Economic Development," in Lerner and Schramm, *Communication and Change,* p. 95.

61. Lucian Pye, ed., *Communications and Political Development* (Princeton, N.J.: Princeton University Press, 1963), p. 24. Editors on Anguilla and Dominica pointed this out. "Most people look at the *Beacon* as me," the Anguillan editor said. On Dominica the editor of the *Chronicle* said that he doesn't go after the news; it comes to him. "I used to have a reporter or two but I don't need them. On big news items the people won't trust a reporter anyway and they bring the information to me," he said.

Speaking about informal media channels in Algeria, there called *Arab telephone,* Fanon felt that information transmitted over these nets was unchallengeable. Fanon, *Dying Colonialism,* p. 78. Possibly, when information is scarce or suppressed and therefore valuable and vital, the distortion rate diminishes. Of course, as Schramm has mentioned, the distortion rate will depend upon the type of information transmitted.

> Word of a great event—Gandhi's death, the fighting in the Himalayas—news like this can be carried effectively by the grapevine. But interpretive material, explanatory and technical material, persuasive material—these are hopelessly distorted, if carried at all, by the grapevine.

Wilbur Schramm, *Mass Media and National Development* (Stanford, Calif.: Stanford University Press, 1964), p. 77. Kurt Lewin, David Manning White, and others would argue, too, that the more gatekeepers involved and the more elongated the news channel, the more distortion possible.

62. Alleyne, "Communications . . . in Jamaica," p. 37.

63. D. Sinclair DaBreo, *The West Indies Today* (St. George's, Grenada: Published by Author, 1971), p. 66.

64. Alleyne, "Communications . . . in Jamaica," p. 37.

65. A similar thing happened on St. Lucia. I was looking for the director of the WIBS substation there when a man came up to me, politely asked what I was looking for, and told me to leave a note at the main desk of this government building. Later in the evening, while at a resort bar, the same man came up to me, asked if I had found the director and told me where he was at that moment. I found out later that this man was the attorney general of the island.

66. Rosalynde Ainslie's term. Ainslie, *The Press in Africa: Communications Past and Present* (New York: Walker & Co., 1968), p. 191.

67. Schiller, *Mass Communications,* p. 127.

68. Sherlock, *West Indies,* p. 12.

69. Roppa and Clarke, *Commonwealth Caribbean,* p. 5. Such isolation was welcomed by colonial authorities during plantation days for it kept the slaves ignorant and conformist, and the islands themselves weak and subservient. Curtin said that the printed media of Jamaica, just before Emancipation, helped keep the people ignorant and the island isolated from the rest of the world by filtering news to fit into the Empire mold. Philip D. Curtin, *Two Jamaicas: The Role of Ideas in a Tropical Colony, 1830–1865* (Cambridge: Harvard University Press, 1955), p. 58.

Hobson, in his classic *Imperialism,* felt misrepresentation of facts and forces was the basis of imperialism, whose gravest peril "lies in the state of mind of a nation which has become habituated to this deception and which has rendered itself incapable of self-criticism." J. A. Hobson, *Imperialism* (Ann Arbor, Mich.: The University of Michigan Press, 1967), p. 211.

70. M. G. Smith, quoted in Singham, *Hero and Crowd,* p. 26.

71. E. Lloyd Sommerlad, *The Press in Developing Countries* (Sydney, Australia: Sydney University Press, 1966), p. 24.

72. Hobson, *Imperialism,* p. 138.

73. Sherlock, *West Indies,* p. 90.

74. Ayeast, *British West Indies,* p. 13. See also Roppa and Clarke, *Commonwealth Caribbean,* p. 57.

75. Carleen O'Loughlin, *Economic and Political Change in the Leeward and Windward Islands* (New Haven, Conn.: Yale University Press, 1968), p. 155.

76. Lewis, *Modern West Indies,* p. 371. Theory of two West Indies refers to the present situation where the region, because of distance and water, is split into Jamaica and the Eastern Caribbean.

77. Gordon K. Lewis, "Danger of Being an Outsider," *Daily Gleaner,* July 27, 1958. See also Singham, *Hero and Crowd,* p. 268.

78. Williams, *History of the Caribbean,* p. 116; Ayeast, *British West Indies,* p. 13.

79. Personal interview, Ray Smith, Director, WIBS, St. George's, Grenada, May 12, 1971.

80. Ibid.

81. Singham, *Hero and Crowd,* p. 67.

82. Lewis, "Danger of. . . ,".

83. Horace Sutton, "The Palm Tree Revolt," *Saturday Review*, February 27, 1971, p. 37.

84. Lewis, *Modern West Indies*, p. 326; see also DaBreo, *West Indies Today*, p. 76. A St. Kitts editor felt that the media should neither hurt the tourist nor "put a blight on the country and damage its investment climate." He accused the opposition paper of doing that on St. Kitts with its articles critical of the government. Personal interview, George Lewis, Editor, *Labour Spokesman*, Basseterre, St. Kitts, May 1, 1971.

85. Personal interview, Sir Etienne Dupuch, Proprietor-Editor, Nassau *Tribune*, Nassau, Bahamas, August 22, 1970.

86. Interview, Reid.

87. Personal interview, Lenn Chongsing, Editor, *Guardian*, Port of Spain, Trinidad, September 1, 1970.

88. Interview, Whitmarsh.

89. Singham, *Hero and Crowd*, pp. 306–7.

90. Roppa and Clarke, *Commonwealth Caribbean*, p. 15. Millikan and Blackmer felt that this was an attitude shared by most colonized peoples. They attributed the reluctance to speak to the hierarchal structure of the society.

> Thus to an individual who has absorbed with his mother's milk the attitude that it is wrong to speak or even think freely until the duly honored elders and persons in superior positions have expressed their opinions, the concept of freedom of thought and expression may be an impossible one to accept.

Millikan and Blackmer, eds., *Emerging Nations*, p. 24.

91. Singham, *Hero and Crowd*, p. 10. See also Millikan and Blackmer, eds., *Emerging Nations*, p. 83.

92. Interview, Boyd. Boyd, while pointing out that all writing in the *Chronicle* is done by him, said that he even writes the letters to the editor. "A lot of higher-ups are afraid to get involved with the government so they come in and give me ideas and then ask me to write a letter to the editor for them. So I write a letter to myself. Other papers are doing the same thing here." While explaining the important role played by letters in his paper, *Royal Gazette*, Bermudian editor E. T. Sayer also discussed anonymity. "It's amazing in a small community like this how many people prefer not to have their names attached to a letter. . . . They say, and it's been an argument I think proved through the years, that people go by the personality writing the letters rather than what is contained in them," he said. Lenora Williamson, "Queen Honors 'Ted' Sayer for Services to Journalism," *Editor & Publisher*, August 22, 1970, p. 34.

93. A. N. Robinson, "Why the Government Should Resign," Trinidad *Express,* August 31, 1970, p. 13.

94. Personal interview, Leo de Leon, Program Director, 610 Radio, Port of Spain, Trinidad, September 1, 1970.

95. Personal interview, A. M. Cruickshank, Editor, *Vanguard,* St. George's, Grenada, May 12, 1971.

96. Personal interview, Wickham; Rick Wayne, Editor, *Voice of St. Lucia,* Castries, St. Lucia, May 7, 1971. Ralph Barney, studying mass media of the Pacific Islands, observed the same characteristic there. "Probably the item with the greatest impact, from a modernization or national development standpoint, is a standard regulation for civil servants which prohibits them from speaking through the media, a condition which strictly limits the amount of information about government that can possibly appear, and which particularly reduces the chances of information on individual initiative and innovativeness to appear in publications. Often, these colonial service regulations are picked up by the country when it gains independence." Letter to Author, Ralph Barney, Assistant Professor, Brigham Young University, October 7, 1971.

97. Lewis, *Modern West Indies,* p. 325.

98. Interview, Archer.

99. Personal interview, Claude Theobalds, Chief Program Officer, WIBS, Kingstown, St. Vincent, May 11, 1971.

100. Personal interview, W. St. C. Daniel, Speaker of House and Former Editor, *Voice of St. Lucia,* Castries, St. Lucia, May 8, 1971.

7

Production and Consumption
of Mass Media

A theoretician on mass media in the developing world, Daniel Lerner, has said that in order to evaluate a communication system, it is wise to begin with the conditions that make for an efficient functioning of all economic processes: the capacity to produce and the capacity to consume.[1]

In order to have the capacity to produce, a nation must have the economic capabilities to construct and maintain the physical plant of the mass media. According to Lerner's checklist, these items are needed for production: plant (buildings, utilities, and facilities), equipment (presses, film, cameras, amplifiers, transmitters, picture tubes, and eventually satellites), and personnel (reporters and editors, printers, scripters, actors, and producers).

The second half of Lerner's model includes the factors that determine whether the capacity to consume media spreads, and how rapidly. These are: literacy, motivation, and money. In other words, do the people have enough literacy training, motivation, and earning power to consume media products?[2]

In the Commonwealth Caribbean the more industrialized, larger islands are faring much better than the Leewards and Windwards in implementing Lerner's economic model for mass media. On the smaller islands at least newspaper patterns seem to revolve around this set of circumstances: with the use of outmoded equipment, inadequate plant, personnel usually poorly trained, and less-than-ideal distribution and transmission methods, a type of medium that is hard to read and expensive to afford is produced. (The frustration endured by most small-media personnel in the British West Indies is exemplified by the Allfrey Story related in Appendix D.)

This chapter will concentrate on the production and consumption factors discussed by Lerner, as well as on two closely related subjects: capital investment needed to start and sustain media production, and social overhead services necessary in the production, transmission, and reception of media messages. Thus, the chapter is organized on this basis: capital is needed to establish and maintain plant and equipment. Also needed concurrently are social overhead services (including what Lerner labels *utilities*) to keep plant and equipment functioning and to distribute the media products to the consumer, who must have the capabilities to understand and purchase them.

INVESTMENT AND MAINTENANCE CAPITAL

Initial investment capital for mass media production is hard to come by in a developing region such as the Commonwealth Caribbean. First of all, the very nature of most colonized society did not lend itself to saving,[3] the result being that there are very few wealthy West Indians. Second, when local entrepreneurs are available in these developing nations-in-a-hurry, they are very reluctant to invest in mass media that, at best, show only long-term profits. Editors on Grenada, St. Lucia, and Barbados confirmed this point.[4]

Finally, local entrepreneurs fear the competition offered by governmental or foreign concerns that have invested, or may possibly invest, in the communications industry. Except for the Trinidad *Express*,* there are very few independent media operations successfully competing with both the governmental and foreign mass media investors found in great numbers in the islands.

Because of these factors, media executives on at least the well-established newspapers can take a complacent attitude about the threat of competition. For example, a Barbadian newspaper executive can feel assured that his paper will not have to face daily competition, despite rumors to that effect, because the "initial costs of starting a daily would be prohibitive."[5] Or a *Gleaner* official can rationalize his paper's monopolistic role in Jamaica by saying that anyone with five million pounds can start his own paper,[6] knowing full well that not very many people of that wealth reside in the nation.

---

* *The Nation* in Barbados and *The Jamaica Daily News* should also be added to this category.

As would be expected, it is difficult to obtain information on the capital structure of Commonwealth Caribbean mass media.[7] This is not unusual; businesses generally are reluctant to release financial information. Because such information is difficult to obtain, the figures in the following two examples, although dated, are provided to give the reader some indication of the large capital outlay necessary to operate the largest media in the region.

The largest mass media corporation in the region is the Gleaner Company, which, by the end of February 1969 used a total investment of £1,978,046, or $4½ million (US). The shares in the company were divided in this manner: in 1965 the Gleaner Company, in order to allow wider investor participation, converted its 550,000 one pound ($4.75 EC) shares into 2,200,000 shares of 5/ par value each. By March 1969, 2,094,324 fully paid shares had been issued, the balance held in reserve. Among the shareholders were 373 Jamaicans. At the same date Gleaner shares were traded at 12/ each on the Kingston Stock Exchange.[8]

In 1966 Trinidad Publishing Company, publishers of the *Guardian* and *Evening News,* included among its investors 479 Trinidadians who held shares totaling $1,500,000 (TT), or $750,000 (U.S.). Foreign investment figures and total amount invested, accordingly, were not available. The 1966 balance sheet of the company gave some indication of its size. Total expenditures in that year amounted to $4,800,000 (TT),[9] or $2,400,000 (U.S.).

Among the region's media the Gleaner Company and Trinidad Publishing Company are exceptional in the amount of capital available and expended. For example, as late as 1968 the four-station Windward Islands Broadcasting Service was operating on a capital of $210,918 (EC), or approximately $105,000 (U.S.). Plans called for doubling that amount once the network was fully reorganized.[10]

Of course, newspapers and magazines on the smaller islands operate on even more limited budgets. *Bim* magazine, for example, keeps $500 (EC) on reserve, $215 of which was donated to the magazine to keep it publishing.[11] Without political party support most small island newspapers would fold, as would nondailies on the larger islands.

Except in a few cases, broadcasting in the islands has not been economically viable. Part of the reason stems from a lack of local capital, but the big ambitions of the broadcasting planners also stand in the way. Developing peoples are noted for being in a hurry, wanting to skip stages of growth that more-developed nations have endured.[12] They want the most of the latest and best, a costly and oftentimes frustrating proposition. Thus, small islands, such as, Dominica, St. Kitts, and Antigua, which in the long run will not be able to afford individual radio and television stations, enter into consortia with governmental and outside interests to develop high-priced broadcasting systems. For example, partly in an effort to keep up with its larger neighbors, the Antigua government, in a consortium of foreign and local interests, set up Leeward Islands Television Services as a full-status system. Today there are only 8,500 television homes in its coverage area, 5,500 of them on Antigua itself.

One small-island television system,[13] St. Lucia Television Service, has maintained its self-sufficiency partly because it has not set unattainable goals. A relay of Caribbean Broadcasting Corporation, the station was designed to require a minimum of facilities, equipment, and personnel. Studio headquarters are in an old, converted, army washhouse, and the equipment consists of only the barest necessities.[14] All programming is kept within the range of the station's earnings, and the staff, for the most part, is borrowed from a rental firm that is the parent organization of St. Lucia Television Service. Ken Archer, director of the station as well as an owner and manager of the rental firm, handles the programming, and two of his rental company employees install and maintain the sets in the homes. One of the latter men also doubles as a cameraman for the station.*

Archer said that television can never be financially successful in the small islands unless it is handled the St. Lucian way. His rationale was:

> We're making a profit which makes us unique in these islands. The bigger stations will have to wait six to seven years to see a return on their investment money. We're unique in that we can

---

* In 1976 I found that St. Lucia Television had not changed much since 1971. However, if government plans to merge Radio St. Lucia and the TV service materialize, an entirely different TV setup will come into existence. There is talk on St. Lucia of attempting to increase the number of TV sets in use from 4,500 to 10,000, of developing color television, and of establishing two TV operations—one by government for St. Lucians, another by Radio Caribbean for neighboring Martinique. Yet, broadcasting personnel told me repeatedly that there is no TV market on St. Lucia, that the island is too poor to support the medium, and too mountainous to make TV reception practicable and profitable. As one official said, St. Lucians cannot afford to pay EC$600 to $800 for a TV receiver. Another said that "TV on St. Lucia is a joke as it stands now. It is not practicable, however, for the government to expand TV, but they might do it anyway" (Personal interviews, Winston Hinkson, director, Radio St. Lucia, Castries, St. Lucia, January 10, 1976; Winston Foster, assistant manager, Radio Caribbean, Castries, St. Lucia, January 10, 1976; Brian Holden, director, St. Lucia Television, Castries, St. Lucia, January 9, 1976).

operate and make ends meet on such a small level. Those stations in the Commonwealth Caribbean broadcasting fulltime on a large scale are getting very little return on their investment.[15]

Pleading for more cooperation among the islands, Archer said:

> Without government ownership, Barbados television would be in big trouble. St. Kitts would have been better off had it set up a relay of Antigua television rather than initiate its own station. Antigua would have been better off as well. What is needed is more cooperation among the expensive media in these small islands. We were hoping to convince St. Vincent, Grenada, and Dominica to do as we have but there has not been much response from them.° St. Vincent has been looking for someone to do it all for them. Cable and Wireless was interested (although they are not now) in loaning facilities to the government there and relaying most programs from Caribbean Broadcasting Corporation in addition to providing some St. Vincent fare as well.[16]

But most islands are not apt to listen to Archer's plan; they would rather depend on outside capital to get the big system, making the following observation by Schiller realistic in the Commonwealth Caribbean:

> The poor, the small and the new states of the world unable to finance independently the establishment, maintenance, and operation of broadcast facilities rely increasingly on either foreign capital to both install facilities and provide packaging in a package deal, which quickly turns the broadcast structures into miniature Western (or Eastern) systems, or on a supply of temporarily low-cost foreign (mostly American) material which originally was produced to the specifications of commercial sponsors.[17]

When these nations feel compelled to adopt Western commercial systems, they also adopt the factors that commercialism depends upon —a mass audience, a standardized appeal, and the "want-creating

---

° In late 1974 the Caribbean Cable Television Company Ltd. began installation work on a cable television system in St. Vincent. The company planned to offer subscribers three channels: Barbados, Trinidad & Tobago, and one from their own studios for local shows, including local news. Caribbean Cable Television is a new company formed by Vincentians residing in the U.S. (*Combroad* [January–March 1975], p. 57.) Dominica since 1971 has reportedly taken the CBC relay; Grenada, a relay from Trinidad and Tobago Television (Personal interview, Brian Holden, director, St. Lucia Television, Castries, St. Lucia, January 9, 1976).

machinery that the consumer goods producers, who sponsor the shows, demand and receive."[18] Commonwealth Caribbean islands have neither mass audiences nor the "want-creating machinery" characteristics; therefore, in many cases, they must accept packages that tie their broadcasting to foreign programming and financial sponsorship.[19]

PRODUCTION: PLANT AND EQUIPMENT

Printed Media

The Commonwealth Caribbean shows the usual wide range of plant and equipment types found in developing nations with uneven distribution of population, resources, and economic base.

For example, a UNESCO report of newspaper equipment in 1968 showed that, of thirty-seven newspapers surveyed (including eight in Belize and Guyana), eleven still relied at least partly on hand composition, while twenty-three others had the use of linotype machines. Ten newspapers were printed on offset presses, usually combined with letterpress, which is used by thirty-four newspapers. Eleven other newspapers were produced on rotary presses, including several that shared the same presses.[20] Other newspapers, one of which was included in the UNESCO survey, use mimeograph.

For example, the Anguilla *Beacon* began operations with a hand-cranked mimeograph machine and moved up to an offset mimeograph when a Bostonian, hearing about the paper's plight in 1968, persuaded A. B. Dick Company to donate the new machine and Pan American Airlines to transport it to the Caribbean free of charge.[21] By using mimeograph perhaps the *Beacon*, as well as the Dominica *Star*, has started its operation in the ideal style for a newspaper in a small, developing nation: within the range of its capital and manpower. The same might be said for the Freeport *News* (Bahamas), which started operations in the early 1960s by flying copy to West Palm Beach, Florida, where the paper was printed. Later, when enough capital was accumulated, the *News* purchased its own offset press.

Largest and most modern of the newspaper plants in the Commonwealth Caribbean is the Gleaner Company on Jamaica. Built in 1969, the multi-million dollar complex occupies approximately two-and-a-half acres of ground space. Among the equipment is a six-unit Crabtree rotary press capable of producing four-color process work and additional spot colors on a number of pages. The Gleaner Company still maintains a 4½-unit Crabtree and web offset presses at its former

Modern plant of The Daily Gleaner, *Kingston, Jamaica.*

plant. The new structure includes conveyer systems to move copy between offices, as well as the largest and most complex air-conditioning unit on the island. Staff members are provided underground parking facilities, locker rooms with showers, cafeteria, restaurant, excellent lighting, and an office for their Provident Society.*

In 1971 the Bermuda newspapers were also contemplating the construction of a new plant. The *Royal Gazette* and *Mid-Ocean News* will convert to offset once they are settled in new quarters. The Bermuda Company has been at the forefront in its use of modern printing facilities; as early as 1965 *Royal Gazette* was among the few newspapers in the world that used computerization in typesetting. According to E. T. Sayer, editor-manager of the *Royal Gazette*:

We were one of the first newspapers to start using a computer for our typesetting. We took the first PDP-8 from Digital Equipment Corporation in Massachusetts in 1965, and we've been using it very

---

* In 1973 the Gleaner Company changed to computerized photocomposition, and by February 1975 the company's daily and Sunday newspapers were wholly produced by that process. (*Editor & Publisher*, April 19, 1975, p. 22.)

successfully since then. We're hoping of course to adapt it to photo composition, which it can easily do.[22]

Among other modern newspaper plants in the Commonwealth Caribbean are the Nassau *Tribune,* completely renovated in 1970, the Nassau *Guardian,* which uses web offset and IBM machines for typesetting, and the Antigua *Times,* an adjunct to a modern, offset printing business that was established in 1971.*

Although not housed in a newly built plant, the Trinidad Publishing Company seems to have sufficient modern equipment to publish its two dailies and *Sunday Guardian.* A Crabtree press is used to print the daily and Sunday *Guardian,* while comics are produced on a Duplex and the *Evening News* and color supplements are printed on a modern Goss.

Contrasted with these newspapers are the small-island nondailies, most of which are poorly housed and equipped. Their situation is especially precarious because most of them are considered too small and insignificant to attract foreign or local governmental help, without which they are not apt to change their status. On the whole, the present small newspapers in the region cannot expect advertising revenue to increase and thus provide funds for equipment and plant improvement. Small newspapers secure enough advertising to cover minimal financial requirements only.

Political party headquarters serve as offices for the main newspapers on Antigua (*Workers Voice*) and St. Kitts (*Labour Spokesman*) and the Dominica *Herald. Workers Voice* of Antigua is housed in an old, unpainted, frame structure that uses chicken wire as a room divider between the presses and union-leader offices. On St. Kitts the *Labour Spokesman* has cluttered quarters in the run-down party house. Confusion describes the scene at election times as people hang around the Labour Party house to be near the action, as well as to pick up their free sweaters, pins, badges, posters, and other election paraphernalia dispensed there. The *Spokesman* editor's desk is next to the window where these political gifts are dispensed.

Still other newspapers, such as the Anguilla *Beacon* and Dominica *Star,* are edited and printed in their editors' homes. The *Crusader* of St. Lucia is produced in an abandoned garage, although the paper's

---

* *The Jamaica Daily News* and Barbados *Advocate-News* are located in modern plants also. The *Advocate-News* moved into new U.S.$1¼ million quarters in 1974. Both newspapers use offset presses. The *Voice of St. Lucia* moved into a more modern building in 1975.

Offices of Workers Voice, *Antigua, housed in the party head-quarters shown here.* (Photo by John A. Lent.)

management plans to sell shares to obtain capital for a new plant.*

What would seem to be necessary equipment and supplies often-times become unaffordable luxuries on smaller Commonwealth Carib-bean newspapers. *Workers Voice* and Antigua *Star* editors complain that they don't have transportation vehicles and can't get to the scene of the news. Other papers face shortages of type faces, uniformly cut newsprint, and typewriters. Some offices are devoid of typewriters; all copy is handwritten.

The results are obvious. For example, the *Crusader* of St. Lucia appears in different tabloid sizes from week to week, depending on where the cheapest newsprint can be found and how it is cut. Other small newspapers, unable to obtain newsprint, have been known to skip issues, appear late, or print on blue or gray sugar paper, as did the Montserrat newspapers of the early 1960s.[23]

In 1965 the amount of newsprint used (all imported) by Common-wealth Caribbean was 450 tons in Bahamas, 900 in Barbados, 870 in

---

* The *Crusader* has moved into better quarters, but certainly not a new plant.

Bermuda, 7,700 in Jamaica, 4,500 in Trinidad, and a total of 200 tons in the other islands.*

Wrong fonts of type are used regularly, not only in the small-island papers but also in political weeklies on the larger islands. When the Grenada *West Indian* runs out of lower-case letters, stories are set in all capitals. The same paper uses an oversized newsprint sheet, the result being half-foot margins of dysfunctional white space.

Other newspapers also use newsprint that is oversized for their forms. For example, *Vanguard* of Grenada fills only 7 x 10½ inches of a 9 x 13½ format, and Dominica *Herald*, 9½ x 13½ of a 12 x 17 sheet. At least fifteen varieties of page sizes, ranging from the 7 x 10-inch *Beacon* of Anguilla to the 17½ x 23-inch *Gleaner*, can be found in the islands. The St. Lucia *Herald*, on an 8½ x 12½-inch format, uses five columns of 1½ inches of type, which makes for much hyphenation and difficult reading.

Some newspapers use incompatible printing techniques that handicap page design and give the poor reader a squinting moment or two. For example, the *Vincentian*, employing linotype and photo-offset, prints stories set on the linotype alongside others that have been photographed from either typewritten copy or London periodicals.

The paucity of photographs in most of the small newspapers adds to the dullness and readability problem. Sampling one day's newspaper content in the islands in November 1968, the UNESCO team found that only thirty-two photographs were used and that they appeared in the region's six largest papers.[24] Only the major newspapers on the larger islands subscribe to a foreign agency's photo service; most of the smaller papers rely on an occasional picture supplied by foreign government information services (mainly British Information Agency and United States Information Agency). At least one other, St. Kitts *Labour Spokesman*, uses photographs issued in conjunction with the publication *Unesco Features*. UNESCO found in 1968 that twenty-two of the thirty-seven area newspapers surveyed had their own block-

---

* Increased prices of newsprint have hampered newspapers in the region recently. Increased costs of newsprint forced the prices of Jamaican dailies from five to fifteen cents in two years (Personal interview, G. A. Sherman, general manager, Gleaner Company, Kingston, Jamaica, January 15, 1976). *The Jamaica Daily News*, like the *Gleaner*, did not make a profit in 1975, partly because of newsprint costs of U.S.$308 to $410 a ton, a 70 percent increase over a two-year period (Personal interview, J. C. Proute, editor, *The Jamaica Daily News*, Kingston, Jamaica, January 16, 1976. Barbadian editors were helped recently when the government dropped the twenty-five percent import duty on newsprint (Personal interview, Harold Hoyte, editor, *The Nation*, Bridgetown, Barbados, January 12, 1976).

making (halftone) facilities.[25] Some block-making is commissioned from commercial printers, locally or in the nearest large territory, usually Trinidad and Barbados. An unusual case is the Grenada *West Indian*, which owns a modern process camera and has engraving equipment available; but it cannot print photographs because the halftone technician left the newspaper to set up his own business. When smaller newspapers have had to depend on neighboring territories for film processing and engraving, the results were similar to that expressed by a former editor of *Voice of St. Lucia*. He said that the *Voice* used to send film to Barbados for processing, but by the time the finished photograph was returned to St. Lucia, its contents were no longer timely.[26]

Thus, generally speaking, the visual effect of most of the small-island newspapers depends solely on headlines and advertisements. As a result, editors[27] have been known to complain that they cannot compete with Trinidadian and Barbadian dailies, which use photographs.

Electronic Media

It would be safe to say that electronic media in the Commonwealth Caribbean are generally better off than printed media when it comes to physical plant and equipment. The reasons are: (1) the relative newness of Commonwealth Caribbean electronic media (especially television) means that physical plants and equipment are usually up-to-date; (2) the at least adequate financial and technical help these media receive from abroad; (3) a number of broadcasting units are owned by island governments that are willing to buy modern plant and equipment.

Among the larger radio stations in the region is Radio Caribbean, a modern 10-kilowatt unit on St. Lucia. The Radio Caribbean building contains 3,600 square feet of office space laid out on open-plan lines to add a "sense of comradeship between administrative, technical and programme staff."[28] In addition to a workshop, store areas, and editing/dubbing, and teleprinter rooms, the station has four studios designed for both one-man and group recording operations. German, Dutch, British, and American technical equipment is used at Radio Caribbean. The transmitter site employs modern 10-KW Collins equipment, served by a VHF link from the studios. Mobile VHF transmitters are used for outside broadcasts such as cycle races and carnival and sporting events.

Technical facilities of Windward Islands Broadcasting Service include: main offices, network studio center, receiver station, two 5-KW shortwave transmitter stations, and a local 550-watt transmitter, all on Grenada. On islands with WIBS substations, the equipment includes: 25-watt relay transmitters on Carriacou and St. Vincent; studio/offices on St. Vincent, St. Lucia, and Dominica; 500-watt local transmitter stations on St. Vincent, St. Lucia, and Dominica; and a new transmitter station under construction on St. Lucia. However, the studio/offices of the three substations are not adequately equipped for the programming needs of those islands.* For example, the Dominica substation is housed in a very cramped, closet-size room in the rear of the island library. In addition, substations do not have adequate record libraries or studio facilities to accomplish prolonged programming, according to WIBS personnel.[29]

Government-owned Trinidad and Tobago Television operates on two channels because of the geographical nature of Trinidad: the island is made up of three mountain ranges (Northern, Central, and Southern). To feed a signal to homes in the South, a transmitter is

Radio Anguilla headquarters; island was one of last to obtain formal mass media. (Photo by John A. Lent.)

---

* Since splitting with WIBS, Radio St. Lucia, Radio Dominica, and Radio St. Vincent have received new quarters.

located on the highest point in the Central range. Other transmitters are located in the Northern range and on Tobago. Channel 13 operates on 2,000 watts and Channel 2 on 33,000 watts; the Tobago transmitter operates on 1,200 watts. Videotape recording equipment was obtained by TTT in 1967; color television facilities in 1972. Outside broadcasts (OB) are done from time to time, although the station does not have its own OB unit.* The centrally located nature of the station and the use of microwave make the outside broadcasts possible.[30]

The Caribbean Broadcasting Corporation physical plant includes both radio and television facilities. Radio Barbados, the CBC radio station, has a control room/studio, recording room/studio, and a mobile van with VHF link. CBC-TV has one two-camera studio and presentation control room; a news/weather/sports remote controlled, single-camera studio; master control room; two black and white television camera chains; two videotape recording machines; and one two-camera mobile unit with link and videotape recording equipment.**

At least one broadcasting company, JBC, has its own airplane, used for public-affairs reporting.

Some broadcasting stations in the region do face problems concerning facilities and supplies.*** For example, the smaller radio stations lack up-to-date record libraries and studio facilities, while television units on Antigua and St. Lucia are hampered by insufficient film supplies. Leeward Islands Television Services, which cannot afford the high costs of producing film, cannot exchange programs with networks and other stations[31] because of the lack of standardization of videotape equipment in the islands.

In an effort to better equip smaller broadcasting units, a 1969 conference of heads of national broadcasting organizations discussed the possible loan of equipment between stations and the exchange of inventory lists of equipment. Also, the group suggested that stations attempt to order compatible equipment in the future, thus facilitating film exchange.

---

* See Deighton Parris, "Inexpensive TV Outside Broadcasting in Trinidad," *Combroad* (April–June 1973), pp. 35–36.

** In 1971 CBC-TV converted to color to become the third Commonwealth nation, after England and Canada, to do so. CBC-TV can also receive live pictures by satellite. By 1974 CBC-TV's general manager announced that the station planned to obtain some of the finest color television equipment in the world. (*Combroad* [April–June 1974], p. 59.)

*** Radio Bahamas until 1975, for instance, maintained separate quarters for the executive and production sectors of the station. An extension to the building now allows management offices and studios to be in the same building. (*Combroad* [April–June 1975], p. 72.)

Jamaica Broadcasting Corporation cannot use some of its new equipment donated by the United States government, because it is not compatible with the station's already existing equipment.* "We've got a political football where we cannot use the equipment, nor can we tell the United States we don't want their aid," an official at JBC said.[32]

A large amount of modern equipment owned by Trinidad and Tobago National Broadcasting is not being used either, but in this case the disuse stems from a lack of personnel trained in its use.[33]

PRODUCTION: PERSONNEL

Most newly emergent nations have found it necessary to start their rebirth with a shortage of communication skills.[34] The few trained communicators in these societies find too many more-lucrative offers to their liking and do not stick with journalism. They either drift off to governmental or industrial agencies or seek their fortunes in a more developed society. Pye, speaking generally of transitional societies, put his finger on the problem when he said:

> In large part the economic poverty of the mass media makes it impossible for the society to support a full community of professional journalists. Journalists in most of the new states tend to be so underpaid that they can hardly feel that they represent an independent force capable of criticizing and judging those who hold political power.[35]

When skilled personnel are available, they usually come from the United States, Canada, or Great Britain, or they were trained there.

---

* In 1974 JBC launched an ambitious modernization and expansion project, enlisting the aid of Nippon Television (Japan) and the BBC. Among priorities of the plan are: the establishment of a central building complex to house JBC, Jamaica Information Service, Educational Broadcasting Service, and other national programs; replacement of worn-out and obsolete equipment; improvement and expansion of transmission; provision of flexible and adequate outside broadcast and production facilities; provision of space and compatibility for the addition of a second program and color to television; development of Radio 2; and improvement of efficiency of administration and operations. (*Combroad* [April–June 1974], p. 54; *Combroad* [April–June 1975], pp. 13–18.) The general manager of JBC said that the expansion project is designed primarily to implement the proposals of the Dunton Report of 1956, the report on which the establishment of JBC was based (Personal interview, Dwight Whylie, general manager, JBC, Kingston, Jamaica, January 14, 1976).

Schiller feels that training of this nature consists of "how to run French, English, American style" media enterprises.[36] In countries with nationalistic aspirations, such as the British West Indies, foreign personnel and training are wanted only until a corps of trained nationals can be created. Once this is accomplished, invariably, at least in the Commonwealth Caribbean, efforts are intensified to remove the expatriates.

Media executives in the Commonwealth Caribbean complain incessantly about insufficient staff, often unsuitable foreign or in-service training, poor salaries causing internal and external migration of staff, and the narrow view of governments that often refuse work permits not only to Britishers and Americans, but also to West Indians from neighboring islands. Therefore, it is not too surprising to read of the closing of an island's only newspaper because the staff emigrated to the United States or Great Britain, as was the plight of Montserrat in 1959.[37] The same fate met the fifty-four-year-old *Daily Bulletin* of St. Kitts in 1968 when its staff left for better-paying jobs in the Virgin Islands.[38]

If expatriates (foreigners residing in the islands) are being denied work permits and local journalists are moving elsewhere, who are the mass media managers of the Commonwealth Caribbean?

In many cases they are individuals who backed into communications through other doors. Although numerous examples abound, the most unusual is that of Rick Wayne,* editor of the *Voice of St. Lucia.* While abroad in the United States and England, Wayne became a popular recording artist, editor of muscle-building magazines, and recipient of a number of awards, not the least of which were "Mr. Universe," "Mr. World," "Mr. America," and "Mr. Britain." With that background, he returned to his native St. Lucia and became editor of the *Voice* in 1971.

A much more common pathway into journalism, especially on the small and medium-sized newspapers, is through politics. Historically, we have seen that newspapers have been used as launching pads for individuals and parties with leadership aspirations. Among contemporary examples in the islands are George Walter, former editor of *Workers Voice,* who became premier of Antigua in 1971, and Grantley Adams, editor of Barbados *Beacon* while leader of the House of Assembly shortly before he headed the West Indies Federation government. Today editors of both papers on St. Kitts; all three on Antigua; all three on Dominica; *Herald, Standard,* and *Crusader* on St. Lucia;

---

* See elsewhere his activities since leaving the *Voice.*

Vanguard on Grenada; and most of the nondailies on the larger islands are in the journalistic profession mainly to push political, religious, or ethnic convictions. For example, A. M. Cruickshank, the barrister-editor of the opposition paper on Grenada, *Vanguard*, is a politician who in 1962 carried his campaign door-to-door in an unsuccessful bid to unseat Premier Eric Gairy.* As another example, Mrs. Reuben Harris, acting editor of Antigua *Times,* is on leave as education officer of that island to campaign against the new Walter government. On Dominica the editor of the pro-Freedom Party weekly, Edward Scobie, is also cofounder of that party and mayor of the Roseau town council.**

In broadcasting the situation is not quite the same. Because a number of the broadcasting systems in the islands are government branches, their managers are usually civil servants, sometimes placed in these positions in return for political services rendered. However, the more sophisticated technical skills needed in the operation of radio and television demand that top personnel be more than just political appointees. Even in a case such as that of Ivor Bird, son of the immediate past premier of Antigua and manager of the family-owned radio station on Antigua, one cannot ascribe purely political reasons for his being in that post. Bird had broadcasting experience dating to his youth (he had his own record show on the government station) and later studied communication techniques at Western Michigan University.

Staff Sizes

Large-island media in the Commonwealth Caribbean generally have large staffs. For example, the Gleaner Company has over 670 employees; Trinidad Publishing Company, over 500; Radio Jamaica, 110; Caribbean Broadcasting Corporation, 80; Trinidad and Tobago Television and TTNBS, 75 each; ZNS in the Bahamas, over 50; and Windward Islands Broadcasting Service, 35, of which 29 are stationed on Grenada.***

But, as we have seen many times before, the situation is different among the smaller-island media. For example, newspapers in the

---

* Disenchanted with governmental interference in journalism, Cruickshank has returned to a full-time law practice.

** Scobie, after his 1972 arrest, left Dominica and now teaches at City College of New York.

*** Barbados *Advocate-News* in 1976 had 140 employees, 24 of whom were in the editorial department.

Leewards and Windwards are normally one- and two-member editorial operations, which is the case with both papers on St. Kitts, all three on Grenada, *Workers Voice* on Antigua, Anguilla *Beacon*, and two of the three Dominica papers.[39] In a few of these instances, the papers were able to have a second editorial worker only when the spouse of the editor helped out.

Even some magazines, *Bim, The Bajan,* and *Spotlight,* are basically one-man editorial operations. *The Bajan* does have a five-member crew, but they are mainly noneditorial personnel. Included in the staff are the editor, his wife who serves as a secretary, three "girl Fridays," and a salesman. Larger newspaper staffs on the Leeward and Windward Islands would have to include the *Voice of St. Lucia* with four editorial workers and the St. Lucia *Crusader* and Dominica *Herald* with three each.*

Production crews are larger, partly because of the job printing upon which so many of these newspapers depend.[40] Technicians are scarce in those departments too, causing many production setbacks. For example, of the Antigua *Star's* twenty-four employees, only one is a linotype operator. At times the *Star* has had to limit its number of pages because type could not be set quickly enough.

Smaller-island broadcasting systems also are undermanned, especially the substations of WIBS. The St. Vincent substation has three employees (a programmer, technician, and secretary), St. Lucia three, and Dominica two.[41] Radio Anguilla is operated by five disc jockeys and a director, while Antigua Broadcasting Service is made up of ten employees. Even a full-status television station such as Leeward Islands Television Services, employs only nine people, including office personnel.

The severity of the problem is such that the regional Caribbean Broadcasting Union needed a head, but most station members could not afford to lose a staff member long enough to operate CBU. Finally, in 1971 a director was found in Guyana.

Because of manpower limitations, some stations cannot meet the requirements of radio in developing countries. St. Lucia WIBS sees a vital need for agricultural information programs but cannot find funds to pay someone to produce one show a week.[42] The three broadcasting outlets on Antigua rely on one civil servant, employed by Antigua Broadcasting Service, for all their news copy. Until recently he was the Reuters stringer as well, but the government

---

* *The Nation* on Barbados has three full-time editorial staff members. The newspaper draws upon volunteer, part-time help.

asked him to relinquish those duties because they were in "conflict with government interests."[43] For years lack of news staff forced a large station such as 610 Radio (then known as Radio Guardian) and later, Trinidad and Tobago Television, to rely on the news material of the Trinidad *Guardian*. Carbon copies of all *Guardian* copy were passed on to the radio and television newsroom, to the displeasure of the newspaper staff.[44] Today these stations have their own news staffs.

Valuable manpower is also conserved by the pooling of news-room resources by the larger radio and television stations belonging to the same corporation. Both Caribbean Broadcasting Corporation radio and television and Jamaica Broadcasting Corporation radio and television have combined newsroom staffs.

Favored Role of the Journalist

The result of these manpower shortages has been a keen competition for the few trained communicators. One Jamaican broadcasting official explained:

> If you can keep 10 per cent of those you train, you're lucky. Our biggest problem is not enough trained staff and then not being able to keep those we train. In a small developing country like Jamaica, with two radio stations, one newspaper company and a TV station, if there is a qualified journalist in the country, he has his pick of the media. This is costly since we have to bring trainees in fresh—people who have never seen a mike before—train them and then lose them. All the time they're being trained, they get paid as well. Salaries are high here but the supply and demand keeps trained people moving from one good job to another.[45]

Personnel turnover is high on other islands as well. The general managers of the three main media of Barbados agreed that as soon as a Barbadian reporter becomes somewhat proficient, he either goes abroad or takes a public relations job with one of the many foreign industries established on the island. On Antigua the only staffer on the government radio station who had received any training during the past five years did not return to the station after his training period.*

---

* On St. Lucia, as Radio St. Lucia planned to expand in 1976, there were complaints of staff raiding from Radio Caribbean.

Journalists in the region are quick to explain that individuals with higher-education backgrounds oftentimes do not want to offer their services to low-paying newspapers. Two comparisons point out journalists' relatively low pay: on Grenada an editorial worker makes $100 (EC) a month, while a bank clerk draws twice that amount;[46] in the Bahamas a reporter gets $160 (Bahamian) a week as a starter, while a good secretary makes $150 (Bahamian). "The secretary may be overpaid but supply and demand keeps it that way," a Nassau *Guardian* official explained.[47] On the other hand, the salary of a Grade C reporter (apprentice) on the Barbados *Advocate-News* is about $300 (EC) a month,* which, according to that paper's general manager, is a higher wage than that received by Grade C civil servants and policemen.[48]

Because of low salaries, a few of the editors who decide to remain in the profession are on dual or even triple payrolls. Some of these people have already been mentioned. In addition, there is Atlin Harrigan, editor of the Anguilla *Beacon,* who works as a full-time electrician and sits on the Island Council. A recent editor of the *Voice of St. Lucia,* W. St. C. Daniel, owned and operated a book shop and served as Speaker of the House while sitting in the editor's chair.

In addition to low pay scales, island journalists also face job insecurity; many of them work for political sheets or state-owned broadcasting outlets and are therefore at the mercy of political party or government shifts in power. Earlier, even on a larger, nonpolitical newspaper such as the Trinidad *Mirror,* jobs were not secured by unions. When the paper folded, a number of journalists were without work because there were not enough local media to absorb them.[49] In recent years several editorial branches of the Union of Commercial and Industrial Workers have been formed. Such branches have been organized at the shop level in some newspapers of Trinidad and Barbados but not in other newspapers in these same countries.** Usually they are affiliated with the Inter-American Federation of Working Newspapermen Organizations.[50]

---

* The 1976 salary range on the *Advocate-News* was U.S.$150 per month for a beginning reporter to U.S.$450 a month for a top reporter.
** In 1976 both CBC and the *Advocate-News* on Barbados were affiliated with the Barbados Workers Union. *The Jamaica Daily News* is also affiliated with a union; the editor complained that the rising cost of labor impinged on the daily's chances of making a profit in 1975. "We concluded a union agreement of a 42 percent increase over the next two years," he added (Personal interview, J. C. Proute, editor, *Jamaica Daily News,* Kingston, Jamaica, January 16, 1976).

However, the transient characteristic of employees on many newspapers does allow for upward mobility among the few staff members. As a *Gleaner* official said, "Some dedicated people have been at the *Gleaner* for 30 or 40 years, but the gap is wide between these few and the many who have been here for only a few years."[51] The lack of trained middle-management people on islands such as Bermuda and Barbados has given some employees unusual opportunities for promotion. One executive said that because unions push for internal promotions, and because trained personnel do not exist at the middle range, a good floorwalker can become supervisor without any of the necessary skills.[52]

Because of the high turnover of personnel and lack of trained middle-management people, many top media positions in the Commonwealth Caribbean are held by relatively young individuals. It is not unusual to find twenty-five- to thirty-five-year-old men editing newspapers or operating broadcasting units. The editors of St. Lucia *Crusader, Voice of St. Lucia,* Anguilla *Beacon,* Antigua *Star,* and St. Kitts *Democrat* were in their twenties or early thirties when they assumed their positions;* the directors of broadcasting units on Antigua, Dominica, St. Lucia, Bahamas, and St. Kitts were in their early thirties. In fact, of the seventy-five or so top media executives this author interviewed, only about a dozen were in their mid-fifties or over. Oldest were Sir Etienne Dupuch, publisher-editor of Nassau *Tribune,* and Frank Collymore, editor of *Bim,* both in their early seventies, and Reggie Clyne, the octogenarian editor of Grenada *West Indian.*

The Expatriate Employee

Complicating the manpower problem is the fact that most islands jealously guard against bringing in foreign personnel to fill journalistic positions. Ainslie, among others, feels that newly emergent nations such as the British West Indies have tired of employing foreign journalists (some completely ignorant of local conditions) to explain their cultures to the world.[53]

As a result, on a paper such as the Jamaica *Gleaner,* only 20 of 670 employees are not Jamaicans; at Radio Jamaica, one of 110 staffers is an expatriate. On Trinidad Publishing Company's 500-man

---

* And more recently, the editors of *The Nation* on Barbados, *The Jamaica Daily News,* St. Lucia *Star,* and Caribbean News Agency.

payroll only one person is not a Trinidadian, and at ZNS (Bahamas) only the general manager* is a nonBahamian. The staffs of the Bermuda newspapers are 90 percent Bermudian, and TTNBS is staffed by Trinidadians only, the policy at that station being not to hire any foreigners. Finally, over 90 percent of all Rediffusion broadcasters in the islands are West Indians. In some cases outside personnel are employed for as long as it takes to train local staff. When plans were jelling for television on Jamaica, one of the stipulations was that, as soon as possible, a Jamaican staff would replace foreign personnel.[54]

Possibly, strict governmental hewing to the law[55] concerning work permits for expatriates has been unfair to mass media on the smaller islands. For example, the *Gleaner* editor said of the situation in the Bahamas:

> The Bahamas has a different tradition from Jamaica. The *Gleaner* has always been run by Jamaicans whereas Nassau has been expatriate-run. The Bahamas are small with limited population so they must seek people from outside to work on newspapers.[56]

The seriousness of the Bahamian problem** was pointed out when, in 1970, the expatriate general manager of the Nassau *Guardian* was ordered by Deputy Prime Minister Arthur Hanna to replace himself with a Bahamian.[57] Six months later, he was no longer in Nassau; his work permit had expired and was not renewed. When the few remaining expatriates on the *Guardian* staff seek work-permit renewals, they are asked to explain what they are doing to replace themselves.[58] Across town, the proprietor-editor of the Nassau *Tribune* is more adamant in his refusal to obey these governmental restrictions. His rationale is that

> the government wants us to replace our staff with Bahamians who are untrained. The *Guardian* did it but I'll close shop before I put inefficient people on the staff. The *Guardian* as a result is now edited by a former linotypist who does not know how to write. If someone does not like you here, he goes to the immigra-

---

* He was recently replaced by a Bahamian.

** Pindling's Bahamanization scheme and independence in 1973 have tightened restrictions on expatriate employees even more so. See *Time,* July 16, 1973, pp. 5–6; *Wall Street Journal,* June 25, 1973, p. 24.

tion board and reports you. When we inquire about work permits, the government refuses to reply.[59]

(See chap. 8 for further discussion on work-permit renewals.)

Even other British West Indians are denied work permits on Commonwealth Caribbean islands. Ken Archer, director of St. Lucia Television, said that he had a well-educated Antiguan who wanted to announce over his station, but the labor minister "came down hard on him," claiming that his work permit did not entitle him to be on television. Archer said that the lack of trust among West Indians was partly responsible for the denial of work permits:*

> The St. Lucia government objects to people from neighboring islands coming here to work. As long as work permits are needed, there will be no cooperation. There must be emigration in these islands. For example, we might have a surplus of economists here but they would go to the United States or England rather than to other West Indian islands where they will not be hired.[60]

Training: Mostly on the Job

Following the British example, the majority of journalists in the Commonwealth Caribbean qualify for their positions through practical experience on media.[61] However, the difficulty with on-the-job training is that editors and broadcasters, especially those on small media, do not have time to provide steady instruction. For example, the director of Radio Anguilla can spend only two hours a week training his disc jockeys, while an ex-editor of the Antigua *Star* devotes a similar block of time to instructing that paper's reporters. The program director of TTNBS on Trinidad said that his station's on-the-job training consists of getting the people with the best "native training, putting them on the air and letting them learn by their mistakes."[62]

The UNESCO team, in 1968, complained that sporadic training efforts of this type "do not contribute much to the improvement of the efficiency and image of journalists."[63] Another source, a television programmer, said that one result of such training is that there are still television reporters in the region who cover a story with pen and pad instead of camera and tape recorder.[64]

---

* In an effort at closer cooperation among Grenada, St. Lucia, and St. Vincent, the premiers of those islands in August 1972 removed the need for work permits for people from neighboring islands.

A few notable attempts at in-depth training have been made in the islands, especially at the Jamaica *Gleaner* and ZNS (Bahamas).

The *Gleaner* advertises for applicants for positions each year, at which time approximately 500 people register. Through tests this number is reduced to 75 to 100 top prospects. More extensive examinations are given and, finally, 15 trainees are chosen for six months of on-the-job instruction. These apprentices are then subjected to three months of intensive training (every Saturday), supervised by experienced *Gleaner* staffers. Upon completion of this last phase, they are graduated to full-time editorial work. However, because of the tremendous turnover of personnel, the *Gleaner* can only expect 5 to 6 of these trained people to be around after 18 months.[65]

In 1971 ZNS instituted a year-long training program, made up of three stages. The first consists of ten weeks of orientation to all aspects of the station; phase two gives the student sixteen weeks of basic training in newsroom, production, and control room procedures; the third stage concentrates on the "deeper involvement of the student in the operations of the Station."[66] After successfully completing the courses, the students are offered employment with ZNS. This program differs from previous ones in that during the apprenticeship students are not on the air nor are they staff members, although they do draw student salaries.[67]

With more programs of this type,* possibly it would not be necessary for an executive, such as the general manager of the Barbados *Advocate-News*, to complain that

> many of my reporters are not aware of what's going on around them. Reporters must exercise the right choice of stories and then know how to handle them. They don't have that know-how here. You can send a man out on assignment here and he spends half a day, brings in seven or eight pages of trash which can be weeded down to two or three paragraphs. Reporters here do not feel responsibilities to be at the scene of the news. They trade notes. For example, if a reporter is late for an assignment, he just gets the notes from another reporter working for another medium.[68]

---

* In 1975, as part of JBC's expansion and modernization plan, it was envisioned that a communications training center would be set up, offering courses in operations, engineering, journalism, production, and presentation. (*Combroad* [April–June 1975], pp. 17–18.)

Formal Journalism Education

Besides the on-the-job training schemes there have been more formal attempts on the part of the media to raise the quality of journalists. During the mid-1960s the Trinidad *Guardian* organized a regional seminar through the Caribbean Publishers and Broadcasters Association (CPBA); however, its attendance was very small because papers in the Leewards and Windwards could not give their employees time off to attend the sessions.[69] CPBA also sponsored a series of lecture courses in various parts of the region in 1967. In 1961 the United States Information Service cooperated with the Press Association of Jamaica (PAJ) in organizing region-wide seminars; the following year the University of the West Indies and PAJ sponsored another series of training seminars. Also in the 1960s, the University of West Indies Extramural Department in Barbados held a three-month long, twice-a-week journalism course for both junior working journalists and school dropouts.* Attendance at all of these seminars was generally poor, according to the UNESCO report.[70]

Working consistently for journalism education in the islands has been the Press Association of Jamaica,[71] founded in 1943 to "foster a high standard of journalism in the island of Jamaica by means of improving the journalistic education of its members and in the furtherance thereof make awards, give scholarships, etc."[72] For years, PAJ has tried to develop a University journalism program in the islands. This goal was realized in October 1972[73] when the University of West Indies offered a diploma course in mass communications with particular emphasis on journalism.[74] The course is open to those with a first degree or equivalent work experience. Financial and technical assistance for the course is provided by the United Nations Development Programme and Jamaica government. The main training center is at the UWI campus at Mona, Jamaica, with subsidiary training to be provided in Trinidad and Guyana.[75] The stimulus for the program was the survey conducted by UNESCO in

---

* In 1975 the Caribbean Broadcasting Union, in conjunction with the Commonwealth Broadcasting Association, planned two training courses—one for broadcasters in the field of radio news production and presentation, and one for those in television program production. The same year CBU agreed to award two annual scholarships for Caribbean broadcasters to attend the Department of Mass Communications at the University of West Indies. (*Combroad* [January–March 1975], p. 43.)

1968, which showed that the main impediment to mass communications progress was the lack of trained personnel.*

Other training schemes that British West Indian media personnel have utilized have been those offered abroad, notably at British Broadcasting Corporation (BBC) and Thomson Foundation, both in England.

BBC has conducted eight- to ten-week training courses for Caribbean broadcasters, both at its London training school and in the Caribbean. Staffers of Thomson newspapers on Trinidad and Barbados have been sent to Great Britain for four to ten months of specialized training through the Thomson Foundation; in other cases they have interned on Thomson newspapers in the United States and Canada.[76] Other Commonwealth Caribbean mass media have also benefited from the program.

The Bahamian government, in its efforts to eliminate expatriates from media staffs, partially supports United States training for a few journalists every year, while ZNS sends trainees to Ryerson Institute of Technology (Canada), RCA Institute, and various universities in the United States. The London-based Center for Educational Television Overseas, as well as TV International Enterprises, helped in the "instant instruction" given ETV personnel in Jamaica when television became a reality there.[77]

DISTRIBUTION: SOCIAL OVERHEAD SERVICES

What Millikan and Blackmer term social overhead services—[78] transportation, telecommunications, and power—are in varying degrees of development in the Commonwealth Caribbean.

---

* For a blueprint of the diploma program, see "One-Year Media Diploma Planned for Phase One," *Express* (Trinidad), July 23, 1973, p. 4. In 1976 the University of West Indies planned to introduce a three-year undergraduate option in mass communication, leading to a bachelor's degree. The program, now called the Caribbean Institute of Mass Communication, moved into new quarters in 1976, provided by Friedrich Ebert Stiftung and the Jamaican government. Among the chief problems the program experienced in its first two years were: lack of equipment, insufficient lead time, and coping with problems of trying to explain the fragmented Caribbean media situation to a group of students from varying disciplines and statuses (Personal interview, Peter Pringle, director, Caribbean Institute of Mass Communication, Kingston, Jamaica, January 15, 1976).

Transportation

Gathering, transmitting, and distributing information in the region is still hampered by transportation problems, although to a lesser degree than a decade ago. Rugged terrain (especially on Dominica, Jamaica, Grenada, and Trinidad), the dispersed nature of the islands (especially the Bahamas), and adverse weather have made it difficult to develop transportation networks on some islands.

In nearly every case the island government designs at least one road that circles its periphery. Some governments, such as that of Dominica, feel that it is better to build a long pothole road than short superhighways; at least with the former, a traveler can get around the entire island. Most roads are constructed of low-grade materials (usually blacktop) and, especially on the smaller islands, are barely wide enough for two automobiles to pass. On larger islands as well, the quality of the road transportation system is inadequate for modern traffic needs. For example, on Trinidad the situation, as described by the writers of the Third Five-Year Plan 1969–1973, is as follows:

> In the rural areas, most of the roads are narrow and tortuous. Many deficient bridges restrict bus and truck movements. In the urban areas, narrow streets, inadequate parking facilities, pedestrian movements, vehicle loading and unloading and intersection conflicts create general disorder; and congestion is widespread during the morning and evening.[79]

The Commonwealth Caribbean is almost entirely reliant upon road transportation for internal movement of people and goods. As a result, the mass media must depend on road travel for gathering news as well as for distributing printed media to the people.

Because some of the world's most densely populated areas are in the Commonwealth Caribbean,[80] on Barbados, Trinidad, and Jamaica, newspapers, at least on these larger islands, have a fairly easy time distributing to most of their subscribers. However, despite this high concentration per square mile, there are numerous, virtually isolated pockets of people in all the territories. Poor transportation facilities into these areas make media distribution prohibitively expensive. The editorial manager of the Jamaica *Gleaner*, for example, said that it was not practical to land the *Gleaner* "at 4,000 feet and drop newspapers at the doorsteps of people in all the isolated villages."[81] He said that the paper hesitated to take pains to distribute copies to these people because they couldn't pay for them anyway.

On the other hand, although the Barbados *Advocate-News* does not feel that it is economical to send its editions into small parishes of only four or five houses, usually off the main road arteries, it does so nevertheless.[82]

On the smaller islands, newspapers make an effort to reach the rural readers, partly because they need all the subscribers they can get, but more important, because they want to promote their political parties and candidates as widely as possible. To cope with the transportation problems that loom much larger on these economically poor islands (many of which are also very mountainous), various methods of newspaper distribution are utilized. For example, political organs such as the *Workers Voice* of Antigua use the party structure to get newspapers circulated. That island has been divided by the Labour Party into fifty sectors, each headed by a party chief. One of his responsibilities is to take the *Voice* to the homes of individual subscribers. Other papers such as the Dominica *Chronicle* depend on the rural people to pick up the papers when they come to town in buses and trucks on market day. Still others depend on bus drivers to drop their papers off in the rural areas.*

Dispersion of the territories hinders at least inter-island transportation (see fig. 1). In the Bahamas many islands are accessible only by weekly mail boat. To travel from one Bahamian territory to another usually involves a return trip to Nassau first, there being no direct routes between a number of islands. However, as a Bahamian radio executive said, most people do not have an occasion to travel to a neighboring island.[83]

As one might imagine, the distribution problems faced by mass media personnel in a nation such as the Bahamas are enormous. The vice-president of the Nassau *Guardian* discussed some of them:

> Transportation is very difficult in the outislands so most of our circulation is on Providence Island. If the paper gets to the outislands, it will possibly be read by 50 people per copy. But air transportation is bad and transportation from the airports to the towns is even worse. So *Guardians* pile up at the airports or are stolen. To send the *Guardian* to Grand Bahama Island, for instance, costs $8

---

* The St. Lucia *Crusader* is distributed by the drivers. The editor said that this type of circulation is inefficient because drivers often forget to drop off the paper. For awhile, the *Crusader* was giving the *Voice of St. Lucia* van drivers a small stipend to distribute the *Crusader*. However, the *Voice* management discontinued this practice (Personal interview, George Odlum, editor, *Crusader*, Castries, St. Lucia, January 9, 1976).

a packet of 50 copies. Thus it costs 16 cents a copy just to send the paper there and it is sold for 15 cents, of which we get 11 and the paperboy 4.[84]

The 1968 UNESCO survey team felt that mass media and information services did not effectively use some of the transportation facilities that already exist in the region, especially inter-island airline services.[85] The reason newspapers hesitate to use airline services for distribution of their issues relates to the high air-freight charges that predominate. Also, as the Nassau *Guardian* official pointed out above, local air services are not always dependable. However, most islands are served by at least one airport, ranging from the Jamaica international terminal, capable of handling 727's, to the dirt strip on Anguilla, where passenger-carrying, inter-island piper cubs land. At least Jamaica, Bahamas, Trinidad, and the Leeward Islands have their own airline services. The latter service, LIAT, is used by the Barbados *Advocate-News* to get that paper to neighboring islands on the day of publication.*

Most of the islands are also connected to the outside world, and in some cases to each other, by shipping routes. Small ships, including sailing vessels, carry on local services among neighboring islands, as well as along the coasts of the larger territories. Larger, tourist-oriented islands, such as the Bahamas, have regular passenger-cargo service to the United States, Canada, Great Britain, South America, and the West Indies. Another large island, Trinidad, has two regional and two coastal vessels. In 1967 the coastal vessels made 245 round trips to neighboring Tobago, carrying 105,708 passengers and 135,000 tons of cargo.[86]

The use made of shipping services by printed media is not known. However, it is not likely that dailies would send their editions to neighboring islands on ships that would require a day or more of travel time. Possibly ships are used to distribute newspaper copies to overseas subscribers, who are more interested in keeping in touch with their homelands than in the timeliness of the news.

---

* The Barbados *Advocate-News* has limited its regional circulation because of difficulties the paper faced concerning air freight (Personal interview, Neville Grosvenor, general manager, *Advocate-News*, Bridgetown, Barbados, January 12, 1976). *The Nation* on Barbados is highly dependent on air freight. The paper is printed by the *Express* in Trinidad at cost, and then transported to Barbados by air freight. During its first year, *The Nation* paid U.S.$25,000 for air freight, and U.S.$19,000 during its second year. By 1977, *The Nation* expected to have its own printing plant in Barbados, at which time the paper would appear more frequently (Personal Interview, Harold Hoyte, editor, *The Nation*, Bridgetown, Barbados, January 12, 1976).

Whether they use air or surface mail, newspapers dependent upon large circulations abroad, for example, Montserrat *Mirror*, *The Caymanian Weekly*, Anguilla *Beacon*, Dominica *Star*, Dominica *Herald*, and Antigua *Workers Voice*, are confronted with high postage bills. The *Star*, for example, spends as much as $900 (EC) a year to send its issues abroad, a very considerable cost for a paper of its circulation.[87]

Telecommunications

Telecommunications systems in most islands are efficient enterprises, usually operated by Cable and Wireless of Great Britain.[88] Cable and Wireless owns all country-to-country cable and radio links and operates internal telephone and telegraph services of a number of countries on behalf of the national authorities. Although improvements have been made, many Commonwealth Caribbean islands continue to lack comprehensive telephone systems. Anguilla, for example, has no public telephone system. The shortage of telephone service to rural areas of other islands has hampered newsgathering because telephones were not available for corrspondents to call in their stories.

The services provided by Cable and Wireless have been described by the UNESCO team as follows:

> Its efficient operation and its constant improvement, development and training effort makes it a tremendous asset to the Region, and any agency concerned with mass communication must inevitably base most of its telecommunications plans on such network.[89]

During the early 1970s, Cable and Wireless was able to provide a high-quality link between any two points in the Caribbean,* but the costs of such a link were not within the budgets of the media.[90] For example, to link Jamaica with the Eastern Caribbean would mean renting cable via Miami, a very expensive proposition, according to one

---

* An 800-mile-long microwave system was being installed in the Eastern Caribbean in 1974. On completion it will link the British, French, and Dutch islands from the British Virgin Islands in the north to Trinidad & Tobago in the south. The chain, being installed by Cable and Wireless in association wth the French PTT and Dutch LRTD, was expected to be completed by the end of 1975. The microwave system will be able to carry 960 simultaneous telephone channels or a combination of many thousands of telegraph or data-transmission circuits. Also, it has considerable capacity to handle inter-island color television transmissions should they be required. (*Intermedia* 2, no. 4 [1974]: 22; *Combroad* [April–June 1974], pp. 12–15.)

regional broadcaster.[91] The alternative of renting direct, permanent circuits between the islands is also out of the price range of Caribbean broadcasting organizations.

In some cases Cable and Wireless has offered cheaper rates for leased circuits rather than keeping them inactive. Yet, the problem of costs still exists and has prevented several mass media, especially those placed peripherally, from benefiting from services such as radio voicecast exchanges and Reuters Caribbean Service.[92] (See Appendix E for existing facilities and operations of Cable and Wireless in British West Indies.)

Cablegram rates set down by Cable and Wireless are also considered too expensive for wide use by Commonwealth Caribbean mass media. UNESCO pointed out that the "only reasonable cheap charge applied at present is the Commonwealth Press Cable Rate of three British pennies per word through the Commonwealth of Nations."[93] Even at this rate it is too costly for media to make use of cablegrams in filing regional stories.

Finally, another area of telecommunications that Cable and Wireless has entered is that of communication satellites. In the early 1970s the company was in the process of developing its fourth satellite–earth station, to be located on Jamaica. Two other satellite–earth stations are planned for the wider Caribbean region, one to be located on Trinidad. The Jamaica station will be equipped for transmission and reception of international television. As the UNESCO team stated, the Caribbean connections with the INTELSAT network of communication satellites is both fortunate and logical—fortunate because the development of "satellite technology has occurred when economic alternatives could not"; logical because a satellite system ideally suits an area as geographically diverse as the Commonwealth Caribbean.[94]

Electric Power

The primary cities of the Commonwealth Caribbean are generally well served with electric power. It is in the rural areas that electric services are lacking. For example, on Jamaica only the main towns are connected to power stations.[95] In the Bahamas, although electrification exists in most major settlements, there are islands where it would be profitless to have electricity, for example, on an island such as Andros with 3,000 people scattered over its 100-mile length.[96] The Bahamas Electricity Corporation generates electricity at three sites on the main island of New Providence and sanctions 27 private generators in the out islands. In 1968–69 BEC generated 247,544,050 annual units (kwh) on New Providence and Paradise Island. During the same period there were 24,136 electricity consumers connected to BEC on New Providence and Paradise Island.[97]

On Trinidad electricity development has been a major part of the five-year plans. During 1968 sales of energy on Trinidad amounted to 650 million kilowatt hours; this figure was expected to increase by 250 million kilowatt hours by 1973. Over the five-year period 1969 to 1973, 37,000 new customers were expected to be added to the system, with 60 percent of the increase in energy sales being absorbed by industrial customers. As a result of proposed development of resorts in northern Trinidad and parts of Tobago, distribution was planned for these areas, too.[98]

Among the smaller islands Anguilla is served only by private generators; Dominica planned island-wide electricity in the early 1970s; and Antigua has had a stable power supply only since November 1970. On St. Lucia a large proportion of the communities are without regular electricity services, causing St. Lucia Television to keep battery-operated videotape equipment ready for use in those areas. St. Lucia does not plan to have island-wide electrification for some time.* In all of the islands the electricity that is available is subject to frequent failure because of weather conditions.[99]

Electric power supplies seem to be adequate for the production needs of the mass media. Only the Barbados *Advocate-News* complained that a new power plant was needed for that paper to function properly.[100] If electric power is to have a profound effect on mass media in the future, it will not be so much in production as in consumption of electronic media products. For example, a Jamaica Broadcasting Corporation official, pointing out the dependence of television upon Jamaica Public Service, showed how television installations have kept pace proportionately with power connections. In mid-1968 there were 84,000 electricity connections and 52,000 television sets on Jamaica; two years later, when the number of electricity consumers increased to 102,000, the number of sets correspondingly jumped to 70,000. The projection for 1975 called for 155,000 power connections and 137,000 television sets on Jamaica.[101]

---

* Government personnel have shown concern about the amount of power expended for Radio St. Lucia's transmitter, and have submitted a proposal to UNESCO for a repeater transmitter (Personal interview, Winston Hinkson, director, Radio St. Lucia, Castries, St. Lucia, January 10, 1976).

CONSUMPTION: LITERACY AND MOTIVATION

If the statistics can be trusted (and they cannot be), literacy would not appear to be a Commonwealth Caribbean problem. On paper all island governments register literacy levels of 80 percent or more; Barbados, Antigua, and St. Kitts-Nevis claim rates as high as 95 percent. But, as in many nations-in-a-hurry, statistics are manipulated to make the states look more developed than they really are.[102] Thus, when the Jamaican government claims 83 percent literacy, one would be wise to ask how functional the literacy happens to be.

Alleyne, discussing Jamaica in the early 1960s, seemed to think that literacy there was quite dysfunctional. He said that an indeterminable percentage of those having received four years of schooling must be considered functionally illiterate. In addition, he felt that

persons in rural communities who are over, say, 40 years, and who have had even the full length of primary education (up to 15 years of age) would, if they had remained in rural communities, most probably have lost their language ability in standard English. Without formal adult education facilities, a person over 21 years with less than four years of schooling in his chiildhood must be considered functionally illiterate.[103]

The editorial manager of the *Daily Gleaner* would agree with Alleyne. He said that literacy on most islands is nonfunctional; on Jamaica, he felt that over 60 percent of the people were functionally illiterate.[104]

Other editors and broadcasters also discredited the literacy rates, saying that they were inflated. One editor questioned the functionality of literacy when so many of the islands still use symbols on election ballots because the people cannot read the names of the parties and candidates.

Numerous reasons were given for the dysfunctional literacy prevalent in these territories. A Trinidadian editor explained that literacy is not so popular now as it was a few years ago when "a person would carry 100 pens in his pocket to show that he writes, and a *Guardian* to show that he reads."[105] A Dominican editor, emphasizing that reading habits have not been developed on that island, said that the upper middle class would "rather be dead than seen reading a book. Instead, they'd rather go to the movies nightly to see cowboys and Indians."[106] And a Jamaican broadcaster felt that the electronic media have detracted from literacy's appeal to the rural people. He said:

A few years ago, one person in twenty could read and the other nineteen gathered around as he read to them. Now all twenty of them just sit around listening to the radio.[107]

There are efforts to revive interest in literacy. The development of educational television programs and the airing of "Sesame Street" are attempts in that direction, as is the *Daily Gleaner's* publishing of *Children's Own* "to get and keep children in the reading habit."[108] However, the most successful program in the region is Jamaica Literacy Project, launched in 1951. Since 1966 the project has developed radio and television programs for adult literacy classes. Approximately 9,000 students, mainly from rural areas, are organized in "media" classes where they are taught reading, word-building, and writing. Classes, which average ninety minutes (including the broadcasts and follow-up instruction), are held in churches, schools, community centers, and even private homes. Radio programs average twenty-nine minutes each; television, twenty-four minutes. Both radio and television literacy classes are broadcast twice a week. Broadcasts are prepared under the authority of the Social Development Commission, in consultation with Jamaica Broadcasting Corporation, Jamaica Information Service, University of West Indies Radio Unit, and UNESCO.[109]

However, high literacy rates, even if functional in nature, do not guarantee a reading public. Lerner observed that "only a literate person *can* read a book, paper or magazine, and only a motivated person *wants* to read."[110]

Findings of the 1968 UNESCO team would indicate that motivation plays some role in Commonwealth Caribbean reading patterns. UNESCO concluded that there was no direct relationship between island literacy rates and readership of newspapers.

> Countries with lower literacy, such as Jamaica and Trinidad, have a much higher circulation of daily papers per head of population than territories like Antigua, St. Kitts and St. Vincent, who, in addition to having a higher literacy rate, also are smaller in area and should therefore have easier distribution problems and less need of radio for reaching every community.[111]

Possibly Jamaicans and Trinidadians are more motivated to read because of the better-quality newspapers published on those islands. In addition, the greater concentration of urbanization that exists on Trinidad and Jamaica could account for higher circulations. In most cases newspapers in the region are published for urbanites, playing up city events and ignoring rural life. Schramm, talking generally, said basically the same thing, that "even when the mass media do come to the villages, they usually are not of and for the villages."[112]

CONSUMPTION: AFFORDABILITY OF MEDIA

After determining the people's ability and motivation to consume mass media, the next question is: do they have the purchasing power to afford the media? Possibly the following two vignettes embody part of the answer for the Commonwealth Caribbean.

Obigah Gardiner of St. Kitts earns twenty-nine dollars (EC) a week in the cane fields, forty dollars if he gets in the full week. A newspaper costs him nearly the price of his twenty-cent shot of rum, which he confesses he prefers to a newspaper.[113]

A merchant on St. Lucia said that he sold 450 small transistor radios during the previous cricket season. After the games were over he neither sold many of these sixteen dollar (EC) radios nor did he have to service any of those he had previously sold. "If the sets go on the blink after the cricket season is over, the people throw them away," he explained.[114]

The answer seems to be that the Commonwealth Caribbean masses can and do buy a medium if it rewards them with the right proportions of prestige, entertainment, and local information while at the same time requiring the least effort to enjoy.[115] Thus, they are reluctant to purchase in great numbers the hard-to-read newspapers that require literacy skills as well as good eyesight or eyeglasses. On the other hand, they are quite willing to put their dollars down on a radio that brings them the cricket matches and horseraces, or on a television set that raises their prestige a notch or two while at the same time providing entertainment.

Printed Media

The consensus of Commonwealth Caribbean editors was that the people do have the financial resources to buy newspapers. These editors felt that they could make this claim despite the fact that the highest per capita incomes in the islands are $734 (US) on Trinidad, $507 (US) on Jamaica, and $476 (US) on Barbados.[116] Only two editors felt that newspapers were too expensive for mass consumption. *Gleaner* editor Theodore Sealy said that the 40-cents-a-week price of his paper will buy the average five-member family codfish for a week;[117] the St. Kitts *Democrat* editor felt that because sugar workers have only five or six months of employment each year, they cannot afford the luxury of a newspaper.[118] The general manager of the Barbados *Advocate-News* said that if the laboring man cannot afford the newspaper all year round, he should be able to be a subscriber during the harvest and tourist seasons, when a "lot of money is circulating on the island."[119]

However, again using sugar-field laborer Obigah Gardiner as an example, it becomes clear that the blue-collar worker has a difficult time justifying the regular purchase of a newspaper.* If Obigah wished to subscribe to a daily newspaper year round, he would have to use over one week's earnings to pay for the subscription. For the sake of comparison, a United States citizen, making the minimum hourly wage, would devote two days' wages for a year's subscription, whereas an average Filipino or Thai laborer would spend twenty to twenty-two days' wages.

As we shall see later in the discussion of television, one does not have to be a purchaser of a medium to consume its contents. Some editors said that the feeling on their islands is that it is better to borrow a newspaper than to purchase one. For example, the Dominica *Chronicle* editor found that in at least one government office forty people were served by one issue of his paper;[120] editors on St. Kitts, Grenada, Barbados, and St. Vincent spoke of similar situations. On St. Kitts the people take turns buying the newspaper; on Barbados it was explained that the *Advocate-News* is passed from house to house until it is nearly in shreds.[121]

Television

A Trinidadian broadcaster used the words *apparent consumer economy* to describe the characteristic whereby peoples of the Commonwealth Caribbean spend money they do not have for luxuries they want, for example, radio and television sets. He said that people live beyond their means to afford television for its show-off value as well as for its entertainment.[122]

Almost from the beginning, when television sets were placed in public squares in Barbados and Jamaica,[123] there has been a demand for the medium in these relatively poor islands.

In the Bahamas it has been significant enough to account for the sales of over 25,000 sets, 10 percent of which are color. Yet the nation does not have local television service. The Bahamians are willing to pay $150 (Bahamian) for a booster antenna required to pick up as little as one hour a day of "fair to rotten" reception from the United

---

* Even more so now that newspaper prices have increased to fifteen U.S. cents on many islands.

States. Television sets cost 30 to 40 percent more in Nassau than they do in the United States, but again, Bahamians continue to purchase them.[124]

Even on media-poor Anguilla, where individually owned generators are the only sources of electric power, about two dozen homes have sprouted television antennae. Anguillans own the sets even though for years they were violating a St. Kitts-Nevis-Anguilla ruling[125] that did not permit the importation of sets, this in spite of the poor reception they get from Puerto Rico, St. Croix, and Antigua stations.[126]

The acceptance of television in the islands can be understood by looking at set ownership figures. In the case of Jamaica, for example, over 70,000 sets have been purchased, penetrating 65 to 70 percent of the Jamaican homes that have electricity.* On the other islands the growth has been equally significant; for example, on Trinidad there are 54,000 sets; on Barbados, 16,000; Antigua, 5,500; St. Lucia, 3,000; and St. Vincent, a "few hundred."[127] (See Table 7.1 for numbers of radio and TV sets.)

TABLE 7.1

NUMBER OF RADIO, TELEVISION RECEIVERS
IN COMMONWEALTH CARIBBEAN, 1970

Country	Population	Radio Receivers	TV Receivers
Anguilla	7,000	5,000	
Bahamas	168,000	100,000	
Barbados	253,000	62,000	16,000
Bermuda	57,000	38,000	17,000
Jamaica	1,915,000	304,000	70,000
Leewards	175,000	56,000	6,000
Trinidad & Tobago	1,031,000	236,000	54,000
British Virgin Islands	6,600	5,100	
Windwards	373,000	61,000	

SOURCE: 1971 World Radio-TV Handbook, p. 290.

---

* Yet, one writer said that television set sales were not very high on Jamaica. He gave an interesting explanation, saying that it was due to easy-going marital customs. "Few males would think of buying the equipment. 'The rule is that when poppa skips out on momma, she keeps everything in the house,' they say. 'So the guy blows the TV set every time.' It's that way in the U.S. too, but with the difference that in Jamaica a fairly active citizen could blow four or five sets in a year." (Al Stump, "Where the Goggle Box Strikes Out," TV Guide, June 17, 1972, pp. 46, 48.)

Television is a very costly medium for nations such as those in the Caribbean, with per capita incomes of $700 (US) or less. For example, a small black-and-white set purchased in Nassau costs $200 (US); color sells for over $600 (US). On Antigua a 21-inch portable model costs over $150 (US); on St. Lucia a 20-inch set can be purchased for $225 (US), plus another $20 for an aerial.

In addition, one must include the cost of electricity, since many islanders purchase this expensive service solely to operate their television sets. On St. Lucia electricity costs a minimum of $8 (EC) a month; on Jamaica the charge is $4 to $8 (Jamaican) monthly. The Trinidad government is helping put electricity within the budgetary range of the common man by spreading the initial charges of installation over a long period of time. This policy has tended to make electricity available to people who could never expect to save enough money to have their homes wired.[128]

Another expense incurred by television owners is the license fee levied on individual sets. On Barbados the annual fee is $12.50 (EC), collected by the Caribbean Broadcasting Corporation and used for programming. Delinquent taxpayers are threatened with legal prosecution.[129] On Antigua the television tax is $10 (EC) yearly. Collection is accomplished through the police department; the revenues go into a common treasury fund but are not allocated to the media.[130]

How do people with per capita incomes of $700 (US) or less afford television sets that sell for at least one-third to one-half of their yearly salaries? In some cases several working members of an extended family pool their wages to purchase a set.[131] Often, however, they do as the previously mentioned Trinidadian broadcaster suggested: they live beyond their means.

On most of the islands people do not have to own the television set they enjoy, rentals being readily available. For example, a third of the 3,000 television sets on St. Lucia are rented.* Rental firms usually charge a flat weekly or monthly fee for the installation and maintenance of sets in the home.[132]

In addition to sales and rentals, government-sponsored community and school sets have allowed island peoples to view television. On Barbados the seven social centers located around the island include sets provided by the Social Welfare branch of government, while at

---

* In 1976 I was told that 90 percent of the 4,500 sets on St. Lucia were owned by their users. TV rental fees on St. Lucia in 1976 were: 11-inch set, US$11 per month; 23-inch receiver, US$15 per month (Personal interview, Brian Holden, director, St. Lucia Television, Castries, St. Lucia, January 9, 1976).

Educational television class in Barbados, early 1970s.

least a dozen schools have television sets, courtesy of the Ministry of Education. Jamaica Broadcasting Corporation and the Jamaican government have donated over 315 sets to educational institutions and another 100 to community centers. Usually Jamaican schools also make their sets available to the adult population.[133] Leeward Islands Television Services on Antigua has provided two community sets for Montserrat, one in the community center, the other in an outdoor park. Community and educational centers on Antigua, however, do not benefit from community sets because the government has not "seen fit to contribute anything to TV's development here."[134]

Radio

The transistor made radio affordable to the British West Indian, although the features that transistors offer—low cost, portability, and nondependence on fixed power sources[135]—were slow in attracting the islanders. The transistor did not really penetrate the Jamaican listenership until 1968 and that of Barbados until 1966.

Just as the urge to hear the broadcast of cricket matches brought the first radio to the islands, so the population's insatiable interest in sports has been partly responsible for the transistor revolution in the islands. For example, transistor sales surged on Trinidad in 1961 while a foreign cricket team was competing there.[136] On all of the islands it is a fact that many transistors are purchased mainly to listen to cricket matches or horseraces.[137]

The price of the transistor is within range of most individual budgets. For example, a Barbadian or Vincentian can purchase a small transistor for $10 (EC); a Jamaican pays $3 (Jamaican). A Dominican can get a radio that will last at least two months for $15 (EC); larger transistors on Dominica range from $80 to $150 (EC). On Trinidad one can buy a transistor for as little as $30 (TT) and up to $400 (TT). The transistor is even more affordable because it does not require electricity and, in the majority of cases, does not have to be licensed.

The license fee on radio sets has been discontinued on most islands because of collection difficulties or political concessions. A few islands still levy a nominal tax on radio sets. For example, on Antigua the rate is two to three dollars (EC) a year, but this rate probably does not dissuade Antiguans from purchasing radios.

Rentals and community listening sets[138] are available for those who cannot afford to purchase a radio. One of the oldest rental firms in the islands is Rediffusion radio, which for nearly four decades has rented loudspeakers and program services to West Indians who could not afford radio sets or the power source needed to keep them operative. Thus, in the mid-1950s, a subscriber to Rediffusion could have wired radio in his home all day for the cost of his daily newspaper.[139]

Because of its ability to skip the requirements of literacy and urbanization, radio will undoubtedly remain for some time the most practical, as well as the most affordable, medium in the islands.

SUMMARY

Production techniques and facilities employed by Commonwealth Caribbean mass media run nearly the full gamut: from the multi-million-dollar Gleaner Company to the nondailies printed in editors' homes; from Jamaica Broadcasting Corporation, using as many as eight transmitters, to St. Lucia Television, a relay of Caribbean Broadcasting Corporation, using as many as eight transmitters, to St. Lucia Television, a relay of Caribbean Broadcasting Corporation operated as an adjunct of a television rental firm.

Because of a shortage of investment capital in the islands, mass media concerns often seek the big package offered by consortia of foreign entrepreneurs and local governments. However, at least St. Lucia Television, Anguilla *Beacon,* and Dominica *Star* have gone another route, keeping production costs within the limits of available capital and resources.

Another production requirement, trained personnel, is lacking on many islands. Individuals with higher educations tend to avoid journalistic work in the islands because of the low wages. Personnel turnover is high because of migration to higher-paying positions abroad and to local government and industry agencies. As a result, upward mobility opportunities on most staffs are plentiful. Island governments jealously guard against bringing in foreign editorial and technical help, thus occasionally necessitating the use of untrained personnel. Training is mostly on the job, although more formal mass media education has been offered at the University of West Indies since 1973.

Social overhead services that affect mass media development are being improved on many islands. Both transportation networks and electric power facilities are undergoing changes that should have beneficial results for the effective transmission and reception of mass media messages. Telecommunications operations are now available on nearly all islands, although certain services offered by Cable and Wireless are still out of the budgetary reach of nearly all the mass media.

British West Indians seem to be motivated to consume mass media products. Newspaper circulation for the entire area is very high, as are purchases of electronic media sets. Radio is the most affordable medium, although a number of people are investing in television sets, despite their high costs in terms of relative consumer buying power. Literacy rates are high enough to allow the majority of the population to enjoy the printed word. However, some West Indians argue that the published literacy rates do not tell the full story, and that functional literacy is actually much lower than the figures would indicate.

NOTES TO CHAPTER 7

1. Daniel Lerner, "Toward a Communication Theory of Modernization," in Lucian W. Pye, ed., *Communications and Political Development* (Princeton, N.J.: Princeton University Press, 1963), p. 337. See also Leonard Doob, *Communication in Africa: A Search for Boundaries* (New Haven, Conn.: Yale University Press, 1961), pp. 154–65.

2. Ibid., p. 338.

3. The inability of developing peoples to save money, an economic necessity for modernity, has been discussed by a number of writers. For example, Ward, pointing the finger of blame at colonialism, described the paradox "of the phrase called 'primitive accumulation'—the first great effort of saving which has to be achieved if the new momentum is to begin. The Western colonial impact on the rest of the world did not create such a momentum." Barbara Ward, *The Rich Nations and the Poor Nations* (New York: W. W. Norton, 1962), p. 35.

In the Commonwealth Caribbean, colonialism dictated that the islands produce raw materials for export and, in turn, import all processed and manufactured goods from the mother country, hardly a situation that would encourage saving. Of course, if the exports brought high prices, saving would have been possible. But they didn't. As Williams has pointed out, West Indian commerce belonged exclusively to the particular metropolitan country involved. The trade philosophy of the metropolitan countries was: (1) colonies must import only metropolitan goods, (2) colonies must send their exports only to the metropolitan country, (3) colonial trade was a rigid monopoly of metropolitan ships and seamen, and (4) colonies must produce raw materials and not manufactured goods. Eric Williams, *From Columbus to Castro, The History of the Caribbean 1492–1969* (London: Andre Deutsch, 1970), pp. 171–72.

4. Personal interviews, Reggie Clyne, Editor, *West Indian*, St. George's, Grenada, May 12, 1971; Stanley Reid, Editor, *Crusader*, Castries, St. Lucia, May 8, 1971; John Wickham, Literary Editor, *The Bajan*, Bridgetown, Barbados, May 14, 1971.

5. Personal interview, Neville Grosvenor, General Manager, Barbados *Advocate-News*, Bridgetown, Barbados, September 7, 1970.

6. Personal interview, Fred Seal Coon, Editorial Manager, *Gleaner*, Kingston, Jamaica, August 26, 1970.

7. Questions were asked about capital structure only if it seemed that the interview would not be hindered by such queries.

8. *Press, Radio and TV*, 1969–70, p. 9. For comparative purposes these are United States dollar equivalents for Commonwealth Caribbean currencies. The East Caribbean dollar, used in Barbados, the Leewards, and Windwards, is equal to approximately fifty U.S. cents, as is the Trinidadian dollar. The Bahamian dollar is worth one U.S. dollar, and the Jamaican dollar is equal to $1.20 U.S. Before Jamaica converted to the dollar/cents system, the Jamaican pound was worth approximately $2.38 U.S., or $4.75 EC. In 1976 the East Caribbean dollar was equal to fifty U.S. cents, as was the new Barbadian dollar.

9. "War Baby Is Now a Giant," Trinidad *Guardian*, May 28, 1967.

10. Source asked for anonymity.

11. Personal interview, Frank Collymore, Editor, *Bim*, Bridgetown, Barbados, May 14, 1971.

12. A number of writers have discussed the phenomenon of developing nations

skipping stages. Von der Mehden has said, "It is not necessary for a state to be as old as the United States in order to approach its level of development." Fred von der Mehden, *Politics of the Developing Nations* (Englewood Cliffs, N.J.: Prentice-Hall, 1964), p. 7. Schramm said something similar, that common men must be lifted from the village to the world almost overnight; nations jump from the oxcart to airplane as quickly. Wilbur Schramm, "Communication Development and the Development Process," in Pye, ed., *Communications and Political Development*, p. 46.. Davison felt that "having only a relatively thin coverage of conventional media, new nations may be able to jump from oral communication systems to the most recent ones." W. Phillips Davison, *International Political Communication* (New York: Frederick A. Praeger, 1965), p. 139. See also C. E. Black, *The Dynamics of Modernization* (New York: Harper & Row, 1967), p. 97.

13. With 3,000 television homes in service area.

14. The station director explained, "We don't use any visual mixers as such and actually we use no professional TV equipment at all."

15. Personal interview, Ken Archer, Director, St. Lucia Television Services, Castries, St. Lucia, May 8, 1971.

16. Ibid.

17. Herbert Schiller, *Mass Communications and American Empire* (Boston: Beacon Press, 1971), p. 114.

18. Ibid.

19. In other words, their economic paths are set by consumerism whether they willed it that way or not. Using Lerner's terminology, they have not used but rather have allowed themselves to be abused by Western communication models. Daniel Lerner and Wilbur Schramm, eds., *Communication and Change in Developing Countries* (Honolulu, Hawaii: East-West Center Press, 1967), p. 310.

20. Guy Roppa and Neville E. Clarke, *The Commonwealth Caribbean: Regional Cooperation in News and Broadcasting Exchanges* (Paris: UNESCO, 1968), p. 19. This survey included eight newspapers of Belize and Guyana, neither of which included in this study.

21. "Press Release," Anguilla *Beacon*, March 31, 1969, p. 5.

22. Lenora Williamson, "Queen Honors 'Ted' Sayer for Services to Journalism," *Editor & Publisher*, August 22, 1970, pp. 34, 36.

23. E. C. Baker, *A Guide to Records in the Leeward Islands* (Oxford: Basil Blackwell, 1965), p. 22.

24. Roppa and Clarke, *Commonwealth Caribbean*, p. 19.

25. Ibid.

26. Personal interview, W. St. C. Daniel, Former Editor, *Voice of St. Lucia,* Castries, St. Lucia, May 8, 1971.

27. Especially the editors of the Grenada papers.

28. From promotional materials from Radio Caribbean.

29. Sources asked for anonymity.

30. Letter to Author, John Barsotti, Assistant Program Director, TTT, August 10, 1971. Besides Trinidad, Jamaica also has had to use relay transmitters to send signals across the mountain ranges. As many as eight transmitters are required to give Jamaica Broadcasting Corporation the power to cover that island properly.

31. Personal interview, Vernon Michaels, Manager, Leeward Islands Television, St. John's, Antigua, May 4, 1971.

32. Personal interview, L. H. Stewart, Assistant General Manager, Jamaica Broadcasting Corporation, Kingston, Jamaica, August 28, 1970.

33. Personal interview, Leo de Leon, Program Director, 610 Radio, Port of Spain, Trinidad, September 1, 1970.

34. For further discussion, see Lerner and Schramm, eds., *Communication and Change,* p. 8.

35. Pye, ed., *Communications and Political Development,* p. 79.

36. Schiller, *Mass Communications,* p. 110.

37. "Montserrat's Only Newspaper Closes," *Daily Gleaner,* October 8, 1959.

38. Personal interview, Stanley Procope, Former Editor, *Daily Bulletin,* Basseterre, St. Kitts, May 1, 1971.

39. The result of such understaffing was explained by the editor of the Dominica *Chronicle.* The newspapers are "no more than scissors and paste operations depending on government handouts." Personal interview, S. A. W. Boyd, Editor, Dominica *Chronicle,* Roseau, Dominica, May 5, 1971.

40. For example, some papers, such as the Montserrat *Mirror,* are secondary to the job printing. The *Mirror* editor said, "My production manager once remarked to me that I was spending too much time on the newspaper." Letter to Author, Dorcas White, Editor, Montserrat *Mirror,* June 10, 1971.

41. Although the new station there will have 11 employees.

42. Personal interview, Winston Hinkson, Director, WIBS, St. Lucia, Castries, St. Lucia, May 7, 1971.

43. Personal interview, Everard Richards, News Editor, Antigua Broadcasting Service, St. John's, Antigua, May 4, 1971.

44. Roppa and Clarke, *Commonwealth Caribbean*, p. 28.

45. Personal interview, Lloyd de Pass, General Manager, Radio Jamaica, Kingston, Jamaica, August 27, 1970. D. G. R. Rowlands of the Thomson Foundation relates this story about the troubles encountered when an island journalist is trained abroad:

> A young man from a small island told me that with three friends he founded a little weekly magazine—partly literary, partly items of local news, announcements of social events and a few advertisements. From a quiet duplicated start they began to print a proper paper, raised funds through fetes and began to make money. Then his three friends were so fired with the thrills of part-time journalism that they all went to Canadian colleges to take journalism courses. "And will they come back?" I asked. He replied, "With training like that they can get good jobs. They will not waste their lives on a small island where, however hard they try, the community can never afford a REAL paper."

46. Personal interview, Elcon Mason, Editor, *Torchlight*, St. George's, Grenada, May 12, 1971. A U.S. dollar was equal to $1.75 East Caribbean at the time.

47. Personal interview, Benson McDermott, Vice-President, Nassau *Guardian*, Nassau, Bahamas, August 24, 1970. One Bahamian dollar was equal to one United States dollar at the time.

48. Interview, Grosvenor.

49. Personal interview, Ken Gordon, General Manager, *Express*, Port of Spain, Trinidad, September 2, 1970.

50. Roppa and Clarke, *Commonwealth Caribbean*, pp. 87–88.

51. Interview, Seal Coon.

52. Interview, Grosvenor.

53. Rosalynde Ainslie, *The Press in Africa: Communications Past and Present* (New York: Walker & Co., 1968), p. 17.

54. "TV: Films Being Test-Transmitted," *Daily Gleaner*, June 21, 1963, p. 1.

55. The law on Jamaica, for example, stipulates that the expatriate must apply yearly for a work permit until he has lived on the island for ten years. At that point he becomes a citizen of the Commonwealth (and automatically a citizen of Jamaica if he applies) and no longer needs a work permit. Laws in the Bahamas specify: "that immigrants do not create unfair competition for employment. Thus, no expatriate may be offered employment in a post for which a suitably

qualified Bahamian is available." The employer must advertise the position and if no local prospects are available, may submit application for an expatriate. If the request is approved, the expatriate must reapply yearly for his work permit.

56. Personal interview, Theodore Sealy, Editor, *Gleaner*, Kingston, Jamaica, August 26, 1970.

57. Personal interview, Chris Evans, General Manager, Nassau *Guardian*, Nassau, Bahamas, August 24, 1970.

58. Personal interview, Leon Turnquest, Editor, Nassau *Guardian*, Nassau, Bahamas, April 26, 1971.

59. Personal interview, Sir Etienne Dupuch, Editor and Proprietor, Nassau *Tribune*, Nassau, Bahamas, April 27, 1971.

60. Interview, Archer.

61. Yet there are still cases where a person is employed for editorial work on the basis of what he achieved in school. "If he can express himself in the proper way, he is hired," one editor said. Personal interview, Nathaniel Hodge, Editor, *Democrat*, Basseterre, St. Kitts, May 1, 1971.

62. Interview, de Leon.

63. Roppa and Clarke, *Commonwealth Caribbean*, p. 90. D. G. H. Rowlands, Director of Editorial Studies of the Thomson Foundation, said that as a result of such training, prospective journalists either "drop out disillusioned or become complacent about their ability." D. G. H. Rowlands, "Caribbean Tour Report 1970," mimeographed (Thomson Foundation).

64. Personal interview, Chris Nuthall, Regional Programmer, Verbatim Inc., St. John's, Antigua, May 5, 1971.

65. Interview, Seal Coon. The *Gleaner* continues to train these individuals even though, once skilled, they do not always remain with the paper. Editor Sealy said that he feels a responsibility to train personnel in media because "we are the only ones who can do it here." Interview, Sealy. A broadcasting executive in the Bahamas said something similar: "We have an awkward situation here. In the United States or Canada, for example, a guy enters broadcasting on a small rural station and works his way up, hopefully to the national services. In these islands, we're the only station. Therefore, we're the training ground as well as the national broadcasting service." Personal interview, John Dodge, General Manager, ZNS, Nassau, Bahamas, April 26, 1971.

66. "ZNS Broadcast Training Course," mimeographed outline in ZNS files.

67. Interview, Dodge.

68. Interview, Grosvenor.

69. Personal interview, Lenn Chongsing, Editor, *Guardian*, Port of Spain, Trinidad, September 1, 1970. The mass media have the same problem for a longer period of time when they send personnel abroad for training.

70. Roppa and Clarke, *Commonwealth Caribbean*, p. 90. In the spring of 1970 a journalistic workshop was held at Codrington College in Barbados, sponsored by the World Council of Churches, among others. Participants are destined to be the backbone of a Church News Service, with the eventual aim of starting an all-Caribbean weekly newspaper guaranteed financially by church funds. It will try, like *The Christian Science Monitor*, to provide people "with worthwhile reading in a way no commercial publisher could attempt." Rowlands, "Caribbean Tour Report 1970."

71. The only other professional organization of journalists in the islands is the Journalists Association of Trinidad and Tobago (JATT), organized in 1971. "Journalists To Draw Up Code," Trinidad *Guardian*, May 11, 1971. Press clubs and publishers' associations have appeared in the Bahamas, but they had generally short lives.

UNESCO, in its 1968 study, proposed that the 400–500 journalists of the region, plus about 800 stringers and part time journalists, join together in a regional association of journalists. PAJ was not enthusiastic, however, because it was felt that a regional group might water down the aims of the national organization by dragging it into arguments between nations. This can be understood when one realizes that Radio Anguilla does not belong to the Caribbean Broadcasting Union because St. Kitts is in the organization. Roppa and Clarke, *Commonwealth Caribbean*, p. 88.

72. Other goals are to "maintain and improve the professional standards of its members," protect rights and privileges of journalists, show recognition to outstanding journalists, and promote the activities in "the interest of public welfare." Roppa and Clarke, *Commonwealth Caribbean*, pp. 86–87. The 150-member group has written a code of ethics, published an annual, *Press, Radio, Television*, and administered the annual journalism awards. Personal interview, Ken Chaplin, Secretary, Press Association of Jamaica, Kingston, Jamaica, August 26, 1970.

73. Originally scheduled to open in October 1970, the program was delayed because of a political wrangle, according to the chairman of the school's general committee, Theodore Sealy. The Trinidad and Barbados branches of UWI, part of the journalism-school program, wanted the headquarters located on their campuses. Interview, Sealy.

74. College-level journalism was attempted in the Bahamas but failed because of lack of response. Interview, McDermott. ZNS in those islands has used the College Technical Center and local Dale Carnegie course to train personnel. Interview, Dodge.

75. "Diploma Course in Communications Set for West Indies University," *UNESCO Features*, no. 610, p. 9. Originally, the diploma course was to be aimed at graduates with at least one year of practical experience, at nongraduates holding other approved professional qualifications, or at exceptional candidates with at least three years' experience. Rowlands, "Caribbean Tour Report 1970."

76. Interview, Grosvenor. See also L. Hunt, "Mass Media in the West Indies," *The Democratic Journalist,* May 6, 1967, p. 63.

77. Personal interview, Inez Grant, Senior Education Officer, Ministry of Education, Kingston, Jamaica, August 28, 1970.

78. Max Millikan and Donald L. M. Blackmer, eds., *The Emerging Nations* (Boston: Little, Brown and Company, 1961), p. 47; see also Doob, *Communication in Africa,* p. 160.

79. Government of Trinidad and Tobago, *Third Five-Year Plan 1969–1973* (Port of Spain, Trinidad: Government Printery, 1969), p. 277.

80. For example, density of population per square mile on Barbados in 1969 was 1,528; on Trinidad, 516; on Jamaica, 447. Source: *Americas* (November–December 1970), p. 46.

81. Interview, Seal Coon.

82. Interview, Grosvenor.

83. Interview, Dodge.

84. Interview, McDermott.

85. Roppa and Clarke, *Commonwealth Caribbean,* p. 72.

86. *Third Five-Year Plan 1969–1973,* p. 283.

87. Personal interview, Phyllis Allfrey, Editor, Dominica *Star,* Roseau, Dominica, May 6, 1971.

88. Except for nationally owned networks in some countries and special radio networks used by civil aviation and meteorological services.

89. Roppa and Clarke, *Commonwealth Caribbean,* p. 73.

90. Ibid.

91. Personal interview, Ray Smith, Director, Windward Islands Broadcasting Service, St. George's, Grenada, May 12, 1971.

92. Roppa and Clarke, *Commonwealth Caribbean,* p. 74.

93. Ibid.

94. Ibid.

95. Interview, Stewart.

96. Interview, Dodge.

97. *Bahamas Handbook 1970–71* (Nassau, Bahamas: Etienne Dupuch, Jr. Publications, 1970), p. 269.

98. *Third Five-Year Plan 1969–73*, pp. 286–87.

99. Weather has been troublesome to both printed and electronic media in the islands. Hurricanes at various times have wiped out Rediffusion networks, the worst instance occurring in 1955 when Hurricane Janet destroyed 10,000 of the 12,000 hookups to the Barbados station. Central Rediffusion Services Ltd., *Commercial Broadcasting in the British West Indies* (London: Butterworth's Scientific Publications, 1956), p. 46.
  Newspaper distribution also has been affected by the weather (see Allfrey Story in Appendix D). The editor of the Trinidad *Evening News* felt that his paper's circulation would increase if the press run were not at noon, height of the daily rainstorm. But he cannot do much about solving the dilemma. As an afternoon paper, the *Evening News* depends on sales to workers in the outlying oilfields before they go home at 5 P.M.; to get the paper there before quitting time, press deadline must remain at noon. Personal interview, Compton Delph, Editor, *Evening News*, Port of Spain, Trinidad, September 1, 1970.

100. Interview, Grosvenor.

101. Interview, Stewart.

102. For example, when an increase in population that was expected in St. Lucia in 1970 did not materialize, the government declined to release census figures for that year. Source asked for anonymity.

103. Mervin Alleyne, "Communication and Politics in Jamaica," *Caribbean Studies* 3, no. 2: 26.

104. Interview, Seal Coon.

105. Interview, Chongsing.

106. Interview, Boyd.

107. Interview, de Pass.

108. Interview, Sealy.

109. John Maddison, *Radio and Television in Literacy: A Survey of the Use of the Broadcasting Media in Combating Illiteracy Among Adults* (Paris: UNESCO, 1971), pp. 9, 48–49.

110. Quoted in Pye, ed., *Communications and Political Development*, p. 337.

111. Roppa and Clarke, *Commonwealth Caribbean*, p. 17.

112. Wilbur Schramm, *Mass Media and National Development* (Stanford, Calif.:

Stanford University Press, 1964), p. 73. The rest of Schramm's quote was: "Illiteracy rapidly decreases the market for printed media outside the city, lack of electricity makes it hard to use electronic media, and a shaky transportation makes it hard to deliver anything." Schramm neglected to mention that the work pattern of rural peoples is a handicap in their use of printed media. As one Caribbean editor said, rural peoples retire early and are in the fields early the next day, allowing very little time for newspaper or magazine reading. Interview, Sealy.

113. Interview in Basseterre rum shop, May 1, 1971.

114. Interview of customers in a St. Lucia restaurant, May 7, 1971.

115. I am indebted to Wilbur Schramm for this notion.

116. These are 1968 figures; more recent income data were not available. "1968 Economic Indexes," *Americas* (November–December 1970), p. S-46.

117. Interview, Sealy.

118. Interview, Hodge.

119. Interview, Grosvenor. Most Commonwealth Caribbean newspapers sell for ten East Caribbean cents, although the *Workers Voice* can be purchased for five and the Bahamian newspapers charge fifteen Bahamian cents. Thus, the range is from three to fifteen United States cents.

120. Interview, Boyd.

121. Interview, Grosvenor.

122. Interview, de Leon.

123. Although the sponsors of the free viewing on Jamaica said that they put the sets in the public square as a public service on the occasion of independence. One of the two sponsors was a European television set manufacturer. "Thousands Enjoy TV in Park," *Daily Gleaner*, August 8, 1962.

124. Interview, Dodge.

125. Since rescinded.

126. A number of islands depend for program services from neighbors. For example, Dominicans in the more mountainous regions of that island can tune in Cuba, Martinique, and Guadeloupe stations; Vincentians get Trinidad and Barbados service.

127. UNESCO statistics as old as 1963 showed that there were 255 television sets per 1,000 population on Bermuda; 24 per 1,000 on Bahamas; and 16 per 1,000 on Trinidad. E. Lloyd Sommerlad, *The Press in Developing Countries* (Sydney, Australia: Sydney University Press, 1966), p. 53.

128.   Interview, de Leon.

129.   Personal interview, Ian Gale, General Manager, Caribbean Broadcasting Corporation, Bridgetown, Barbados, September 4, 1971.

130.   Interview, Michaels.

131.   Millikan said that where life is economically precarious, as in traditional societies, it is common for all members of a group of relatives to share their income. Millikan and Blackmer, eds., *The Emerging Nations*, p. 24.

132.   St. Lucia Television Rentals assesses the following weekly fees: $4 EC for an 11-inch set; $5 EC, 20-inch set; $5.50 EC, 24-inch set. After one year of service the customer is given a dollar-a-week reduction. The billing is done by mail every four weeks. The firm does not encounter collection problems because billing is eight weeks in advance. Interview, Archer. On Jamaica a 19-inch set rents for $6.50 Jamaican per month plus an initial installation charge of $10.70 Jamaican. Interview, Stewart. On Barbados there are several rental companies, including Rediffusion. A 19-inch television rents for $14 EC a month; 23-inch set, $17. When color arrives, a 19-inch color set will rent for $25 EC a month. Interview, Gale. And on Trinidad three firms, including Rediffusion, handle rentals. An average-size television there rents for $17 TT a month. Interview, de Leon.
   Rentals of a more personal nature are also prevalent in the islands. On Jamaica, for instance, there are people who charge neighbors twenty cents for a night of television viewing, as well as shopkeepers who allow customers to watch television "as long as they buy a beer now and then." Interview, Stewart.

133.   Personal interview, Roy Lawrence, Public Relations Director, Jamaica Broadcasting Corporation, Kingston, Jamaica, August 28, 1970.

134.   Interview, Michaels.

135.   One writer said that previous to the transistor's introduction to the British West Indies, "for economic consumption of electricity and for long preservation of batteries in rural areas that are not electrified, radio owners frequently practice selective listening." Alleyne, "Communications and Politics in Jamaica," p. 36.

136.   Interview, de Leon.

137.   A Jamaican broadcaster said that the transistor's effect on the lower strata of society was to increase gambling. "Both radio and television air horseracing and this has tremendously increased transistor sales. People buy them to listen to the races. Every day a race is broadcast and on Saturdays, there are six live races on television." Personal interview, Roy Lawrence, Public Relations Director, Jamaica Broadcasting Corporation, Kingston, Jamaica, August 28, 1970.

138.   As early as the 1930s the ZNS (Bahamas) manager traversed the mail-boat circuit of those islands, installing community radio sets so that out islanders could hear war news and hurricane warnings. Interview, Dodge.

139.   Central Rediffusion Services, *Commercial Broadcasting*, p. 49.

8

Mass Media
and West Indian Governments

The relativity of the concept of freedom of the press is exemplified by mass media in the Commonwealth Caribbean.

Item: Ask a Trinidadian television official employed by the government outlet about his station's relationships with the Williams government, and he will reply that they are "very cordial indeed."[1]

Item: Ask the same question of a black-power newspaper editor on St. Lucia, and he will answer that "government-media relationships are not good at all," and that the government is completely unaware of the importance of mass media in projecting an image.[2]

Item: Inquire about the nature of mass media freedom in the islands, and the answers from media personnel will range from "we get away with practically anything" on Jamaica,[3] to "don't be surprised if the government closes us down" on St. Kitts.[4]

In the light of this varying spectrum of belief, this chapter will first explore the concept of freedom of the press in the developing nations of the Commonwealth Caribbean, and then, using a categorization plan conceived by Siebert[5] in 1948, government relationships with the mass media of the Commonwealth Caribbean will be studied under these headings: government as a regulatory agency, as a restrictive agency, as a facilitating agency, and as a participating agency.

CONCEPT OF FREEDOM OF THE PRESS

Sommerlad classified the nations of the world in three broad categories with regard to their attitudes concerning freedom of the press:

251

authoritarian, liberal, and evolving.[6] The first two categories are familiar to students of freedom of the press; the third, according to Sommerlad, includes those nations in the

> no man's land where social institutions are still being shaped, where democracy is in the balance and one-party states are developing, and where the relations between press and government are ill-defined. The press is caught up in an ideological whirlpool and there is little ground for optimism that the western concept of a free press will survive.[7]

Because of the transitional nature of these societies, government leaders feel that a modification of traditional concepts of freedom of the press is in order.* They claim that in emerging nations unusual powers are sometimes necessary to force decisions that will benefit the people. Acting as benevolent dictators, they ask that the mass media show restraint in criticizing government. Press magnate Roy Thomson, who owns a number of media in the evolving world, agrees with these leaders:

> From my own experience, I am convinced that in some of the new nations of the world, criticism of Governments may legitimately be subject to some degree of restriction. Some of the journalists in these developing countries do not have a sufficient background of knowledge, experience and judgment to enable them to restrain themselves from destructive or inflammatory criticism which, exposed to populations which have not yet learned the art of political stability, could lead to serious unrest and even revolutionary activity.[8]

Although mass media in the Commonwealth Caribbean evince an evolving-world attitude toward freedom of the press, they can also be characterized as being influenced by authoritarian and liberal concepts. This is natural in any country, and especially so in evolving cultures that borrow extensively from both authoritarian and liberal philosophies.

---

* Caribbean communicators, discussing media usage for developmental purposes in 1974, agreed that freedom of the press was a concept that originated under different circumstances in other parts of the world and was then transferred into the region. They added that the concept was based on the availability of sufficient resources to allow for a plurality of media. Since resources are scarce in the Caribbean, they felt that the concept should be replaced with institutionalized forms of public accountability and public accessibility as applied to formal media. (*Intermedia* 2, no. 4 [1974]: iii.)

Governments of newly independent nations such as those of the Commonwealth Caribbean do have authoritarian tendencies, oftentimes the result of their colonial upbringing.[9] Singham, referring indirectly to the Commonwealth Caribbean, has said that despite their espousal of egalitarian and democratic ideas, these developing countries

> tend to have basically authoritarian personalities. . . . Even those who rebel against the repression of colonialism retain their authoritarianism when they achieve power and try to introduce change.[10]

Although the two-party system of government predominates in the region, most islands are controlled by strong, charismatic leaders. One-man rule is particularly evident on islands such as Grenada and St. Kitts. For example, Eric Gairy of Grenada is involved in nearly everything that takes place in his government, including the hiring and firing of secretaries, road-construction workers, and policemen. Some Grenadian editors claim that the people have given Gairy "Christ-like reverence."[11] Robert Bradshaw of St. Kitts-Nevis and Eric Williams[12] of Trinidad and Tobago are nearly as powerful. The relatively long tenures of office of these leaders (in the case of Williams dating to the mid-1950s) have lent themselves to the setting up of authoritarian governments.

Because of the smallness of the islands and the heavy reliance upon government services, leaders often perpetuate themselves in office through personal contact and patronage of the public. As one writer concluded:

> In a small island of 50,000 or 100,000 people, dominated by a single political party, it is very difficult to prevent political abuse. Everybody depends on the government for something, however small, so most are reluctant to offend it. The civil servants live in fear; the police avoid unpleasantness; the trade unions are tied to the party; the newspapers depend on government advertisements, and so on.[13]

On almost every island, at varying times, authoritarian actions have been taken against the mass media. Licensing regulations have been tightened to silence certain opposition newspapers,* expatriate

---

* At a meeting in 1974 of Caribbean developmental communicators, it was suggested that the licensing system used in broadcasting be extended to print media, such an arrangement being seen as contractual, with rights and duties on both sides. (Supplement to *Intermedia* 2, no. 4 [1974]: iv.)

journalists have been denied work-permit renewals (thus being forced from the islands), a printing press was confiscated, economic sanctions have been levied, and in some cases traditional news sources have been replaced by government press releases. But the seriousness of these incidents does not compare with what happened in Greece, Burma, Indonesia, or Cuba during the past decade, where whole segments of the nations' mass media operations were suppressed. Except for a few rare cases, most of the overt government action against mass media in the Commonwealth Caribbean has been individual in nature, with specific media or journalists coming under attack.

Of course, the island governments are capable of larger-scale suppression. One writer pointed out that although the government of Trinidad & Tobago is powerful enough to completely control mass communications, self-restraints are used to assure freedom of the press.

> In a small country like Trinidad, despite a press it did not control, the political regime dominated the public communications system. With a strong party, led by a strong personality, this tendency is enhanced so that, in effect, self-constraints had to be exercised by political leadership to assure an open system as far as the media were concerned.[14]

Others would argue that a government such as that of Trinidad & Tobago does control the mass media, but through indirect means. Of the four nongovernment-owned media on that island, three are in the hands of foreign enterprises.* Apparently Prime Minister Williams's regular outbursts against foreign ownerships keep them in line.[15] On other islands similar situations exist. The Bradshaw government on St. Kitts owns the radio-TV broadcasting outlet, controls one of the newspapers through the dominant political party, and threatens the expatriate editor of the other newspaper with expulsion if he gets too critical. On Grenada the broadcasting outlet is completely under government control, as is one of the newspapers. Grenadian newspaper editors complain that most of their news sources are drying up, while the government attempts to rule by press releases and police action.

Oppositionist Press

On the other hand, the strong oppositionist presses in the islands make for a paradox: editors complain about government suppression

---

* Since 1975 the *Guardian* and *Evening News* have been predominantly in the hands of Caribbean enterpreneur Charles McEnearney.

ALEONG Jan. 29, 1959

New style, 1959.

Cartoon depiction of a Williams press conference in 1959; the same can be said of many island premiers today.

at the same time that their presses grind out strongly worded condemnations that would not find their way into print in many Western democracies.

Pye has said that an oppositionist press is a natural by-product of independence; editors who criticized every colonial act find it very difficult being anything but critical and negative about national governments after independence. Thus their criticism is usually unconstructive and hostile.[16] The same is true in the Commonwealth Caribbean. Except for those owned by ruling political parties, most newspapers in the region, especially on the smaller islands, are very critical of governmental actions. Larger-island dailies generally offer a more constructive type of criticism than the political nondailies, which resort to name-calling and character assassination.

That this criticism is tolerated in the newly independent Commonwealth Caribbean is an indication that local governments have accepted some liberal points of view of freedom of the press. Commenting on postcolonial societies as a whole, Fagen said that they cannot tolerate disruptive criticism and therefore usually tighten their controls over media channels.[17] Yet, in the Commonwealth Caribbean, a great deal of disruptive criticism is still voiced, to the extent that newspapers on Grenada, on Dominica, and in the Bahamas refer to government officials as Hitlerites and Gestapo imitators.* A nondaily in Trinidad espouses Mao philosophies, and militant black-power newspapers appear from time to time on St. Lucia, Jamaica, Trinidad, Dominica, and Grenada. Normally, when the black-power papers disappear, the cause of death stems from economic starvation, not from government suppression.[18] However, the economic starvation might be linked with governmental denial of legal notices to these papers.

Because a large proportion of broadcasting in the region is government owned, criticisms of government have not been so intense on these media.** As some broadcasters point out, for a public broadcasting system to criticize its government owner is equivalent to an editor blasting his publisher in the publisher's own newspaper.[19]

---

* In Dominica a recent headline declared that the premier's wife "cannot make love to any man; how can she love her country?" (Personal interview, Edward Scobie, former *Herald* editor, Castries, St. Lucia, January 9, 1976). The December 25, 1975, issue of St. Lucia *Crusader* carried a page-one drawing of the premier chained to capitalism, exploitation, and imperialism, at the same time he was using the whip on poor St. Lucians. The greeting read, "It's Merry Hell this Xmas!! and Happy-Hell in the New Year."

** Judging from comments made by the CBU president in 1973, there have been recent instances of broadcasters being fired by government authorities for dabbling in politics and for their reporting on certain political matters. (*Combroad* [March–April 1974], pp. 44–45.) A popular disk jockey who used patois was fired by Radio Caribbean on St. Lucia because he angered a chief advertiser in 1975. A priest who was critical of the Dominican government was banned by Radio Dominica in 1975; the officials said he was using his religion show to espouse political ideas. Another priest was censored by Radio Caribbean for denouncing political violence on St. Lucia. On Trinidad, the new director of 610 Radio fired five key broadcasters in 1975, including the chief newscaster, chief sportscaster, and director of programs. Apparently these individuals were released because they advocated oppositionist views or disagreed with station management policies ("The Rolling of Heads at 610 Radio," *Caribbean Contact* [October 1975], p. 24).

Privately owned broadcasting units have been freer in their criticisms of government, as indicated in this description of Radio Jamaica talk shows:

> People would call in and say the most inflammatory things—and get away with it. Then one night on a talk show, a fellow asked if it were true what he'd heard about the sex life of a certain highly placed government official. He put it in the baldest terms. They cut him off the air, but not before the damage was done. The official didn't say a thing. But we've been careful since then to pre-record all the talk shows.[20]

Island governments are extremely sensitive about the oppositionist press,[21] although they do not always react to its outpourings. The small size of the political units in the British West Indies tends to magnify internal problems, so that even a whispering campaign does not go unnoticed. Therefore, when an oppositionist newspaper blows up a governmental problem or anomaly, the officials feel that they have reason to be concerned. As a result, authorities keep an eye on media content: on Jamaica, by monitoring radio and television shows and clipping newspapers; on St. Lucia, by police monitoring of radio shows; on Trinidad and other islands, by direct complaints from government ministers to the media. Again, because of the geographical smallness of the islands, the relationship between media personnel and the highest government officials is highly personal. For example, prime ministers have been known to telephone editors and broadcasters to complain about content; on Antigua a high official calls ZAL-TV to tell the general manager which shows he enjoys.[22] This example from the author's journal points out the personalness of the relationship between government and mass media on these small islands:

The 10 A.M. newscaster on Trinidad Broadcasting Company's "Radio Trinidad" casually mentioned that a number of hotel employees had been called out on strike that day, hardly significant news during normalcy. But in August 1970 Trinidad was far from being in a normal state, having lived under emergency rule for over four months. Among the many provisions of the emergency were: (1) striking was illegal, (2) the media, especially broadcasting, were restricted as to what they could say. I was sitting in the office of Sam Ghany, sales manager of Trinidad Broadcasting Company, when the strike news broke. Within five minutes after the announcement, the minister of labor of Trinidad had Ghany on the phone, asking about the validity of the newscast, its source, and why the station ran the news. Especially since the emergency rules went into effect in April 1970, such personal (and sometimes intimidating) calls from high governmental officials—even as high as Prime Minister Eric Williams himself—have not been uncommon.

Evolving Concept and Press Responsibility

Realizing that the free-swinging, often libelous, and mostly disruptive nature of criticism of the press in the postcolonial period cannot continue without serious governmental interference, some people are pushing for more responsible mass media in the region. Some of the newspapers themselves are discussing a "deliberately guided" press, while the few press associations in the region are setting up professional codes of ethics.

The deliberately guided press principles match up closely with those Sommerlad classified as evolving. For example, a Trinidadian editor, Raoul Pantin, writing on the eighth anniversary of his island's nationhood, said that criticism by the mass media must be more constructive than it has been and that a journalist

> should criticise a group, be it a Political Party, a Government or any other sector in that society, for fooling around with the national effort. But always, underlying every criticism, must be an appreciation for the fact that the national effort is necessary. . . . Deliberate guidance from within the Press itself is vital. This has to do with the Press itself assessing its responsibilities and then fulfilling them. For inevitably, if the Press does not do this, it will lay itself open to sanctions from other sectors of the society. In contemporary times, it can be said, and it has been said, that the Press in Trinidad and Tobago is free. But on closer examination, such freedom has been purely technical since the local media has [sic] emasculated itself (more in anticipation than from any genuine testing of freedom) and has therefore provided its own safeguards against clashing with forces that can impose sanctions. In such a situation, the Press may be said to be free but it cannot be said to be responsible.[23]

Pantin felt that the freedom of the press conceptualized by the late Tom Mboya, former minister of economic planning and development in Kenya, was what his nation needed. Mboya wanted to see the press maintain enough freedom to protect people against corruption and abuse by junior officials, but he also argued that

freedom of the press in a new country . . . has got to be limited: not
so much by legislation; but rather, deliberately guided; for its main
functions include not only giving news but also taking part in the
national effort and contributing towards the building of a nation.[24]

Editors on at least Jamaica and St. Lucia have reassessed their responsibilities to the people and nation. The editor of the Jamaica
Daily Gleaner contrasted his paper's concept of freedom of the press
with that of the United States as follows:

> The American press thinks a newspaper's role is to solve the
> problems of the world. That is all right, but we feel it is the govern-
> ment's business to run the government, not the newspaper's. In the
> United States, they use the press as a political apparatus. We are
> not in that sphere. We provide a forum for the community in which
> the community itself carries out the action. It is not our function to
> run the country, but rather to take part in a discussion of the coun-
> try's operations.[25]

The *Voice of St. Lucia* has stopped criticizing the government directly;
instead, its editor allows the government to criticize itself through
background and interpretative stories. "We put a mirror up to the
government officials and let them show themselves," he said.[26]

At least three professional groups of journalists in the region see
the need for more responsible mass media. The relatively young Caribbean Broadcasting Union hopes to make broadcasters more responsible
through better training schemes; the Journalists Association of Trinidad
& Tobago, during its first sessions upon organization in 1971, formu-
lated a code of ethics for journalists. The Press Association of Jamaica
(PAJ), which includes both newsmen and broadcasters among its
members, is concerned with freedom of the press, but at the same time
acts as a disciplinary body toward members who deviate from the
organization's code of ethics. PAJ claims that it has made a stand not
only against misbehaving journalists, but also against publishers, other
media organizations, and the government.[27]

A team of UNESCO investigators in 1968 proposed that a Caribbean Association of Journalists be formed to raise the dignity, standard,
and role of journalists throughout the region, and to introduce—and
enforce by self-disciplinary action—an ethical code of professional
conduct.[28] However, as of 1972 such an organization had not been

established in the region. Nor has the regional press council, proposed by UNESCO, been implemented.*

Constitutional Guarantees

Freedom of press/speech is covered in most constitutions that have been written in the Commonwealth Caribbean since independence.[29]

An example of the freedom-of-expression guarantee found in island constitutions is this statement from the Jamaica (Constitution) Order in Council, 1962:

> 22.—(1) Except with his own consent, no person shall be hindered in the enjoyment of his freedom of expression, and for the purposes of this section the said freedom includes the freedom to hold opinions and to receive and impart ideas and information without interference, and freedom from interference with his correspondence and other means of communication. (2) Nothing contained in or done under the authority of any law shall be held to be inconsistent with or in contravention of this section to the extent that the law in question makes provision—(a) which is reasonably required—(i) in the interests of defence, public safety, public order, public morality or

---

* Although a policy-making board for regional media has been set up, resulting from a December 1974 seminar on Communications and Information for Development Purposes in the Caribbean Area, held in Guyana. The body, National Information Communication Council (NICC), will deal with communication policy, planning, regulation, and evaluation. Made up of representatives of government, media management, development-support communication units, and citizen and community groups, NICC will examine issues such as the development of formal media infrastructures and progress of development-support communication. (*Asian Mass Communication Bulletin* [March 1975], p. 14. Fuller account published as supplement to *Intermedia* 2, 4 [1974]: i–iv.) A press council for the Caribbean was planned to take effect in mid-1976. The dean of the University of West Indies law faculty will head the council that will include four journalists, four representatives named by the Caribbean Publishers and Broadcasters Association, and eight lay members chosen by the council head. The council will be organized along the lines of similar bodies in Scandinavia and Great Britain. It will be self-regulatory. There is "very strong opposition against the press council" emanating from both journalists and some government media personnel, who feel the council will mean government interference with the press (Personal interview, J. C. Proute, editor, *The Jamaica Daily News*, Kingston, Jamaica, January 16, 1976). The general manager of the Gleaner Company in Jamaica said that he has washed his hands of the press council, because his newspapers feel that "the government has no right to get involved in the news flow." His main complaint was that the irresponsible presses of the region, not being CPBA members, will not come under the council aegis. Also, he did not appreciate other islanders' sitting in judgment on Jamaican media, and vice versa (Personal interview, G. A. Sherman, general manager, Gleaner Co., Kingston, Jamaica, January 15, 1976).

public health; or (ii) for the purpose of protecting the reputations, rights and freedoms of other persons, or the private lives of persons concerned in legal proceedings, preventing the disclosure of information received in confidence, maintaining the authority and independence of the courts, or regulating telephone, telegraphy, posts, wireless broadcasting, television or other means of communication, public exhibitions or public entertainments; or (b) which imposes restrictions upon public officers, police officers or upon members of a defence force.[30]

As the Farquharson Institute of Public Affairs in Kingston interpreted the Jamaican constitution,* the right of freedom of speech is not absolute, unlimited, or unqualified. For example, limits have been placed on freedom of expression where it is necessary to maintain justice or fair-trial guarantees.

GOVERNMENT AS A REGULATORY AND RESTRICTIVE AGENCY

In earlier times the function of government in the field of communications was in regulatory and restrictive capacities. This still holds true to a great extent. In most nations a number of regulations have been enacted to protect individuals and societies against harmful publication. Usually these laws are meant to protect individual interests

---

* Examples of other constitutional guarantees follow: The Trinidad and Tobago Constitution already guarantees freedom of the press; a new constitution under consideration would do likewise, stating that no restrictions shall be placed on any person in the exercise of his right to freedom of expression, and that, specifically, no law shall restrict the freedom of the press or any other mass media (David Renwick, "Press As an Ombudsman," *The Nation*, November 30, 1975, p. 9). The Barbados Constitution does not specifically mention freedom of the press, but does read:

Except with his own consent, no person shall be hindered in the enjoyment of his freedom of conscience and for the same purpose of this section the said freedom includes freedom of thought and religion, freedom to change his religion or belief, and freedom, either alone or in a community with others, and both in public and in private, to manifest and propagate his religion or belief in worship, teaching, practice and observance. Except with his own consent, no person shall be hindered in the enjoyment of his freedom of expression, and for the purpose of this section the said freedom includes the freedom to hold opinions without interference, freedom to receive ideas and information without interference, freedom to communicate ideas and information without interference and freedom from interference with his correspondence or other means of communication ("Constitution," *The Nation*, November 25, 1975, p. 46).

against untruthful and unjustifiable publication, defend common standards of the community, and protect against internal disorders and interferences with the operation of government. Specifically, the laws that come under these categories guard against libel, sedition, importation of publications detrimental to the common good, obscenity, invasion of privacy, and the misuse of broadcasting services.

Press Laws

Probably the laws having the most serious effects upon newspapers in the Commonwealth Caribbean are those dealing with libel and sedition. Both have been used, and sometimes misused, by island governments to restrict newspaper operations. Although private West Indian citizens are protected by the libel laws, most of the suits of any magnitude are brought by government or political figures. This is understandable because of the politically oppositionist nature of the papers; most of their attacks are directed against politicians and government officials, rather than against private individuals. Also, island newspapers are not protected by libel laws when dealing with public officials,[31] as United States mass media are protected by the *New York Times* v. *Sullivan* decision.

It is not unusual for heads of government and ministers to bring libel suits against Commonwealth Caribbean newspapers; both Eric Gairy of Grenada and Eric Williams of Trinidad have done so.[32] Grenadian editors go so far as to accuse Gairy of intimidating media, both foreign and domestic, with libel suits.[33] In the two-year period 1969 to 1971, Gairy either threatened or actually brought libel suits against *Look* magazine, some London media,[34] and *Torchlight* and *Vanguard* on Grenada. According to the *Vanguard* editor, the four libel suits Gairy brought against his paper during the two years were meant to

> cripple us financially. He pursues his libel cases with the *Vanguard* to the end. In one case, we lost $12,000 (EC), but the public came up with the money for us. Party people and anti-government citizens donated money to pay for our libel case.[35]

Newspapers on Antigua and St. Kitts have also been subjected to government pressure through libel laws. In January 1972 both Antigua opposition newspapers, *Workers Voice* and *Times*, were forced to shut down because of the enactment of amendments to the Newspaper Registration Act and the Newspaper Surety Ordinance. The first amendment requires that newspapers pay an annual license fee of $300 (US); the second imposes a bond of $5,000 (US) on the papers to cover expenses that might be caused by libel actions. The newspapers have takn the matter to the local courts* and the Inter American Press Association.[36]

Similar types of laws were expected to be passed on St. Kitts.** Because of increasing governmental threats, the St. Kitts *Democrat*, an opposition weekly, has taken the precaution of having all copy read by a party lawyer for possible libel.[37]

Protection of internal security has been used by a number of islands to restrict press operations. In 1972 the Inter American Press Association was investigating the possible misuse of sedition acts by the governments of St. Kitts, Trinidad, and Grenada.

The St. Kitts Press and Publications Board Bill of 1971 was presented to Parliament after Premier Robert Bradshaw's government won reelection in May of that year.*** Bradshaw had promised during his campaign that, if reelected, he would close the opposition weekly, St. Kitts *Democrat*.[38] It seems that the enactment of this bill was his way of attempting to kill the paper. However, the stated purpose of the bill (ultimately made into law) was to prohibit "undesirable pub-

---

* And apparently, higher. In mid-1975 the British Privy Council ruled that neither act contravened the nation's Constitution. (*The Times* of London, May 20, 1975, p. 23.)

** Of course, laws of this nature have been on the books for generations; they just had not been used much previously. For example, on St. Lucia there is "An Ordinance To Regulate the Printing and Publishing of Newspapers and To Assimilate the Law of The Colony in This Respect to the Law of England, 28 May 1844." It stipulates that newspapers must register with the government, file copies of each edition with the Registrar, and post bond against possible libel fines. However, one lawyer said that the extent to which the law has been used can be gauged by the fact that he himself has never read the law. In 1975 Grenada passed the Newspaper (Amendment) Act, which stipulates that it is illegal to print or publish any newspaper unless an annual payment of EC$500 is made for a license, as well as a bond of EC$960 and a cash deposit of EC$20,000. Of the five weeklies and biweeklies, only the government's *West Indian* is published in the context of the law ("Grenada," *Caribbean Monthly Bulletin* [July 1975], p. 12). A clause of the Grenada Act states: "Where a Justice of the Peace is satisfied by information on oath that there is reasonable ground for suspecting that an offence under this Act is being, has been, or is about to be committed on any premises, he may issue a warrant in writing authorizing any police officer to enter those premises, if necessary by force, at any time within 14 days from the time of the issue of the warrant and search them" (Rickey Singh, "Press Freedom Is Taking a Beating," *The Nation*, November 30, 1975, pp. 10–11).

*** By the end of 1975 the premier of St. Kitts-Nevis had not rescinded the Press and Publications Board Bill, and, according to the Inter American Press Association, publishers continued to operate in fear of prosecution.

lications calculated to harm the national interest." Bradshaw denied that the new law would diminish freedom of the press on St. Kitts.[39]

One of the potentially dangerous internal security laws, designed to muzzle the press, was The Seditious and Undesirable Publications Act,* passed on Dominica in 1968. This law, which gave the authorities broad powers of interpretation, provided for the closing of suspected newspapers until a judicial decision could be reached, seizure or banning of imported or local publications, banning of publishers and editors from newsrooms for one year, closing of convicted newspapers for one year, and seizure of mail suspected of containing prohibited publications. In addition, citizens could be forced to surrender banned publications to the police, and break/enter/search warrants could be used in the confiscation of such materials.[40] Edward Scobie, editor of the Dominica *Herald*, told how the act came about:

> In 1968, the government was getting repeated criticism from the press, especially from the *Herald*. The premier said that I was destroying his image by talking of government incompetence. He tried to close the paper in various ways, first by trying to entice me into giving it up. He promised me he'd put me in charge of national radio or commission me to write the island's history, if I gave the *Herald* up. Then he tried to get at me on charges that the paper did not pay its debts. When the Seditious and Undesirable Publications bill was proposed, we three editors got together and campaigned. We said if one of us was forced to close down, others would close with token strikes.[41]

While the bill was being debated in the House of Representatives, Scobie, *Chronicle* editor S. A. W. Boyd, *Star* editors Robert and Phyllis Allfrey, and nearly 3,000 Dominicans demonstrated outside the building. Despite this public reaction, the bill was only slightly amended and passed. The resentment caused by the passage of the sedition act encouraged the formation of the Freedom Party by Scobie, the Allfreys, and other anti-government sympathizers. The main campaign issue of the Freedom Party in succeeding elections was the sedition act.[42] The law itself has never been repealed, nor has it been enforced,

---

* In 1975, when a priest was banned from Radio Dominica, one writer stated that the incident happened to warn that the Seditious and Undesirable Publications Act was in effect (Rickey Singh, "Press Freedom Is Taking a Beating," *The Nation*, November 30, 1975, pp. 10–11).

probably because it would make a martyr of the press.* According to the Trinidad *Evening News*, the Dominican press has given the government ample reason to enforce the law. In August 1968 the *Evening News* reported:

> Trinidad & Tobago has not seen in recent years anything in the nature of such personal and near-libellous attacks on Ministers of Government as those found in the Dominican newspapers.[43]

Whereas most of these bills have resulted from government sensitivity to criticism, there have been occasions where island governments initiated press legislation because of serious threats to internal security.

After the black-power revolt on Trinidad in April 1970, emergency regulations were clamped on the mass media, as they were on all sectors of the society. In effect for approximately seven months, the Emergency Powers Regulations were geared to keep to a minimum the publicity given the April insurgents.[44] For example, there was a complete ban on the publication of pictures of the revolt leaders (and their relatives), as well as any of their court testimony. Media were allowed to identify the revolutionaries only by their names, addresses, occupations, ages, and the charges brought against them. During this period the government had the power to control and censor media content and ban publication; however, it did not use these powers, despite critical comments in the press.[45]

On the heels of the emergency was a proposed Public Order Act, which drew tremendous fire from Trinidadians of all walks of life. Among numerous other rules, the proposed bill stated that anyone publishing "threatening, abusive or insulting" matter, or distributing such literature at a public meeting or on a public march, was subject to arrest.[46] After much discussion the bill was dropped. However, in early 1972 the IAPA reported that a new sedition law had been enacted on Trinidad, which the "journalists of that country consider dangerous to the free practice of their profession."[47]

Feeling a threat to internal security following black-power demonstrations in late 1970, and nutmeg workers' and nurses' strikes of early

---

* Since this was written, it has been enforced. By the way, Scobie, his Freedom Party, and *Herald* were involved in an attempt to take over the Dominican government on December 16, 1971. Scobie and five others were arrested on charges of committing violence and inciting to violence. Scobie was acquitted; he said the acquittal was a political move on the part of the government. Scobie left Dominica in early 1972; the *Herald* folded shortly after (Personal interview, Edward Scobie, former editor, *Herald*, Castries, St. Lucia, January 9, 1976).

1971, the Grenadian government proposed a strong amendment to the Public Order Act, promulgated on that island in 1951. The amendment stated that

> a person is guilty of an offense if (a) he publishes or distributes written material which is threatening, abusive or insulting, or (b) he uses in any public place or at any public meeting or proceeding, words which are threatening, abusive or insulting.[48]

Persons found guilty of these offenses were liable to a fine not to exceed $2,500 (EC) or 12 months in prison, and not less than $1,000 (EC) or six months in prison. The act was still hanging over the heads of the media in mid-1971.

Other instances in which states of emergency* have hindered press functioning were Jamaica in 1967, Antigua in 1968, and Montserrat and Anguilla in 1969. During the Antigua state of emergency, the Bird government summoned mass media personnel to the premier's office to tell them what he expected to be published and broadcast. According to one editor, the media were cooperative because they did not want to damage the island's image abroad.[49]

Island governments have also banned the importation of foreign media, considered possible threats to internal security.[50] Sometimes this action is carried out without the use of internal security laws. For example, a National Broadcasting Company commentator said that the Jamaican government exercises a selective form of censorship, preventing circulation of books that might foster black consciousness. "Titillating books are allowed, but nothing by Malcolm X or Stokely Carmichael. That is government policy," he added.[51] In other cases, a movie, "Halls of Anger," was banned by the St. Lucia Film Censors Board in 1971, because it dealt with the race problem; the Anguilla *Beacon* was prohibited on St. Kitts during the 1969 troubles between those two islands. An 1877 Newspaper Act (revised in 1961) was used to keep out the *Beacon*. It stipulated that no person may sell or deliver on St. Kitts any paper or pamphlet without first registering with the Supreme Court.[52]

It does not appear that there is much banning of foreign publi-

---

* Various emergency periods have existed in the region in recent years. In March 1973 Bermuda was declared in a state of emergency after the murder of the island's governor. In June 1973 Dominica was placed under emergency rule after widespread protests against the transfer of a popular disc jockey. Grenada was paralyzed economically by island-wide strikes at the time it received its independence in February 1974. Bahamas was in a threatening position at the time of its independence in July 1973; some of the outer islands, such as Abaco, made noises of secession.

cations that would be considered obscene or pornographic in some cultures. American and British male magazines, usually *Playboy* or *Penthouse,* are readily available on most islands,* as are a number of the "restricted" movies from the United States. There have been a few instances of movie censorship because the films were considered potential threats to the morals of the community. For example, in 1970 Trinidadian film censors banned the showing on that island of "Midnight Cowboy" and "Bonnie and Clyde."[53] On the Windward islands, where the populations are predominantly Roman Catholic, there have also been cases of movie censorship.[54]

Newspapers, even the most radical black-power weeklies, refrain from the use of profanity and obscenity in advertisements and news copy. Although newspapers on tourist islands use an abundance of photographs of girls in bikinis, they do not portray nude females as do a number of Asian newspapers. License requirements of most broadcasting stations emphatically stipulate that obscene material cannot be used in commercials or programs.

Broadcasting Laws

Laws prohibiting harmful broadcasting are generally more detailed than press laws in the Commonwealth Caribbean. Government licenses, under which broadcasting units operate, spell out what the stations can and cannot do. On a few islands broadcasting authorities, designed somewhat like the Federal Communications Commission in the United States, watch over individual broadcasting units. Oldest and most active of these island regulatory bodies is the Jamaica Broadcasting Authority,** in existence since the late 1950s.[55] The Jamaica Broadcasting Authority investigates content and format of JBC radio and television and of Radio Jamaica, but it admits that its random checks are not effective because of a shortage of manpower to monitor stations.[56] However, the board has reprimanded radio and television stations for using too much foreign programming, cramming too many

---

* However, in 1976 I was told by a bookstore employee on St. Lucia that magazines of this type have been banned by the post office.

** The Authority was under severe criticism in 1975 for not functioning effectively as a monitor and arbiter of broadcast policy, standards, and programming, partly because of lack of continuity of personnel and policies. The JBC modernization and expansion plan recommends the establishment of a broadcasting commission, made up of representative membership, reflecting the most important sectors of society. JBC would be answerable to the commission on matters of program policy and content, technical and commercial standards. The commission, in turn, would be answerable to Parliament. (*Combroad* [April–June 1975], p. 18.)

commercials into prime time, programming a minstrel show offensive to a part of the black population, and not "Jamaicanizing" commercials.[57]

At the dawn of the 1970s Trinidad still had neither a permanent regulatory body for broadcasting nor a telecommunications act, although both were in the thinking stage of development.[58] An interim board, sponsored by the government but composed of civilians, provides direction for broadcasting on Trinidad. On other islands the broadcasting regulatory body usually consists of one man, the premier. Broadcasting personnel on the larger islands of Jamaica, Barbados, and Bahamas also claim that, despite the presence of broadcasting boards, the prime minister (or premier) is actually the officer in charge of broadcasting.[59] For example, ZNS in the Bahamas is under the supervision of an independent five-man commission appointed by the governor, in consultation with the prime minister. Actually, however, the prime minister appoints members to the commission.[60] On Dominica, as plans were shaping up for a new national broadcasting system, the manager-designate tried to persuade government that he needed a broadcasting board to serve as a buffer between him and his staff and the government.* In other words, he did not want the station to be a division of the premier's office, as is the case on some of the smaller islands.[61] On Anguilla an advisory group, the Anguillan Broadcasting Committee, offers suggestions to the radio station. The committee, appointed by the Anguilla Council, has no legislative power.[62]

Usually the broadcasting laws set down in government licenses are rather inclusive, dealing mainly with advertising practices, but

---

* The St. Lucia Broadcasting Corporation Act of October 28, 1974, was designed to provide a corporation to develop broadcasting in St. Lucia. The body is made up of five to seven members appointed by the governor. Its purposes are to "undertake all broadcasting equipment, facilities, programmes at present managed by Radio St. Lucia," to promote and manage all aspects of radio-TV broadcasting, and to appoint the manager to carry out the day-to-day work of the Corporation. Media personnel on St. Lucia seemed vague about the working of the corporation. The government public relations officer did not know the duties of the corporation; the director of Radio St. Lucia said that it was a board to promote and manage the stations and to listen to citizens' complaints about broadcasting. As it is written, the act is meant only for Radio St. Lucia, he said, but the language in the act allows some control of other broadcast media. "It is not clear and will have to be tested," he added (Personal interviews, Albert Mason, public relations officer, government of St. Lucia, Castries, St. Lucia, January 9, 1976, and Winston Hinkson, director, Radio St. Lucia, Castries, St. Lucia, January 10, 1976).

also covering deceptive programming, privacy, libel, and political broadcasts.

On Jamaica the stations are regulated by the Sound Broadcasting Regulations of 1963, which stipulate that the licensee shall "not permit to be broadcast obscene, profane. . . , malicious, scandalous and defamatory matter in contravention of the laws of Jamaica." In addition, stations are not permitted to broadcast false or deceptive advertising or false or misleading news. Newscasts must be objective, fair, accurate, free from bias, and factual. Advertising requirements prohibit broadcasting of "any matter which describes repellently any function or symptomatic results of disturbances of the human body or relief in such disturbances through the use of any appliance or medicament," any promotion for schools that offer an inducement for enrollment (such as promises of employment), any advertising of matrimonial agencies, fortune telling, astrology, obeah, occultism, or palm reading. Furthermore, liquor, wine, and beer advertisements cannot directly urge purchase or consumption of such products, and drugs and medicine advertisements must comply with the provisions of the Drugs and Poisons Law. Advertising content must not exceed five minutes in any half-hour program segment, or twelve minutes in an hour. Stations are ordered to refrain from the use of material that encourages or incites to crime or a breach of the peace. Concerning political broadcasting, the Jamaica broadcast rules stipulate that sponsors and political parties, on whose behalf a speech or address is made, must be identified before and after the broadcast. Also, dramatized political broadcasts are not permitted on Jamaican stations.[63]

The Bahamas Broadcasting Act of 1956 (revised 1965 and amended 1969) sets the rules for ZNS-1 and ZNS-2. The minister in charge of Bahamian broadcasting is provided with wide administrative powers by the 1969 amendment. For example, he may make rules "to control the character of any and all programmes broadcast or televised by the Commission; to determine the proportion of time which may be devoted to advertising in any programme and to control the character of such advertising," as well as to prescribe the amount of time devoted to political advertising. He also has the right to stop certain broadcasts at will.

The 1965 revised edition of the Bahamas Broadcasting Act prohibits advertising of spirits (although beers and wines can be advertised) and soliciting of funds during religious programs. In addition, it stipulates that in any one-hour period, not more than eight minutes of advertising (in not more than eight announcements) are permitted.

Emergency messages may be accepted for broadcast to out islands not adequately served by telegraph or a radio telephone station. The messages must be limited to fifty words each and a fee must be assessed. In the case of messages concerning illness or death confirmed by a doctor or hospital, they may be accepted free of charge.[64]

CBC radio and television on Barbados are regulated by the Caribbean Broadcasting Corporation Act of 1963. It, too, gives a cabinet minister far-reaching powers over broadcasting. For example, no person can be appointed general manager of CBC without prior approval of the minister. In addition, he must approve all salaries over $6,000 (EC) a year, as well as all dismissals from the staff.[65]

All three broadcasting systems on Trinidad operate under government licensing. An official at government-owned Trinidad & Tobago National Broadcasting System (formerly 610 Radio) claimed that the licenses are wholly unrestrictive and that any limitations that do come up are individual by practice.[66] However, an official at the rediffusion station countered that "licenses by the government cover almost all points; it is as if we had controls." He cited license provisions that allowed another station to come into Radio Trinidad's territory and that granted the government the right to check regularly on programming.[67] The television license does not permit sponsorship of shows, because big businesses would buy the bulk of the programs, thus depriving small advertisers of air time.[68] In one-hour shows Trinidad and Tobago Television is allowed up to four two-minute breaks; in half-hour programs, as many as two two-minute commercial periods. Radio licenses on Trinidad provide for a maximum of ten minutes of advertisements per hour.

The broadcasting license issued by the St. Lucian government follows the format of most licenses in the region, according to the director of Radio Caribbean.[69] Advertising practices are emphasized. Radio Caribbean cannot accept advertisements that exaggerate a product, disparage an opponent's advertisements, or offer medical cure-alls. No "bulletin or flash type commercials" can be broadcast, nor those that "describe graphically or repellently any internal or external body function, or dramatises colds, influenza and coughing by the use of sound effects." Harsh noises, war themes, and obscenity are not to be used in commercials. Raffles cannot be advertised on the air, although the names of winners of such raffles can be broadcast. Contraceptives should not be advertised, but family-planning services can be announced. St. Lucia radio and TV stations cannot advertise more than a minute in a five-minute programming span, or more than twelve minutes an hour.

Regulations Preventing Access

In the Commonwealth Caribbean, coverage of the legislative and judicial branches of government have, in a number of cases, been hampered by laws promulgated to close legislative sessions or limit reporters in their coverage of them.

Probably the law of this nature that has raised the most protest from press circles is the Powers and Privileges Act, passed by the Bahamian legislature in 1969.* It stipulates that a reporter who publishes a false or misleading report on legislative proceedings is liable to contempt and, as a result, can forfeit his right to cover either chamber of government for a year. Once a reporter is banned, all other staff members of his medium can be barred from legislative proceedings for the same period of time. In addition, no recourse to a court of appeal is provided in such cases.[70] Shortly after the bill was passed, the speaker of the House informed reporters that henceforth they would have to possess passes signed by him to enter legislative sessions.

On the affirmative side, a Barbadian bill was defeated in mid-1971 that would have canceled speaking immunity to members of Parliament, thus inhibiting the press from quoting legislators.[71]

On other islands as well, rules tend to restrict rather than facilitate coverage of public meetings. For example, on St. Kitts public meetings are not open to the media during nonelection times;[72] on Anguilla the *Beacon* has campaigned unsuccessfully to have Council meetings open to the press and Council minutes available for publication.[73] On St. Lucia a number of people have requested live WIBS broadcasts of debates in the House, but, according to the WIBS director there, such broadcasts could be dangerous.

---

* In August 1975 the proprietor of the Nassau *Tribune* complained that the government attempted to "intimidate and harass" his paper by bringing charges of contempt and breach of House privileges. The charges stemmed from a *Tribune* story that quoted documents attached to an opposition minority report. The government said that the documents had not been formally presented and should not have been published (G. A. Sherman, "Report on Freedom of the Press Caribbean Area," presented to IAPA General Assembly, São Paulo, Brazil, October 20–24, 1975).

The mass media have tremendous impact on politicians' careers here. We would not want to cover the House debates live, because there is one legislator who has a terrible lisp and it would be unfair to him to air his House comments.[74]

An example of the obstacles placed in the path of newsmen in their coverage of the judicial process is that of Jamaica. The Jamaican law of contempt is severely enforced against newsmen who violate regulations placed on the coverage of the courts. Among such rules are: a prisoner under arrest cannot be photographed, the fact that a defendant has had a previous conviction cannot be revealed in the media, and photographs within the precincts of the court are outlawed. Even people going in and coming out of the court precinct cannot be photographed. Names of offenders under seventeen years of age are not mentioned in the press, and no information is published that might tend to identify them. However, teenagers' names may be used in murder cases once the trial commences. Identities of young girls involved in rape cases are not revealed; the police also "contrive to cover up the names of adults who have been raped." Names of jurors in criminal trials are not published, except at the end of trials.[75]

Other Pressures

Besides regulations against harmful publication and broadcasting, there are other governmental pressures used to control media content that is considered discomforting or embarrassing to the authorities.[76] Among such pressures are: use of licensing and tax powers to punish media, deportation of expatriate journalists critical of island governments, granting of governmental advertising and printing contracts to favored media, confiscation of a printing press, and public denunciations and threats leveled at anti-government newspapers. In the previous section we also saw how sedition and libel laws have been used to pressure anti-government media.

One of the chief ways a government can restrict mass communications is through the economic lifelines of the media. This can be accomplished by levying high taxes and license fees, by depriving certain media of lucrative governmental advertising and printing contracts, or by withholding newsprint and foreign exchange allocations.[77] In the Commonwealth Caribbean most economic restricting of mass media is carried out through the issuance of printing and advertising contracts and by some licensing. Of course, other methods have been applied, but usually in isolated instances.* In the Bahamas, for example, a Progressive Labour Party official asked the people not to advertise in the *Tribune* because it had been unfriendly to the government;[78] on Antigua the minister of commerce and industry told Antiguans not to buy shares in ZDK radio.[79]

Governmental withdrawal of printing contracts can be disastrous to smaller-island newspapers, which are heavily dependent on this additional source of income. Thus, it should not be surprising to hear the editor of the Montserrat *Mirror* say that her paper "never takes up serious governmental matters in print because the printery's biggest customer is the government."[80] Experience has shown that island governments will withdraw printing contracts from newspapers that have been critical. The editor of the Grenada *Torchlight* has seen this happen to his paper. Since it became critical of the Gairy government, the *Torchlight* has noted a marked reduction in the number of government printing orders received.[81]

A more complex arrangement concerning governmental printing contracts exists in the Bahamas. For years it was usual for the government to print tenders for the publication of its *Bahamian Times*, the contract going to the lowest bidder. The firm that received the *Times* printing job was also contracted to print governmental legal notices. Both the Nassau *Tribune* and Nassau *Guardian* competed vigorously for the contract; in fact, both were willing to print the *Times* at their own expense in order to obtain the more rewarding legal-notices contract. In 1969 the new deputy prime minister, feeling that the *Tribune* and *Guardian* were too critical of government, arbitrarily decided to give the printing contract for the *Times* to the *Times* itself, and no bids went out. Of course, the *Times* did not have printing facilities, so the *Guardian* was hired to print the government paper.[82] The whole point of this maneuver by the deputy prime minister was to make sure that the *Times* retained the legal notices contract. Thus, the dominant party-owned newspaper, published twice weekly, printed the government legal notices that people depended on daily. Approximately a year later a number of government ministers quit their posts and the dominant party, PLP. In turn, they formed the Free PLP that retained control of the *Bahamian Times*. Shortly after the party

---

* On St. Lucia the government had the mortgage on the building occupied by the *Crusader*. The government attempted to evict the newspaper; the case is now in court (Personal interview, Peter Josie, member of Parliament, Castries, St. Lucia, January 9, 1976).

split the government took both the printing and legal notices contracts from the *Times* and awarded them to the *Guardian*.[83]

There have not been many outcries from the press concerning government advertisements, although in most cases they are not distributed equitably.* There have been cases where the government has used the advertising contract as a control device. In 1964 the Barbados *Advocate-News* lost all governmental advertising for a short time because the paper had editorialized for federation rather than for national independence.[84] Also, Sir Etienne Dupuch of the Nassau *Tribune* has complained to the Inter American Press Association that the Bahamian government had penalized his paper by refusing to place advertisements in it.[85]

On Dominica the government sends most of its advertisements to the *Chronicle*, the "least objectionable of the three weeklies."[86] However, both the *Herald* and *Star* also receive governmental advertisements.** The *Herald* claims that it receives the legal notices because "we reach the masses, and the government has respect for the power of the masses";[87] the *Star* believes that the government must use its pages to advertise because "we hit the youth market and the government advertises a number of jobs that young people qualify for."[88] The Grenada *Vanguard* does not receive any governmental advertising support; for a while even merchants would not advertise in the paper because of fear of governmental retribution.[89]

On the larger islands newspapers do not seem concerned about government advertising, probably because they are not so heavily dependent upon it. In 1959, when Eric Williams and the Trinidad *Guardian* were having heated exchanges, the prime minister announced

---

* Pressures through granting of advertising contracts hit the *Vincentian* in 1975. The *Vincentian* editor wrote: "Until the current government became displeased with our expressed disagreement with their manipulation of the Constitution to manoeuver [sic] the appointment of a leader of the Opposition of its own choice, the Government was an important source of our advertising revenue. Subsequently, government advertising, including that submitted through it by overseas territories has been sent only to the ruling St. Vincent Labour Party's organ, *The Star*. Continued opposition by the *Vincentian* on issues regarded as detrimental to democratic principles in general and our state in particular have not been well received by the authorities" (G. A. Sherman, "Report on Freedom of the Press Caribbean Area," presented to IAPA General Assembly, São Paulo, Brazil, October 20–24, 1975).

** Since the Freedom Party attempt to overtake the government in 1971, the government has pulled its advertisements from the *Star* (Personal interview, Edward Scobie, former editor, *Herald*, Castries, St. Lucia, January 9, 1976).

in a radio broadcast that Trinidadian newspapers were subsidized by governmental advertising. The *Guardian* replied editorially that the charge was "absurd."[90]

Until 1971 most Commonwealth Caribbean mass media did not see any real threats from their governments' use of tax and license powers.* Radio Caribbean personnel on St. Lucia complain about the 30 percent import duty and 10 percent consumption tax on new equipment but point out that all businesses on that island have to pay these taxes, not just the media.[91] On Antigua ZDK radio and ZAL-TV must pay $1,000 (EC) and $5,000 (EC) annual license fees, respectively, while no fee is required of the government station, Antigua Broadcasting System. However, radio and television personnel affected by the fee do not really complain; they merely say that the government is not about to tax itself. Even when, in the late 1960s, Grenada's registrar asked a black-power newsletter to post a $10,000 (EC) publication bond, not much was made of the incident.[92] The newsletter simply folded.

But the response was different in 1971, when the Antiguan government enforced the Newspaper Surety Ordinance and Newspaper Regulations Act, both mentioned earlier. The $300 (US) annual license fee and $5,000 (US) surety bond required of newspapers were seen as attempts to destroy the Antiguan oppositionist press.[93] In a cabled message to Antigua Premier George Walter, the Inter American Press Association condemned the action in this fashion:

> The Inter American Press Association, acting in behalf of its wide newspaper membership throughout the Western Hemisphere, expresses its grave concern over the passing of amendments to the Newspaper Registration Act and the Newspaper Surety Ordinance and their promulgation into law, as a result of which two newspapers in Antigua have ceased publication. The IAPA considers this legislation undesirable and that it has had and will continue to have far-reaching consequences in suppressing freedom of the press. We are particularly disturbed by the imposition of prior restraint, which is contrary to the laws and the traditions under which the

---

* In 1975 the St. Lucia government was accused of misusing its tax powers. As Radio Caribbean planned to revive its English language service in 1976, the government, seeing this as competition for its own Radio St. Lucia, offered to drop all import/export duties on Radio Caribbean material if the station broadcast only in French (Personal interview, Winston Foster, assistant manager, Radio Caribbean, Castries, St. Lucia, January 10, 1976).

people of Antigua have lived. We earnestly urge you to reconsider the wisdom of breaching the freedom to publish, which in all free and democratic countries is not only a right of the press but concerns also the basic right of the people to be fully and freely informed. We therefore trust that you will restore this fundamental right to the newspapers and the people of Antigua.[94]

The Antigua government had not heeded the IAPA request as of early 1976.[*] Considered among the most menacing problems of Commonwealth Caribbean mass media are governmental attitudes concerning expatriate journalists. On a number of occasions governments have denied work-permit renewals to foreign-born journalists who have been critical of official policy and action. In other cases the threat of work-permit withdrawals hangs over the heads of a number of island journalists. The Anguillan-born editor of the opposition paper on St. Kitts, for example, said that he regularly receives threats from government supporters who feel that he must be shipped home.[95]

The editor of the St. Lucia *Crusader* said that the government has no need to use legal means to restrict the media as long as there are those subtle controls through work permits. He expressed it thus:

---

[*] The imposition of press laws on Antigua and Grenada has made the situation on those islands explosive. When the Privy Council in England ruled in favor of the Antigua government, the authorities seized copies of opposition newspapers that had been circulating in defiance of the law. Only the progovernment newspaper paid the required sum and published. The fortnightly *Outlet*, organ of the Afro-Caribbean Liberation Movement, complained of police harassment (Rickey Singh, "Press Freedom Is Taking a Beating," *The Nation*, November 30, 1975, pp. 10–11). The political climate of the island has not facilitated opposition newspapers raising the necessary money to post bond. The *Workers Voice* was distributed free of charge in 1975 in an effort to avoid the law, but the government amended the act granting the Cabinet authority to approve the publication of a newspaper.

On Grenada, unauthorized publications are seized. Persons who are caught either selling, or purchasing, or reading any newspaper that does not meet the requirements of the Newspaper (Amendment) Act of 1975 are arrested. Photographers who are caught taking pictures of policemen seizing newspapers and arresting people, or of armed police and defense-force patrols on the streets, have their cameras seized and smashed. The photographers have been beaten with axe handles and pieces of wood (G. A. Sherman, "Report on Freedom of the Press Caribbean Area," presented to IAPA General Assembly, São Paulo, Brazil, October 20–24, 1975). On July 18, 1975, Kenrick Radix, a leader of the oppositionist New Jewel Movement, was beaten and shot while attempting to photograph near riot scenes in St. George's when police clashed with vendors of the *Jewel*, the movement's weekly. Nine Movement members were arrested and charged with distributing the *Jewel* ("More Trouble on Grenada," *Caribbean Contact* [August 1975], p. 20). The *Jewel* has gone underground. Police have set up road blocks at other times to search vehicles and pedestrians for concealed copies of *Jewel* ("Grenada," *Caribbean Monthly Bulletin* [July 1975], p. 12).

Most people who have been concerned with the mass media here have been expatriates. Government gets at the media through these people.[96]

In 1970 the St. Lucian government used this control by asking Barbadian-born Denzil Agard, editor of *Voice of St. Lucia*, to leave the island, after he had been denied a work permit for criticizing a cabinet minister's Labor Day speech.[97]

Other examples abound in the region. On Dominica the government pressured expatriate newspapermen in 1964 by telling them that if they expected to purchase local property they had better not write critically about the government.[98] In the same year the Jamaican attorney general sought to punish immigrants who wrote negatively about the authorities, but refrained from taking any action when the media voiced a complaint.[99]

In 1967 the Barbados government refused a residual permit to Ronald Batchelor, Reuters Caribbean representative, because of what government officials termed security reasons. The IAPA felt that the real reason was that the prime minister had heard reports of Batchelor's background reporting in the area and did not want him prying into Barbadian governmental affairs.[100] Reuters transferred Batchelor to another area.

Immediately after the Antiguan elections of 1971, the new Walter government deported Dorcas White, editor of the Antigua *Workers Voice*. Very little reason was given for the sudden interest by the government in her lack of a work permit, but a number of Antiguans assumed that she was deported because of the editorials she wrote in the *Voice* and broadcast over ZDK radio.[101] The pro-government newspaper, Antigua *Star*, said that the deportation resulted because the former Bird government had got its use out of Miss White, and when she was no longer needed, they dropped her. As the *Star* put it:

She who had stood on political platforms and lied and slandered and libelled for the hierarchy of the Labour Party was left in the lurch.[102]

Miss White's version of the deportation was as follows:

After the February 13, 1971 victory for the PLM, that party carried out its promise of rewards to friends, punishments to enemies. I was summoned to the immigration office to have my immigration status reviewed and was given until March 5 to leave the country. I was to apply for a work permit and do no work until I got it. I applied to the minister of home affairs (who is empowered to grant or withhold permits at his discretion). But I was asked to leave on February 26. My impression is that I have been victimised. However, I was not surprised.[103]

Another occasion when the Antiguan government used the denial of a work-permit renewal to suppress a journalist occurred in 1968. Television commentator Bobby Margetson was forced to leave the island for political broadcasts that he made. According to Everard Richards, news editor of Antigua Broadcasting System, Margetson's case developed in this manner:

A number of us, including Bobby Margetson, interviewed a government minister who had resigned the Bird cabinet. I wrote the story and gave a carbon copy to ZAL-TV to broadcast. The same story was broadcast over ABS and ZAL-TV, yet, Bobby was prosecuted for lack of a work permit as a result of his broadcasting the story. Nothing happened to me, although I wrote the release and aired it over ABS.[104]

One of the founding editors of the Anguilla *Beacon,* Canon C. R. G. Carleton, was forced off that island during its crises of 1969. The reason given by leader Ronald Webster was that he wanted to get British subjects (Carleton was British) off the island before British troops could use their evacuation as an excuse to invade Anguilla. But Carleton feels that Webster wanted him out of the way because Carleton was editing the *Beacon* and keeping London media informed of island happenings through letters to the editor.[105]

Probably the Commonwealth Caribbean journalists who feel that they have been hit hardest by the discriminatory use of immigration laws are those in the Bahamas. A number of outsiders apparently agree that Bahamian print media have been subjected to unnecessary manpower restrictions. For example, IAPA in 1969 accused the Bahamian government of using immigration laws to restrict recruitment of newspaper staffs.[106]

Most of the troubles between the Bahamian government and the press started in 1969, when the islands' first black government was seated. Using the rationale that he believed in a free press but not the "right to distort," the new prime minister, Lynden O. Pindling, helped pass the Powers and Privileges Act of 1969. The original wording would have given the speaker of the legislature (who characterized newsmen as "evil pushers of the pen") the right to bar indefinitely from the islands any dissenting reporter. After IAPA protests, the act was amended to give reporters a second chance, but only if their reportorial error was minor, not deliberate, and if the paper published a satisfactory apology.[107]

Since then the Pindling government* has forced one newspaper general manager to leave, threatened to expel the editor of the Grand Bahama *Tribune*, and boosted the costs of annual work permits from $30 to $150 (Bahamian).[108] In addition, the government has not granted a new application for a journalist's work permit since coming into office.[109]

Chris Evans, the British-born general manager of the Nassau *Guardian*, was given less than a year to replace himself with a Bahamian. In April 1971, when his work permit was not renewed, he left the island. Among other cases, the chief reporter on the *Guardian* was given a work permit for six months, but before two months had elapsed, he received notice that he must be replaced by a Bahamian.[110]

Etienne Dupuch, editor-proprietor of the *Tribune*, threatens to close the Grand Bahama *Tribune* for lack of staff. His editor there, Bernard Murphy, who operates the paper virtually single-handedly, is also having troubles getting his work permit renewed and faces expulsion by the government. As Dupuch has pointed out in numerous emotion-laden editorials in the Nassau *Tribune*, the Bahamian government insists that newspapers use local personnel when such trained people are not available. The work-permit-renewal dilemma confronts the Nassau *Tribune* as well.[111] For example, Dupuch's British-born son-in-law, an editor of the *Tribune*, cannot get his work permit renewed. Because of such governmental harassment, Dupuch claims that he has done two things since the Pindling government came into office: he has financially secured his family outside the Bahamas in case they must leave; he has exposed the situation of the press in the Bahamas to the world press organizations.[112] Thus, International Press Institute, Inter American Press Association, and Commonwealth Press Union have all heard Dupuch's complaints and pleas concerning Bahamian freedom of the press.

Besides economic sanctions, a number of other pressures have been used against mass media in the Commonwealth Caribbean. One involved the theft of the Anguilla *Beacon* press, an act for which Anguillan leader Ronald Webster was blamed. Editor Atlin Harrigan recounted that incident in this way:

My A. B. Dick Duplicator offset press was taken from my home

---

* Pindling's Progressive Liberal Party was returned to power in 1972.

by a gang I believe was sent there by Webster. They came in and said, "Webster wants the press, where is it?" They hauled it out and took it to the police station. They had guns and knives when they entered my home. Later, I met Webster and asked if he sent seven men to get the press. He said no. But, he did say he would look into the matter. I told him it was my press and I wanted it returned. The next morning, the police officer and one of his prisoners pulled the press up here and said Webster sent it. It was out of order when they returned it.[113]

Webster's explanation of the theft was, "The press was taken by citizens who believed the *Beacon* printed news that was treasonable."[114]

Another form of direct pressure, precensorship, is practiced by a few island governments, especially in cases where the governments own their own broadcasting stations. Prior censorship is particularly evident on Grenada, where all press releases must be signed by the premier or his cabinet secretary. Once signed, they are assured of being aired in their original format because the news editor of Grenada WIBS is not allowed "to add or subtract, amend or correct in any way news items reaching that station from government information services."[115] The Bird government on Antigua censored all local news before it went over the government station. In this case it was the permanent secretary who was responsible for reading and approving all news before broadcast. This prepublication censorship has ceased under the new Walter government, a government employee said.[116]

A newspaper that has sustained a great deal of pressure from government is the Grenada *Vanguard*. Subtle, as well as rather open, forms of harassment have permeated all aspects of that paper's operations, according to media personnel on the island. Editor A. Michael Cruickshank related some of *Vanguard's* difficulties that result from governmental pressure:

There is no direct pressure against *Vanguard*. The government does threaten people connected with the paper. Anonymous letters are sent to us saying we will be burned out in our cars. People are therefore afraid to attach their names to letters to editor; they are afraid of mayhem and victimizing by the Gairy government. Only a few people will come to our office to pick up copies of the paper. Downtown, if a person buys the *Vanguard*, he hides it inside a Trinidad *Express* or *Guardian*, so no one will know he bought it. There is nothing official about government repression. Civil servants are not allowed to read *Vanguard* in public or in their offices. The paper is not allowed in the libraries. If you're seen with *Vanguard*, you're automatically blackballed. If we get a letter from a reader, we take it downstairs, rewrite it so the government boys cannot trace the handwriting. Then we burn the original copy and set the letter in type. Government gangs have threatened members of our staff with beatings and rape. I used to send the *Vanguard* on buses to various villages but some drivers refused to transport the paper. On many occasions, I had to haul the paper around the country myself. It's like an underground paper in that some shops that take it for distribution, keep it under the counter. In the villages, it is sold by party members who own shops. The government here searches homes for guns and ammunition. A member of our editorial board had his home searched. We have not been associated with any subversive activity and that is the reason the *Vanguard* people have not been arrested.[117]

Public Denunciations, Threats, Intimidation

Governmental officials in the islands regularly denounce mass media performance on public platforms. This is especially true during election campaigns. Sometimes the denunciations take the form of veiled threats and intimidating words; most times, however, they are only part of the standard political rhetoric. One gets the impression that to chastise the mass media publicly is as much a part of the political-meeting format as the hymns, steel bands, and long speeches. In only a very few cases do the politicians or governmental officials attempt to carry out their threats.

Probably the man who has been most instrumental in promoting the taunting of mass media is Eric Williams, prime minister of Trinidad & Tobago. Although he has let up a little now that his government owns TTNBS and TTT, for years Williams strongly castigated both foreign and domestic mass media. His favorite target was the Trinidad *Guardian*, which at various times he accused of downplaying his speeches, scaring away foreign investors, and peddling United States and British propaganda. At one time he told his party leaders to attack the *Guardian* "without mercy"; on another occasion he threatened to cancel the annual queen contest sponsored by that paper.[118] He has used an assortment of dramatic acts to get his point across to the public. While speaking in Port of Spain's Woodford Square (Williams calls this his "University of Woodford Square"), the prime minister has shown his distaste for the *Guardian* by cleaning his shoes with it and, on one occasion, by consigning it to hell. Here is a 1960 account of the latter incident:

Dr. Eric Williams, Premier of Trinidad and Tobago, stood dramatically on a bandstand, an open fire burning in front of him. In his hand, he held a copy of the Trinidad *Guardian*. With a flourish he tossed it into the fire and pronounced the awesome sentence: "I consign it to the flames—to hell with it!"[119]

Williams usually tells his audiences which sectors of the Trinidadian society are detrimental to the nation's welfare; the mass media are nearly always included in what he once termed the "seven deadly sins." Before the national elections in 1971, he narrowed the public enemies to three: big business, the press, and the church. In a speech condemning these institutions, he made the following comments, which give the reader a glimpse of the vagueness of his charges:

> We (PNM) have never depended on a newspaper; it is they (the opposition) who have a newspaper party. One day—the day of reckoning, will come. That is a different story. We do not have time for it now. We'll have a lot to deal with . . . total distortion of the news and attempts to use the so-called impartiality of the press to suppress information.[120]

There are some who believe that Williams's constant haranguing about the mass media is having some effect upon the public and the media themselves. For example, in 1959, when Trinidadian reporters were being intimidated by political hooligans, the *Guardian* attributed this action to Williams's stirring up hate for the press.[121] Ten years later the IAPA felt that the media themselves had been affected by the public denunciations. "There is known censorship carried out by all media because of fear of reprisals from both government and business interests," the *IAPA News* reported.[122]

Media on other large islands also hear governmental threats shouted from the political platform.* The general manager of the Barbados

---

* For example, in 1972 Jamaica's Minister of Housing called the *Daily Gleaner* the "Daily Misleader," "number one enemy of the people," and "totally intolerable" (*Daily Gleaner*, September 4, 1972; *Daily Gleaner*, September 5, 1972, p. 1). In 1975 four ministers attacked the *Daily Gleaner* again, calling upon the paper's management to place 51 percent of the company's shares on the public market. Other officials also called the newspaper a "capitalist monopoly." The prime minister assures his audiences, however, that he does not wish to threaten freedom of the press on Jamaica. Some media personnel are apprehensive, especially in light of the prime minister's brand of "democratic socialism" and close ties with Cuba (J. C. Proute, "Press Freedom Comes Face-to-Face with Democratic Socialism: Change without Chains," *The Nation*, November 30, 1975, pp. 41, 45). However, the general manager of the *Daily Gleaner* and editor of *The Jamaica Daily News* did not place much importance in these ministerial outpourings and thought that freedom of the press was rather safe on Jamaica. On Barbados, government officials recently attacked the press, especially *The Nation*, but again, the editors did not take the criticism to mean freedom of the press was in danger.

Advocate-News said that his paper hears governmental threats made publicly, but that no real pressures against the press emanate from the government.[123] A Jamaica *Gleaner* editor said:

> I can't really say there is any threat to the press here. Occasionally, a politician comes out with a statement that the *Gleaner* should be suppressed, but no government has done anything about the threats. Politicians like to call us monopolistic on the political platforms.[124]

On most of the smaller islands, public denunciations of mass media operations are quite frequent. In some cases, they cannot be taken lightly. For example, Antiguan governmental officials on a number of occasions in 1971 announced that they would introduce legislation against opposition media. The result was the promulgation of the Newspaper Surety Ordinance and Newspaper Regulations Act, discussed earlier. In early 1971 the Walter government warned that it would legislate against the *Workers Voice* to keep it from abusing cabinet ministers. In fact, ex-newspaperman George Walter himself said that he would close any papers that attacked his ministers.[125] In April the minister of home affairs told a public gathering that newspapers fell within his portfolio, and, because of some recent writings in the *Voice*, he planned to introduce legislation to make newspapers act responsibly.[126] Apparently the *Voice* did not take him seriously. Here was that paper's response:

> I really wonder if Halstead (minister of home affairs) had in a few drinks so that he didn't know what he was saying, because when he omitted the Antigua *Star*, the chief misleading and propagandist paper. . . . that paper is the paper solely responsible for a lot of treachery and falsehood to this State of ours, making investors decide against Antigua for doing some sort of business.[127]

At about the same time, the Antiguan minister of public utilities used another political meeting platform to tell his audience that Reuben Harris, columnist and part owner of the Antigua *Times*, owed him $3,000 (EC) for electricity consumed at three businesses Harris owned. He warned that if the bills were not paid the next morning, Harris's electricity would be stopped, and he would have to use lamplight to write his column. Harris replied in print that, once adjusted, the sum he owed was actually $33.21. As for writing his column by kerosene light, he said he was accustomed to that, "so it will not hurt. I know that the articles hurt and these I will continue to write even in the dark."[128]

Recent developments on St. Kitts have also deterred press personnel from shrugging off government threats to the media. The editor of the St. Kitts *Democrat,* for example, said that the constant verbal attacks by government do not allow him to "feel free to say what I want."[129] He cited two incidents that have intimidated the media of that island. In 1967 Bradshaw's Labour Party accused a number of opposition party leaders of conspiracy to overthrow the government. Twenty-two people were imprisoned for five months. Among them was the leader of the opposition, Dr. William Herbert, who also owns the *Democrat.* Although there were no newsmen among the twenty-two arrested, the link-up between Dr. Herbert, PAM, and the *Democrat* had an intimidating effect on that paper's staff.[130] The other incident occurred in 1969. Vivienne Fieulleteau, then editor of the *Democrat,* was charged with conspiracy and libel for an article she printed entitled "Unsolved Nevis Murders? Why?" The Bradshaw government said that Miss Fieulleteau knew who had written the article but refused to reveal her source. The IAPA reported that a great deal of apprehension surrounded the case, which she subsequently won.[131] However, because of this incident and the numerous attacks and threats on her by the government, she decided to leave the island in 1969.

In 1971 Bradshaw was on the platform again, this time threatening to close the *Democrat.* He was upset because the paper had criticized his government for sending police to the homes of several civil servants in the middle of the night to deliver dismissal notices. Bradshaw accused the *Democrat* of giving the nation a bad image abroad.[132]

On Dominica government officials have also publicly denounced the opposition press. At various times speakers have instructed the people not to read the *Herald,* and Premier E. O. Le Blanc* has threatened publicly to "make the *Herald* inactive" because of its anti-government articles.[133] One government official showed his scorn for the *Herald* by tearing up a copy at a political meeting.

Edward Scobie, *Herald* editor, thinks that government action of this type has an effect upon the public. He said that he receives anonymous letters from government supporters threatening to burn his press building and kill him. During the last elections, Scobie, a candidate for public office, said that he was stoned at public gatherings.[134] The other opposition paper on Dominica, *Star,* has also been the subject of the "government's thundering against media on the political platform." However, *Star* editor Phyllis Allfrey said that the use of irony

---

* The new premier of Dominica is Patrick John.

in stories makes it difficult for government officials to attack the paper. She said, "for a politician to explain to the illiterate common man how the *Star* has done the politician dirt is difficult when the story is couched in irony."[135]

Other island newspapers have experienced the same types of verbal abuse by government officials. The editor of the Grenada *West Indian* said that Eric Gairy frequently mounts the political platform to "lambaste us," leaving the impression with people that the island newspapers do not count.[136] Another media executive on Grenada said that if his medium publishes something derogatory to the Gairy government, the premier publicly accuses it of being disloyal to the nation.[137] Finally, on Anguilla, Ronald Webster has attacked the *Beacon* for "false articles engineered by a Britisher" and for being "anti-Anguilla."[138]

GOVERNMENT AS A FACILITATING AGENCY

The government can facilitate the functioning of mass media in a number of ways. Among them are: (1) by making government information readily available to the media, (2) by providing government services and concessions that aid in the dissemination of news, and (3) by initiating or cooperating with fairness and equal-time regulations.

This section is meant to deal predominantly with facilitating acts of government, but one must remember that there are instances where services designed to aid the mass media have been turned into restrictive agencies of government. This is certainly true in the Commonwealth Caribbean.

Availability of Government Information

One of the chief ways that Commonwealth Caribbean governments communicate with the mass media and with the public is through government information services. News media, especially small-island nondailies without adequate reportorial staffs, rely heavily on these services.

The structure and organization of government information services in the region present a highly unbalanced picture. UNESCO reported in 1968 that Jamaica Information Service had a staff of 128, while other operations, for example, those on Antigua, St. Kitts, and St.

Lucia,* were handled by one-man staffs.[139] Even large islands such as Barbados and Trinidad had relatively small information staffs in 1968. Barbados Information Services had two officers; Trinidad, one information officer, three specialists, and a few technicians. The situation was expected to improve on Trinidad as the planners of the Third Five-Year Plan, 1969–73, envisioned over $½ million (TT) being spent on GIS over a five-year period.

By 1971, however, some of the islands were enlarging their government information staffs. For example, St. Vincent GIS now has seven employees, more than the combined staffs of the *Vincentian* and St. Vincent WIBS, the island's only media. Grenada also has a relatively large governmental information apparatus.

A wide diversity was also shown in budgets allocated to government information services. The 1968–69 budget of Jamaica Information Service was £204,000 (or $980,000 EC) out of a total national budget of £100,795,000, while that of Antigua was $55,000 (EC) out of a total of $16,700,000. Dominica's information service was budgeted $12,800 (EC), while the national budget was $8,000,000 (EC).[140]

Jamaica Information Service** is divided into six specialized sections: press and photography, publications and campaigns, distribution and mobile units, radio, film, and television. UNESCO reported in 1968 that JIS, despite its own impressive organization, was not happy with the network of information officers in government departments. Only two ministries have public relations officers placed under JIS; a third is independent of JIS.[141]

On other islands there is also a wide scope of coordination. For example, Grenada's director of the Department of Information Services has no jurisdiction over the broadcasting unit, whose head reports directly to the premier. A number of Grenadian government services more directly connected with information (agricultural extension, health education, adult education) handle their own information.

UNESCO condemned the situation in the islands where government staff members issue releases in addition to those written by information officers. This is especially true on Antigua, where government headquarters issued their own press releases, which could not

---

* In 1976 St. Lucia still had a one-man government information service. The officer said that his job involved writing five or six releases on "pieces and bits" of news, administering the showing of films at village community centers, and acting as the premier's public relations officer (Personal interview, Albert Mason, public relations officer, government of St. Lucia, Castries, St. Lucia, January 9, 1976).

** The Jamaica service is now called the Agency for Public Information.

be edited by either information officers or government radio. UNESCO felt that the government department should either have its own public relations officer or leave the responsibility of drafting releases to the qualified government information officers.[142]

Normally the information services in the Commonwealth Caribbean come directly under the offices of the prime minister or premier.[143] JIS comes under the minister of finance and planning; Antigua, under the minister of social services.

The objectives of government information services vary from island to island, while the description of the quality of service provided differs from source to source.

On St. Vincent the stated objectives of GIS are to "project government's policy adequately in economic development, education, health and social development," to provide an expression for public reaction to government policies, and to spearhead general education among the masses.[144] The director, Cameron King, said that his staff tries to stay out of political-election canvassing, because in "a small place like this, it is very easy to be construed as being a political arm of the government." As for his office's role with the government, King said that no one from the executive or legislative branches tries to "poke anything down GIS's throat," that his office operates under set policies. King is answerable to the permanent secretary, who in turn is responsible to the premier. On many issues GIS deals directly with the premier.[145]

When one talks with Weston H. Lewis, editor of St. Vincent's only newspaper, a different picture of GIS emerges. Lewis said that he gets a number of news releases from GIS, but most of them are of the political propaganda type. He also said that GIS has made reprisals against him for stories he has written in the *Vincentian.*

> GIS has withheld information from us. Sometimes deliberately, other times because of untrained underlings. More recently, however, GIS has withheld the information deliberately. For example, when ministerial changes occurred, we were not informed. The press here is not invited to many functions of the government. The House of Assembly agendas are no longer sent to me in advance. The last two debates, I didn't even receive the bills. The government public relations man has done a lot that the people do not approve of. He controls the local WIBS outlet, for example. As a result, there is a lot of government public relations on WIBS.[146]

Little doubt exists as to the function of GIS on Grenada; nearly everyone, including a former director of the service, is in agreement that GIS serves as a propaganda outlet for Premier Eric Gairy.* One source on the island provided this description of Grenada GIS:

GIS in Grenada is more highly staffed and more active than similar services in other islands. That is why it seems that the gov·ernment controls media content here. It does. The GIS tries to give a release on everything. Its rationale is that it is trying to supplement the poor newsgathering on Grenada. Other news sources are just about dried up here, so that the community now sends news tips directly to GIS. Of course, not every item sent to GIS will be heard. The government comes down hard on anyone who tries to hurt its image.[147]

Almost immediately after assuming office, Gairy decided that his government did not need an information officer, but instead a public relations director who would be directly responsible to him.[148] From that point on, most releases that emanated from the Grenadian government were designed to promote Gairy's image, not that of the government. A number of actions attest to that point of view.

For example, the only release from GIS on May 11, 1971, was a twenty-three-inch account of sporting events in which Gairy had participated.** Excerpts follow:

The Premier and his team of "Cavalier Cricketers" continue to dominate the cricket scene in Grenada. . . . After being sent to bat by skipper E. Gairy. . . . Gairy, in the meantime, was on a length with some medum-fast bowling that caused the Carriacou team to panic. . . . But Tyrone Harbin and E. Gairy came together and featured in a 4th wicket stand. . . . After the game, Premier Gairy described the game as not an easy one and congratulated the opposing team on their team spirit. On the more serious side, the Premier told the Carricouans that they are seeing for themselves progress on the island which was never seen before. . . . In lawn tennis . . . E. Gairy and Paul Slinger beat[149]

All three editors on the island agree that the Gairy government is trying to rule by press release. The editor of *Torchlight* said:

---

* By 1974 Grenadian journalists had formed the Grenada Press Association, partly as a defense against Gairy.
** Examples of 1975–76 press releases of another Windward Island, St. Lucia, follow: "Lady Minister Opens New Community Centre," "Agriculture Minister Opens WINBAN Meeting," "Independence, Theme of Caribbean Studies Association Conference," or "Canadian Grant for Resurfacing Hewanorra Airport Runway."

The government rules by press releases. All releases deal with Gairy. *Torchlight* and *West Indian* do not use releases from the government. Government information is just a public relations service for Gairy. Government has no regular press conferences where you can get information directly from the officials.[150]

Vanguard editor A. Michael Cruickshank said that all releases are "ego centered for Gairy, and oftentimes libelous and personal. Gairy chooses an enemy and blasts him through releases read over WIBS."[151] Gairy is also in control of all content that emanates from WIBS main headquarters on Grenada. "If the newspapers say something good about Gairy, it is quoted over WIBS. If it is bad comment, WIBS ignores it," one editor said.[152]

A man who has worked at both WIBS and GIS on Grenada is Leslie Seon, a frequent critic of Gairy. Seon said that while he was program director of WIBS, Gairy would bring in items for broadcast that were libelous. On a few occasions Seon did not use the Gairy releases; for this action he was subsequently transferred to GIS, with "an empty desk and no responsibility over the staff."* He was not fired, because his position on WIBS was paid for by the premiers of all four governments associated with WIBS. Thus, he sat out the remainder of his three-year contract doing virtually nothing in GIS.[153]

Media personnel on a number of islands complain that public officials do not facilitate their obtaining timely, accurate, and detailed information about governmental happenings. On the larger islands the complaint is not so frequent or loud, mainly because the mass media are not entirely dependent upon government sources for government news. Their large reportorial staffs are able to probe for and expose some of this information without much outward cooperation from the government. Even on a few of the smaller islands, there are media personnel satisfied with the news output of government agencies. For example, the editor of St. Lucia *Crusader* feels that he has "reasonably free access to government information; all the information that we require." He said that the government sends him six to eighteen press-release packages (each package containing six to eight stories) a week.[154] The editor of the pro-government St. Kitts *Labour*

---

* A similar incident happened on Dominica in mid-1973, when then Premier Le Blanc moved a popular radio announcer, Daniel Cauderion, to a less-public position in the civil service. Le Blanc accused Cauderion of selling his personal brand of sociopolitics in a radio commentary on the Watergate bugging scandal, as well as permissive views on sex. Numerous protests resulted until a state of emergency was declared. (Reuters dispatch in *Straits Times* [Malaysia], June 18, 1973.)

Spokesman said that he has no trouble getting information from the government. "You can't sit down and wait for it; you have to dig sometimes," he added.[155]

However, in a number of cases, newspapers have an extremely difficult time getting comments from their governments. The Nassau *Guardian,* for example, resorts to devious means to obtain information from the Pindling government.

> The government here passes the buck, and reporters are passed from one man to another. So, when the *Guardian* cannot get confirmation on a story, we run it as a rumor. The government immediately comes out and denies the rumor and says we are trying to bring down the government. On other occasions, when the government won't talk, we go to the opposition for comment. Their anti-government remarks usually elicit a response from government.[156]

In other instances, press releases are not sent to newspapers that have been critics of government. Grenada *Vanguard* is not provided with GIS materials; neither is the Dominica *Herald.* The *Herald* editor said that the Dominican government quit sending him releases after he wrote the following headline over a release that said that Dominicans were subject to fines and prison for stealing electricity poles: "Communications Minister Threatens Public with Imprisonment."[157]

Press conferences are not regular items on the schedules of officials in the region. On Dominica the premier has not held a press conference for over four years;[158] before the 1970 black-power revolt on Trinidad, Eric Williams had not held a press conference for over five years.* However, from April to August 1970, he held four such conferences.[159] In the 1950s and early 1960s, when he did hold regular conferences, the media complained that they were only political propaganda sessions. In fact, in 1959 the *Guardian, Evening News,* and Radio Guardian boycotted Williams's press meetings, calling them "propaganda conferences." At that time, the action did not deter Williams; he said that the press conferences would continue even if the press did not show up.[160]

Possibly a reason that authorities neglect to hold regular press conferences is that they do not feel secure enough to field questions from the mass media. But, on the smaller islands, where access to

---

* The Bahamian prime minister, in his first eight years in office, never met regularly with media. However, in 1975 Lynden Pindling consented to meet the mass media on a current events radio program, "Contact," broadcast one hour every second Monday. (*Combroad* [April–June 1975], p. 72.)

public officials is more easily obtained, the need for press conferences may not be urgent. For example, the editor of the *Voice of St. Lucia* said that, although press conferences are very infrequent, it is not difficult to get to the premier or a minister when an issue does arise.[161] On St. Vincent the director of GIS said:

> I wouldn't say there are regular press conferences of the premier. On a small island like this, the premier and ministers are always available. They are out with the people—breaking ground at some new building site, showing up at film showings in the countryside. They talk to the people on a first hand basis. They are also out with the people during political meetings which are held almost weekly.[162]

Facilitating Dissemination/Reception of Messages

Most island governments facilitate the dissemination of news by granting newspapers special mailing rates. In fact, as early as 1941 all island governments were providing newspapers with mailing subsidies. For example, newspapers on Bermuda could be mailed at one-eighth the rate for first-class letters; on Bahamas, one-third; on Trinidad, one-eighth; on Barbados, one-twelfth; on Leewards, one-eighth; on Grenada, one-sixteenth; on St. Lucia, one-third; and on Dominica, one-eighth.[163] Today, in the Bahamas, newspapers approved by the postmaster can be airmailed to out islands at a rate of three cents per copy. Airmail letters going to the same destinations cost eight cents for two ounces. Newspapers can be airmailed to other islands in the Caribbean and to foreign nations at about one-third the rate of first-class mail. Newspapers shipped inter-island by surface mail are not charged a rate, if approved by the postmaster. Magazines are also given special mailing rates, which are slightly less than first-class costs.[164]

In Jamaica local newspapers are shipped by inland post at a rate of ½d per copy, while letters weighing two ounces or less go at the rate of 2d. Newspapers can be mailed by overseas post at the rate of 2d for the first two ounces, while letters cost 3d to 6d for one ounce or less.[165]

Another area where some governments have made concessions, so that mass media messages can more easily reach the general public, concerns the license fee on radio receiving sets. In the Bahamas the tax was dropped because it was impossible to determine who in the out islands had radio sets, let alone trying to collect fees on them.[166] On St. Vincent and Dominica, however, the governments have dispensed with the tax as a concession to the masses. The WIBS director on Dominica explained why his government has stopped taxing radio sets, although television receivers will probably be licensed:

> We have a socialist type of government here that hates to license because of the outcry from the public, which would cost them votes. There is no license on TV sets yet but when we get our own station, sets will be licensed. The thinking is that unless there is a conscious move to help TV pioneers get revenue, there will be no television. Plus the government thinks any television that is not educational is a luxury and the people should pay for their luxuries. Political thinking tells you too that it is not every man who will be able to buy a set. The common masses who vote wouldn't be able to afford a set, thus the voting masses will not be upset by a TV set license fee.[167]

Fairness and Equal Time

Merrill and Lowenstein said that whereas the "old attitude favored government intervention to bring the press to the people, the latest plea is for government intervention to bring the people into the press." They pointed out that postal subsidies facilitated bringing the press to the people; equal time and fairness regulations promoted bringing the people into the media.[168]

In politically motivated regions such as the Commonwealth Caribbean, fairness and equal-time considerations are definitely needed. The fact that a number of the media, especially broadcasting units, are owned by government necessitates the setting up of clearly defined rules on political broadcasts. Most government broadcasting systems in the region either have a set of regulations to provide equal time or avoid the issue by banning all political broadcasts. Or they can completely boycott the opposition from their programs.

Among the most stringent policies* concerning political broadcasts is that delineated by ZNS in the Bahamas. During an election year any candidate is entitled to one fifteen-minute broadcast, while each recognized political party is allowed two fifteen-minute broadcasts. Because there are usually two candidates for each of the thirty-eight seats in the Assembly, plus a number of independents, the time devoted

---

* New information reveals that Barbados also has a stringent policy. Speaking in early 1976, the Minister of Information and Public Relations on Barbados said that, except at election time, no political party is entitled to time on CBC radio or television. He said that when government ministers use electronic media, the opposition asks for equal time, but the ministerial broadcasts are to inform the public of governmental actions and to seek public support for them ("Minister Defends Policy of CBC," Barbados *Advocate-News*, January 10, 1976, p. 2).

to political broadcasting totals as many as 100 quarter hours. In 1967 the station divided the time slots in this fashion,

> Once the nominations were closed, we knew how many candidates there were. We figured we needed 108 broadcasts. We chose three times a day for a total of 45 minutes to broadcast the speeches —7:30–7:45 P.M., 9:15–9:30 P.M. and 10:15–10:30 P.M. Independents were given their picks of those times, because they could be on only once, not having a party to represent them a second time. We assigned times to party leaders who had to let us know who would be their spokesmen. Toward the end, just before election day, we put on five to ten per cent more time for the laggers. All speeches had to be prerecorded, and all had to be paid for in advance. Content was subject to the approval of the station management to avoid libel. Direct accusations could not be included in speeches.[169]

By law, ZNS should have political broadcasting only during election years, but the station does cover politicians' news conferences and speeches at other times. The opposition is provided with equal time, to the extent that if a government report is aired, the opposition is given a chance to respond. Also, the station grants the government the right to respond to newscasts that might be hazy about some governmental action. Immediately following a newscast, the government has the option of preparing a three-minute commentary on the news, if it feels that an explanation of government policy is needed.

The St. Vincent WIBS policy concerning election-year campaigning allows each party a half-hour broadcast. The party is allowed to decide how the time will be used, either by five-minute announcements or in toto. All political broadcasts are suspended on St. Vincent WIBS the day before election day. During nonelection periods, both the dominant and opposition parties are allowed to broadcast announcements of their meetings as news items.[170]

Some privately owned stations have set up their own equal-time guidelines concerning political broadcasting. Radio Jamaica, for example, specifies that political parties can buy fifteen-minute segments up to a certain maximum, which depends on the number of members the party has in Parliament.* The station will not accept payment from

---

* At JBC each political party, including that of the government, is permitted ten radio broadcasts during an election campaign. Each broadcast is confined to one speaker and can be no longer than fourteen minutes. JBC has a number of public access shows that allow other viewpoints to be expressed. National broadcasts by ministers are not to include promotional material for the ruling political party nor attacks on the opposition. An infringement upon this policy was committed by the prime minister in November 1975; the matter was under litigation in early 1976 (Personal interview, Dwight Whylie, general manager, JBC, Kingston, Jamaica, January 14, 1976).

individual candidates during election periods, only from parties involved in the elections. Political speeches must be submitted to Radio Jamaica beforehand as a protection against libel.[171]

Among broadcasting units that avoid all politically oriented information is ZAL-TV on Antigua. Under the terms of its license, the station is not allowed to broadcast any "political information or announcements."[172] As the head of the station pointed out, this becomes a difficult task in an area such as Antigua, where nearly anything can be termed political.

Last year, there was a civil service strike. We dealt with it very fully on television. Some people said it was a political matter, and we should not have covered it. This year, we did not cover the Labor Day parade because it has political overtones.[173]

St. Lucia WIBS has been instructed by the premier on that island not to broadcast any political materials, not even announcements of political-party meetings.* ZDK on Antigua is allowed to broadcast announcements of political meetings, but nothing more political than that.

At least four government-owned stations do not feel that it is necessary to practice equal-time objectives; they don't allow the opposition any air time. On Grenada the situation has been so unfair that, during parliamentary debate, only the government arguments were broadcast. After much criticism, the Grenadian government consented to allow the opposition party one half hour of time during legislative broadcasts. Opposition-party announcements and advertisements are not accepted by Grenada WIBS. In 1971 the announcement of the death of an opposition-party leader was not permitted to be broadcast by the station.[174]

The situation on Dominica is similar. Dominica WIBS director Jeff Charles described the use that the government makes of his station:

No matter how much the opposition party begs, it cannot obtain

---

* The leaders of the opposition said that the policy is prejudicial in favor of the government. "The opposition is not allowed radio time, and no opposition views are heard. We are mentioned only when the government calls us names or accuses us," a member of Parliament said (Personal interview, Peter Josie, member of Parliament, Castries, St. Lucia, January 9, 1976). The government public relations officer and the director of Radio St. Lucia both said that there is no formula for use of opposition views on the air.

air time on WIBS.* The government, on the other hand, uses the station regularly. A year ago, government used the station for its own purposes more than now. Government officials would come to the studio to tape speeches or to borrow one of our tape recorders. Some ministers pressured WIBS to put their speeches on the air without enough warning to avoid upsetting our program format.[175]

The opposition is not provided broadcast time over government-owned ZIZ on St. Kitts.** The station claims that it does not get involved in any political broadcasting, but Kittitians say that this is not true. For example, in 1967 Premier Robert Bradshaw went on the air to accuse the opposition party, PAM, of trying to overthrow his government. PAM was denied rebuttal time.[176]

Until 1971 Antigua Broadcasting System did not allow opposition political parties broadcast facilities. Even parliamentary proceedings were edited to keep the opposition voice off the air. Neither announcements of opposition party meetings nor the opposition's paid advertisements were welcome at ABS. According to the ABS news editor, these policies have been relaxed since the Walter government came into power in 1971.[177] On the other hand, the opposition claims that not much has changed.[178]

GOVERNMENT AS A PARTICIPATING AGENCY

Siebert defines government's role as a participating agency in this manner:

By this I do not mean the informational activities of the government designed to supply the private media with material which it may or may not transmit to the people. I mean direct contact between the government and the people through government instruments.[179]

He goes on to explain that by "government instruments" he means government-owned mass media.

---

* The situation has not changed on Dominica. On official occasions, the station allows a heavily censored broadcast of the opposition leader. Paid announcements of public meetings of the opposition are occasionally allowed (Personal interview, Edward Scobie, former editor, *Herald*, Castries, St. Lucia, January 9, 1976).

** By 1976 the opposition was not allowed radio-TV exposure even during an election campaign.

In previous chapters I have discussed the participating roles played by governments or dominant political parties as mass media owners (see chaps. 3, 4, and 5). In broadcasting, governments own at least two-thirds of the electronic media on Trinidad, Jamaica, and Barbados; one-half of those on Montserrat, Antigua, and St. Lucia; and the sole outlets on Grenada, St. Vincent, Dominica, the Bahamas, and St. Kitts. In chapter 5 the programs provided the public by government stations were analyzed and in another part of this chapter I discussed the restrictions that government-owned stations place on opposition parties. Government- or dominant party-owned newspapers and magazines have been similarly treated.

Since government's participating role in media ownership has already been covered, this section will explore other contacts that exist between Commonwealth Caribbean governments and the people. Chief among these are governmental use of radio and television programs, mobile film units, and political meetings to reach the masses.

Government Broadcasting Programs

A number of government- and privately owned stations in the region are required to set aside a portion of time for government programs. These shows, usually produced by GIS, are regarded not as propaganda, but as necessary information in the area of public affairs. The 1968 UNESCO report said that although Commonwealth Caribbean governments have been generally happy with the broadcasting service of the commercial stations, they have nevertheless found it necessary to "supplement station programmes with one or two more programmes produced by government broadcasters."[180]

In Trinidad both radio stations must give one hour and fifteen minutes daily to government broadcasts—thirty minutes of which is information about government and community activities, thirty of parliamentary affairs, and fifteen of local music. Government Information Service provides the material on tape. The required amount of time devoted to government information on the Barbados stations is thirty minutes thrice weekly. The government broadcasts must be aired at the same time on both of the island's stations. UNESCO, questioning the popularity of government shows, said:

> The care taken in both Trinidad and Barbados not to allow any alternative to the listeners when the government programme is on, may indicate some misapprehensions as to the popularity of such programmes.[181]

CBC-TV devotes a half hour a week to government programming. Usually the show is designed to inform the public about what is happening in Barbadian industry and agriculture.

In the smaller islands the governments also use the stations for special information programs. Radio Caribbean on St. Lucia, for example, is required by license to devote one hour daily to government shows, but the government seldom comes near meeting that quota. Instead, the station airs government programming forty minutes twice a week. In addition, three 15-minute school broadcasts that originate with the government are included on the station's weekly log.[182]

Plans are also being developed for a half-hour weekly ministerial show over Antigua Broadcasting System;[183] in the Bahamas a government information department was established in 1970 that has produced several shows for ZNS. St. Kitts radio has dropped its regular government broadcasts because of a lack of listeners. If something important in government occurs, a St. Kitts minister gets on the air to talk to the people.

The St. Lucian government is permitted to use up to one hour of television time daily (out of one to one-and-a-half hours of local programming per day) to communicate to the people. So far, the government has not taken advantage of this time allotment. At ZAL-TV in Antigua, no set amount of time is allocated to government programming, but the station is required to give the authorities free time during emergencies. On St. Vincent GIS provides the local radio substation, WIBS, with three one-hour shows a week and five news releases daily. The GIS director on St. Vincent said that islanders identify his office with WIBS. "Some people forget we are not WIBS. They call us at GIS and request music," Cameron King said.

Mobile Film Units

Most island governments have mobile film units that are used to take feature, educational, and informational films to rural areas. During the showings government personnel are available to talk directly with the people. The GIS film director on St. Vincent described his unit's operations in rural areas as follows:

St. Vincent GIS communicates government messages to the people through a weekly newsletter, radio programs and the mobile film unit. The film unit started operations in early 1971. We try to hide government programs in between a Cassius Clay fight or Trinidad Carnival feature. For example, we show a film of the Carnival, then one on Trinidad development, and then the premier or a cabinet minister talks and answers questions on St. Vincent's development. We close the night's performance with a Clay fight picture. One minister always travels with us to talk to the people.

For some of these people, it is the first time they have seen a film. One picture we showed was "Mrs. Indira Gandhi in Trinidad," followed by a discussion of women's roles in St. Vincent. We weave aspects of the film into Vincentian society. We show agriculture films and tell people that, although we don't have big machines like those in the film, here is what we can do with what we have.[185]

On an island such as St. Vincent, which has only three movie houses (one of which is outside the capital city), the mobile film units prove to be extremely effective. The government units have attracted crowds of up to 2,000 for a night's performance. Even in Kingstown, which has two theaters, the government can get as many as 1,000 people to come out to see the films. As another example, the two mobile units of the Barbados Education Department give performances five nights a week to an annual audience of nearly 200,000.

Film production is undertaken by the larger information services, especially those on Trinidad and Jamaica. For example, Jamaica Information Service produces at least four documentaries and several newsreels annually.

Political or Street Meetings

Probably one of the chief means by which island governments maintain contact with the public is the street (also called political) meeting. Alleyne has said that, whereas in North America the political meeting has declined as a propaganda and information medium, on an island such as Jamaica it is still of enormous importance. He added:

It is by means of these meetings that the most comprehensive picture of the political, social and economic state of the country can be obtained. . . . The political meeting then becomes, with interpersonal contact, the principal source of information and the principal opinion director. It is unfortunately also the most biased source.[186]

On island after island one hears about the importance of political meetings in keeping communications open between the governmental hierarchy and the masses. Eric Williams, for example, spends a number of nights a year in Woodford Square talking directly with the people.

At one point he also instituted a "Meet the People" program, designed to provide and obtain information at the local community level. In the early 1960s, for example, Williams traveled to nearly every Trinidad and Tobago hamlet discussing his programs. Questions were solicited in advance from the local people so that Williams could bring relevant ministers to provide answers.[187]

During Anguilla's revolt in the late 1960s, leader Ronald Webster used a public address system to get his people together in villages, where he gave them the latest reports.[188] St. Vincent GIS officials point out that press conferences of government leaders are not necessary because the premier and his ministers are with the people on a regular basis. Political parties hold weekly meetings in the Kingstown public square, even during nonelection periods. Government has such a meeting every Thursday, at which time officials clarify points brought up during the week by the opposition.

Bahamian leader Lynden Pindling uses mass meetings and his Bahamian dialect to reach the masses, and does it most effectively, according to one source.[189] His mass-meeting speeches are often taped for later radio broadcast.

On all of the islands the street meetings are held year round in an effort to maintain the enthusiasm of party supporters. Most are held outdoors: in a park, public square, or at a convenient crossroads. The format of the meetings does not change much: opening prayer, followed by mass singing (sometimes of party songs) to gain rapport, and then the long speeches. Usually the last speech is that of the party leader. Ayeast felt that one of the main attractions of the meetings is the free show provided for these people, many of whom cannot afford any other kind of entertainment.[190]

SUMMARY

A number of men who write about freedom of the press have been trying to come up with a philosophy that will take into account the presses of the developing regions of the world. One such philosophy is the evolving concept, discussed by Sommerlad. It probably suits the Commonwealth Caribbean mass media better than do the authoritarian or libertarian concepts, although tenets of both are included in the evolving philosophy. Basically, this philosophy allows for the fact that sometimes emerging nations' presses must be deliberately guided to fit national goals and programs.

This chapter has dealt primarily with regulations and restrictions under which British West Indian mass media function. Among regulatory acts of government are the press and broadcasting laws. Press laws that have been most restrictive to media in the region are those of libel and sedition. A number of instances of misuse of these laws have been noted, especially in Trinidad, Grenada, Antigua, and St. Kitts. Broadcasting laws in the region deal mainly with advertising content, although they also cover deceptive programming, libel, and political programming.

A number of subtle forms of suppression exist in the islands. For example, economic sanctions, through tax and license powers and government printing and advertising contracts, have affected certain media. In 1971 the government of Antigua threatened the freedom of the press through instituting an excessively high license fee on oppositionist newspapers. Bahamian newspapers complain that they have been discriminated against by governmental withholding of printing contracts. Denial of work-permit renewals to expatriate journalists critical of the government has hampered mass media operations on a number of islands. However, again, it was in the Bahamas where this restriction has been most menacing to newspapermen.

Still other restrictive actions taken against area mass media include: confiscation of a printing press, precensorship of broadcasting content, and the continuous public denunciations, threats, and intimidations, usually issued from political platforms.

Governments in the islands also facilitate mass media operations. Without the services of GIS, many smaller-island media would be without sources of news and information. However, some of the government information offices have also been turned into agencies that restrict, rather than aid, mass media. This has been the case on Grenada. Access to government information is hindered in some cases through discriminatory use of press releases, lack of press conferences, and closed meetings and records.

Other areas where the government has facilitated the functioning of mass media have been through postal subsidies granted to printed media, and fairness and equal-time rulings designed for electronic media.

The island governments also perform as participating agencies, owning a large number of the broadcasting units, as well as publishing their own newspapers and magazines. In addition, Commonwealth Caribbean governments have made efforts to keep contact with the masses, through information programs aired over radio and television, mobile film units that bring movies and public officials to the country-side, and political meetings.

NOTES TO CHAPTER 8

1. Letter to author, John Barsotti, Assistant Program Director, Trinidad and Tobago Television, Port of Spain, Trinidad, August 10, 1971.

2. Personal interview, Stanley Reid, Editor, *Crusader*, Castries, St. Lucia, May 8, 1971.

3. Novelist Peter Abrahams, quoted in David Butwin, "From Colony to Black Republic," *Saturday Review*, September 14, 1968, p. 52.

4. Personal interview, Nathaniel Hodge, Editor, *Democrat*, Basseterre, St. Kitts, May 1, 1971.

5. Fred S. Siebert, *Communications in Modern Society* (Urbana, Ill.: University of Illinois Press, 1948).

6. E. Lloyd Sommerlad, *The Press in Developing Countries* (Sydney, Australia: Sydney University Press, 1966), p. 141. Lowenstein uses the term *social centralist* to describe basically the same traits Sommerlad calls evolving. Social centralist is a modern modification of the authoritarian philosophy. The difference is that this philosophy controls the press not "primarily to keep it from doing harm to the ruling elite, but to channel the power of the media into what the state sees as constructive educational, developmental and political machinery." John C. Merrill and Ralph Lowenstein, *Media, Messages, and Men* (New York: David McKay Company, 1971), p. 187.

7. Sommerlad, *Press in Developing Countries*, p. 142.

8. Quoted in Sommerlad, ibid., p. 143.

9. DaBreo, discussing the British West Indies, said that colonial experiences of regional politicians determined their actions both before and after independence. "Many of them have suffered psychologically during the colonial period and after it, tend to take revenge. This leads them to the point where they are either incapable of making decisions or where they make rash ones." D. Sinclair DaBreo, *The West Indies Today* (St. George's, Grenada: Published by Author, 1969), p. 6.
  Millikan said that in transitional societies (such as the Commonwealth Caribbean), there has been a steady, but accelerating drift toward authoritarian practices, partly because of the general dissatisfaction with the slow rate of change, and partly because of the absence or weakness of institutions and political parties capable of resisting the state. Max Millikan and Donald Blackmer, eds., *The Emerging Nations* (Boston: Little, Brown & Co., 1961), p. 83. See also W. Phillips Davison, *International Political Communication* (New York: Frederick

A. Praeger, 1965), p. 139; John Hohenberg, *Free People, Free Press: The Best Cause* (New York: Columbia University Press, 1971), p. 464.

10.   A. W. Singham, *The Hero and the Crowd in a Colonial Polity* (New Haven, Conn.: Yale University Press, 1968), p. 10.

11.   Personal interview, Reggie Clyne, Editor, *West Indian*, St. George's, Grenada, May 12, 1971.

12.   Possibly Williams's power was shown in the results of the 1971 national elections. Williams's People's National Movement won all 36 seats in Parliament. As a result, Williams had to either appoint opposition leaders or run a de facto dictatorship. He chose the former. Probably the reason his party won all 36 seats was because the opposition withdrew from the race. "Trinidad-Tobago: Hollow Victory?" *Newsweek*, June 7, 1971.

13.   Sir Arthur Lewis, *The Agony of the Eight* (Bridgetown, Barbados: Advocate Commercial Printery, n.d.), p. 16.

14.   Morton Kroll, "Political Leadership and Administrative Communications in New Nation States," *Social and Economic Studies* (March 1967), p. 28.

15.   See *IAPA News* (October 1969). Apparently, even the only locally owned newspaper on Trinidad has means of knowing when government objects to its content. Editor Ken Gordon of the *Express* said: "But there are indirect ways that we get the message that government is unhappy with us. The *Nation*, government paper, from time to time carries what we call '*Express* supplements.' From the criticism of us in the *Nation*, we learn that government is dissatisfied." Personal interview, Ken Gordon, General Manager, Trinidad *Express*, Port of Spain, Trinidad, September 2, 1970.

16.   Lucian Pye, ed., *Communications and Political Development* (Princeton, N.J.: Princeton University Press, 1963), p. 102.

17.   Richard Fagen, *Politics and Communication* (Boston: Little, Brown & Co., 1966), p. 116.

18.   For example, *Abeng* on Jamaica died of lack of finance and organizational weaknesses; the paper on Dominica, *Flambeau*, lasted only three issues because its student editor could not afford to keep it going.

19.   Personal interview, John Dodge, General Manager, ZNS, Nassau, Bahamas, April 26, 1971.

20.   Butwin, "Colony to Black Republic," p. 52.

21.   Sommerlad said that evolving nations generally have political leaderships that are extremely sensitive to criticism. He attributed this to their lack of security and lack of acceptance of the role of an opposition. Sommerlad, *Press in Developing Countries*, p. 144.

22. Personal interview, Vernon Michaels, Manager, ZAL-TV, St. John's, Antigua, May 4, 1971.

23. Raoul Pantin, "The Press in a Less Developed Country," Trinidad *Express Independence Magazine*, August 30, 1970, p. 3.

24. Ibid.

25. Personal interview, Theodore Sealy, Editor, *Daily Gleaner*, Kingston, Jamaica, August 26, 1970.

26. Personal interview, Rick Wayne, Editor, *Voice of St. Lucia*, Castries, St. Lucia, May 7, 1971.

Some broadcasters said basically the same thing: that they had quit criticizing politicians; instead, the worth of the politician comes through by the way he is interviewed by the broadcasting people.

27. Guy Roppa and Neville Clarke, *The Commonwealth Caribbean: Regional Co-Operation in News and Broadcasting Exchanges* (Paris: UNESCO, 1969), p. 87.

28. Ibid., p. 89.

29. Although the constitutions were not reviewed by this author, Trinidad, St. Kitts, and Dominica, according to editors on those islands, guarantee freedom of expression in their constitutions. It is likely that the other islands also have such guarantees.

30. Government Printing Office, *The Handbook of Jamaica for 1962* (Kingston, Jamaica: GPO, 1962), pp. 73–74.

31. Interview, Sealy.

32. For example, Trinidad *Evening News* lost a libel case to Williams in 1963. He has sued media on other occasions. "PM's Claim for Libel Settled," Trinidad *Guardian*, May 21, 1963.

33. For example, Elcon Mason, Editor of *Torchlight*, said that Gairy instituted libel suits against his paper two years previously "but doesn't bring it forth." Mason said that Gairy used libel suits to harass *Vanguard*. Personal interview, Elcon Mason, Editor, *Torchlight*, St. George's, Grenada, May 12, 1971.

34. In mid-1971, Gairy was considering a suit against a London columnist who gave an adverse review of a documentary on Grenada. David Renwick, "Grenada Goes on TV and Creates a Stir," *Sunday Guardian*, May 9, 1971, p. 17.

35. Personal interview, A. Michael Cruickshank, Editor, *Vanguard*, St. George's, Grenada, May 12, 1971.

36. "IAPA Blasts Antigua Law That Shut Down Two Papers," *IAPA News* (January–February 1972), p. 7. See also Tony Cozier, "Caribbean Islands Press Threatened," *Editor & Publisher,* July 31, 1971, p. 20; *IAPA News* (August 1971), p. 1; Associated Press dispatch, February 22, 1972.

37. Interview, Hodge.

38. Ibid. However, apparently not too many people took him seriously. A former editor, Stanley Procope of St. Kitts *Daily Bulletin,* said that Bradshaw was just playing with words. "It is a political trip here for a politician to say he will do the *Democrat* in if his party gets in." Personal interview, Stanley Procope, Former Editor, *Daily Bulletin,* Basseterre, St. Kitts, May 1, 1971.

39. Associated Press dispatch, February 22, 1972.

40. Alvin Austin, "Infringements on Freedom of the Press in Latin America," *North Dakota Quarterly* (Spring 1969), p. 63.

41. Personal interview, Edward Scobie, Editor, Dominica *Herald,* Roseau, Dominica, May 5, 1971. Basically the same points were made by the editors of the *Chronicle* and *Star* in interviews with this author.

42. Ibid.

43. Ulric Mentus, "Enter Dominica's Freedom Fighters," Trinidad *Evening News,* August 14, 1968. More information on the act and succeeding events can be found in "Dominica Press Gags Bill Passed at Rowdy Sitting," Trinidad *Guardian,* July 9, 1968; "IAPA Condemns New Press Law in West Indies," *Editor & Publisher,* August 31, 1968, p. 22.

44. Personal interview, Lenn Chongsing, Editor, Trinidad *Guardian,* Port of Spain, Trinidad, September 1, 1970. See also John Babb, "Emergency Regulations Amended," Trinidad *Guardian,* June 5, 1970.

45. Personal interview, Compton Delph, Editor, Trinidad *Evening News,* Port of Spain, Trinidad, September 1, 1970. Another source, writing at the time of the revolt, said that Williams and the police commissioner of Trinidad banned all news from foreign countries "until further notice." Radio stations were told that references to the mutineering army had to be cleared by the government. Robert Maynard, "Trinidad Trickery Nabs Trio," Denver *Post,* May 3, 1970.

46. Hollis Boisselle, "The Public Order Bill and Freedom of Movement," Trinidad *Guardian,* August 15, 1970; "Justice Raps Proposed Act," Trinidad *Guardian,* August 24, 1970, p. 1; Editorial in Trinidad *Guardian,* April 24, 1970.

47. "Freedom of Expression Under Siege," *IAPA News* (January–February 1972), p. 5.

48. "Public Order (Amendment) Laws During Emergency," Grenada *Vanguard,*

March 12, 1971, p. 1; "Public Order Amendment Act a Means of Repression," Grenada *Torchlight*, March 17, 1971, p. 1.

49. Personal interview, Bentley Cornelius, Editor, Antigua *Star*, May 4, 1971. To cite one more case, when Bermuda was having race problems in the late 1960s, restrictions were placed on the reporting of events there. John Hilton Bassett, editor of a Black Power paper, was jailed for inflammatory writing. It was against the law to be found with a copy of his paper. At the time of his arrest, Bassett remarked that it was impossible to get a fair trial in a "fascist pig court." For that statement, he was arraigned. A local radio station and newspaper that reported the remark were arraigned as well. Horace Sutton, "The Palm Tree Revolt," *Saturday Review*, February 27, 1971, p. 17.

50. For example, St. Kitts, until mid-1971, banned the importation of television sets. This move was interpreted by some commentators as an effort on Premier Bradshaw's part to keep people ignorant. He said that he didn't want TV sets on the island because they would cause discontent. When the law was lifted, a United States firm was granted the license, at $18,000 (EC) a year, to import, sell and repair the sets. Placing the television-set monopoly in a foreign business's hands caused added controversy. The St. Kitts *Democrat* wrote: "The whole thing is a phantasmagoria of fiscal marauding by the authorities, trampling disdainfully on the rights of the business community, not to mention those of the masses." "A Closing Reign," St. Kitts *Democrat*, May 1, 1971, p. 3.

51. "First Tuesday," NBC, April 6, 1971.

52. "St. Kitts Government Outlaws Unregistered Newspapers," Trinidad *Guardian*, January 10, 1969; "Editorial," Anguilla *Beacon*, February 15, 1969.

53. "The Cowboy and the Censors," Trinidad *Express*, September 3, 1970, p. 4.

54. Especially on St. Lucia there was concern about the powers of the board of censors. But there it was the police, not the church, that was restricting movie fare.

55. "Broadcasting Authority To Be Set Up," Jamaica *Gleaner*, June 17, 1958.

56. "Broadcasting Authority's Report on Local TV, Radio Stations," Jamaica *Daily Gleaner*, January 25, 1966.

57. Personal interview, Roy Lawrence, Public Relations Director, Jamaica Broadcasting Corporation, Kingston, Jamaica, August 28, 1970. See also "Complaints of Distorted News Justified in Some Instances," Jamaica *Daily Gleaner*, September 23, 1964.

58. Personal interview, Sam Ghany, Sales Manager, Trinidad Broadcasting, Port of Spain, Trinidad, September 2, 1970; Personal interview, Leo de Leon, Program Director, 610 Radio, Port of Spain, Trinidad, September 1, 1970. According to the Third Five-Year Plan of the island (p. 337), "A broadly based

Authority will be set up under a Telecommunication Act to supervise and regulate all sound and visual broadcasting, its criteria of operation being to ensure high standards, the promotion of local goods and services, and the development of a national style, image and outlook."

59. This was told to the author by Lawrence at JBC, who said that the prime minister is the officer in charge of Jamaican broadcasting; by Gale on Barbados who said "there is a broadcasting authority in Barbados who is the prime minister really." Interview, Lawrence; Personal interview, Ian Gale, General Manager, Caribbean Broadcasting Corporation, Bridgetown, Barbados, September 4, 1970.

60. Interview, Dodge.

61. Personal interview, Jeff Charles, Manager-Designate, Radio Dominica, Roseau, Dominica, May 6, 1971.

62. Personal interview, Roy Dunlop, Director, Radio Anguilla, The Valley, Anguilla, April 29, 1971.

63. Sound Broadcasting Regulations of 1963, Jamaica. Xeroxed copy from Radio Jamaica files.

64. Bahamas Broadcasting Act. Copies provided author by John Dodge, ZNS.

65. Caribbean Broadcasting Corporation Act 1963-36 (Supplement to *Official Gazette*, November 11, 1963). Copy provided author by Ian Gale, CBC.

66. Interview, de Leon.

67. Interview, Ghany.

68. Letter, Barsotti.

69. Personal interview, John Whitmarsh, Station Manager, Radio Caribbean, Castries, St. Lucia, May 7, 1971.

70. Personal interview, Sir Etienne Dupuch, Editor-proprietor, Nassau *Tribune*, Nassau, Bahamas, April 27, 1971; Personal interview, Benson McDermott, Vice President, Nassau *Guardian*, Nassau, Bahamas, August 24, 1970; Elsa Gilbert, "Press Freedom Bahama Style," *Overseas Press Bulletin*, December 17, 1969, p. 3; "Bahamian Newsmen Face Government Pressure," *IAPA News*, No. 200, p. 8; "Bahamas Bill Worries the Press," *IPI Report* (January 1969), p. 5; "Revised Press Bill Stiffer Than Original," Nassau *Guardian*, March 20, 1969; "Should Be Left To Die," Nassau *Guardian*, March 21, 1969, p. 4; "Amendment Bid Fails As Press Bill Passes," Nassau *Guardian*, March 27, 1969, p. 1; Donn Selhorn, "Bahamas Puts Press Under Severe Rules," *Editor & Publisher*, May 3, 1969.

71. "Caribbean Press Facing Subtle Pressures," *IAPA News* (August 1971), p. 1.

72. Interview, Hodge.

73. Editorial, Anguilla *Beacon*, February 3, 1968. Interview, Dunlop.

74. Personal interview, Winston Hinkson, WIBS Director, Castries, St. Lucia, May 7, 1971.

75. Interview, Sealy.

76. Merrill and Lowenstein term these "pressures against 'harmless' publication." Merrill and Lowenstein, *Media Messages, and Men*, p. 206.

77. Media personnel did not mention any instances of government using newsprint or foreign exchange allocations as methods of control. The same cannot be said for Guyana.

78. Interview, Dupuch.

79. Because the station is owned by the Bird family, opponents of the present government. Personal interview, Leslie John, Chief Reporter, *Workers Voice*, St. John's, Antigua, May 4, 1971.

80. Letter to author, Dorcas White, Editor, Montserrat *Mirror*, Plymouth, Montserrat, June 10, 1971.

81. Interview, Mason.

82. Interview, McDermott.

83. Interview, Dupuch. Dupuch said that the deputy prime minister was quoted as saying that he would not deal with the *Tribune*. The contract was given to the *Times*, which had no circulation, he said.

84. Personal interview, Neville Grosvenor, General Manager, *Advocate-News*, Bridgetown, Barbados, September 7, 1970.

85. Sir Etienne Dupuch, "Preservation of Democracy as Great a Concern as Freedom of the Press," Nassau *Tribune*, October 28, 1970.

86. Interview, Scobie.

87. Ibid.

88. Personal interview, Phyllis Allfrey, Editor, Dominica *Star*, Roseau, Dominica, May 6, 1971. Mrs. Allfrey said that the government does not like to give the *Star* its advertising, but has been reasonably fair in its distribution of legal notice advertisements.

89. Interview, Cruickshank.

90. "We Can Only Try," Trinidad *Guardian*, February 17, 1959; "Government Subsidy to Press Denied," Trinidad *Guardian;* February 17, 1959.

91.   Interview, Whitmarsh.

92.   The registrar felt that the listed proprietors were "strawmen," according to Cruickshank. Interview, Cruickshank.

93.   See note 36 for sources.

94.   "IAPA Blasts Antigua Law. . . ,"

95.   Interview, Hodge.

96.   Interview, Reid.

97.   Interview, Wayne. Commenting on the Agard incident, IPI said that the St. Lucian politicians would not stand for criticism from outsiders. *IPI Report* (September 1970), p. 7.

98.   *IAPA News* (October 1964).

99.   Ibid.

100.   *IAPA News*, March 31–April 1, 1967. See also "IPI Protests at Bar on Reuters Man," *IPI Report* (March 1967), p. 1; "Reuters Correspondent Banned by Barbados," *Press of the Americas* (April 1967), p. 1; "Reuters Correspondent Batchelor Is Not Permitted To Enter Barbados," *Press of the Americas* (August 1967), pp. 3–4.

101.   Personal interview, Ivor Bird, Manager, ZDK, St. John's, Antigua, May 4, 1971; Interview, John.

102.   *Star* said that she was the victim of "callous, calculated neglect by the very members of the Labour Party whom she had gone way out on a limb to defend." "Now Who Really Forced Dorcas To Leave Antigua?" Antigua *Star*, March 10, 1971, p. 2.

103.   Letter; White.

104.   Personal interview, Everard Richards, News Editor, Antigua Broadcasting System, St. John's, Antigua, May 4, 1971.

105.   Letter to author, Canon C. R. G. Carleton, Former Editor, Anguilla *Beacon*, Inagua, Bahamas, June 29, 1971.

106.   *IAPA News* (October 1969).

107.   Gilbert, "Press Freedom Bahama Style."

108.   "Report of the 1970 SDX Advancement of Freedom of Information Committee." Apparently, the Bahamian government has used the denial of work permits to regulate others besides mass media personnel. According to one source,

the Pindling government started withholding work permits to break the hold on Freeport imposed by foreign concessionaires and builders there. The result was that some owners of businesses on Grand Bahama suddenly found themselves unable to work in their own establishments. Sutton, "The Palm Tree Revolt."

109.   Personal interview, Chris Evans, former General Manager, Nassau *Guardian,* Nassau, Bahamas, August 24, 1970.

110.   Ibid.

111.   Sir Etienne Dupuch, "Gestapo at Work," Nassau *Tribune,* April 24, 1971, p. 3; Interview, Dupuch.

112.   Interview, Dupuch. In 1968 the Bahamas Senate sought to censure Dupuch for his criticism of the government. The motion failed. See *IAPA News* (April 1968); "Bahamas Bid To Censure Editor Fails," *IPI Report* (December 1967), p. 2.

113.   Personal interview, Atlin Harrigan, Editor, Anguilla *Beacon,* The Valley, Anguilla, April 29, 1971.

114.   "Freedom of Speech and Press," Anguilla *Beacon,* April 12, 1969, p. 2. Webster is accused of suppressing the second newspaper on Anguilla. An article in one of the issues of *Observer* was critical of the Anguillan president; he stopped that issue's circulation. Interview, Harrigan.

115.   Personal interview, Leslie Seon, former WIBS Program Director and former GIS Director, St. George's, Grenada, May 13, 1971.

116.   Interview, Richards.

117.   Interview, Cruickshank.

118.   "The Right to Criticize," Trinidad *Guardian,* January 26, 1963; "Stones on Glass Houses," Trinidad *Guardian,* April 14, 1960; "Premier Replies to Sir Gerald," Trinidad *Guardian,* January 26, 1963; "PM Attacks 'Old Enemies,'" Trinidad *Guardian,* September 27, 1963; "Trinidad Chief Threatens Press," *Press of the Americas,* August 1, 1957; "No 'Mercy' for Guardian," Trinidad *Guardian,* October 9, 1960.

119.   "Williams' Infernor," *Press of the Americas,* May 1, 1960, p. 3.

120.   "Dr. Williams: The Press, Church, Big Business Against PNM Again," Trinidad *Express,* April 29, 1971, p. 3.

121.   "Stamp Out Hooliganism," Trinidad *Guardian,* October 20, 1959.

122.   *IAPA News* (October 1969). Also *IAPA News* (October 1964).

123.   Interview, Grosvenor.

124. Personal interview, Fred Seal Coon, Editorial Manager, *Daily Gleaner*, Kingston, Jamaica, August 26, 1970.

125. Interview, John.

126. Rowan Henry, "What Does the Future Hold?" Antigua *Times*, May 1, 1971, p. 4.

127. "The Truth Hurts," *Workers Voice*, April 27, 1971, p. 2.

128. Reuben Harris, "Watt, Where Are Your Principles?" Antigua *Times*, April 28, 1971, p. 4.

129. Interview, Hodge.

130. Ibid.

131. *IAPA News* (October 1969). Also Interview, Hodge; "St. Kitts Editor Arrested," Trinidad *Guardian*, January 22, 1969.

132. "St. Kitts Paper Under Pressure," *IAPA News* (June 1971), p. 8.

133. "Dominica CM Threatens Press," Trinidad *Guardian*, February 12, 1966.

134. Interview, Scobie.

135. Interview, Allfrey.

136. Interview, Clyne.

137. Source asked for anonymity.

138. Homer Bigart, "Anguillans Have Big Plans for Their Republic," Charlotte Amalie *Daily News*, March 20, 1969, p. 6; Personal interview, Ronald Webster, President, Anguilla, The Valley, Anguilla, April 29, 1971.

139. Roppa and Clarke, *Commonwealth Caribbean*, p. 67.

140. Ibid.

141. Ibid., p. 68.

142. Ibid., p. 69.

143. In at least one case, it was felt that this arrangement hindered the obtaining of government information. An Antiguan editor said that now that the government has a press information officer, directly under the premier, no one can say anything to the press unless the premier allows it. Interview, John.

144. "Statement of Objectives," mimeographed (St. Vincent Government Information Service).

145. Personal interview, Cameron King, Public Relations and Information Officer, Government Information Service, Kingstown, St. Vincent, May 10, 1971.

146. Personal interview, Weston H. Lewis, Editor, *Vincentian*, Kingstown, St. Vincent, May 10, 1971.

147. Source asked for anonymity.

148. Singham, *Hero and Crowd*, p. 209.

149. The Grenadian editor who provided me with this copy of the release instructed me to "keep it under your hat." The reason: he said that government releases are private communication between the premier and press on Grenada.

150. Interview, Mason.

151. Interview, Cruickshank.

152. Interview, Clyne.

153. Interview, Seon.

154. Interview, Reid.

155. Personal interview, George Lewis, Editor, *Labour Spokesman*, Basseterre, St. Kitts, May 1, 1971.

156. Personal interview, Leon Turnquest, Editor, Nassau *Guardian*, Nassau, Bahamas, April 26, 1971.

157. Interview, Scobie.

158. Ibid. Scobie added that press relations with the Dominican government have always been poor. The premier's public relations are hopeless, he said. "When I started as editor of the *Herald*, I prompted him to have press conferences. But he quit having them because he resents the press," Scobie added.

159. Interview, Delph. Delph added that Williams is not kindly disposed to the press.

160. " 'Guardian' Boycotts Press Conference," Trinidad *Guardian*, January 25, 1959.

161. Interview, Wayne.

162. Interview, King.

163. *West Indies Yearbook Including Also The Bermudas, The Bahamas, British Guiana and British Honduras 1941-2* (Montreal, Canada: Thomas Skinner & Co., 1942).

164. *Bahamas Handbook* (Nassau: Etienne Dupuch Jr., 1970), p. 337.

165. Government Printing Office, *The Handbook of Jamaica for 1962*, p. 597.

166. Interview, Dodge.

167. Interview, Charles.

168. Merrill and Lowenstein, *Media, Messages, and Men*, p. 209.

169. Interview, Dodge.

170. Personal interview, Claude Theobalds, Chief Program Officer, WIBS, Kingstown, St. Vincent, May 11, 1971.

171. Personal interview, Lloyd de Pass, General Manager, Radio Jamaica, Kingston, Jamaica, August 27, 1970. At St. Lucia Television political broadcasts are allowed as long as equal time is provided all parties. The station is not permitted to advertise political messages but can broadcast political programs. Personal interview, Ken Archer, Director, St. Lucia Television Services, Castries, St. Lucia, May 8, 1971.
     Radio Caribbean, also on St. Lucia, broadcasts announcements of political meetings but must restrict the notices to the names of speakers, time and place of speech. The title of the speech cannot be broadcast in the announcements. Interview, Whitmarsh.

172. Interview, Michaels.

173. Ibid.

174. Interview, Cruickshank; Interview, Clyne.

175. Interview, Charles.

176. Interview, Hodge.

177. Interview, Richards; "Halstead Wants Antigua Radio Destroyed," *The Journal*, April 24, 1969.

178. Interview, John.

179. Siebert, *Communications in Modern Society*.

180. Roppa and Clarke, *Commonwealth Caribbean*, p. 26.

181. Ibid.

182. Interview, Whitmarsh.

183. Interview, Richards.

184. Interview, Archer.

185. Personal interview, Leon Huggins, Film Director, GIS, Kingstown, St. Vincent, May 10, 1971.

186. Mervin Alleyne, "Communications and Politics in Jamaica," *Caribbean Studies* 3 no. 2: 39.

187. Kroll, "Political Leadership . . . States," p. 27.

188. Interview, Webster.

189. Interview, Turnquest.

190. Morley Ayeast, *The British West Indies: The Search for Self-Government* (London: George Allen & Unwin, 1960), p. 217.

9

Conclusion

Mass media came to the islands as part of the British cultural implantation, and for years they remained as institutions within the British colonial apparatus. From the time of emancipation, a number of independent newspapers (even some that were very critical of the British colonial system) appeared on the scene. But, underlining the whole communications structure of the region was the presence of foreign influences. Later, when broadcasting came to the islands, it, too, was patterned after the British system in both structure and function.

Despite political independence, mass media in the region are still pervaded by British, as well as United States, influences, so that in many cases both ownership and content are in foreign hands. Roy Thomson, Rediffusion of London, Columbia Broadcasting System, and National Broadcasting Company are names that one finds among media owners of the region. Rock and soul music, in place of native calypso and steel bands, and Hollywood movies fill radio and television logs and movie marquees. Reuters, Associated Press, and United Press International serve as the chief news dispensers in the Commonwealth Caribbean, while American and British feature syndicates furnish comic strips, crossword puzzles, and columns. Radio news in many cases is BBC news; books and magazines for sale are American and British products. For example, when one finds a bookstore that does handle Caribbean materials, invariably the books are placed in sections called "West Indies," as if they were foreign publications.

Basically, two points of view are expressed concerning the foreign impact on Commonwealth Caribbean mass media. Many writers on the West Indies, including DaBreo, Lewis, and Williams, feel that cultural extinction is imminent if the large powers keep flooding newly emergent regions with mass media products. They tend to agree with Schiller, who, speaking more generally, warned that electronic communications from the developed nations were "menacing the cultural integrity of many developing nations . . . with extinction."[1] Others argue that these developing nations need foreign mass media materials, not being able to produce their own.

In this connection, it must be remembered that the developing nations (such as the Commonwealth Caribbean) themselves made the final decisions concerning their relationships with foreign media. Foreign conglomerates do not forcibly take over media plants; they just make island governments and media personnel offers that are too attractive to turn down. Along the same lines, island media are not required, legally or otherwise, to purchase or subscribe to foreign news and entertainment services. Instead, they do so because they feel that large, foreign concerns can offer a better product than the island media can produce, and do so at a lower cost.

So actually, the problem stems more from actions on the part of the islands than from the foreign entrepreneurs. The process probably starts in this fashion: Once independent, nations such as the Commonwealth Caribbean want to jump overnight out of the horse-and-cart stage into the jet age. They impatiently want to get on with the most of the latest in the quickest time. They want all the prestige and recognition they were denied for so long under British colonial tutelage. But getting into the jet age requires capital, equipment, and knowhow that many of the islands do not possess. Therefore, to get the big media package, which they feel they need for prestige, the islands tie themselves to the United States or Great Britain. In turn, they accept the foreign ownership and content orientation that go with the deal.

Once mass media development of this type is initiated, it seems to build a momentum of its own, which in the end can become too quick-paced for a region such as the Commonwealth Caribbean. For example, once people purchase television sets, they demand more hours of programming, which, because of the prohibitively high costs of local production, must be imported. At the same time, once educational and literacy development are stimulated, a demand for reading material is created; to meet the demand, printed media are forced to fill more and more pages. The convenient sources for this space-filling are the international news agencies and syndicated feature services.

It seems to me that if the island elites feel that such large amounts of foreign communications represent a threat, they should attack the problem at its source—at the local government stage. They should not allow their governments to go after the big package; instead, the elites should offer alternatives that would make more use of interpersonal networks that would be more modest in format. But they should also be realistic enough to recognize that no matter which alternative they choose, they will have to depend upon outside help of some sort. They will have to take note that most of the production materials of mass media—presses, newsprint, transmitters—are not made in the islands. Nor are the basic raw materials, from which this technology is produced, indigenous to the area.

I see both good and bad results from the imported media content. In some ways such content might bring rural dwellers out of their villages and, at least psychically, expose them to the outside world. On the other hand, a large percentage of United States broadcast programming, for example, would not present a realistic picture of life in an industrialized nation. Instead, many times false stereotypes are represented, so that developing peoples think that all Americans are middle class or wealthy, as shown on television and in the movies.

Again, using broadcasting as an example, if island stations cannot afford to produce local drama shows because of the cost factor, they could at least provide more story hours where only a reader is needed. A few stations have made attempts in that direction. The region has an abundance of important writers whose works deserve the attention of broadcasting, and print, media. Also, why would it not be possible for the works of West Indian authors to be produced for worldwide consumption that in turn would be shown in the region? With the shortage of new and interesting material on United States and British television, it would seem that television directors in those two countries might be interested in producing certain works of West Indian authors who use universal themes. Actually, what I am putting forth here is the Lerner proposal—that developing peoples adapt, rather than adopt, the industrialized world's communication patterns.

By adapting foreign media products to local usage, the British West Indian elites would be accomplishing what I believe they really want: a decision-making role in the direction taken by their mass media.

So far only the elites of the islands are being heard. Possibly this results from the fact that the common man is for the most part satisfied with the foreign content of his mass media; every year the mass audiences grow in these islands. If he is satisfied, and if the overexposure to foreign media content is detrimental to local cultural values, then the elites will have to act immediately, before the masses become so imbued with foreign programs that they shun local shows.

If the islanders insist upon the big media package, while at the same time wanting only minimum foreign involvement, then they will have to resort to government and political party sponsorship. With a few major exceptions, only these local agencies seem able and willing to invest in large-scale mass media operations in the islands. Even now, large proportions of broadcasting are in government hands and most nondaily newspapers are politically backed. In many cases locally prepared media content implies high usage of GIS releases.

Because most governments in newly emergent nations are extremely sensitive to criticism and, if not checked, are prone to authoritarianism, mass media often find themselves pushed into the roles of government apologists and defenders.

The serving of political goals has always been the chief mission of a large sector of the Commonwealth Caribbean mass media. During crisis-filled periods in the past, newspapers throve on political content that supported their side's arguments while blasting opposite viewpoints. The situation has intensified since independence. First, a larger portion of the mass media has, since the mid-1950s, come under government or political-party control. Also, the stirring of nationalism and black-power movements in the islands during the past decade has augmented the political content of most media.

Political comments in most media are hostile and unconstructive, probably a carry-over from preindependence days when editors felt that their main task was to attack the colonial authorities, no matter what they said or did. The governments of the region, still immature and unstable, tend to be extremely sensitive and suspicious of this criticism. The result: numerous instances of suppression by Commonwealth Caribbean authorities. These restrictive acts are usually subtly carried out because the officials do not wish to stir up negative regional-and-world public opinion while their governments are still in this insecure state.

Probably in larger, more developed states, a number of these restrictive acts would not be accorded much attention; however, the smallness of the islands accentuates any governmental actions.

Overall, there is definitely a swing to authoritarian governmental practices concerning island mass media. For example, if one were to assume that a free press is one that is relatively free of government, he would have to adjudge the island media as being very unfree. Commonwealth Caribbean mass media are heavily dependent on government, many units being owned by the authorities, others still relying on government for newsgathering and distribution services, as well as for advertising and printing contracts. In addition, as noted elsewhere, there is the tendency of island governments to restrict, rather than facilitate, oppositionist media operations.

The numerous restrictions placed on regional media might be assessed as an indication that newspapers and broadcasting stations are doing good jobs, assuming that their chief purpose is to check on government. On the other hand, this optimistic view is offset by the fact that many media, especially small nondailies, are fulfilling this function not so much for the welfare of their nations, but for the sake of garnering additional political payoffs from their subsidizers.

The oppositionist nature of mass media is common among newly independent countries. In some ways, the press of the Commonwealth Caribbean is reminiscent of the Philippines before 1972 martial law. The Philippines had been under Spanish, American, and Japanese rule for about 350 years. When liberation from the Japanese occurred in 1945, and finally independence from the United States in 1946, newspapers sprouted everywhere in the islands. In almost every case the papers were oppositionist and hostile. These same traits were discernible in Philippine media examined by this writer as late as the mid-1960s.

Describing the Philippine press immediately after independence, one editor said:

> Never had the press been so free, never had it wielded such power and influence. The government was but recently established and uncertain of its strength. It was extremely sensitive to public opinion and the press took advantage of this healthy state, pouncing on government's least mistakes and making national issues of them . . . . The power of the press was utterly out of proportion to the circulations of the various papers. None could claim a sale of more than a few thousand copies.[2]

In recent years—as the Philippine government grew more confident, as media consolidated to form larger, more commercially conscious units, and as self-regulatory press organizations developed—the Philippine mass media have settled down somewhat.

Some Commonwealth Caribbean mass media, especially the larger units, seem to be following the same path. Realizing that they cannot continue their destructive criticism of government without serious repercussions, some island media are initiating self-regulatory guidelines.

Self-regulatory codes of ethics, press councils, and other press institutions are worthy projects and should be encouraged, as long as they come from within media ranks. However, in territories such as the Commonwealth Caribbean, where government ownership of media is significant, one must question whether the press is regulating itself, or whether the government is regulating the press through its own media outlets.

On some islands, especially Trinidad and, to a certain degree, Jamaica, media and government personnel have promoted the concept of a deliberately guided press. Under this philosophy, the media are urged to show restraint in their criticism of government for the sake of the accomplishment of national goals. There are merits to such a theory, although one readily recognizes it as a modified form of authoritarianism. But it is also a very idealistic principle that assumes that men in power will, on their own volition, lessen press restrictions once their governments are more stable and national goals have been met.

In the emerging Commonwealth Caribbean, where authoritarian personalities are in control of islands for long periods of time, such a philosophy would seem to strengthen their rule and perpetuate them in office for even longer periods of time.

Thus, unconstructive and hostile as it may be, press criticism is needed in the islands until the governments learn to appreciate the necessity for an opposition. Hopefully, the criticism will take a more constructive turn once the governments themselves better organize national development aims.

From the foregoing, four major conclusions might be drawn:

1. The nature of mass media in the Commonwealth Caribbean is still heavily dependent upon outside factors in the areas of ownership, programming, and technology.

2. A number of the mass media problems in the region are those typical of emerging nations in a hurry to become modernized. Basically, these problems relate to one central point: developing areas are in need of those sources that they are least able to afford, and that, oftentimes, are least indigenous to their cultures.

3. One of the main purposes of mass media in the islands is to serve political functions. Although this is a function of mass media in many nations, the distinguishing factors in the Commonwealth Carib-

bean are the nature of the political intention and the intensity of usage of political items.

4. Freedom of the press on most islands is shaky, with authorities tending to intimidate the press through laws, suits, and financial favors.

In addition, these observations are offered:

1. Because growth of the press keeps pace with the speed of economic growth generally, more industrialized islands such as Trinidad and Jamaica appear to be far ahead in their mass media development than smaller, agrarian-oriented islands.

2. As islands become more economically independent, local governments start thinking in terms of replacing foreign media ownerships with local government control.

3. Broadcasting appears to be the chief medium of the region. This results from government direction and the relatively inexpensive transistor radio, and also because broadcasting is less hampered by problems of literacy, education, and distribution than are the other media.

4. A crucial area in the national development process that has been slighted in the region concerns mass media's role relative to rural dwellers. As noted elsewhere, media operations are concentrated in capital cities; media contents are designed for urbanites. Efforts are being made to reach the common man in the countryside, but probably not seriously enough.

(UNESCO in 1968 made a number of conclusions concerning Commonwealth Caribbean media. See Appendix F.)

Hopeful Trends

So that the reader does not assume that the Commonwealth Caribbean mass media are caught in revolving doors with no doorway, three significant trends in the islands will be discussed.

It becomes increasingly apparent that the most likely way Commonwealth Caribbean mass media will overcome economic, political, and social hindrances to their development is through regional cooperation. Hopeful signs are on the horizon. Generally speaking, the islands have moved toward regionalization in recent years. Economically, they are tied together in the recently created Caribbean Development Bank and the Caribbean Free Trade Area (CARIFTA).*

---

* Since mid-1973 the Commonwealth Caribbean has been served by CARICOM, a new common market and offspring of CARIFTA. See Compton Delph, "A New Common Market Is Born," Gemini dispatch in *Straits Echo* (Malaysia), August 27, 1973.

Politically, they are considering a revival of the West Indies Federation.

There have been corresponding attempts in the field of mass communications. The region now has a news service, although foreign controlled, in the Reuters Caribbean Desk;* it has a training scheme in the planned University of the West Indies journalism-diploma program; and there is a regional broadcast exchange bureau in the Caribbean Broadcasting Union. In addition, government information service heads in the early 1970s were considering regionalization. Windward Islands Broadcasting Service, one of the first regional media operations, is reorganizing, so that better service might be provided for its St. Vincent, St. Lucia, and Dominica substations, and also to keep the organization itself intact. Caribbean Broadcasting Corporation on Barbados is still promoting the idea of direct television link-ups, hoping that St. Vincent, Dominica, and Grenada will receive the CBC-TV signal by relay and thus form a regional television network.

Additionally, Caribbean Broadcasting Union hopes to regionalize program exchanges and provide more linking of radio stations for events of national importance. At least one broadcaster,[3] looking further into the future, envisions island stations joining the satellite age by buying as a group extremely costly satellite time through Caribbean Broadcasting Union. Broadcasters feel that use of satellites will help disseminate regional materials abroad, and vice versa, as well as facilitating inter-island programming exchange.

Some of these projects are closer to fruition than others; some will never leave the proposal stage, and, generally, regionalization on a large scale will take considerable time.** But, eventually, island pride and jealousy must step aside to make room for regionalization. There is no other viable way for the island media operations to untangle themselves from the webs in which they are caught. As the UNESCO team stated in 1968:

It is the view of this Mission, repeatedly expressed in this Report, that it is precisely because of the difficulties arising from the imbal-

---

* And since January 7, 1976, the region has its own news service, Caribbean News Agency (CANA).

** The developments in Caribbean mass communications during the four years since this book was written prove this statement. WIBS is defunct, while other regionalization goals are reaching fruition: CANA is operating, as is the University of West Indies mass communication program; CBU is successful in developing broadcast exchanges; regional-type publications such as *Caribbean Contact* are rather popular; CPBA is hard at work setting up a regional press council, and so on.

ance of development in general, and of mass communication potential in particular, that regional cooperation is necessary.[4]

Another encouraging trend is that toward more professionalization among mass media personnel. In recent years the region has seen the birth of journalists' associations, the establishment of codes of ethics, and the designing of a journalism diploma course at the University of the West Indies. The move from on-the-job training to the more formal instruction that the UWI program provides should benefit the mass media immensely. It has been evident in other developing regions that the initiation of journalism education programs has had beneficial results on the quality of the media products, and the same effect can be expected in the Commonwealth Caribbean.

Finally, the changing technology of mass communications should help media in the islands. Medium- and large-size newspapers will benefit from offset machinery and, in some cases, computerization. Regional cooperation of broadcasting units will allow for satellite hook-ups. Long-term benefits of such electronic machinery, which allows for specialization, flexibility, feedback, and inexpensiveness, are conducive to developing regions such as the Commonwealth Caribbean.

NOTES TO CHAPTER 9

1.   Herbert Schiller, *Mass Communications and American Empire* (Boston: Beacon Press, 1971), p. 109. See also Arthur Goodfriend, "The Dilemma of Cultural Propaganda: 'Let It Be,'" *Annals of the American Academy of Political and Social Science* (November 1971), p. 106.

2.   Teodoro Locsin, quoted in John A. Lent, *Philippine Mass Communications: Before 1811, After 1966* (Manila, Philippines: Philippine Press Institute, 1971), p. 14.

3.   Personal interview, Ian Gale, General Manager, Caribbean Broadcasting Corporation, Bridgetown, Barbados, September 4, 1970.

4.   Guy Roppa and Neville Clarke, *The Commonwealth Caribbean: Regional Co-Operation in News and Broadcasting Exchanges* (Paris: UNESCO, 1968), p. 80.

List of Known Newspapers
in Commonwealth Caribbean

Founded	Name	Frequency	Year of Last Known Issue
Bahamas:			
1783–84	The Bahama Gazette	W, Bi-W	1857
1804	The Royal Gazette & Bahama Advertiser	Bi-W	1837
1810	Bahama Gazette	Bi-W	1814
1831	The Bahama Argus	Bi-W	1837
1836, 1838	The Bahamian (renamed The Observer	Bi-W	1838
1844	Nassau Guardian	D	continues
1849	Bahama Herald	Semi-W	1877
1861	The Nassau Advertiser		1865 (discontinued)
1869	The Nassau Times		1895
1886	The Freeman		unknown
	The West Indian Guardian		1891–92
1898	The Bahama News		1901 (discontinued)
	Parthenon		unknown
1901	The Watchman		1906
1904	The Tribune	D	continues
1908	The Witness		
1922	Observer Weekly (later Nassau Leader)	W	unknown
1935	Bahama News		unknown
1937	Nassau Herald	W	1941

Founded	Name	Frequency	Year of Last Known Issue
1938	The Mirror		1940 (discontinued)
	Business Men's Monthly	M	1941
1940s	The Voice		unknown
1944	The Liberator		unknown
1964	Bahamas Weekly	W	unknown
	Bahamian Times		continues
	Freeport News		continues
	Inagua Record		unknown
	Bimini Bugle		unknown
	Eleuthera Palm (Governor's Harbour)		unknown
	Searchlight (Inagua)		unknown
1968	Grand Bahama Tribune	D	continues

Barbados:

Founded	Name	Frequency	Year of Last Known Issue
1731	Barbados Gazette (continued as the Barbados Gazette, or General Intelligencer (1783-92)	W, 2 x W	
1762	The Barbados Mercury (continued as The Barbados Mercury and Bridge-Town Gazette (1805-48)	W	
	Barbados Chronicle or Caribbean Courier		1807-09
1814	Barbados Times		unknown
1819	Barbados Globe, Official Gazette and Colonial Advocate	Bi-W	1913
1822	The Barbadian	Bi-W	1861
1827-28	Barbados Globe and Demerara Advocate		unknown
1833	The West Indian	Bi-W	1885
1836	West India Magazine		1840
1836	New Times	W	1836
1837	Liberal		1859
1840	The Sun		1840 (discontinued)
1840	Morning News		1840 (discontinued)
1844	The Standard		1846 (discontinued)
1862	The Times	Bi-W	1895 (discontinued)

Founded	Name	Frequency	Year of Last Known Issue
1862	The Barbados Agricultural Reporter	Bi-W	1930 (discontinued)
1865	The Official Gazette	W	1910
1876	The Barbados People & West Indian Gazette	Bi-W	1876
1876 (?)	Pepper Punch		unknown
1876 (?)	Saturday Review		unknown
1876	Penny Paper	W	1876
1877	Barbados Herald	Bi-W	1884
1877 (?)	Two Penny Paper		unknown
1877 (?)	Sentinel		unknown
1886 (?)	Bridgetown Ledger	D	1887
1895	The Barbados Advocate	D	present
	Barbados Bulletin		1896
1904	The Weekly Illustrated Paper	W	1915
	Daily News	D	1904–5
	Illustrated Sunday News 1905–41, then as Sunday News 1941–43, then Illustrated Sunday News again in 1944 and Illustrated & Midweek News after 1944	W	1944
	Recorder Weekly	W	1905–10
1908	The Sparklet	W	1920s
1909	The Barbados Standard	D	1927 (discontinued)
1911	Agricultural News	Fort.	1930
1912 (?)	Speightstown Review		1920s
1913	Democrat		1916
1919	The Barbados Herald	W	1930
1920 (?)	Barbados Times		1928
	Barbados Sporting News		1923
1934	Observer	W	continues
	Barbados Commercial		1941
1941	Barbados Recorder	3 x W	1960 (discontinued)
1946	Beacon	W	continues
1946	Torch		1960
1954 or 5	Truth		continues
1956 (?)	Barbados News		1964
1960	Calypso (Sunday supplement)	W	1966

Founded	Name	Frequency	Year of Last Known Issue
1960	Barbados Daily News	D	1968
1969	Democrat	W	continues
1973	The Nation	W	continues
1973	Manjak	Bi-W	continues

Bermuda:

1784	The Bermuda Gazette and Weekly Advertiser	W	1822
1810	Royal Gazette and Bermuda Advertiser		unknown
1819	The Bermudian (St. George's)	W	1822
1828	The Royal Gazette	W	continues
1842	The Bermudian	W	1842
1863	The Mirror	D	1868
1865	The Bermuda Colonist (St. George's)		1875
1866	The Bermuda Colonist		1915
1871	The Bermuda Times and Advocate	W	1875
1899	The Mid-Ocean	Bi-W, D	1941
1920	The Royal Gazette and Colonist	D	unknown
1925	The Recorder	W	continues
1930	Bermudian	M	unknown
1964	Bermuda Sun	W	continues

British Virgin Islands, Cayman Islands, Turks Islands:

1853	The Royal Standard and Gazette of the Turks and Caicos Islands	W	1884
	The Island Sun (BVI)	W	continues
1959	Tortola Times (BVI)	W	unknown
1964	Caymanian (Cayman Islands)	W	continues
	Conch News (Turks Islands)	Irregular	continues

Jamaica:

1718	The Weekly Jamaica Courant	W	1755 (discontinued)

Founded	Name	Frequency	Year of Last Known Issue
1745	Jamaica Gazette (elsewhere listed as The Jamaica Gazette, established in 1761)	W	1788
1755	The St. Jago de la Vega Gazette		1840 dis-continued)
1756	The Saint Jago Intelligencer	W	1768
1756	The Kingston Journal	W	1789 (dis-continued)
1772–73	Cornwall Chronicle or County Gazette, then The Cornwall Chronicle and General Advertiser (weekly) in 1776, then Cornwall Chronicle and Jamaica General Advertiser in 1781.		
1776	The Kingston Journal and Jamaica Universal Museum		unknown
1779	The Jamaica Mercury and Kingston Weekly Advertiser, later known as The Royal Gazette, also as The Royal Gazette and Jamaica Times from 1838 and Royal Gazette and Jamaica Standard from 1842		
1782	The Cornwall Mercury and Savanna-la Mar Weekly Advertiser	W	1791
1787	The Kingston Morning Post		unknown
1788	The Savanna-la Mar Gazette	W	1788
1790	The Daily Advertiser	D	1804
1791	Jamaica Mercury and Trelawny Advertiser (Falmouth)		unknown
1792	The Times		unknown
1795	The Diary and Kingston Daily Advertiser	D	1802

Founded	Name	Frequency	Year of Last Known Issue
1801	The Kingston Mercantile Advertiser		unknown
1805	Jamaica Courant, later called Jamaica Courant and Public Advertiser in 1813; then Jamaica Courant and Daily Advertiser in 1828.	D	1828
1805	The Kingston Chronicle and City Advertiser	D	1837 (discontinued)
1811 (?)	Cornwall Chronicle		unknown
1818	Cornwall Gazette and Northside General Advertiser (Falmouth)	W	1825
1822	The Trifler, later changed to Buccatoro Journal in 1823 and The Gossip in 1826 (Montego Bay)	W	1827 (discontinued)
1823	The Jamaica Journal and Kingston Chronicle	W	1830 (discontinued)
1825	Cornwall Courier		unknown
1826	Montego Bay Gazette		unknown
1826 (?)	Cornwall Chronicle or Country Gazette		1826
1827	Isonomist	possibly D	unknown
1829	The Watchman and Kingston Free Press	Bi-W	1832 (discontinued)
1829	The Struggler (Montego Bay)		unknown
1831–32	Christian Record		1832
1830s	Jamaica Gazette		1853
1831	Cornwall Advertiser	D	1834
1832	Jamaica Despatch, Chronicle and Gazette; later Jamaica Despatch and Shannon's Daily Messenger, 1832–37; then Jamaica Despatch and New Courant and Jamaica Despatch		

Founded	Name	Frequency	Year of Last Known Issue
1832 (Cont.)	and Kingston Chronicle.	D	1837
	Kingston Chronicle and Jamaican Journal	D	1827
1832 (?)	The Jamaica Watchman		unknown
1832	The Patriot		unknown
1833	De Cordova's Advertising Sheet		unknown
1833	Commercial Advertiser		unknown
1832–33	The West Indian	W	unknown
1834	Falmouth Post, or Jamaica General Advertiser		1874 (discontinued)
1834	The Loyalist		unknown
1834	Jamaica Standard	D	unknown
1834	The Baptist Herald		1843 (discontinued)
1834	The Daily Gleaner and Weekly Compendium of News	W, D	continues
1835	Jamaica Herald and Commercial Advertiser		unknown
1836	The Conservative and Constitutional Advocate		unknown
1838	The Morning Journal	D	1870 (discontinued)
1838	The Polypheme and De Cordova's Advertiser	D	unknown
1838	De Cordova's Mercantile Intelligencer	irregular	1844 (discontinued)
1838	De Cordova's Prices Current		unknown
1840s	The Family Journal		unknown
1839 (?)	The Colonial Reformer (Spanish Town)		1839
1840	Paul Pry (satire)	Semi-W	1841 (discontinued)
1841	The Middlesex Gazette, later became Middlesex Gazette and Jamaica Agricultural Reporter		1845 (discontinued)
1843	The Reporter	D	1844 (discontinued)
1843	The Old Harbour Mirror	W	unknown

Founded	Name	Frequency	Year of Last Known Issue
1844	Advertising Sheet		1846 (discontinued)
1845	Jamaica Guardian and Patriot		1847 (discontinued)
1849	Political Satirist		1851 (discontinued)
1850 (?)	Despatch	D	1883
1850s	The Daily Advertiser and Lawton's Gazette		unknown
1852	The Banner of the People		unknown
1852	Creole Miscellany	W	1855 (discontinued)
	Trelawney		1852–53
1854	Nune's Advertising Sheet		1874 (discontinued)
1855	Gall's Family Newspaper, later became Gall's Newsletter, Country Edition in 1862		1890
1863	The Jamaican	W	1865 (discontinued)
1863	The Sentinel	Semi-W, D	1865
	The Jamaica Tribune and Daily Advertiser	D	1859
1860	Jamaica Guardian		1868–69 (discontinued)
1865	Jamaica Daily Express	D	unknown
1871 (?)	The Jamaica Instructor		1871
1874	The Budget	D	1885
1874 (?)	The Trelawny and Public Advertiser		1874
1878 (?)	Jamaica Witness		1878
1879 (?)	Westmoreland Telegraph and Planters Gazette		1879
1879	The Creole and Daily Record, called the Creole by 1882	D	1883
1882	The New Century, also called the Nineteenth Century and St. James Chronicle	Bi-W	unknown / 1917
1883 (?)	Jamaica Colonist		1883
1883 (?)	The Westmoreland Telegraph and County of Cornwall Gazette		1883

Founded	Name	Frequency	Year of Last Known Issue
1885	West Indian Field, also Jamaica Field		1886 (discontinued)
1885	The Evening Express	D	1887 (discontinued)
1887	Jamaica Post and West Indian Advertiser, later Jamaica Daily Telegraph	D	unknown 1898 (discontinued)
1888	The Tri-Weekly Budget		1891
1889	Jamaica Post	D	1890
1893	The Jamaican	W	unknown
1894	The Evening News		unknown
1894	The Jamaica Advocate	W	1899
1894	The West Indian Graphic		1894
1896	Catholic Opinion	W	continues
1897	Jamaica Daily Telegraph and Anglo-American Herald, successor to Jamaica Post	D	1907
1897 (?)	The Newsletter		1897
1898	The Jamaica Times, also Weekly Times	W	1941
1904	The Leader		unknown
1905	The Presbyterian	M	1913
1907	The Northern News and Provincial Advertiser, also Northern News from 1913–21 (Montego Bay)	D	1921
1908	The Jamaica Guardian		unknown
1908 (?)	Jamaica Tribune		unknown
1910	Daily Chronicle	D	1913
1910	The Jamaica Telegraph and Guardian (merger of Jamaica Telegraph and Jamaica Guardian)		1912
1910	The Daily News		unknown
1913 (?)	The Sentinel		unknown
1913 (?)	Public Opinion		unknown
1917 (?)	The Trelawny Advocate		unknown
1918 (?)	The Western Echo		unknown
1922 (?)	The Herald		unknown

Founded	Name	Frequency	Year of Last Known Issue
1926	The Jamaica Mail		unknown
1926	Negro World		unknown
	Our Own		unknown
1928 (?)	Sunday Morning Post	W	unknown
1929 (?)	The Blackman		unknown
1931 (?)	The Commercial Advocate		unknown
1932	Jamaica		1948
1932 (?)	The New Jamaican	D	unknown
1933 (?)	The Voice of Jamaica		unknown
1935 (?)	Plain Talk		unknown
1937	Public Opinion	W, D, W	continues
1938 (?)	Weekly Searchlight	W	unknown
1938	Jamaica Standard		unknown
1939	Pagoda	Alternate Weeks	unknown
1939	The Worker	D	1941
1939 (?)	Jamaica Labour Weekly	W	unknown
1940 (?)	News Bulletin	D	unknown
1941 (?)	Evening Post		unknown
1941	Daily Express	D	1951
1941 (?)	The National Negro Voice		unknown
1941 (?)	The New Negro Voice		unknown
1943 (?)	The Masses		unknown
1944 (?)	The Democrat		unknown
1944 (?)	Jamaica Patriot		unknown
1944 (?)	The Young Jamaican		unknown
1945 (?)	The People's Voice		unknown
1945 (?)	The Weekly Observer	W	unknown
1947 (?)	The Mo-Bay Times		unknown
1947 (?)	Spanish Town Tribune		unknown
1947 (?)	The Western Sun		unknown
1947	West Indian Sportsman		unknown
1948	Chinese Public News	3 x W	continues
1950 (?)	The Leader		unknown
1950 (?)	The Times		unknown
1950	Children's Newspaper, now Children's Own	W	continues
1951	Star	D	continues
1951	Jamaica Weekly Gleaner	W	continues
1952 (?)	The People		unknown
1952	The Advocate, incorporating Agricultural Advocate		unknown
1952	The Voice of Jamaica	W	continues
1953 (?)	The Tribune		unknown

Founded	Name	Frequency	Year of Last Known Issue
1955	Farmer's Weekly	W	continues
1957 (?)	The Cornwall Guardian		unknown
1957 (?)	The News Express		unknown
1958 (?)	Chung San News	3 x W	continues
1964 (?)	The Beacon (Montego Bay)	3 x W	continues
1968	Moko, A Serious Review	Fort.	continues
1969	Abeng	W	1970
	The New Nation		continues
	The Visitor, Resort Weekly	W	continues
	The Bell		continues
	Catholic Standard	W	continues
1970s	The Labrish	3 x W	continues
1973	The Jamaica Daily News	D	continues

Leeward Islands:

Anguilla

Founded	Name	Frequency	Year of Last Known Issue
1967	The Beacon	W	continues
1969	Observer		1969 (discontinued)

Antigua

Founded	Name	Frequency	Year of Last Known Issue
pre-1755	The Antigua Gazette	W, D	1819
pre-1769	The Antigua Mercury or St. John's Weekly Advertiser	W	1777
1783 (?)	The Antigua Chronicle		1788
1797	Antigua Journal	W	1799
1813	The Weekly Register, continued as the Antigua Weekly Register after 1843	W	1883 (discontinued)
1824	The Antigua Free Press		1829
1832	The Antigua Herald and Gazette, also called Weekly Herald	W	1859
1835	The Antigua Messenger	W	1836
1843	The Antigua Observer	W	1903
1851	The Antigua Times, also The Antigua Weekly Times	W, D by 1866	unknown

Founded	Name	Frequency	Year of Last Known Issue
1870	The Antigua New Era	Bi-W, W	1881
1872	The Royal Gazette of the Leeward Islands (irregular), changed to The Leeward Islands Gazette (weekly) from 1891 to 1956, then to Antigua, Montserrat and Virgin Islands Gazette (weekly) from 1956–62.		
1872 or 1883	The Antigua Standard	W	1908 (discontinued)
1907	The Sun	D	1920
1909	Antigua News Notes		1911 (discontinued)
1922 (?)	Antigua Magnet	D	1941
1936	Antigua Star	3 x W	continues
1944	Workers Voice	W	continues
1945	Antigua Newsletter	W	1946
1947	Angelus	M	continues
1956	The Anvil	3 x W	1959 (discontinued)
1971	Antigua Times	W	discontinued
1970s	Outlet	Bi-W	continues
1975	Leader	W	continues

Montserrat

Founded	Name	Frequency	Year of Last Known Issue
1875	The Montserrat Chronicle	W	1876
1898	The Montserrat Herald		1910
1909	The Searchlight		1910
1941	The Observer	W, Bi-W	1959 (discontinued)
1952	The Standard	Bi-W	1955
1959	Montserrat Mirror	W	continues

Nevis

Founded	Name	Frequency	Year of Last Known Issue
1871	The Nevis Guardian	W	1871
1873	The Liberal (new series)		unknown
1953, 1954	Nevis Weekly Recorder	W	unknown
	Nevis Voice		unknown
	Nevis Review	W	continues

Founded	Name	Frequency	Year of Last Known Issue
	St. Christopher (St. Kitts)		
1747	The St. Christopher Gazette and Charibbean Courier, by 1771 called St. Christopher Gazette or The Historical Chronicle	W	1908
1768	The Charribbean and General Gazette of the St. Christopher Chronicle	Bi-W	1775
	St. Christopher Journal		1780
1781	Homes' Royal Charribbean Gazette, or the St. Christopher Chronicle		1781
1782, 1783	The St. Christopher Advertiser and Weekly Intelligencer	W	1908
1800	The Charribbean Courier or St. Christopher Chronicle		unknown
1865	St. Christopher News-Letter	W	1887
1875	The Voice of the People	W	1880
1879	The Official Gazette of St. Christopher	W	unknown
1881	The West Indies Weekly Herald and St. Christopher Chronicle		unknown
1881, 1882	The Daily Express of the St. Christopher Advertiser		1882
1881	The St. Christopher Daily Bulletin	D	1881
1881	The St. Christopher Daily Express	D	1915
1882	St. Christopher Independent	W	1886
1888	St. Christopher Commercial News	W	1888
1890	The Lazaretto	Fort.	1891 (discontinued)

Founded	Name	Frequency	Year of Last Known Issue
1891	The St. Christopher Daily Telegram	D	1893
1896	The Leeward Islands Churchman	M	1896
1904	The Official Gazette of St. Christopher-Nevis	W	1962
1907	The Reporter	M	unknown
1915	The St. Kitts-Nevis Daily Bulletin	D	1968
1921	The Union Messenger	M, D, 3 x W	1958
1941	The Workers' Weekly	W	1956
1949	The Democrat	W	continues
1957	The Labour Spokesman	D	continues
	The St. Christopher-Nevis Weekly Bulletin was publishing #4347 in 1930, still publishing in 1958		unknown

Trinidad & Tobago:

pre-1790	Gazeta		1790
1796 or 1799	The Trinidad Weekly Courant, changed to The Trinidad Weekly Courant and Commercial Gazette in 1808 and to the Trinidad Courant and Commercial Gazette (2 x W) in 1813		1817
1807	Tobago Gazette	W	1898
1820	Trinidad Gazette, changed to Port of Spain Gazette in 1825 (Bi-W), then daily from 1829		1956
1825	Trinidad Chronicle		1959
1831	The Colonial Observer and Trinidad Gazette		1833
1831	The Royal Gazette (Port of Spain)		1832
1833	The Trinidad Royal Gazette		1943
1834 (?)	The Mirror	D	1914

Founded	Name	Frequency	Year of Last Known Issue
1837	The Trinidad Standard and West India Journal	Bi-W	1846
1845 (?)	Trinidad Spectator		1847
	Trinidadian		1848–53
1850	San Fernando Gazette		1896 (discontinued)
	Trinidad Mercantile Advertiser		1850
	Trinidad Free Press		1851–53
	Trinidad Examiner		1854
	Trinidad Palladium		1854
	Herald		1853–54
1856	Trinidad Sentinel		1864 (discontinued)
	Trinidad Press		1860
	The Colonist		1861–63
	Star of the West		1862–71
	The Review		1869–70
	The Echo of Trinidad		1870–75
	The New Era		1870–89
pre-1866	The San Fernando Reporter		unknown
pre-1866	The Trinidad Reporter		unknown
1876	La Critique		1878 (discontinued)
	Fair Play		1881–82
1884	Public Opinion		1896 (discontinued)
1892	The Catholic News	W	unknown
	Creole Bitters		1904
1911	Argus	D	1913
pre-1917	Mirror		unknown
1917	Trinidad Guardian	D	continues
	East Indian Weekly	W	1922
1931	The Beacon	M	1934–38 (discontinued)
1936	Evening News	D	continues
1941	Observer	M	continues
1948	The Clarion	W	1952
1956	PNM Weekly, also The Nation		continues
1959	The Democrat	W	continues
1959	Sun	W	unknown
1960s	Cheng Chi	W	unknown

Founded	Name	Frequency	Year of Last Known Issue
1961	Statesman	W	continues
1965	We the People		unknown
1965	Vanguard	W	continues
1967	Daily Express	D	continues
1969	Tapia	M	continues

Windward Islands:

Dominica

1765	The Freeport Gazette or the Dominica Advertiser	W	1767
1770	The Freeport Gazette or the Dominica Chronicle	W	1775
1783	The Dominica Gazette or General Intelligencer		1786
1784	Gazette des Petites Antilles Charibbean Register or Ancient and Original Dominica Gazette		Aug. 29, 1787 is #911
1790	Gallaher's Weekly Journal and Charibbian Advertiser		Dec. 18, 1790 is # 31
1790	L'Armide la Liberté, et L'Enemi de la Licence		Dec. 18, 1790 is # 11
1790	Mrs. Browne's Roseau Gazette and Dominica Chronicle		1792
1790	Courrier des Petites Antilles		1790
1791	Le Furet Colonial et le Reviseur Universel	2 x W	1791
pre-1810	The Dominica Journal or Weekly Intelligencer	W	1810
1813	The Dominica Chronicle (and Roseau Gazette)	W	1827 (dis- continued)
1825	The Dominica Colonist	W	1866
1837	The Dominica Standard		1837
1839	The Dominican	W	1911

Founded	Name	Frequency	Year of Last Known Issue
1871	The New Dominican	W	1873 (discontinued)
1873	The Dominican Advertiser	W	1873
1873	The Dominica Jewel	W	1873
1874	The Dominica Courant	W	1874
1875	The Beacon	W	1876
1877	The People	W	1880
1880	The Dominica Courier	3 x W	1880 (discontinued)
1882	The Dominican Dial	W	1893
1884 or 1893	The Dominica Guardian	W	1924
1902	Cable News		unknown
1905	The Leeward Islands Free Press (Roseau)	W	1908
1906, 1907	The Ecclesiastical Bulletin of Roseau	M	1942 (discontinued)
1909	The Pioneer	W	1910
1909	The Dominica Chronicle	2 x W	continues
1909–11	The Voice of Dominica	W	1915
1924	The Dominica Tribune, incorporating the Dominica Guardian, weekly, then two times week after 1933, ceased publication, then revived		1951
1938	The Caribbean Monitor	W	1939
	The West India Times	W	1940–48
	Dominica Welfare News, succeeded by Dominica Welfare Review, quarterly, 1964	M	1947–63
1951	The Clarion		1951
1955	Dominica Herald	W	discontinued 1972
1959	The Star	W	continues
1961	Onward (PR Dept.)	M	1963
1962	Dominica Chamber of Commerce Journal	Qtry	1964
1970	Flambeau		

Founded	Name	Frequency	Year of Last Known Issue
	Grenada		
1764, 1765	The Royal Grenada Gazette		1775
1784	St. George's Chronicle and New Grenada Gazette	W	1791
1798	St. George's Chronicle and Grenada Gazette, later The Chronicle and Gazette	W, D	1913
1826	Grenada Free Press and Weekly Gazette, also Grenada Free Press and St. George's Gazette	W	1842
1828	The St. Andrews Journal and La Bouse (?) Miscellany		1828
1829	The Star or Occidental Comet		unknown
1846	The Carriacou Observer and Grenadines Journal		unknown
1854	The Weekly Record	W	1854
1863	The Grenada Phoenix		1865
1867	The Grenada Reporter		1867
1876	Excelsior		1876
1878	The New Era		1880
1882	The Equilibrium		1887
1883	The Grenada People		unknown
1885	Daily Tidings	D	1887
1896	The Federalist		1901
1901	The Federalist and Grenada People to 1907, then as Federalist again	W	1920
1915	The West Indian	D	continues
	The Grenada Guardian		1930–35
1955	The Torchlight		continues
1957	The Citizen's Weekly (GIS)	W	1961
1959	The Star		unknown
	Thunder		unknown
1964	Public Relations Officer's Newsletter		unknown
	The Vanguard	W	discontinued
1970s	Jewel	W	continues

Founded	Name	Frequency	Year of Last Known Issue
	St. Lucia		
1788	La Gazette de Ste. Lucie, then in 1789 to Gazette de Sainte-Lucie Nationale et Politique		1794 (discontinued)
1819	La Gazette de Sainte Lucie ou Courrier des Antilles		unknown
1820	La Courrier des Antilles		1823 (discontinued)
1823	L'Impartial Journal Politique, Commercial et Litteraire de Sainte Lucie	W	1830 (discontinued)
1831	The St. Lucia Gazette and Public Advertizer		1831 (discontinued)
1832	The St. Lucia Gazette		unknown
1836	The News	W	1836 (discontinued)
1838	The Palladium and St. Lucia Free Press, in 1844–48 known as The St. Lucia Palladium and Public Gazette	W	unknown
1839	The Independent Press	W	1847 (discontinued)
1850	The Sentinel		1850 (discontinued)
1851	The Union		unknown
1863	The St. Lucian	W	1873
1874	St. Lucia Observer, continued as The Observer after 1876	W	1876
1877	The Narrator		unknown
1877	The Voice	W	1882 (discontinued)
1885	The Voice of St. Lucia	W, D	continues
1898	Daylight	Fort.	1901 (discontinued)

Founded	Name	Frequency	Year of Last Known Issue
1901	St. Lucia Guardian	W	1911 (discontinued)
1911	The Herald of St. Lucia	Bi-W	1914
1927	The Advertiser	2 x W	1930 (discontinued)
1934	The West Indian Crusader	W	continues
1952	The Workers' Clarion	W	1958
1957	The People's Gazette	W	unknown
1957	The Castries Catholic Chronicle	Fort.	unknown
1962	The St. Lucia Herald	W	continues
1967	The Standard		continues
1968	Winban News		continues
1969	The St. Lucia News		unknown
1970s	The Vanguard	irregular	discontinued
1975	The St. Lucia Star	M	continues

St. Vincent

1817	The Royal St. Vincent Gazette and Weekly Advertiser	W	1839
1825	The Royal St. Vincent Gazette		unknown
1834	St. Vincent Chronicle and Public Gazette		1840
1840	The New Era		unknown
1840	The St. Vincent Mirror		unknown
1855 or 1862	The St. Vincent Witness		1886
1858, 1859	St. Vincent Guardian and Government Gazette, continued as St. Vincent Guardian after 1868		
1876	The Mail News and Advertiser		unknown
1876	The St. Vincent Gazette and Planters' Magazine		unknown
1887	The Sentinel		1888
1890	The Sentry	W	1932
1898	The Rambler	W	1913
1899	The St. Vincent Times		unknown
1919	The Vincentian	2 x W	continues

Founded	Name	Frequency	Year of Last Known Issue
1919 (Cont.)	The Times	W	1941–45
	The Investigator		1941
1951	Challenge (Govt. PR Dept.)	Fort.	1962
1960	New Era	W	unknown
1966	Daily Model	D	1966
1970s	The Star	W	continues
1975	The Tree	M	continues

SOURCES: The author compiled this list of newspapers, which is the first of its kind in the Commonwealth Caribbean, from the following sources, as well as from interviews he conducted in the region: E. C. Baker, *A Guide to Records in the Leeward Islands* (Oxford: Basil Blackwell, 1965); E. C. Baker, *A Guide to Records in the Windward Islands* (Oxford: Basil Blackwell, 1968), pp. 29, 48, 62–63, 71, 73, 87–88; Barbados *Advocate-News* 75th Anniversary Supplement, October 1971; Frank Cundall, "The Press and Printers of Jamaica Prior to 1820," *Proceedings of the American Antiquarian Society* 26 (1916): 355–56; Frank Cundall, *A History of Printing in Jamaica from 1717 to 1834* (Kingston, Jamaica: Institute of Jamaica, 1935), pp. 51–52, 61–63; catalogues of newspaper files of Nassau Public Library, Institute of Jamaica, Barbados Free Library, Barbados Department of Archives, St. Kitts Archives reports; Waldo Lincoln, "List of Newspapers of the West Indies and Bermuda in the Library of the American Antiquarian Society," *Proceedings of the American Antiquarian Society* (April 1926), pp. 131–55; Lowell J. Ragatz, "Early West Indian Newspapers and Periodicals I Have Come Across," manuscript in Institute of Jamaica files; Isaiah Thomas, *The History of Printing in America with a Biography of Printers and an Account of Newspapers* (Albany, N.Y.: Joel Munsell, 1874); Theodore Sealy, "Caribbean Newspapers: A Record of Vigorous Development," *The Times Review of the British Colonies* (September 1951); Irene Zimmerman, *A Guide to Current Latin American Periodicals: Humanities and Social Sciences* (Gainesville, Fla.: Kallman Publishing, 1961); Arthur Gropp, *Guide to Libraries and Archives in Central America and the West Indies, Panama, Bermuda, and British Guiana* (New Orleans, La.: Tulane University, 1941); Michael Craton, *A History of the Bahamas* (London: Collins, 1962), pp. 294–95; E. M. Shilstone, "Some Notes on Early Printing Presses and Newspapers in Barbados," *The Journal of the Barbados Museum and Historical Society* (November 1958), pp. 19–33; Douglas McMurtrie, "The First Printing in Dominica," *British and Colonial Printer and Stationer* (May 1932); Dominica *Chronicle*, July 8, 1931, p. 6; Philip D. Curtin, *Two Jamaicas: The Role of Ideas in A Tropical Colony 1830–1865* (Cambridge: Harvard University Press, 1955); Clifton Neita, *One Hundred Years of Famous Pages from the Press of Jamaica 1853–1953* (Kingston, Jamaica: The Gleaner Co., 1953); *Daily Gleaner* Souvenir Edition, December 31, 1966, pp. 12–13; Jamaica *Times*, January 21, 1899; Douglas McMurtrie, *Notes on the Beginning of Printing on the Island of Trinidad* (Fort Worth, Tex.: National Association for Printing Education, 1943); Donald Wood, *Trinidad in Transition* (London: Oxford University Press, 1968); unpublished manuscripts on the early presses of Bahamas, St. Kitts, and St. Lucia written by Mary Moseley, Stanley Procope, and Robert Devaux.

Appendix B

Advent of Television
on Bermuda

Television had its birth on Bermuda when the United States Air Force set up a station for American servicemen at Kindley Field. In 1956 the Air Force station applied to the insular government for permission to telecast on an island-wide basis to serve the families of the 900 airmen who lived off the base.

The Bermuda Executive Council granted the request. Their feeling was that there was nothing to fear since Bermuda citizens did not own sets and an embargo had been placed on American-made sets. British sets were permitted entry only if they had been engineered so as not to receive United States programs. However, shortly after the Council's decision, a television manufacturer in England sent over five sets adapted to receive the Kindley Field signal. The government next made it illegal to erect television antennae. But the urge for television had already permeated the island, and the law was repealed under pressure. The repeal really came about because English set manufacturers were buying American parts, building them into English sets, and selling them on Bermuda. The American Consulate objected to an embargo under these conditions. See Robert Lewis Shayon, "Bermuda Holiday," *Saturday Review*, April 13, 1957, p. 25.

Appendix C

Chronology
of Significant Dates

1623	Earliest British settlement in Commonwealth Caribbean, St. Christopher (St. Kitts).
1624	Barbados becomes second British settlement in area.
1628	Nevis claimed by British.
1632	Antigua and Montserrat settled.
1650	Sugar becomes main crop of region.
1655	Jamaica captured by British from Spain.
1688	Anguilla settled by British.
1717	First known newspaper in Commonwealth Caribbean, *Weekly Jamaica Courant.*
1730	Barbados *Gazette,* probably second region newspaper, started.
1734	First *Jamaica Almanac.*
1741	First book of region published on Barbados.
1747	First known press on St. Christopher (St. Kitts).
1748	Earliest known newspaper on Antigua.
1751	First Jamaican book published.
1763	Dominica ceded to Great Britain.
1765	Dominica and Grenada obtain first newspapers.
1781	*Jamaica Magazine or Monthly Chronicle* established, probably first magazine in islands.
1783–84	First newspapers on Bermuda and Bahamas.
1788	St. Lucia's earliest newspaper published.
1790	Earliest record of newspaper on Trinidad.

1807	First known press on Tobago.
1817	First newspaper on St. Vincent published.
1828	Oldest newspaper in islands, *Royal Gazette* of Bermuda, founded.
1830s	*Watchman* published as pro-black, Jamaican newspaper.
1834	Act of Emancipation promulgated; slavery ends in Commonwealth Caribbean.
1834	*The Daily Gleaner and Weekly Compendium of News* founded.
1836	*New Times,* first pro-black newspaper on Barbados.
1836	Famous *The Liberal* started on Barbados.
1837	Regular fortnightly mail service from England to West Indian ports.
1844	Nassau *Guardian* established.
1871	First known newspaper on Nevis.
1870s	Telegraph service comes to areas of Commonwealth Caribbean.
1876	First known newspaper on Montserrat.
1885	*Voice of St. Lucia* founded.
1895	Gale starts Barbados *Advocate.*
1904	Nassau *Tribune* established by Dupuch.
1909	Dominica *Chronicle* founded by Roman Catholic Church.
1910	Marcus Garvey starts his journalistic career.
1915	St. Kitts-Nevis *Daily Bulletin* founded.
1915	Marryshow creates *West Indian.*
1917	Trinidad *Guardian* published for first time.
1919	*Vincentian* established.
1919–30	Wickham and Inniss publish Barbados *Herald.*
1921	One of first union newspapers established, St. Kitts *Union Messenger.*
1934	First broadcasting service comes to region, on Barbados.
1934	St. Lucia *Crusader* founded.
1935	Trinidad gets local broadcasting service.
1936	ZNS Radio established on Bahamas.
1936	Trinidad *Evening News* and Antigua *Star* founded.
1938	Strikes and riots in Commonwealth Caribbean.
1938–44	Establishment of popular governments in islands.
1939	First newsmagazine created in islands, *Spotlight.*
1939	ZQI, first radio service on Jamaica, established.
1943	*Bim* literary magazine started.
1943	Bermuda officially starts radio service.

1944	*Workers Voice* published on Antigua.
1949	St. Kitts *Democrat* begins publication.
1950	*Children's Newspaper* (now *Children's Own*) founded.
1951	Jamaica *Star* and Jamaica *Weekly Gleaner* established.
1953	*The Bajan*, Barbadian newsmagazine, founded.
1954–55	Windward Islands Broadcasting Service created.
1955	Grenada *Torchlight* and Dominica *Herald* begin publishing.
1957	St. Kitts *Labour Spokesman* published for first time.
1958–62	West Indies Federation.
1958	ZBM-TV becomes first local television service in region.
1958	Jamaican government initiates Jamaica Broadcasting Corporation.
1959	Montserrat *Mirror* and Dominica *Star* created.
1961	Radio Caribbean developed.
1962	Trinidad and Jamaica receive independence status.
1962	Trinidad and Tobago Television initiated.
1963	Jamaica Broadcasting Corporation television goes on air.
1963	Caribbean Broadcasting Corporation's Radio Barbados established.
1964	Caribbean Broadcasting Corporation television commences.
1965	ZFB-TV developed on Bermuda.
1966	Cecil King sells his Commonwealth Caribbean media interests.
1967	First newspaper founded on Anguilla.
1967	Trinidad *Daily Express* founded after *Mirror*'s demise.
1967	Commonwealth Caribbean government heads propose regional news agency.
1968	UNESCO team surveys media potentialities and problems.
1968	Reuters Caribbean Desk begins service to region from Barbados.
1969	Government takes control of Trinidad and Tobago Television and Trinidad and Tobago National Broadcasting radio (formerly Radio Guardian and 610 Radio).
1969	Radio Anguilla becomes first broadcasting station on that island.
1969	CARIFTA regionalizes economies of islands.
1969	Reorganization of WIBS commences.
1969–70	Caribbean Broadcasting Union formed.
1970	State of emergency declared on Trinidad after black-power riots.
1971	Antigua *Times* established.

1972   University of West Indies develops journalism training program; first courses in 1973.

1972   Walter government closes two Antigua newspapers.

1972   Pindling and Gairy returned to power on Bahamas and Grenada, respectively; Michael Manley became prime minister of Jamaica.

1972   RJR and JBC started FM stereo service.

1972   Radio Grenada began operations independently of WIBS, which was dissolved December 1971.

1972   St. Kitts-Nevis received its own television service.

1973   Bahamas granted independence.

1973   Bermuda and Dominica were temporarily under emergency rule.

1973   Sir Etienne Dupuch retired from his editorship of Nassau *Tribune*.

1973   CARICOM replaced CARIFTA as regional common market.

1973   Jamaica *Daily Gleaner* started using computerized photo-composition.

1973   *The Jamaica Daily News* and *The Nation* (Barbados) began publishing.

1974   Grenada received its independence.

1974   800-mile long microwave system initiated in Eastern Caribbean.

1974   Cable television installed on St. Vincent.

1974   Radio Dominica began full operations independently of WIBS.

1974   610 Radio opened a FM channel on Trinidad & Tobago.

1974   A West Indies Television Network served the Caribbean region.

1974   JBC started its modernization and expansion program.

1974   *Caribbean Contact* begins publication.

1974   Seminar on Communications and Information for Development Purposes in the Caribbean Area held; NICC formed as result.

1975   British Privy Council ruled that Antigua press laws do not contravene that nation's Constitution.

1975   Grenada Newspaper Act imposed.

1975   Frenchman purchases Radio Caribbean.

1975   McEnearney-Alstons purchases major stock of Trinidad *Guardian* and *Evening News*.

1975   Antigua government purchases Leeward Islands Television
         Service.
1975   *Hers: The Barbadian Magazine for Women* appears.
1975   *People* magazine starts publishing in Trinidad.
1976   Caribbean News Agency (CANA) launched.
1976   Other islands (St. Lucia, St. Kitts-Nevis, *etc.*) prepare for
         independence.
1976   Undergraduate mass communication degree option offered
         at University of West Indies.
1976   CPBA plans Caribbean Press Council.

Appendix D

The Allfrey Story

It was Thursday, and Thursday was press day for Dominica's three Saturday newspapers—Saturday because that is market day. The editors of one of the weeklies, the *Star*, did not have time to sit down for an interview and took this author on their rounds instead.

Robert and Phyllis Allfrey, the editors of the *Star*, came to the journalistic profession with outstanding credentials, having accomplished a great deal in many fields and a little in journalism. Robert had been a British mechanical engineer who came to the islands on holiday and never returned to England. Phyllis, whose grandfather was the famous Sir Henry Nicholls whose "Fabian Socialism has not stifled in her an obvious pride in belonging to the 'Royal Family of Dominica,'" was born and raised on Dominica. At various times in her career, she has been minister of labor and social affairs and holder of six portfolios in the West Indies Federation cabinet, founder and leader of two political parties on Dominica, novelist, poet, housewife, and mother of five children, three of whom were adopted.

The *Star* was founded by the Allfreys in 1965. It is unusual in that it is printed in two different offices and uses two types of printing processes. The editors cut stencils for the paper at their converted millhouse home on the fringes of Roseau and shuttle them to their Roseau "depot," a twelve-by-fifteen-foot dining room in a friend's home, loaned to the Allfreys for production and distribution purposes. The paper employs a combination of Roneo mimeograph and lithograph; page one and all advertisements are done by paste-up, the other pages stenciled. Headlines are hand set. The result, according to Robert, is a "poor newspaper for people with bad eyes." He added that the most frequent criticism of the *Star* is that its print is too small and dull. "People here cannot afford eyeglasses and without them they cannot see what we write." The total equipment used to publish the *Star* involves a Roneo 795 mimeograph machine located in the middle of the former dining room, some hand-set type for advertisements, and a photoengraver and typewriter, both of the latter kept at the mill-house home, where Robert said he "can keep it under my eye."

On this particular press day, the routine took this form:

> Phyllis had just brought a stencil to the "depot" to be duplicated. She gave the boy operating the Roneo meticulous instructions and then phoned a couple of reporters who had failed to cover their stories. All the time, a young employee was pondering what 12-point type was. She showed him from a past issue. Before we could get out of the "depot," a man came in to sell raffles; Phyllis took time out to buy a couple and asked about the raffle seller's wife and father.

> We got into the Allfrey's green dune buggy for a trip across town to pick up a picture of a girl who had won a beauty contest the week before. After spending a few moments with the girl's mother, Phyllis returned to the vehicle. The picture was too small to use. On the way back to the "depot," Phyllis told me, between stops and honks to greet neighbors, about her printer. "He makes at least one or two mistakes in every headline and if I ask him to correct them, he makes more. So I just say forget it," she explained, shrugging her shoulders. "He's a member of the Black Power group here and we expect any day for the whole paper to go up. Just last week, our writers went to the Black Power meeting at deadline time and we didn't get the paper out on time. We lost sales of 1,000 copies because of that." It is extremely important to get newspapers out early in Dominica, even though they are weeklies, because the paperboys go to the newspaper office that has its issues ready and they start selling. When they tire themselves out, they do not return to circulate newspapers that have the later press runs.

> Back at the "depot," Phyllis called a government communications official to apologize because her reporter failed to cover a meeting. Hanging up the phone, she sighed, "I get into enough trouble with the government; I don't want them to accuse me of not holding to what I say I'll do."

> Finally, we were on our way, over extremely bumpy roads, to the millhouse home-office-plant. Although the distance between the two offices can be covered in "seven minutes flat" under normal weather conditions, Dominica doesn't have much of the latter. Frequent slides and an occasional bridge washout hamper the shuttle service employed by the Allfreys. On the way, Phyllis remembered

Phyllis and Robert Allfrey, editors Dominica Star, *at their mill-house office.* (Photo by John A. Lent.)

that the first issues of the *Star* did not go over well; only 300 copies were sold. "The people didn't like the paper because it was stapled," and prestige newspapers are not stapled, she explained. Once the paper quit stapling and began running off issues on a new Roneo obtained from England, circulation went up. "But we almost needed an engineer to run the machine at first." Today, the circulation of the *Star* is 2,000 on good weeks and when there is nothing exciting happening, 1,600. If it rains on the day of issue, the paperboys and papers get sopped and circulation falls off tremendously.

Noticing a stalled vehicle on the side of the road, Phyllis stopped to see if she could be of help. "Haven't seen you for a long time. How's the family?" she greeted the driver. And at that point I made the connection: these greetings were more than just casual remarks; they were also questions to gather information for next week's issue.

At the former millhouse a table was set up on the patio and there, in the outdoors with lush foliage and a clear stream only inches away, Robert and Phyllis Allfrey typed stencils, answered correspondence, laid out advertisements, fed their adopted Carib Indian children and talked about the *Star* and island politics. Robert recounted how the paper came about. "Phyllis and I were running the *Herald* (another Dominican weekly) for awhile for an old blind man who was easily influenced on most matters. In the *Herald* building, the blind man also had a drinking place where he imbibed quite a bit. I split with him after an argument and as people began asking about getting duplicating jobs done, we set up this operation." The *Star* does not pay for itself so these job printing chores help make up the deficit.

Over a lunch of fish and breadfruit, the conversation turned to politics. The Allfreys are still in politics "more or less" with Phyllis on the executive board of the Freedom Party. "Oh yes, we support the Freedom Party openly," she said, giving the reason why they support that group and not the Labour Party of which she was president at one time. "When the Federation collapsed, my political teammate (now the premier of Dominica) was afraid I'd return to Dominica and stand for election as premier. He chucked me out of the party although I was president. His excuse was that I criticized my own land."

How has the *Star* survived with an expatriate as editor? Phyllis answered. "They'd like to get Robert out but it would be like chucking the prince out of Buckingham. I'm one of the few white people here who is indigenous and I have held some powerful positions. They'd like to get Robert out and then shut down the *Star*. Robert runs the paper really and I'm the strength because they cannot get the *Star* out of the way as long as I'm behind it."

Another stencil was finished, ready to be hauled to town; the children had eaten lunch and were waiting to be taken back to school, and I had a plane to catch—three good reasons to get back into the dune buggy and head for Roseau.

Appendix E

Facilities and Operations of Cable and Wireless in Commonwealth Caribbean Relative to Regional Communications, 1968

Antigua: Microwave link carrying two groups (each sixteen circuits) to Barbados, and one group each (sixteen circuits) to Bermuda, Tortola, and St. Thomas. Tropospheric-scatter links to Barbados, via St. Lucia, and to Tortola, carrying a maximum capacity of four and five groups respectively. A microwave link of twelve channels reaches St. Kitts. Telex channels to Barbados are available.

Barbados: In addition to the handling of traffic from the major trunk routes, Barbados is also the clearing center for traffic to and from the company's smaller branches in the region, and circuits are also worked to Curaçao, Paramaribo, Martinique, and Santo Domingo (morse). Cable circuits are worked to Georgetown (Guyana) and São Luis (Brazil), and Barbados is an intermediate traffic station on the New York-Rio de Janeiro telegraph-cable chain. Telex trunks from all smaller islands in the area and all main international trunks are terminated at Barbados. A receiving station at Carrington is the terminal of the Link from the scatter station sited on Mount Misery; the external system from there consists of: two sixteen-channel groups to Trinidad;

one sixteen-channel group to the U.S.A.; two sixteen-channel groups to Antigua; one sixteen-channel group to St. Lucia; one six-channel group to St. Vincent on VHF; one sixteen-channel group to Guyana (operative in March 1969).

Dominica: One five-unit telegraph circuit, as a terminal on the selective Barbados-St. Lucia-Dominica chain. Telex service available. VHF radio site is connected by landline. C & W own and operate the telephone system, which is automatic. International telephone is via ringdown circuits via Barbados and St. Lucia.

Grenada: Telex channels to Barbados are available via Trinidad on the Eastern Caribbean system. Nine 4kHz channels are operated to Trinidad by VHF at present, but the link is being upgraded to twelve channels. A single channel VHF link gives telephone connection to Carriacou (Grenadines). The international telephone service is manual to Barbados and semi-automatic to Port-of-Spain.

Jamaica: Scatter terminal of the Cayman Islands-Jamaica link. Circuits derived from the Jamaica-Florida coaxial cable are routed by a microwave system from the cable terminal to the C.T.C. All international telex calls handled on a switchboard in the CTO.

Montserrat: VHF equipment providing link to St. Kitts. International telephony is provided via ringdown circuits to Antigua, St. Kitts, and Barbados. The Antigua service will be semi-automatic in the direction Antigua to Montserrat. One public five-unit telegraph circuit and telex service are available.

St. Kitts: The telegraph bearer to Barbados is being reequipped for twelve-channels, and a six-channel system to St. Maarten has been supplied. The Montserrat bearer is also upgraded to six channels. Telex channels to Barbados are available. VHF links to Antigua (twelve circuits) and Montserrat (six circuits) are operated by a station connected by landline to the CTO.

St. Lucia: International telephony is provided via circuits to Barbados; there is also one circuit to Dominica. St. Lucia is on a shared five-unit telegraph circuit Barbados-St. Lucia-Dominica. Telex is also available with two channels to Barbados. Tropospheric scatter station with links to Barbados (500-watt output power) and Antigua (1-Kw output).

St. Vincent: International telephone provided via ringdown circuits to Barbados. One five-unit telegraph circuit to Barbados and two telex channels, carried on VHF relay links.

Trinidad: Tropo scatter system, with 1-Kw transmitter to Barbados (2 groups, 32 circuits), Bermuda (1 group, 16 circuits), Grenada (1 group, 12 circuits). A scatter system to Guyana, with 10-Kw transmitters (16 circuits) is expected to be operative in March 1969. VHF link to Grenada, equipped with 9 channels and 3 more are on order. HF transmitting station and facilities, providing for telephone services to Miami, Jamaica, Guyana, Venezuela, and Surinam. Direct telex channels to London and Barbados, and through these points to the world network.

Tortola (British Virgin Islands): It is the "A" terminal of the Bermuda-Tortola submarine eighty-circuit (N type) coaxial-cable system. Tropospheric scatter link to Antigua, also carrying five groups (eighty circuits). Microwave link to St. Thomas carried a twelve-circuit group for Tortola-St. Thomas service and a sixteen-circuit through group for Antigua-St. Thomas circuits.

Cayman Islands: "Thin-line" tropospheric scatter system to Jamaica. Links are provided between Grand Cayman and Cayman Brac ("thin-line" scatter), and between Cayman Brac and Little Cayman (VHF).

SOURCE: This listing was taken directly from: Guy Roppa and Neville E. Clarke, *The Commonwealth Caribbean: Regional Co-Operation in News and Broadcasting Exchanges* (Paris: UNESCO, 1968), pp. 74–76.

UNESCO Conclusions Concerning Commonwealth Caribbean Mass Media

a. There is a general desire in the Commonwealth Caribbean Region to make use of the mass media to promote better understanding within the Region and to help surmount the problems encountered in moving towards closer social and economic co-operation.

b. The use of the mass media for these purposes cannot be achieved effectively without close collaboration between the media themselves and coordination of the efforts of the media and all other related institutions and organizations in the context of mass communication serving regional developments.

c. Doubts expressed in the Region about the feasibility of regional co-operation in the mass communication field stem mainly from the fear that the regional problems in terms of finance, human resources and the distribution of administrative, financial and technical responsibility would be insurmountable.

d. The solution to these problems lies in co-ordination of available sources of technical assistance, a comprehensive training programme and a carefully planned and co-ordinated distribution of responsibilities.

e. The desired increased exchange of news and programmes within the Region is to a large extent dependent on the exchange of professional journalists of all media. By working in other countries of the Region, they would contribute to the mutual appreciation of national problems, and to the gradual development of a regional outlook and approach.

f. As in other developing areas, more pressing needs have relegated the development of the mass media to a very low place in national priorities. The result has been that the media are either unable to perform their functions effectively or are dominated by interests external to the Region. This is one aspect of the traditional pattern of communications in the Region that originates from its former colonial status and is continued by the natural tendency for communications to flow outwards from developed countries.

g. Regional co-operation and the co-ordination of national efforts, supported as far as possible from local resources, leading to the creation of arrangements better suited to the Region can help to counteract this situation.

h. The historical, geographical, ethnical, social and economic complexities of the Region, the imbalance existing in the capability of its mass media, and the communications gap existing between different areas, and between authorities and citizens, call for the organization and application in depth of mass communication research—as a vital contribution to many mass communication developments in the Region.

i. In their role as contributors to regional understanding, education and development, the mass media must be considered in their entirety, without division between press and broadcasting and other media. It is vital to avoid a plethora of arrangements and regulating bodies. As far as possible, in view of the relatively small size of the operation in each branch of the media, one unified regional arrangement should cover all their needs. While maintaining the initiative and independence of all bodies involved in mass communication, their activities should be concentrated under one regional umbrella.

SOURCE: Guy Roppa and Neville Clarke, *The Commonwealth Caribbean: Regional Co-Operation in News and Broadcasting Exchanges* (Paris: UNESCO, 1968), pp. 94–95.

Recommendations
for Further Research

To successfully implement further research on Commonwealth Caribbean mass media, one must first make sure that island academicians
are aware of the need for, and usefulness of, such study. According to
the 1968 UNESCO report, the need has been felt:

> The academic authorities have long felt that mass communica-
> tion was one of the big gaps in their research programme and felt
> that that gap should be filled, as mass communication was very
> relevant to social and economic development—the objective of the
> present research programme of the University of the West Indies.

With the development of a journalism program at the University
of the West Indies, a natural home for such research projects has
been provided. Therefore, UWI journalism faculty and students should
begin to fulfill the following research needs:

1. A clearing house to handle any information relating to mass
communications should be developed at the Univeersity of the West
Indies. Such a clearinghouse could be a starting place for all future
research projects on the region. As matters stand now, it is extremely
difficult to accomplish library research on mass communications in the
islands, the main drawback being that the information is scattered in
different offices and libraries in the islands, the United States, and
Great Britain.

2. The University of the West Indies, in conjunction with the
Institute of Jamaica, should coordinate newspaper files in the islands.
At the least, UWI should find out where the copies of British West
Indian newspapers are and record the data in a catalogue listing that
would be available to scholars. At the same time, newspapers and

libraries should be encouraged to keep files of back issues and, more important, keep them safe from weather and insects. In many cases newspapers do not have issues dating back even a few weeks. Many volumes of newspapers at other libraries and in newspaper morgues are uncatalogued, worm-eaten, and weather damaged.

3. As a stimulus for more research into Commonwealth Caribbean mass communications, it would be wise for the University of the West Indies to create a mass-communication journal—modest in the beginning—to provide an outlet for writers in the field. The only publication now devoted to journalism in the islands is the twenty-page *Press, Radio and TV*, issued annually by the Press Association of Jamaica and devoted predominantly to *Gleaner* and PAJ activities. A few journalists in the islands have prepared manuscripts on the history of their newspapers but cannot find publication outlets for such limited subjects.

4. The establishment of a journalism history and biography series is also urgent. It is important that the history of Commonwealth Caribbean newspapers be written while the files of the oldest papers are still in semi-readable form. Also, biographies of journalism pioneers should be written. If the manpower is not yet available for the writing of biographies, at least the interviews should be accomplished while some of the men who have initiated significant media enterprises are still alive. Such primary data would be invaluable to future researchers.

5. Studies concerning interpersonal communication networks should be accomplished. The islands, because of their smallness and compactness, could provide valuable information to researchers interested in trying to understand how traditional forms of communication occur. Along the same lines, studies of rumor should be attempted, as well as studies concerning the possible link-up of traditional and modern forms of communication.

6. Audience and content analyses are sorely needed by many media. In many instances, it seems that island mass media are publishing and broadcasting without very clear ideas about characteristics of their audiences: needs, likes, and problems. In the same vein, content studies of contemporary newspapers and broadcast program schedules are almost nonexistent. Again, media personnel guess about the amount of space and time they devote to various news and entertainment subjects.

Most of these are rudimentary studies. However, the present state of mass communications research in the islands demands that these projects be accomplished first, after which more sophisticated research efforts can be undertaken.

Bibliography

This bibliography attempts to pull together information available on mass communications in the Commonwealth Caribbean, especially those sources used in the present research. A number of general sources (histories, travelogues, yearbooks, and handbooks) are included because much of the data on mass media is found piecemeal in these works.

Detailed studies of mass communications in the Commonwealth Caribbean have been written, but usually as feasibility papers, in connection with plans for the possible setting up of new media. Important along these lines was a survey performed by the Canadian Broadcasting Corporation of Caribbean broadcasting. W. Y. Martin, executive assistant of CBC, explained it was a "feasibility study prepared at the request of the Canadian government on the possibility of establishing a radio network to service the Commonwealth islands in the Caribbean," but that the study was classified because it contained confidential data provided by the Caribbean governments.

The United States Information Agency has surveyed Commonwealth Caribbean media also, but the results of its searches are classified. A third regional study resulted from a UNESCO mission in 1968 designed to look at the possibility of developing regional news exchanges. Of course, other more general UNESCO yearbooks and papers on mass communications have been useful for their statistics on West Indian media.

The British press in the Caribbean has been covered adequately historically, especially by Douglas McMurtrie and Frank Cundall. In addition *Proceedings of the American Antiquarian Society*, during the first three decades of this century, compiled histories and lists of British Caribbean newspapers. Two books published in London give historical background on Commonwealth Caribbean broadcasting: Central Rediffusion's *Commercial Broadcasting in the British West Indies* and the *Handbook on Broadcasting Services in the Colonies Etc. 1956*.

Data for this bibliography were gathered from the following libraries: Free Library, Bridgetown, Barbados; *Guardian* files, Port of Spain, Trinidad; Institute of Jamaica, West Indies Reference, Kingston, Jamaica; University of West Indies Library, Mona, Jamaica; Library of Congress; the public libraries in Nassau, Bahamas; The Valley, Anguilla; Roseau, Dominica; Castries, St. Lucia, and Kingstown, St. Vincent; the main libraries at the University of Iowa, University of Illinois, Temple University, and University of Wyoming.

Journals checked closely for information on Commonwealth Caribbean mass communications are listed here to forestall the need for prospective researchers to duplicate what I have already done. Bibliographies within most of these journals were also perused with the intent of finding sources. The journals were: *Press of the Americas* (1955–1971), *Proceedings of the American Antiquarian Society* (1880–1969), *Journal of Developing Areas* (1966–1976), *Caribbean Quarterly* (1961–1975), *Caribbean Studies* (volumes 1 through 14, 1974), *Caribbean* (1965–1968), *Quill* (1958–1976), *Journalism Quarterly* (volumes 1 through 18, 22–38, 40–present), *Public Opinion Quarterly* (1937–1976), *Gazette* (volumes 1 through 4, 13–present), *Journalist's World* (1963–1968), *EBU Review* (1968–1976), *Hispania* (1938–1947), *IPI Report* (1952–1976), *IAPA News, Journal of Inter-American Studies,* Trinidad *Guardian* files on newspapers, and Institute of Jamaica files on newspapers and broadcasting. More recent issues, up to 1976, of other journals were searched. Also looked at were the lists of theses and dissertations that have appeared in *Journalism Quarterly*: Ph.D. dissertations on communications, 1945–1953; masters' theses, 1949–1952; graduate research for 1955–1957, 1962, 1964, 1965–66, 1968; lists of unpublished theses in journalism from 1902–1934.

The few bibliographies that provided additional sources were: Lambros Comitas's *Caribbeana 1900—1965, A Topical Bibliography* (Seattle, Wash.: University of Washintgon Press, 1968); S. A. Bayitch's *Latin America and the Caribbean: A Bibliographical Guide to Works in English* (Coral Gables, Fla.: University of Miami Press, 1967); Lawrence Lichty's *World and International Broadcasting: A Bibliography* (Washington D.C.: Association for Professional Broadcasting Education, 1971); Albion Ross's *English-Language Bibliography on Foreign Press and Comparative Journalism* (Milwaukee, Wis.: Marquette University, Center for the Study of American Press, 1966). Yielding fewer data on Commonwealth Caribbean mass communications were: Kantor's *A Bibliography of Unpublished Dissertations and Masters Theses . . . of Latin America;* Price's *The Literature of Journalism;* Price and Pickett's *Journalism Bibliography; Directory of Newspapers and Magazines* (London: Haymarket); Weaver's *Latin American Development;* Brode's *The Process of Modernization: An Annotated Bibliography on the Socio-Cultural Aspects of Development;*

Deutsch and Merritt's *Nationalism and National Development: An Interdisciplinary Bibliography;* Wolseley's *The Journalists Bookshelf;* Blum's *Reference Books in the Mass Media;* Watkins's *Bibliography of Printing in America;* Skolnik's *A Bibliography of Selected Publications on Foreign and International Broadcasting;* Hansen and Parsons's *Mass Communication: A Research Bibliography; Journalism Abstracts,* 1968–1971, and Rogers's diffusion-of-innovations bibliographies.

In addition, the following guides and indexes were surveyed for articles on mass media of the region: *Business Periodicals Index,* July 1965 to January 1971; *Public Affairs Information Service,* 1965 to February 1971; *Readers Guide to Periodical Literature,* March 1966 through February 1971; *Wall Street Journal Index,* 1966 through 1970; *London Times Index,* September 1968 through February 1970, 1974–76; *Topicator,* 1965 through 1974; *New York Times Index,* 1959 through 1970.

Reports of the freedom of press committee of the Inter American Press Association (1954, 1955, 1964–1975) also provided some insights into freedom of the press in the islands.

Also important to the researcher of Commonwealth Caribbean are the files of newspapers of the region, available in a number of places. One of the best collections in the United States is in the American Antiquarian Society Library. In the West Indies, the Institute of Jamaica has the most complete collection of Commonwealth Caribbean newspapers. A number of old Barbadian newspapers are stored in the Barbados Free Library, and Bahamian papers are in the Bahamas Public Library, Nassau. Both collections are suffering from weather and insect damage. Original St. Kitts newspapers can be found in the St. Kitts Government House Archives, and scattered issues of Windward Island newspapers are available in the libraries of Grenada, St. Vincent, and Dominica. University of West Indies (Mona, Jamaica) newspaper files include publications of Antigua, Barbados, Trinidad, Jamaica, and St. Lucia. Old newspapers of the Bahamas, Barbados, Bermuda, Grenada, Jamaica, St. Lucia, Tobago, and Trinidad have been microfilmed by Micro Photos, Inc., 1700 Show Ave., Cleveland, Ohio (see *Caribbean Studies* 2, no. 4: 77–79).

Caribbean Studies has scheduled for publication a bibliography on Commonwealth Caribbean mass communications, written by this author (see *Caribbean Studies* 14, no. 2).

GENERAL

Ainslie, Rosalynde. *The Press in Africa: Communications Past and Present.* New York: Walker & Co., 1968.

Almond, Gabriel A., and Coleman, James S. *The Politics of the Developing Areas.* Princeton, N.J.: Princeton University Press, 1970.

Berlo, David, ed. *Mass Communication and the Development of Nations.* East Lansing, Mich.: International Communication Institute, 1968.

Black, C. E. *The Dynamics of Modernization.* New York: Harper & Row, 1967.

Boorstin, Daniel J. *The Image: A Guide to Pseudo-Events in America.* New York: Harper & Row, 1964.

Braddon, Russell. *Roy Thomson of Fleet Street.* London: Collins, 1968.

Coller, Richard. *Social Effects of Donated Radios on Barrio Life.* Quezon City, Philippines: Community Development Research Council, 1961.

Cross, Malcolm. *West Indian Social Problems.* Port of Spain, Trinidad: Columbus Publishers, 1969.

Davison, W. Phillips. *International Political Communication.* New York: Frederick A. Praeger, 1965.

Dizard, Wilson. *Television: A World View.* Syracuse, N.Y.: Syracuse University Press, 1965.

Doob, Leonard. *Communication in Africa: A Search for Boundaries.* New Haven, Conn.: Yale University Press, 1961.

Fagen, Richard. *Politics and Communication.* Boston: Little, Brown & Co., 1966.

Fanon, Frantz. *Studies in a Dying Colonialism.* New York: Monthly Review Press, 1965.

Gottschalk, Louis. *Understanding History.* New York: Alfred A. Knopf, 1969.

Hohenberg, John. *Free People, Free Press: The Best Cause.* New York: Columbia University Press, 1971.

Hobson, J. A. *Imperialism.* Ann Arbor, Mich.: The University of Michigan Press, 1967.

Horowitz, Michael M. *Morne-Paysan: Peasant Village in Martinique.* New York: Holt, Rinehart & Winston, 1967.

Lerner, Daniel, and Schramm, Wilbur, eds. *Communication and Change in the Developing Countries.* Honolulu, Hawaii: East-West Center Press, 1967.

———. *The Passing of Traditional Society: Modernizing the Middle East.* New York: The Free Press, 1958.

Markham, James W. "Investigating the Mass Communication Factor in International Behavior." In *Mass Media and International Understanding.* Ljubljana, Yugoslavia, 1968.

Mehden, Fred von der. *Politics of the Developing Nations.* Englewood Cliffs, N.J.: Prentice-Hall, 1964.

Milbrath, Lester. *Political Participation.* Chicago: Rand McNally & Co., 1965.

Millikan, Max, and Blackmer, Donald, eds. *The Emerging Nations.* Boston: Little, Brown & Co., 1961.

Pye, Lucian, ed. *Communications and Political Development.* Princeton, N.J.: Princeton University Press, 1963.

Rogers, Everett. *Diffusion of Innovations.* New York: The Free Press, 1962.

————. *Modernization Among the Peasants: The Impact of Communication.* New York: Holt, Rinehart & Winston, 1968.

Rostow, W. W. *The Stages of Economic Growth.* New York: Cambridge University Press, 1969.

Schiller, Herbert. *Mass Communications and American Empire.* Boston: Beacon Press, 1971.

Schramm, Wilbur. *Mass Media and National Development.* Stanford, Calif.: Stanford University Press, 1964.

Sommerlad, E. Lloyd. *The Press in Developing Countries.* Sydney, Australia: Sydney University Press, 1966.

Ward, Barbara. *The Rich Nations and the Poor Nations.* New York: W. W. Norton, 1962.

Williams, Eric. *Capitalism and Slavery.* London: Andre Deutsch, 1964.

Wolseley, Roland. *The Black Press, U.S.A.* Ames, Iowa: Iowa State University Press, 1971.

THE WEST INDIES

Augier, F. R. *Sources of West Indian History.* London: Longmans, Green & Co., 1964.

Austin, Alvin E. "Infringements on Freedom of the Press in Latin America." *North Dakota Quarterly,* Spring 1969, pp. 60–71.

————. "The Situation in Latin America: The Throttling of the Free Press and the Free Flow of Information in Cuba and Elsewhere in Latin America." Mimeographed. Grand Forks, North Dakota: University of North Dakota, 1962.

"Available West Indian Newspapers on Microfilm." *Caribbean Studies* 2, no. 4: 77–79.

Ayeast, Morley. *The British West Indies: The Search for Self-Government.* London: George Allen & Unwin, 1960.

Bell, Wendell. *The Democratic Revolution in the West Indies.* Cambridge, Mass.: Schenkman Publishing, 1967.

Benn Brothers Ltd. *Benn's Guide to Newspapers and Periodicals of the World.* 119th issue. London: Benn Brothers Ltd., 1970.

Blundell, Margaret. "Caribbean Readers and Writers." *Bim* 11 (1966): 163–67.

Burns, Sir Alan. *History of the British West Indies.* London: George Allen & Unwin, 1954.

"Canadian Broadcasting Corporation Weighs Center for Commonwealth Broadcasts in Indies." *Advertising Age* 37 (October 31, 1966): 94.

"Caribbean Press Facing Subtle Pressures." *IAPA News,* August 1971, pp. 1, 4.

"Caribbean Radio Is Heard by a Million." *World's Press News* 57, no. 1456 (February 8, 1957): 29.

Central Rediffusion Services Ltd. *Commercial Broadcasting in the British West Indies.* London: Butterworth's Scientific Publications, 1956.

Chilcote, R. H. "The Press in Latin America, Spain and Portugal." Special issue of *Hispanic American Report,* August 1963.

Cozier, Edward L. "The Press in the New West Indies." *Bajan,* April 1958, pp. 22–23.

Cozier, Tony. "Caribbean Islands Press Threatened." *Editor & Publisher,* July 31, 1971, p. 20.

DaBreo, D. Sinclair. *The West Indies Today.* St. George's, Grenada: Published by Author, 1971.

Editor & Publisher. *Editor & Publisher Yearbook 1969.* New York: Editor & Publisher, 1969.

Fishman, Joshua A.; Ferguson, Charles A.; and Gupta, Jyotirindra das, eds. *Language Problems of Developing Countries.* New York: John Wiley & Sons, 1968.

―――, ed. *Readings in the Sociology of Language.* The Hague, Netherlands: Mouten, 1970.

Foreign Broadcast Information Service. *Broadcasting Stations of the World.* Parts I, III, IV. Washington, D.C.: Foreign Broadcast Information Service, 1969.

Freitas, G. V. de. "Press and Radio." *The Statist,* September 1956, pp. 69–70.

Gropp, Arthur E. *Guide to Libraries and Archives in Central America and the West Indies, Panama, Bermuda and British Guiana*. New Orleans, La.: Tulane University, 1941.

Hallett, Robert. "Newspaper Growing Pains in New Nation." *IPI Report*, November 1957, pp. 3–4; February 1958, pp. 3–4.

Harris, William H. "The West Indian Radio Newspaper." In *The Economic Future of the Caribbean*, edited by E. F. Frazier and E. Williams. Washington, D.C.: Howard University Press, 1944.

Hearne, John. "The Creative Society in the Caribbean." *Saturday Review*, September 14, 1968, pp. 62, 99.

Hunt, L. "Mass Media in the West Indies." *The Democratic Journalist* 4 (1967): 52–54; 5–6 (1967): 63–65.

"IAPA Group Reports on Press Freedom in Caribbean." *Daily Gleaner*, November 22, 1963, p. 1.

Information Department of Colonial Office. *Handbook on Broadcasting Services in the Colonies Etc. 1956*. London: Information Department of Colonial Office, 1956.

Laing, Michael. "Radio Comes to the West Indies." *New Commonwealth* 30, no. 11 (November 1955): vi–vii, 28.

Lent, John A. "The Government and Broadcasting in the Commonwealth Caribbean." Paper presented at Global Broadcasting, Dimensions, Problems and Promises: A Centennial Symposium, April 24, 1971, at Ohio State University. Mimeographed.

Lewis, Gordon K. *The Growth of the Modern West Indies*. London: Macgibbon & Kee, 1968.

Liebling, A. J. "Wayward Leeward and Windward Press." *New Yorker* 28, no. 29 (September 6, 1952): 92, 99.

———. "Wayward Press: Caribbean Excursion." *New Yorker*, April 10, 1948, pp. 60–67.

Lincoln, Waldo. "List of Newspapers of the West Indies and Bermuda in the Library of the American Antiquarian Society." *Proceedings of American Antiquarian Society*, April 1926, pp. 130–55.

"Major Changes in Former Carib. Press Association." *Daily Gleaner*, July 14, 1963, p. 2.

Merrill, John C.; Bryan, Carter R.; and Alisky, Marvin. *The Foreign Press*. Baton Rouge, La.: Louisiana State University Press, 1970.

Mitchell, Sir Harold. *Contemporary Politics and Economics in the Caribbean*. Athens, Ohio: Ohio University Press, 1968.

Morrison, Hugh P. "Radio for the Community." *Caribbean Quarterly*, September 1968, pp. 42–49.

O'Loughlin, Carleen. *Economic and Political Change in the Leeward and Windward Islands.* New Haven, Conn.: Yale University Press, 1968.

Oswald, John Clyde. *Printing in the Americas.* New York: Gregg Publishing Co., 1937.

Pearcy, G. Etzel. *The West Indian Scene.* New York: Van Nostrand Co., 1965.

Pitman, Frank Wesley. *The Development of the British West Indies 1700–1763.* London: Frank Cass & Co., 1967.

Prakke, Henk J. *Handbuch der Weltpresse.* Cologne & Opladen, West Germany: Westdeutscher Verlag, 1970.

"Press Still Free in British Caribbean." *Daily Gleaner,* October 31, 1964, p. 1.

Proctor, Jesse Harris. "British West Indian Society and Government in Transition." *Social and Economic Studies* 2, no. 4 (December 1962): 273–304.

Ragatz, L. J. *A Guide for the Study of British Caribbean History, 1763–1834.* Washington, D.C.: Government Printing Office, 1962.

Richardson, Willy. "The Place of Radio in the West Indies." *Caribbean Quarterly* 7, no. 3 (December 1961): 158–62.

Roppa, Guy, and Clarke, Neville E. *The Commonwealth Caribbean: Regional Co-Operation in News and Broadcasting Exchanges.* Paris: UNESCO, 1969.

Sealy, Theodore. "Caribbean Newspapers: A Record of Vigorous Development." *The Times Review of the British Colonies,* September 1951.

Sherlock, Philip. *West Indies.* London: Thames & Hudson Ltd., 1966.

Springer, Hugh. "Problems of National Development in the West Indies." *Caribbean Quarterly,* March–June 1965, pp. 3–12.

Stanley, E. L. "Notes on Advertising for West Indies Markets." *Canada-West Indies Magazine* 28, no. 8 (September 1939): 26–27.

"Statutes of the Caribbean Broadcasting Union." Mimeographed. Grenada: Windward Islands Broadcasting Service, 1971.

Sutton, Horace. "The Palm Tree Revolt." *Saturday Review,* February 27, 1971, pp. 15–19, 36–37.

Television Digest. *Television Factbook 1970–1971.* 2 vols. Washington, D.C.: Television Digest, 1970.

Thomas, Isaiah. *The History of Printing in America With a Biography of Printers and an Account of Newspapers.* Albany, N.Y.: Joel Munsell, 1874.

Ullman, James, and Dinhofer, Al. *Caribbean Here and Now*. London: MacMillan & Co., 1968.

UNESCO. *The Daily Press: A Survey of the World Situation in 1952*. Paris: UNESCO, 1953.

―――. *Newsprint Trends 1928–1951*. Paris: UNESCO, 1954.

―――. *Statistics of Newspapers and Other Periodicals*. Paris: UNESCO, 1959.

―――. *World Communications: Press, Radio, Television, Film*. Paris: UNESCO, 1964.

―――. *World Press: Newspapers and News Agencies*. Paris: UNESCO, 1964.

―――. *World Radio and Television*. Paris: UNESCO, 1965.

"West Indian Politicians and the Press." *Sunday Gleaner*, April 28, 1957.

West India Royal Commission Report. Presented by the Secretary of State for the Colonies to Parliament by Command of His Majesty. London: His Majesty's Stationery Office, 1945.

West Indies Yearbook Including Also The Bermudas, The Bahamas, British Guiana and British Honduras 1941–2. Montreal: Thomas Skinner & Co., 1942.

Williams, Eric. *From Columbus to Castro: The History of the Caribbean 1492–1969*. London: Andre Deutsch, 1970.

Willing's Press Guide 1969. London: James Willing Ltd., 1969.

Zimmerman, Irene. *A Guide to Current Latin American Periodicals: Humanities and Social Sciences*. Gainesville, Fla.: Kallman Publishing, 1961.

BAHAMAS

"Bahamas Bid To Censure Editor Fails." *IPI Report* 16, no. 8 (December 1967): 2.

"Bahamas Bill Worries the Press." *IPI Report* 17, no. 9 (January 1969): 5.

"Bahamian Newsmen Face Government Pressure." *IAPA News*, February 1971, p. 8.

Cole, Bill. "Amendment Bid Fails As Press Bill Passed." Nassau *Guardian*, March 27, 1969, p. 1.

Craton, Michael. *A History of the Bahamas*. London: Collins, 1962.

"Dupuch Masterminded Powers and Privileges Bill." Nassau *Guardian*, March 22, 1969, p. 1.

Dupuch, Sir Etienne. "Children Playing With Fire." *The Tribune* (Nassau), August 18, 1970.

———. "Gestapo at Work." *The Tribune* (Nassau), April 24, 1971.

———. *Tribune Story*. London: Ernest Benn Ltd., 1967.

Gilbert, Elsa. "Press Freedom Bahama Style." *Overseas Press Bulletin*, December 17, 1969, p. 3.

"Island Paper Gambles on Glowing Prospects." *Editor & Publisher*, May 27, 1967, p. 30.

Moseley, Mary. "Newspapers of the Bahamas 1784–1944." Nassau *Guardian*, November 23, 1944.

———. "The Colony's Oldest Newspaper." Nassau *Guardian*, November 23, 1944.

"Not So Balmy Breezes from the Bahamas." *IPI Report* 18, no. 8 (December 1969): 12.

"Preservation of Democracy As Great a Concern As Freedom of the Press." *The Tribune* (Nassau), October 28, 1970.

Rediffusion International Ltd. "The Bahamas: Radio Audience Survey No. 1." London: Rediffusion International, 1970.

Selhorn, D. "Bahamas Puts Press Under Severe Rules." *Editor & Publisher* 102 (May 3, 1969): 42.

White, P. Anthony. "The Shameful Blackout." Nassau *Guardian*, April 23, 1971.

BARBADOS

Archer, Thomas A. "Radio in Barbados." *The Bajan*, March 1964, p. 29.

Barbados Advocate-News. Anniversary supplement. October 1, 1970. 24 pp.

"Barbados' First Paper Appeared in 1731." Barbados *Advocate*, November 21, 1961, p. 8.

"Barbados Press Freedom 'Challenged.'" *IPI Report* 15, no. 11 (March 1967): 2.

Barbados Ministry of Education. *Barbados Independence Magazine*. November 1966.

"Barbados *Recorder* Suspends Publication." *Daily Gleaner*, January 8, 1960.

Barbados Rediffusion Service Ltd. "Market Profile Edition No. 2." London: Rediffusion International, 1965.

——. "This Is a Rediffusion World." Bridgetown: Barbados Rediffusion Service Ltd., March 1962.

Baugh, Edward. "Frank Collymore and the Miracle of BIM." *New World* 3, nos. 1–2 (1966–67): pp. 129–33.

Bridgetown. Caribbean Broadcasting Corporation. "Caribbean Broadcasting Corporation Radio and Television Services: Organization and Inter-Relation" [by Ian Gale].

——. "The Future of National Radio and Television Link-Ups in the Caribbean Area" [by Ian Gale].

"Broadcasting and Television." *The Bajan*, July 1965, pp. 7–10.

Caribbeana. Containing Letters & Dissertations, Together With Poetical Essays, on Various Subjects and Occasions; Chiefly Wrote by Several Hands in the West Indies, and Some of Them to Gentlemen Residing There. London: Printed for T. Osborne and W. Smith, 1741.

"CBC TV." *Bajan*, December 1964, pp. 21–22; January 1965, pp. 22–24; February 1965, p. 23.

Chandler, M. J. *A Guide to Records in Barbados.* Oxford: Basil Blackwell, 1965.

"Extracts from The Liberal Newspaper." *The Journal of the Barbados Museum and Historical Society* 26, no. 1 (November 1958): 9–19, 56–162.

"First Radio Station for Barbados." *The Bajan*, February 1960, p. 22.

"From One Man's Idea in 1894, a Paper Is Born." Barbados *Advocate*, November 21, 1961, p. 1.

Hamilton, Bruce. "BIM Comes of Age." *The Bajan*, December 1963, p. 9.

Hoyos, F. A. *Our Common Heritage.* Bridgetown: Advocate Press, 1953.

"IPI Protests at Bar on Reuters Man." *IPI Report* 15, no. 11 (March 1967): 1.

McMurtrie, Douglas C. *Early Printing in Barbados; Being an Account of the Establishment of the Press on That Island and of the Known Work of David Harry, Samuel Keimer, William Beebe, William Brown, G. Esmand, John Orderson, Thomas W. Perch, Isaac W. Orderson, and W. Walker.* London: Privately printed, 1933.

——. *A History of Printing in the United States.* New York: R. R. Bowker Co., 1936.

Morrison, Hugh. "Live Arts." *The Bajan,* February 1965, p. 26.

"October 1 1895—Red Letter Day." Barbados *Advocate,* November 21, 1961, p. 1.

"Oldtimer Celebrates." *Newday,* October 1957.

"Reuters Correspondent Banned by Barbados." *Press of the Americas,* April 1967, p. 7.

"Reuters Correspondent Batchelor Is Not Permitted To Enter Barbados." *Press of the Americas,* August 1967, pp. 3–4.

Schomburgh, Robert H. *History of Barbados.* London, 1848.

Sharp, G. F. "The Barbados Publicity Committee: Its Origin and History." *Journal of the Barbados Museum and Historical Society* 31, no. 2 (May 1963): 60–71.

Shilstone, E. M. "Some Notes on Early Printing Presses and Newspapers in Barbados." *Journal of the Barbados Museum and Historical Society* 26, no. 1 (November 1958): 19–33.

"Sound Broadcasts." *The Bajan,* December 1963, pp. 14–15.

Vaughan, H. A. "Samuel Prescod: The Birth of a Hero." *New World* 3, nos. 1–2 (1966–67): 55–60.

BERMUDA

"Bermuda—a Fairy Environment—But Oh, Those Professional Atrocities." *World's Press News* 47, no. 1205 (April 18, 1952): 24.

"Bermuda Lawmakers Want Gag on Press." *Editor & Publisher,* January 12, 1952, p. 10.

"Bermuda TV Station, ZBF-TV, Hamilton, To Start July 1." *Broadcasting,* June 28, 1965.

Cole, George Watson. *Bermuda in Periodical Literature.* Boston: The Boston Book Co., 1907.

"Freedom Issue in Bermuda Dates to 1762." *Editor & Publisher,* December 22, 1951, p. 10.

Greene, W. Maxwell. "Bermuda (Alias Somers Islands) Historical Sketch." *American Geographical Society Bulletin* 33, no. 3 (1901): 220–42.

Hayward, Walter. *Bermuda: Past and Present.* New York: Dodd Mead, 1926.

"Lone Fight of Bermuda Paper for Right to Press Freedom." *World's Press News* 46, no. 1192 (January 18, 1952): 22.

McMurtrie, Douglas C. *A Project for Printing in Bermuda, 1772.* Chicago: Privately printed, 1928.

"Private Station Gets Franchise Despite Fear It Might Advertise Liquor." *New York Times,* May 31, 1943, p. 19.

Shayon, R. L. "Bermuda Holiday." *Saturday Review,* April 13, 1957, p. 25.

Simmonds, Peter Lund. "Statistics of Newspapers in Various Countries." *Statistical Society of London Journal* 4, no. 2 (July 1841): 111–36.

"The Press in Bermuda." *Bermuda Pocket Almanack 1893.* Pp. 158–63.

Williamson, Lenora. "Queen Honors 'Ted' Sayer for Services to Journalism." *Editor & Publisher,* August 22, 1970, pp. 34, 36.

JAMAICA

Alleyne, Mervin. "Communications and Politics in Jamaica." *Caribbean Studies* 3, no. 2: 22–61.

Ashenheim, L. E. "Speech of *Gleaner* Chairman." *Daily Gleaner,* May 30, 1964, p. 25.

"Bill Empowering Govt. To Grant TV Franchise Passed by House." *Daily Gleaner,* December 21, 1962, pp. 19, 37, 40.

Binns, Graham. "Broadcasting in Jamaica." *Jamaica and West Indian Review* 2, no. 5 (Spring 1965): 18–19.

"Broadcasting Authority Report Before House." *Daily Gleaner,* July 6, 1960.

"Broadcasting Authority's Report on Local TV, Radio Stations." *Daily Gleaner,* January 25, 1966.

"Church, State and the Press." *Public Opinion,* December 7, 1957.

"Contempt of Court." Kingston: Farquharson Institute of Public Affairs, June 1970.

Cundall, Frank. "Benjamin Franklin's Connection with Jamaica." Jamaica *Mail,* September 26, 1929.

———. "Early Jamaica Printing." *American Book Collector,* January 1927.

———. "Early Printing in Jamaica." *The West India Committee Circular* 41, no. 719 (April 22, 1926): 150–51.

———. *History of Printing in Jamaica from 1717 to 1834.* Kingston: Institute of Jamaica, 1935.

———. "Jamaica's First Newspaper." Jamaica *Standard,* March 24, 1938.

———. "The Press and Printers of Jamaica Prior to 1820." *Proceedings of the American Antiquarian Society* 26 (1916): 290–412.

Curtin, Philip D. *Two Jamaicas: The Role of Ideas in a Tropical Colony 1830–1865*. Cambridge, Mass.: Harvard University Press, 1955.

Dunbar, Rudolph. "Jamaica Needs TV for Rural Development." *The Star* (Jamaica), November 24, 1962.

Durham, Vivian. "Television: How Much Longer Must Jamaica Wait?" *Sunday Gleaner*, September 20, 1959.

Eddy, George S. "B. Franklin and Jamaica," Jamaica *Mail*, July 27, 1929.

Eisner, Gisela. *Jamaica, 1830–1930*. Manchester, England: Manchester University Press, 1961.

Faber, Michael. "Twenty Questions and Answers About Jamaican TV." *Daily Gleaner*, July 23, 1962.

Findley, Eleanor Elizabeth. "A Content Analysis Comparing Symbols of Nationalism, Socialism, and Scientism as Found in the Jamaica *Daily Gleaner* in 1954, 1960, and 1966." Master's thesis, University of Washington, 1969.

Forkman, John. "T.V., Jamaica and the Canute Way." *Farmers Weekly*, January 23, 1960.

Gabe, D. R. "Problem Child—One Year Old." *Daily Gleaner*, August 9, 1951.

Gill, F. T. "A New Look in Communication." *Canada-West Indies Magazine* 26, no. 11 (1937): 28–30.

"*Gleaner* Declines TV Offer." *Daily Gleaner*, November 24, 1962, p. 1.

"*Gleaner* Opens $8M Building." Trinidad *Guardian*, April 27, 1970.

"*Gleaner*-Philips TV Tie-Up a Roaring Success." *Sunday Gleaner*, August 12, 1962.

"Government Awards TV Franchise to Jamaica Broadcasting." *New York Times*, November 11, 1962, p. 140.

Government Printing Office. *The Handbook of Jamaica for 1949–50*. Kingston: Government Printing Office, 1950.

———. *The Handbook of Jamaica for 1956*. Kingston: Government Printing Office, 1956.

———. *The Handbook of Jamaica for 1962*. Kingston: Government Printing Office, 1962.

"Government States TV Principles." *Daily Gleaner*, May 17, 1962.

"House Passes Television Resolution." *Daily Gleaner*, December 19, 1962.

"Independence: Monumental Task for Press—Glasspole." *Daily Gleaner*, October 31, 1961.

Information Officer. "Looking Back on 1940 . . . ZQI Broadcasts 1940–43." Kingston: Information Officer, n.d.

Jacobs, H. P. "The Press and Radio." *Daily Gleaner*, July 28, 1962.

Jamaica Broadcasting Corporation. "Educational Broadcasting Service Performance Report 1969–70." Mimeographed. Kingston: JBC-TV, 1970.

"Jamaica May Get TV Soon." *Daily Gleaner*, January 17, 1962.

"JBC Inaugurates Educational TV." *Daily Gleaner*, September 12, 1964, p. 2.

"JBC—The Challenge and Contribution." *Daily Gleaner*, June 22, 1963, p. 24.

"JBC To Start TV August 1." *Daily Gleaner*, November 8, 1962, p. 1.

"JBC-TV Continues To Show Profit." *Daily Gleaner*, April 29, 1966, p. 27.

"John Grinan—He Showed the World." *Spotlight*, December 1964, p. 79.

Judah, George. "The Newspaper History of Jamaica." Jamaica *Times*, January 21, 1899.

Kingston. Institute of Jamaica. "A Brief History of Radio Jamaica."

———. "Jamaica Almanacs" [by Frank Cundall].

———. "Jamaica Newspapers."

———. "The Handbooks of Jamaica" [by Harry Vendryes].

Kingston. Jamaica Broadcasting Corporation. "ETV Comes to Jamaica" [by Inez Grant].

MacKenzie, K. C. "Whither Jamaican TV?" *Sunday Gleaner*, November 11, 1962, pp. 7–8.

Maddison, John. "Radio and Television in Literacy: A Survey of the Use of the Broadcasting Media in Combating Illiteracy Among Adults." Paris: UNESCO, 1971.

Makin, William J. "Earthquakes and Sudden Death in the Caribbean." *World's Press News* 19, no. 484 (June 9, 1938): 5.

Marshall, H. V. Ormsby. "The Press and Us." *Sunday Gleaner*, October 16, 1955.

McFarlane, Basil. "The Rise and Fall of 'The Times.'" *The Welfare Reporter* 22, no. 1 (February 1963): 25–26, 29.

McMurtrie, Douglas C. "A Broadside Issued at Mobile (Now in Alabama) in 1763, But Printed on the Island of Jamaica in the Same Year." Chicago: Chicago School of Printing, 1939.

———. "The Early Press of Jamaica." Metuchen, N.J.: Privately printed, 1934.

———. "The First Printing in Jamaica, With a Discussion of the Date of the First Establishment of a Press on the Island by Robert Baldwin. With a Facsimile of the Earliest Extant Jamaican Imprint, the Second Edition of Pindarique Ode, . . ." Evanston, Ill.: Privately printed, 1942.

————. "The First Printing on the Island of Jamaica." Metuchen, N.J.: Privately printed, 1934.

Milner, Harry. "The Jamaica Broadcasting Corporation." *Sunday Gleaner,* December 5, 1965, p. 6.

Moss, W. Stanley. "Teleview." *Daily Gleaner,* August 6, 1963, p. 1.

Murray, K. T. "Nationalisation and Broadcasting." *Daily Gleaner,* December 6, 1949.

Neita, Clifton. *One Hundred Years of Famous Pages from the Press of Jamaica 1853–1953.* Kingston: The Gleaner Co., 1953.

Press Association of Jamaica. *Press, Radio and TV,* 1969–1970 issue. (Annual).

"Promises Unkept." *Spotlight,* December 1964, p. 77.

"Public Radio-Government Plan." *Daily Gleaner,* February 5, 1958, p. 1.

"Radio and TV." *Spotlight,* December 1964, p. 77.

Radio Jamaica. "Jamaica Survey No. 6. Audience Research in Jamaica." Kingston: Radio Jamaica, 1969.

————. "Jamaica Market Profile 1965." London, October 1965.

"Recollections of Evon Blake." *Spotlight,* December 1964, pp. 7–8.

Rennalls, Martin A. "Development of the Documentary Film in Jamaica." Master's thesis, Boston University, 1968.

"Sealy Sees Success in Fight To Maintain Freedom of Press." *Daily Gleaner,* September 24, 1963, p. 21.

"Standards Higher; But Too Much Rock; Poor Rural Reception." *Daily Gleaner,* November 6, 1962, pp. 8, 15.

Stevens, G. R. "Advertising in Jamaica." *Canada-West Indies Magazine* 10, no. 7 (May 1922): 180–81.

"Television Will Publicize Life in Rural Jamaica—Lecturer." *Daily Gleaner,* July 31, 1963, p. 8.

The Daily Gleaner Souvenir Edition, December 31, 1966.

"The Gleaner Company Limited." Brochure. Kingston: Gleaner Co., 1969.

The Government Printer. *Annual Report on Jamaica for the Year 1955.* Kingston: The Government Printer, 1956.

————. *Annual Report on Jamaica for the Year 1956.* Kingston: The Government Printer, 1957.

————. *Annual Report on Jamaica for the Year 1958.* Kingston: The Government Printer, 1959.

———. *Annual Report on Jamaica for the Year 1961.* Kingston: The Government Printer, 1962.

"Thousands Enjoy TV in Park." *Daily Gleaner,* August 9, 1962.

"TV: Films Being Test-Transmitted." *Daily Gleaner,* June 21, 1963, p. 1.

White, Paul F. "Early Newspapers." *Daily Gleaner,* November 23, 1964, p. 12.

"Who Listens to What—And Why." *Sunday Magazine (Gleaner),* September 19, 1965, p. 10.

LEEWARD ISLANDS

Baker, E. C. *A Guide to Records in the Leeward Islands.* Oxford: Basil Blackwell, 1965.

Brisk, William. *The Dilemma of a Ministate: Anguilla.* Columbia, S.C.: University of South Carolina, Institute of International Studies, 1969.

Eames, Wilberforce. "The Antigua Press and Benjamin Mecom, 1748–1765." *Proceedings of American Antiquarian Society* 38 (1928): 303–48.

"Government Bans Import of TV Sets on Ground That They Would Create Discontent." *New York Times,* October 11, 1968, p. 25.

McMurtrie, Douglas C. "Early Printing on the Island of Antigua." Evanston, Ill.: Privately printed, 1943.

Michelow, Michael, ed. *Antigua, Official Independence Magazine,* 1967.

"Montserrat's Only Newspaper Closes." *Daily Gleaner,* October 8, 1959.

"Now Who Really Forced Dorcas to Leave Antigua?" Antigua *Star,* March 10, 1971, p. 2.

O'Loughlin, Carleen. "Problems in the Economic Development of Antigua." *Social and Economic Studies,* September 1961, pp. 236–77.

Procope, Stanley. "History of the Press of St. Kitts-Nevis-Anguilla." Manucsript given to author by Procope (n.d.).

"Purge in Anguilla Civil Service; Newspaper Closed." Trinidad *Guardian,* March 15, 1969.

Richards, Novelle. *The Struggle and the Conquest.* St. Johns, Antigua: Workers Voice Printery, ca. 1964.

"St. Kitts Editor Arrested." Trinidad *Guardian,* January 22, 1969.

"St. Kitts Government Outlaws Unregistered Newspapers." Trinidad *Guardian,* January 10, 1969.

"St. Kitts Paper Under Pressure." *IAPA News,* June 1971, p. 8.

The Beacon (of Anguilla), issues of April 20, 1968, September 27, 1967, December 28, 1968, April 12, 1969, March 31, 1969, September 6, 1970, April 11, 1970, September 27, 1969.

TRINIDAD AND TOBAGO

Alleyne, C. G. "When a Reporter Had To Keep Pace with a Train." Trinidad *Guardian,* September 24, 1967.

Babb, John. "Cinemas: 'To Hell and Back.'" Trinidad *Guardian,* May 17, 1970, p. 1.

Barrat, George. "Our Fighting Editors." *Express* (Trinidad), June 9, 1968, pp. 45–46.

"Bed Time Stories Days Are Over." *Sunday Guardian* (Trinidad), October 28, 1962.

"Birth of a Newspaper." Trinidad *Evening News,* August 23, 1963.

Boisselle, Hollis. "The Public Order Bill and Freedom of Movement." Trinidad *Guardian,* August 15, 1970.

"'Bomb Explodes' in T'dad Soon." Trinidad *Evening News,* February 17, 1970.

"Capildeo Heads the 'Statesman.'" Trinidad *Guardian,* June 24, 1964.

Carmichael, Gertrude. *The History of the West Indian Islands of Trinidad and Tobago. 1498–1900.* London: Alvin Redman, 1961.

Cartar, Lloyd. "Thomson Acquires 'Guardian.'" Trinidad *Guardian,* April 12, 1961.

Chongsing, Lenn. "40 Years of Progress." *Sunday Guardian,* September 1, 1957.

———. "History in Headlines." *Sunday Guardian,* September 1, 1957.

"Concern Over Trinidad." *Press of the Americas,* December 1, 1959, pp. 3–4.

Daniel, Edward W. "The Introduction of Printing into Trinidad de Barlovento." Port of Spain: Historical Society of Trinidad and Tobago, 1949.

"End of the Line for DLP Newspaper." Trinidad *Daily Mirror,* June 4, 1964.

"ETV-AV for Trinidad-Tobago." *AV Instructor,* April 1966, p. 292+.

"First Commercial Station Opening Set." *New York Times,* August 14, 1947, p. 46.

"Freedom of Press in West Indies." *Press of the Americas*, February 1, 1961, p. 2.

"Government and the Press." Trinidad *Guardian*, April 28, 1962.

"Government Subsidy to Press Denied." Trinidad *Guardian*, February 17, 1959.

"Great Stride by WI Press Seen." *Daily Gleaner*, September 2, 1958.

Grimes, John. "News News News: Your 'Evening News,' How It Started." Trinidad *Guardian*, May 16, 1956.

"'Guardian' Boycotts 'Press Conference.'" Trinidad *Guardian*, January 25, 1959.

"IAPA Sees Freedom of Press in Trinidad." Trinidad *Guardian*, November 22, 1963.

"IAPA Told CM Threatened Press." Trinidad *Guardian*, October 18, 1957.

"In Trinidad—A Leading W.I. Chinese Paper." *The Nation*, August 12, 1960.

Jacobs, Carl. "War Baby Is Now a Giant." Trinidad *Guardian* May 28, 1967.

"Jamaican for the 'Chronicle.'" *Newday*, September 1958.

James, C. L. R. *Party Politics in the West Indies*. San Juan, Trinidad: Vedic Enterprises, circa 1962.

John, G. R. "What's This We've Been Hearing About a Foreign Press?" Trinidad *Daily Mirror*, September 29, 1964.

Kingston. Institute of Jamaica. "The First Printing on the Island of Tobago."

Kroll, Morton. "Political Leadership and Administrative Communications in New Nation States." *Social and Economic Studies* 16, no. 1 (March 1967): 17–33.

Layne, Lancelot. "Continuing Cultural Obliteration." *Tapia*, August 9, 1970, p. 5.

"Life Begins at 40." *Newday*, November 1957.

McMurtrie, Douglas C. "Notes on the Beginning of Printing on the Island of Trinidad." Fort Worth, Tex.: National Association for Printing Education, 1943.

Mahabir, Dennis. "The Impact of Television in Trinidad." *Enterprise* (Trinidad), March 1964, pp. 11–13.

"No 'Mercy' for 'Guardian,' Says Premier." Trinidad *Guardian*, October 9, 1960, p. 1.

Pantin, Raoul. "'Tapia'—Signs of the Times." Trinidad *Guardian*, October 2, 1969.

"Party Press To Roll Again." Trinidad *Guardian,* June 9, 1964.

Perez, Z. A. "The Company (Guardian) Today." Trinidad *Guardian,* September 24, 1967.

———. "The Pace-Setters Who Have Passed Through Our Doors." Trinidad *Guardian,* September 24, 1967.

"PM Attacks 'Old Enemies.'" Trinidad *Guardian,* September 27, 1963.

"PM's Claim for Libel Settled." Trinidad *Guardian,* May 21, 1963.

"Premier Replies to Sir Gerald." Trinidad *Guardian,* January 26, 1961.

Radio Trinidad. "Market Profile Trinidad." Port of Spain: Radio Trinidad, November 1967, August 1969.

Renwick, David. "Capital Increased 100 Times Since Its Birth." *Sunday Guardian,* September 1, 1957.

Roach, Eric. "Fifty Years of Public Service." Trinidad *Guardian,* September 24, 1967.

Robinson, A. N. "Why the Government Should Resign." Trinidad *Express,* August 31, 1970, pp. 12–13.

"State of Emergency." *Evening News,* April 21, 1970, p. 1.

"'Statesman' To Be Revived." Trinidad *Guardian,* March 18, 1966.

"Strange Obsession of Peter Farquhar." Trinidad *Guardian,* October 14, 1963.

"Television for Trinidad." Trinidad *Guardian,* November 1, 1962, p. 10.

"The 'Mirror' Closes; Thomson Takes Over $2M Assets." Trinidad *Guardian,* September 3, 1966.

"The 'Nation' and the 'Evening News.'" Trinidad *Guardian,* August 27, 1967.

"The Pioneers." Trinidad *Guardian,* September 24, 1967.

"The Press- and the Public." Trinidad *Guardian,* July 1, 1967.

"Thomson Taking Over 'Guardian.'" *Daily Gleaner,* April 12, 1961.

"Threatening the Press." Trinidad *Guardian,* October 27, 1957.

"Time to Think for Ourselves." Trinidad *Guardian,* November 2, 1962.

"Trinidad Chief Threatens Press." *Press of the Americas,* September 1, 1959, p. 4.

Trinidad Guardian, issues of September 7, 1966, April 24, 1970, September 3, 1968, February 1, 1967, May 16, 1970, April 14, 1958, May 17, 1956, September 2, 1964, March 24, 1946, October 23, 1959, September 11, 1966, September 2, 1963, April 22, 1970, April 28, 1946, September 24, 1967, June 15, 1955, December 8, 1957, December 11, 1965, April 22, 1970, January 26, 1963, November 1, 1960, October 20, 1959, April 14, 1960, March 11, 1968, May 27,

1964, October 29, 1968, May 29, 1954, May 14, 1968, December 31, 1966, June 8, 1959, February 2, 1967, October 9, 1960.

"Trinidad *Guardian* Sounds the Alarm." *Press of the Americas,* September 1, 1959, p. 4.

"Trinidad Starts TV Operation." *Broadcasting,* October 29, 1962.

"20 Per Cent Trinidadians Don't Go." Trinidad *Evening News,* December 7, 1967.

" 'Vanguard' Bombed Again." Trinidad *Evening News,* April 28, 1970.

Williams, Eric. *History of the People of Trinidad and Tobago.* London: Andre Deutsch, 1964.

"Williams' Infernor." *Press of the Americas,* May 1, 1960, p. 3.

Wood, Donald. *Trinidad in Transition.* London: Oxford University Press, 1968.

WINDWARD ISLANDS

Baker, E. C. *A Guide to Records in the Windward Islands.* Oxford: Basil Blackwell, 1968.

Devas, Raymund P. *The History of the Island of Grenada 1850–1950.* Bridgetown, Barbados: Advocate Printery, 1965.

Devaux, Robert. "History of Newspapers in St. Lucia 1788–1970." Castries, St. Lucia: St. Lucia Archeological and Historical Society, forthcoming.

"Dominica CM Threatens Press." Trinidad *Guardian,* February 12, 1966.

"Dominica Press Gags Bill Passed at Rowdy Sitting." Trinidad *Guardian,* July 9, 1968.

Duncan, Ebenezer. *A Brief History of St. Vincent.* Kingstown, St. Vincent: Graphic Printery, 1970.

"IAPA Condemns New Press Law in West Indies." *Editor & Publisher,* August 31, 1969, p. 22.

Jesse, Rev. C. *Outlines of St. Lucia's History.* Castries, St. Lucia: The Voice Publishing Co., 1964.

Kay, Frances. *This—Is Grenada.* Trinidad: Caribbean Printers, 1966.

McMurtrie, Douglas C. "The First Printing in Dominica." London: Privately printed, 1932.

Mentus, Ulric. "Enter Dominica's Freedom Fighters." Trinidad *Evening News,* August 14, 1968.

"Newspaper Marks Golden Jubilee." *Daily Gleaner,* January 20, 1959.

"Paper Banned in St. Lucia." Trinidad *Guardian,* February 20, 1966.

Singham, A. W. *The Hero and the Crowd in a Colonial Polity.* New Haven, Conn.: Yale University Press, 1968.

Windward Islands Broadcasting Service. "Report on the Reorganization of Broadcasting in the Windward Islands." Mimeographed. St. George's, Grenada: Windward Islands Broadcasting Service, 1969.

CORRESPONDENCE

Letters from Ralph Barney, Assistant Professor, Brigham Young University, Provo, Utah, September 10, 1971, October 7, 1971.

Letter from John Barsotti, Assistant Program Director, Trinidad and Tobago Television, Port of Spain, Trinidad, August 10, 1971.

Letter from W. D. Bodden, Editor, *The Caymanian Weekly,* Grand Cayman, July 23, 1971.

Letter from Jack C. Brockman, Office of Assistant Director for Latin America, United States Information Agency, Washington, D.C., October 23, 1970.

Letters from Canon C. R. G. Carleton, Former Editor Anguilla *Beacon,* Inagua, Bahamas, May 15, 1971, June 29, 1971.

Letter from Paul Fisher, Director, FOI Center, Columbia, Missouri, April 22, 1971.

Letter from W. Y. Martin, Executive Assistant, Canadian Broadcasting Corporation, Ottawa, Canada, October 1, 1970.

Letter from Karney Osborne, General Manager, ZIZ Radio, Basseterre, St. Kitts, May 1, 1971.

Letter from Jack A. Rickel, Jack A. Rickel Associates, Inc., Washington, D.C., August 23, 1971.

Letter from Charles O. Thomas, Information Assistant, United States Information Service, Bridgetown, Barbados, November 19, 1970.

Letter from Dorcas White, Editor, Montserrat *Mirror,* Plymouth, Montserrat, June 10, 1971.

INTERVIEWS

Allfrey, Robert and Phyllis, eds. Dominica *Star,* Roseau, Dominica, May 6, 1971.

Archer, Ken, director, St. Lucia Television Services and owner St. Lucia Rentals, Castries, St. Lucia, May 8, 1971.

Bird, Ivor G. T., manager, ZDK Radio, St. John's, Antigua, May 3 and 4, 1971.

Boyd, S. A. W., ed. Dominica *Chronicle*, Roseau, Dominica, May 5, 1971.

Buntin, William, vice president Antigua Trade and Labour Union and former president Senate, St. John's, Antigua, May 4, 1971.

Chaplin, Ken, secretary, Press Association of Jamaica, Kingston, Jamaica, August 26, 1970.

Charles, Jeff, manager designate, Radio Dominica, Roseau, Dominica, May 6, 1971.

Chongsing, Lenn, ed. Trinidad *Guardian*, Port of Spain, Trinidad, September 1, 1970.

Clarke, Austin, general manager, Caribbean Broadcasting Corporation, Bridgetown, Barbados, January 12, 1976.

Clyne, Reggie, ed. *The West Indian*, St. George's, Grenada, May 12, 1971.

Collymore, Frank, ed. *Bim*, Bridgetown, Barbados, May 14, 1971.

Coon, Fred Seal, editorial manager, *Daily Gleaner*, Kingston, Jamaica, August 26, 1970.

Cornelius, Bentley, ed. Antigua *Star*, St. John's, Antigua, May 4, 1971.

Cruickshank, A. Michael, ed. *Vanguard*, St. George's, Grenada, May 12, 1971.

de Leon, Leo, program director, 610 Radio, Port of Spain, Trinidad, September 1, 1970.

Delph, Compton, ed. *Evening News*, Port of Spain, Trinidad, September 1, 1970.

de Pass, Lloyd, general manager, Radio Jamaica, Kingston, Jamaica, August 27, 1970.

Dodge, John, general manager, ZNS Radio, Nassau, Bahamas, April 26 and 27, 1971.

Duesbury, Gary, general manager, Radio Barbados, Bridgetown, Barbados, September 7, 1970.

Dunlop, Roy, director, Radio Anguilla, The Valley, Anguilla, April 29, 1971.

Dupuch, Sir Etienne, editor-proprietor, Nassau *Tribune*, Nassau, Bahamas, August 22, 1970 and April 27, 1971.

Evans, Chris, general manager, Nassau *Guardian*, Nassau, Bahamas, August 24, 1970.

Foster, Winston, assistant manager, Radio Caribbean, Castries, St. Lucia, January 10, 1976.

Gale, Ian, general manager, Caribbean Broadcasting Corporation, Bridgetown, Barbados, September 4, 1970.

Ghany, Sam, sales manager, Trinidad Broadcasting, Port of Spain, Trinidad, September 2, 1970.

Gordon, Ken, general manager, *Express,* Port of Spain, Trinidad, September 2, 1970.

Gordon, Michael, director, *Voice of St. Lucia,* Castries, St. Lucia, January 10, 1976.

Grant, Inez, senior education officer and ETV director, Ministry of Education, Kingston, Jamaica, August 28, 1970.

Grosvenor, Neville, general manager, *Advocate-News,* Bridgetown, Barbados, September 7, 1970; January 12, 1976.

Harrigan, Atlin, ed. Anguilla *Beacon,* The Valley, Anguilla, April 29, 1971.

Harris, Mrs. Reuben, acting ed. Antigua *Times,* St. John's, Antigua, May 4, 1971.

Hillary, Sam, Jamaica Information Service, Kingston, Jamaica, August 26, 1970.

Hinkson, Winston, St. Lucia WIBS director, Castries, St. Lucia, May 7 and 8, 1971; January 10, 1976.

Hodge, Nathaniel, ed. *Democrat,* Basseterre, St. Kitts, May 1, 1971.

Holden, Brian, director, St. Lucia Television, Castries, St. Lucia, January 9, 1976.

Hoyte, Harold, ed., *The Nation,* Bridgetown, Barbados, January 12, 1976.

Huggins, Leon, film director, Government Information Service, Kingstown, St. Vincent, May 10, 1971.

John, Leslie, chief reporter, *Workers Voice,* St. John's, Antigua, May 4, 1971.

Josie, Peter, member of Parliament, Castries, St. Lucia, January 9, 1976.

King, Cameron, public relations and information officer, Government Information Service, Kingstown, St. Vincent, May 10, 1971.

Lawrence, Roy, public relations director, Jamaica Broadcasting Corporation, Kingston, Jamaica, August 28, 1970.

Lewis, George, ed. *Labour Spokesman,* Basseterre, St. Kitts, May 1, 1971.

Lewis, Weston H., ed. *Vincentian,* Kingstown, St. Vincent, May 10, 1971.

McDermott, Benson, vice president, Nassau *Guardian,* Nassau, Bahamas, August 24, 1970.

Mason, Albert, public relations officer, government of St. Lucia, Castries, St. Lucia, January 9, 1976.

Mason, Elcon, ed. *Torchlight,* St. George's, Grenada, May 12, 1971.

Mayers, Harry, head, Caribbean News Agency, Christchurch, Barbados, January 12, 1976.

Michaels, Vernon G., manager, ZAL-TV, St. John's, Antigua, May 4, 1971.

Nuthall, Chris, regional programmer, Verbatim, Inc., St. John's, Antigua, May 5, 1971.

Odlum, George, ed., *Crusader,* Castries, St. Lucia, January 9, 1976.

Owen, Jody, program director, ZDK Radio, St. John's, Antigua, May 4, 1971.

Pringle, Peter, director, Caribbean Institute of Mass Communication, Kingston, Jamaica, January 15, 1976.

Procope, Stanley, (former) ed. *Daily Bulletin,* Basseterre, St. Kitts, May 1, 1971.

Proute, J. C., ed., *Jamaica Daily News,* Kingston, Jamaica, January 16, 1976.

Rawlins, Randolph, Jamaica radio commentator, Basseterre, St. Kitts, May 1, 1971.

Reid, Stanley, ed. *Crusader* and *Link,* Castries, St. Lucia, May 8, 1971.

Richards, Everard S. A., news ed. Antigua Broadcasting Service, St. John's, Antigua, May 4, 1971.

Daniel, W. St. C., Speaker of House and (former) ed. *Voice of St. Lucia,* May 8, 1971.

Scobie, Edward, ed. Dominica *Herald,* Roseau, Dominica, May 5, 1971; January 9, 1976.

Sealy, Theodore, editor, *Daily Gleaner,* Kingston, Jamaica, August 26, 1970.

Seon, Leslie, former WIBS program director and former GIS director, St. George's, Grenada, May 13, 1971.

Sherman, G. A., general manager, *Daily Gleaner,* Kingston, Jamaica, August 26, 1970; January 15, 1976.

Smith, Ray, director WIBS and head Caribbean Broadcasting Union, St. George's, Grenada, May 12, 1971.

Stewart, L. H., assistant general manager, Jamaica Broadcasting Corporation, Kingston, Jamaica, August 28, 1970.

Theobalds, Claude, chief program officer, WIBS, Kingstown, St. Vincent, May 11, 1971.

Turnquest, Leon, ed. Nassau *Guardian,* Nassau, Bahamas, April 26, 1971.

Wayne, Rick, ed. *Voice of St. Lucia,* Castries, St. Lucia, May 7, 1971.

Webster, Ronald, president, Anguilla, The Valley, Anguilla, April 29, 1971.

Whitmarsh, John, station manager, Radio Caribbean, Castries, St. Lucia, May 7, 1971.

Whylie, Dwight, general manager, Jamaica Broadcasting Corporation, Kingston, Jamaica, January 14, 1976.

Wickham, John, *The Bajan* and *Bim,* Bridgetown, Barbados, May 14, 1971.

BIBLIOGRAPHIC ADDENDUM, 1976

"All Ah We—The Issue of West Indian Identity." *Caribbean Contact,* July 1975, p. 17.

"A National Council Is Planned for Caribbean." *Asian Mass Communication Bulletin,* March 1975, p. 14.

"And Now—Television." *Caribbean Contact,* July 1975, p. 19.

"Antigua Newspaper Laws Not Unconstitutional." *Times* (London), May 20, 1975, p. 23.

"Antigua: Site of Deutsche Welle-BBC Relay." *Islander* 2, no. 4: 44.

"At Last, Our Own News Service." *Caribbean Contact,* July 1975, p. 18.

Bard, David R., and Baker, William J. "The American Newspaper Response to the Jamaican Riots of 1865." *Journalism Quarterly,* Winter 1974, pp. 659–63, 709.

"Bermuda Press Ltd. Separates Divisions." *Editor & Publisher,* May 21, 1968, p. 50.

"Brave Warrior (Dupuch) for 50 Years." *Editor & Publisher,* June 14, 1969, p. 38.

"Broadcasting Authority's '71–'72 Report." *Daily Gleaner,* August 2, 1973, pp. 5–7.

"Broadcasting Corporation of the Bahamas." *Combroad,* April–June 1974, p. 63.

Brown, Robert U. "Hemisphere Danger." *Editor & Publisher,* April 14, 1973, p. 60.

Brunton, Leslie, "St. Kitts Must Hold on to Democracy." Trinidad *Express,* January 11, 1976, p. 7.

"Cable Television in St. Vincent." *Combroad,* January–March 1975, p. 57.

"CAIC Object to Press Laws." *Caribbean Contact,* December 1975, p. 19.

"CANA Must Be Free of Political Control—Gordon." Trinidad *Express,* January 9, 1976, p. 4.

"Caribbean Broadcasting Corporation (Barbados): New Colour Television Equipment." *Combroad,* April–June 1974, p. 59.

"Caribbean Broadcasting Corporation (Barbados): OB Unit Converted to Colour." *Combroad,* April–June 1975, p. 71.

"Caribbean Broadcasting Corporation (Barbados): Tenth Year of Television." *Combroad,* January–March 1975, pp. 60–61.

"Caribbean Broadcasting Union: Fifth Annual General Assembly." *Combroad,* January–March 1975, pp. 41–44.

"Caribbean Broadcasting Union: Fourth General Assembly." *Combroad,* March–April 1974, pp. 44–46.

"Caribbean Broadcasting Union: Sixth General Assembly." *Combroad,* October–December 1975, pp. 46–48.

"Caribbean News Agency and Press Council in '76." *Caribbean Contact,* December 1975, p. 18.

"Caribbean Press Seminar: Can Censorship Code Help Democracies Win Cold War?" *Editor & Publisher,* May 17, 1958, pp. 11, 60–61.

Cave, Roderick. "Printing Comes to Jamaica." *Jamaica Journal* 9, nos. 2–3 (1975): 11–17.

"CBA On-Site Training—in Africa and the Caribbean." *Combroad,* April–June 1975, pp. 51–53.

"CBC Bans Hatch." *The Nation,* December 14, 1975, p. 1.

"CBU Urged to Work for Good of Region." *Caribbean Contact,* October 1975, p. 9.

Chambers, Audrey. "Selected List of Serials Published in Jamaica." *Jamaica Library Association Bulletin,* 1975, pp. 35–39.

Commonwealth Broadcasting Association 1974. London: Commonwealth Broadcasting Association, 1974.

"Constitution (of Barbados)." *The Nation,* November 25, 1975, p. 46.

"Cozier Making Changes on St. Lucia *Voice.*" *Editor & Publisher,* July 18, 1953.

Critchlow, Cheddie. "Oh, No, Mr. Bain! Are You Serious?" *Caribbean Contact,* April 1975, p. 19.

Cuthbert, Marlene, ed. *Caribbean Women in Communication for Development.* Barbados: Cedar Press, 1975.

"*Daily Gleaner* of Jamaica Goes Modern Via Computer." *Editor & Publisher,* April 19, 1975, p. 22.

Darville, Vernon M. "The Bahamas Press: A Study of the Editorial Coverage of the 1967–1968 General Election by the Two Nassau Dailies, the Nassau *Guardian* and the Nassau *Tribune.*" Masters thesis, University of Florida, 1972.

"Ewing Helps Staffers Build Trinidad Paper." *Editor & Publisher,* March 2, 1968, p. 35.

"Expansion of Radio Bahamas." *Combroad,* April–June 1975, pp. 71–72.

"General Manager—CANA." *Caribbean Contact,* August 1975, p. 18.

Gordon, Lorna. "The Jamaica Broadcasting Corporation Geared To Serve a Developing Nation." *EBU Review* 23, no. 3: 25–27.

"Gordon Tells Govts Where They Are Wrong." *Caribbean Contact,* December 1975, p. 19.

"Harold Hoyte on Who Should Own the Media: Definitely Not Lord Thomson!" *The Nation,* November 25, 1975, pp. 17, 21.

Honolulu. East-West Communication Institute. "Caribbean Seminar and Training Course: Radio and Television for Out-of-School-Education, Kingston (Jamaica) 16th April–14th May 1971."

————. "Readings on Population Information and Education: Background Papers for a Ford Foundation Meeting on Population, Elsinore, Denmark—June 1972." See: James W. Trowbridge, "Jamaica's Mass Media Campaign: A Case Study of a Public Information Program for Family Planning," pp. 169–83.

Hosein, Everold. "Mass Media Preferences, Media Credibility and CARICOM Awareness in Urban St. Lucia." *Caribbean Monthly Bulletin,* July 1975, pp. 14–20.

————. "Regional Television Programming for the Commonwealth Caribbean." *Combroad,* October–December 1973, pp. 13–17.

Hunter, Neville. "Caribbean Microwave Scheme." *Combroad,* April–June 1974, pp. 12–15.

"Jamaica Broadcasting Corporation: Modernisation and Expansion Project." *Combroad,* April–June 1974, pp. 54–56.

"Jamaican Minister Appeals to Press." Barbados *Advocate-News,* January 10, 1976, p. 1.

"Journalism Must Be Honest, Responsible." Barbados *Advocate-News,* January 11, 1976, p. 6.

"Kingston *Gleaner* Closed by Walkout." *Editor & Publisher*, April 23, 1966, p. 116.

Lent, John A. "British Caribbean Mass Communications Bibliography." Mimeographed. Iowa City, Iowa: School of Journalism, University of Iowa, 1971.

———. "Commonwealth Caribbean Mass Communications: A Case Study." Buffalo, N.Y.: Council on International Studies, University of Buffalo, 1975. Monograph.

———. "Commonwealth Caribbean Mass Media: Historical, Cultural, Economic and Political Aspects." Ph.D. dissertation, University of Iowa, 1972.

———. "Commonwealth Caribbean Mass Media: History and Development." *Gazette* 19, no. 2 (1973): 91–106.

———. "Cultural Confusion and Media Infusion Leave Few Options for the Commonwealth Caribbean." *Journal of Communication*, Spring 1975, pp. 128–35.

———. "Developing a Medium for Island Masses: Stapling the Pages Clipped Circulation." *IPI Report*, November 1972, pp. 8–9.

———. "How Independent Are Commonwealth Caribbean Mass Media. . . ?" Paper presented at Caribbean Studies Association, Castries, St. Lucia, January 8, 1976.

———. "Press Freedom in the Commonwealth Caribbean." *Index on Censorship*, Autumn 1973, pp. 55–70.

———. "Small Caribbean Media Avoid Foreign Ownership." *Journalism Quarterly*, Spring 1975, pp. 114–17.

Lindo, Cecil. "Jamaica." In *International Handbook of Advertising*, edited by S. Watson Dunn. New York: McGraw-Hill, 1964, pp. 280–82.

Lindo, Cedric. "Jamaica Makes a Film To Shock Its People." Penang, Malaysia *Sunday Gazette* (Gemini dispatch), January 6, 1974.

"Literacy Through Radio and Television in Jamaica Social Development Commission." *Educational Television International* 4, no. 1 (1970): 50–54.

Lowenthal, David, and Comitas, Lambros, editors. *The Aftermath of Sovereignty: West India Perspectives*. Garden City, N.Y.: Doubleday, 1973.

"*Manjak's* First Two Years." *Manjak*, no. 11 (1975), pp. 3–4.

Maxwell, Austen, "Television Production Training in the Caribbean." *Combroad*, October–December 1975, pp. 53–55.

Meisler, Stanley. "Report on Calypso: Trinidad Analyzes Politics with

Wit and Rhythm." *Philadelphia Inquirer*, March 25, 1975, p. 8-A.

"Mission Perturbed by Visit to Caribbean Islands (of Antigua, St. Kitts)." *IAPA News*, March–April 1972, p. 3.

Moore, Carl. "The Long History of Journalism." *The Nation*, November 25, 1975, p. 19.

"More Trouble in Grenada." *Caribbean Contact*, August 1975, p. 20.

"Nassau *Tribune* Fights for Right of Independence." *Editor & Publisher*, October 18, 1969, p. 24.

"National Television Audience Survey Jamaica 1971." Prepared for Jamaica Broadcasting Corporation by CRAM International (W.I.) Ltd., n.d.

"New Media in Curriculum Development and Teacher Training in the Caribbean." *Educational Broadcasting International*, September 1974, pp. 148–51.

"Newspapers from 1730." *The Nation*, November 25, 1975, p. 21.

Noel, Elaine. "Printers and Publishers in Jamaica." *Jamaica Library Association Bulletin*, 1975, pp. 11–12, 15.

"Not Only a Free Press Needed, But the Right to Disagree." *Caribbean Contact*, December 1975, p. 18.

"One-Year Media Diploma Planned for Phase One." Trinidad *Express*, July 23, 1973, p. 4.

Pantin, Raoul. "*The Guardian* Goes 'Trinidadian'?" *Caribbean Contact*, May 1975, p. 8.

Parris, Deighton. "Inexpensive TV Outside Broadcasting in Trinidad." *Combroad*, April–June 1973, pp. 35–36.

"Perry Building Plant for Paper in Bahamas." *Editor & Publisher*, May 10, 1969, p. 52.

"Portrait of a Premier." *Caribbean Contact*, March 1975, p. 13.

"Press (of Antigua) Wins Out." *IAPA News*, June–July 1973, p. 5.

"Press Freedom Under Fire." *Caribbean Contact*, July 1975, p. 19.

"Press Must Be Free, Says Compton." *St. Lucia Star*, November 15, 1975, p. 1.

"Priest Banned, Another Censored." *Caribbean Contact*, August 1975, p. 4.

Proute, J. C. "Change Without Chains: Press Freedom Comes Face-to-Face with Democratic Socialism." *The Nation*, November 30, 1975, pp. 41, 45.

"Radio St. Vincent and the Grenadines." *Combroad*, April–June 1974, p. 59.

Rambachan, Surujrattan. "Advertising in a Developing Society (the

Commonwealth Caribbean)." *Combroad*, April–June 1974, pp. 22–27.

"Sam Flood Fired; Freedom of Speech Threatened." *Crusader*, November 29, 1975, p. 1.

"Seminar on Communications and Information for Development Purposes in the Caribbean Area." *Intermedia* 2, no. 4 (1974): i–iv of supplement.

"Seminar Strengthens News Unions (in Caribbean)." *Guild Reporter*, April 12, 1963, p. 3.

Sing, Louislee. "Two Different Journalism Courses." *Caribbean Contact*, February 1975, p. 8.

Stump, Al. "Where the Goggle Box Strikes Out: Sooky and His Jamaican Friends Refuse To Pay. Any Attention to TV." *TV Guide*, June 17, 1972, pp. 44–46, 48.

Taylor, Jeremy. "How Do You Blend the Cultures." *Caribbean Contact*, December 1975, p. 9.

————. "If TTT Would Only Do Its Job." Trinidad *Express*, January 5, 1976, p. 8.

"Television for Dominica." *Combroad*, July–September 1974, pp. 50–51.

"The Caribbean's 800 Mile Microwave Chain." *Intermedia* 2, no. 4 (1974): 22.

The Center for Research Libraries: Newspapers. Chicago: The Center for Research Libraries, 1969. 176 pp.

"The National Lie in Grenada." *Caribbean Contact*. December 1975, p. 1.

"The Rolling of Heads at 610 Radio." *Caribbean Contact*, October 1975, p. 24.

"Trinidad Newsmen Win Contract." *Guild Reporter*, February 8, 1963.

"Virgin Islands and CANA." *Caribbean Contact*, July 1975, p. 18.

"We're Two." *The Nation* (Barbados), November 30, 1975, p. 1.

"What Is Communication for Development? Caribbean Workshop in Communications and Development." Georgetown, Guyana: United Nations Development Programmes, 1973.

Whylie, Dwight. "The Future of the Jamaica Broadcasting Corporation." *Combroad*, April–June 1975, pp. 13–18.

"Who's Who in Commonwealth Broadcasting 1975." *Combroad*, January–March 1975, supplement.

Index

393